next: Trends for the Near Future

next:

Trends for the Near Future

Ira Matathia and Marian Salzman

with Ann O'Reilly
and the staff of Brand Futures Group

Preface by Ed Vick

The Overlook Press
WOODSTOCK & NEW YORK

Visit the *Next: Trends for the Near Future* Website
at www.nowandnext.com

Visit the Overlook Press Website at
www.overlookpress.com

First published in the United States in 1999 by
The Overlook Press, Peter Mayer Publishers, Inc.
Lewis Hollow Road
Woodstock, New York 12498

Library of Congress Cataloging-in-Publication Data

Matathia, Ira.
Next : trends for the near future / Ira Matathia & Marian Salzman.
p.   cm.
1. Forecasting. I. Salzman, Marian. II. Title
CB161.S245   1999   303.49'09'05—dc21   99-11457

Manufactured in the United States of America
Book design and type formatting by Bernard Schleifer
FIRST EDITION
1 3 5 7 9 8 6 4 2
ISBN 0-87951-943-6

Contents

Preface

*I*T'S ON THE COVER OF EVERY MAGAZINE you read. It's broadcast live on television and via the Internet. Everyone—from business people to students and educators—heralds its arrival. This all-encompassing obsession? The information revolution. And at the dawn of the millennium, we've got front row seats.

There's really no doubt about it. Information and knowledge *are* transforming our society. In the not-so-distant past, America was made over in the image of great manufacturers: those companies that used knowledge to revolutionize the production of steel, oil, and cars. Names like Carnegie, Rockefeller and Ford—these were the icons that represented not just vast wealth, but the bulk of our culture as well. Not since these titans reshaped the global landscape, tipping hegemony toward the west, has there been such a radical transformation.

Yet, moving faster than any prior generation could have even imagined, the men and women at the vanguard of the information revolution have become America's new icons. Bill Gates, Andy Grove and Steve Jobs. Not to mention Michael Dell and Steve Case. We see their faces in print and on television. We use their products and visit their web sites. Ultimately we are collectively embracing their vision of the world.

And these folks don't just promise a different future. They deliver it. They've changed the rules and set new standards. Who would have thought that a company that customizes computers would not only take over the PC market, but redefine the way we expect all goods and services to be produced and delivered? Or that innovations in computer software and chip design would forever change the where and when and how of work? Not to mention our basic assumptions about productivity and its effect on economics.

Actually, the authors of this book, Marian Salzman and Ira Matathia, foretold the proliferation of many of these trends well before they occurred. They hailed the importance of individually-tailored products that let consumers express who they are and what they can achieve, in everything from their choice of fragrances to their financial portfolios.

Their view of the future also included the now-popular assertion that blue is **the** color of the millennium. Gleaned from a survey of their Young & Rubicam colleagues around the world, Marian and Ira's blue-hued prediction has been borne out in the introduction of products ranging from the American Express blue card, to the Bondi blue iMac, and of course, the blue m&m.

That's because, unlike so many "futurists," Marian and Ira have a genuine capacity to generate knowledge about trends and social movements that business people can actually use. In a world where just keeping up with life is a defensive proposition, that's one of the most valuable skills around.

Communications and media are at the center of the information revolution. It's here that technology and innovation are moving at the most breathtaking pace. We're creating enough gadgets to keep us busy pretty much every waking hour. And that's getting to be all 24, since we can go on line all night long—to check a stock market halfway around the world, or buy everything from a paperback to a three-bedroom apartment.

As consumers and corporations alike teeter on the brink of overload, who has time to think ahead? Or to try and understand the impact all this change will have on our world, our attitudes—everything?

Of course, there's also a huge opportunity in all this uncertainty. But only if you understand people's current concerns, all over the globe. The companies and individuals that want to thrive in the years to come will also have to anticipate where technology, social trends and other change agents are leading. The kind of intelligence you'll find in this book is the most vital resource we bring to the digital table.

ED VICK
Chief Operating Officer
Young & Rubicam Inc.

next: Trends for the Near Future

Introduction:
Welcome to the Near Future

WE'RE LIVING IN A FASCINATING AGE. Even those people who claim to be immune to millennium fever can't help but wonder what lies on the other side of the date we've long used to represent the future. In these last days of the twentieth century, we're focused not so much on the triumphs of the last hundred years as on the promise and uncertainty of the years to come. If this century saw the global adoption of automobiles and electric lights, men walking on the moon and advances in medicine that have extended the average life expectancy well into our seventies, what might the next century bring? How will those of us who will be alive in 2050 be living? What will our homes look like? How will we get from one place to another? How will we shop—and what will we be shopping *for*?

As we travel toward the future, the one constant we will confront is the reality of accelerating change. Change is naturally unsettling. In writing this book about what you can expect to happen over the next five to ten years, we hope to provide some practical tools with which you might confront, evaluate, and process what these changes will mean for you.

We ourselves are by no means immune to the forces of change. And although we have been living and working for some time with the information *Next* will unfold for you in these pages, our own circumstances have changed substantially since we undertook the development of a manuscript for publication in The Netherlands about three years ago. At that time, our business, The Department of the Future, part of the TBWA International advertising agency, was based in Amsterdam. Living and working abroad gave us a unique opportunity to observe, firsthand, how the future was developing itself in environments outside the United States. Our travels took us across Europe, to Africa, the Far East and beyond.

We are back in the United States now based in New York City, with our team intact and known as the Brand Futures Group, part of the Young and Rubicam Inc. family of companies. We still do our share of traveling, but enjoy the advantage of monitoring change from this more familiar, but equally trendsetting environment. In fact, the contrast in vantage points has been instrumental in shaping our process and our work.

There are two essential reasons for the evolution of *Next* into a travelogue of what's coming in the next five to ten years but no later: one is the need to be broad because no book can be instantly produced. The other is because we have learned firsthand that those far removed from the marketing business are future-obsessed, or at least concerned that they be in the know about what's around the bend.

Following the notion that the future guarantees accelerated change, a lot has changed for us since we first began *Next*. Much of it has confirmed our hypotheses; some of it has stunned us. And even once we submit this revised—correction, thoroughly recreated book—there is a lag time of four to six months before publication, which is about the quickest reality of the conventional book publishing business today. In chapter 18 we address how this industry will confront its own future in terms of instant access to content, which will shorten the timeline from development to publication of a book. For now, we ask you to rely on our companion Web site (www.nowandnext.com), on which we will continue to update content from the book, as well as provide an ongoing monitor of the trend work we continue to assemble daily.

While we endeavor to give you as fresh a view on the near future as possible, please understand that what you have in your hands is not, and could never be, always absolutely current. And in the futures business, yesterday to today can be a very long time indeed. So visit the Web site—often.

With the insights of our American publisher, Peter Mayer, we've come to realize that the relevance and utility of *Next* are far broader than we ever thought they would be when we began. *Next* is a road map. No matter what your background, social station, or job (be it registered nurse or CEO), the future, the idea of accelerating change, is scary. Professionals, homemakers, and just about everyone will find something in these pages that separates the hype from practical realities, something that offers a practical way to think about what's ahead. What kinds of jobs will be available in 2010? How will families stay in touch as mobility increases? Will computer-mediated "relating" replace courtships? What destinations will be hot for vacations? Will religion and religiosity determine where and how you live over the next decade? (The kind of hype we're seeking to avoid is that seemingly linked only to a future with little relation to the present—for some, the future is filled with airplanes falling from the sky as a consequence of overcrowded air highways, motherhood being written off as a job for robots pre-programmed by Microsoft or one of its competitors, and sexual predators robbing innocent teenagers of their virtual virginity in America Online chat rooms. The reality is that the future will be a rapid evolution of life today.) If the calls we get from journalists based on our advance press are any indication, there's a dearth of information out there on this subject. *Next* will supply some of the answers we're all seeking, and, more importantly, it will raise even more questions and provide you with ways of assembling your own toolbox of "tricks" to find answers about what to expect in your near future.

To a businessperson, insights into new working styles, access to global markets, new channels of distribution, and new means of economic transaction are some of the most significant areas *Next* will explore. The book is rich with usable information for confronting and capitalizing on the future.

Of course, because we're professional marketers, we hope the book continues to be an important tool for practitioners. It shows how accelerated change will influence marketplaces and "marketspaces," the stewardship of brands, and the changing habits, preferences, and motivations of consumers. We'll also show how new "messaging" and media options will affect the face of the future.

* * *

Although literature abounds with long-term prognostications about life in the distant future, our view is more pragmatic than most of these. Here's why. Our focus is international. Global. Worldwide. We're living in what we *used* to call "the future." By way of example, *Wired* magazine just reported that freelancing is out for 1999 and "e-lancing" is in—we've employed e-lancers since 1994 and have built our business these last five years using that particular employment approach. It has given us a low overhead and raised the quality of life of our colleagues.

Those of us who spent part of the '70s contemplating the work of Marshall McLuhan recognize that we are already living in McLuhan's "global village," and we understand how essential it is to decode our present rather than live with both eyes on the rearview mirror. The present is an enormously important tool for those in the trendtracking business and especially for those in global marketing communications. Today, it's not only true that the medium is the message, it's also true that the message is the medium. If you've ever received an "instant message" via the Internet or a commercial online service, you know what we mean. The 1998 film *You've Got Mail* illustrates just how real intimacy can be online—and also makes clear how rapidly and intensely dialogues, and even relationships, can progress in the world of cyberspace.

Being "on trend"—cognizant of events here, now, and *Next*—has been our thing for most of our careers, although our motivations for guessing ahead of the curve have shifted over the years. Why do people with a background in advertising care about trends? And why does an understanding of these trends have importance for a general public that is interested in the future but not in advertising or marketing and not necessarily even in the business world?

Taking advantage of emerging trends ahead of the competition is a goal of any business, from selling shoes to building communications networks. Now that so many of us work in a global market, we must know whether local trends have broader implications. Some trends, such as snowboarding and hip-hop, spread relatively quickly among youth from one continent to the next. Other trends never make it beyond a particular city or region or continent. Kinders, for instance, the popular children's egg toys made by Ferrero in Italy, are all the rage in parts of Europe, but a similar product failed miserably in the United States. Japan's Tamagotchi "virtual pets" have enjoyed tremendous success in Asia and were subsequently introduced in North America and Europe with real success. After the 1998 Christmas season in Britain, it looks as though the American Beanie Baby craze will soon be giving Kinders a run for their money there.

It's the mission of advertising agencies and marketing communications firms to connect people to brands. Current thinking speaks to the fact that an ad either registers with a target consumer or it doesn't—all the hammering home of the message doesn't make much difference. What does make a difference is a holistic approach that integrates the campaign launch with a proactive "educational" campaign to ensure that the consumer is told what to expect and then hears what he or she was expecting. To connect people to brands, brand partnerships must work together on everything from setting realistic market-share targets to determining the appropriateness of pricing premiums to choosing the most beneficial brand image, relevant packaging, and role of sponsorships. Innovative consumer research provides the smarts in terms of connecting people to brands and then reinforcing this connection through savvy media picks, layered messaging, and the use of nontraditional media.

We view the future through contemporary popular culture. Advertising is one of the world's common cultural touchpoints. From Ronald McDonald to the dancing California raisins to the hyperactive Energizer bunny, advertising's icons are a part of popular culture around the globe. These figures and their tag lines tie us together with consumers in other countries, serving as a common reference for conversation in just about any language.

A trend we first recognized in Amsterdam that will be adopted in other multicultural cities (and America is becoming more and more multicultural as Spanish becomes ever more widely spoken) is the use of signage and outdoor advertising in which symbols and graphics have replaced copy (which is increasingly scant) as the conveyer of the essence of messages. As more brands become global, we can expect to see greater emphasis on logos and other symbols that provide a clear voice for a brand without regard to language or culture.

* * *

Trendtracking is becoming so trendy that Reuters carried a September 1998 caution from Pope John Paul II that we believe might just be targeted at us and at all futurologists and secular mystics. As Reuters wrote, the Pope "urged people to turn to prayer rather than psychics and astrology when they're looking for guidance, delivering a tough message in a nation [Italy] where horoscopes and lucky lotto numbers preoccupy many." Speaking from his retreat outside Rome, the Pope had said, "No one but God knows our future and can guide our steps in the right direction." He's more right than not, but as our former colleague Adam Morgan, a brilliant strategic thinker now based in London, noted, if you can guesstimate the speed and the direction of change, there's a darn good chance of harnessing it for practical advantage. For example, we realized back in 1994 that pets had become essential family members. This has resulted in everything from pet greeting cards and daycare centers to books about traveling with pets and nutraceutical products to enhance the quality of life for dogs and cats. Over the past five years, pet-related industries have boomed. And so we go—tracking patterns, linking seemingly unrelated developments, and doing our best "witchcraft," tying together art and science to ensure we've got a bird's-eye view of Now and Next.

REFLECTING ON NOW

"Historians and archaeologists will one day discover that the ads of our time are the richest and most faithful reflections that any society ever made of its entire range of activities."

—MARSHALL MCLUHAN

It's often said that advertising is a window on culture. We think that's true, and that's why anything that can be used to monitor change and change agents is a fundamental tool for effective marketing communications. So in our work as advertisers we have come to appreciate the degree to which accurate trendtracking is both critical to the marketing process and to those people who want to master the future, ahead of their friends, neighbors, and colleagues. In our day jobs, accurately spotting and forecasting trends is of fundamental importance in determining whether an ad is a genuine asset to a brand (ideally by becoming a part of popular culture) or simply a negligible wave over which channel surfers pass. But the same process is critical to the work and lives of those who want to live profitably and comfortably in the near future.

Having been charged with taking our former agency's intelligence unit global, we spent over twenty months living and working in Europe from bases in Amsterdam and Milan and telecommuting to a Dutch office from home offices in Lutz, Florida, and Austin, Texas. Conducting trend research with the assistance of agency offices in cities ranging from Hong Kong to Johannesburg, Frankfurt to Toronto, we all had an opportunity to explore trends taking shape on a global scale. *Next* is a product not only of our work as international intelligence analysts, but also of insights and points of view honed by years of experience inside and outside the advertising industry.

Think of trends as humans, with their own life cycles. That is, they are sown or fertilized, they gestate, grow, mature, age, and eventually die. Some trends spring up again a decade or more later, often in a slightly different form. Cher has been fashionable more than once; so has Eric Clapton, and so have bell bottoms and platform shoes.

How do we track trends? Like other major trendtrackers, our approach is interdisciplinary. We study and analyze traditional (newspapers, magazines, newsletters, transcripts of television news broadcasts) and nontraditional media (Internet news sources, Web sites, e-zines, and outdoor billboards) meant for both a specialized (advertising, marketing, technology, retailing, etc.) and a general audience. Because opportunity is missed by those who view the world only through the eyes of their chosen profession, we are confirmed generalists, tracking scores of themes daily. (Some of the most engaging themes we consistently study are lifestages, people, and their relationship to money, sensuality, and sexuality, business travel, work styles—the list runs to 450 subjects at any given time, occasionally even more.) When we begin to see a pattern, we turn to the experts—and then consider their points of view. Notice how often so-called experts disagree and restate the obvious to emphasize their particular take on a situation or scenario. Notice too that "expertness" is empowering; some predictions are self-fulfilling as a result of media hype. For example, it's gotten to that point that Y2K coverage has convinced all media that Y2K is something that all media must cover. (*Wallpaper** magazine offers insights into building "fab forts" stocked with "Quaker oatmeal, amoxycillin tablets, and Evian," as well as many other nonperishables for trading during the temporary period in which the "global economy is reduced to a feudal barter system.")

When all is said and done, trendtracking, like communication, is part art, part science. An effective trendtracker must have a talent for the rhetorical as well as a pragmatic view of the message's impact. At some point, most of us wonder, What will trend X mean for me? For everyone else? (One example: Does the imminent demise of the permanent employer mean I will be short of cash, or does it mean I will need to think of myself the way I'd think of a brand and manage my own marketing and selling to ensure I'm valuable to organizations that will contract for my services/the goods I produce?) According to futurist Wendell Bell, "The primary goal of futurists is not to predict the future but to uncover images of possible, probable, and preferable futures that enable people to make informed decisions about their lives." Our trendtracking style is to identify the probable for life and work *Next*—and to show the likely implications if the probable actually happens. Essentially, our process results in customized maps that look at various approaches to a destination and point out key landmarks that will be passed en route.

January 1, 2000: What to Expect

Although the third millennium technically won't begin until January 1, 2001, the world's celebration of it will take place a year earlier. So what will the dawn of that day bring (other than some pretty serious hangovers)? Here's a sample of what we can expect.

Although there are other contenders, the Chatham Islands in the South Pacific are the most likely to be the first inhabited land mass to witness the dawn of the millennium. On the summit of Mount Hapeka on Pitt Island, at 3:59 on the morning of January 1, 2000, the new-millennium sun will rise. (And, of course, TV companies around the world are vying for the film rights.)

Who *won't* be partying the night before? Nearly two-thirds of the world's population (primarily in non-Christian countries), but that leaves about two billion observers. (Also not in a party mood will be those staffing suicide hotlines. Suicide runs at record levels on New Year's Eve, and 1999's is expected to set new records.)

In China, the dawn of the year 2000 is expected to mark the beginning of a baby boomlet—not because of the millennium but because it's a year of the dragon, an auspicious time to be born.

The Western media will make it virtually impossible to ignore the millennium. Since the beginning of '99, print, radio, and TV have been featuring retrospective histories of human civilization and our achievements over the last 100, 1,000, and 2,000 years. Apocalyptic expectations, millennial cults and prophecies are also being spotlighted, as are prognostications for the next 100 and 1,000 years.

And now for the bad news. We've all heard about the "millennium bug" (a.k.a. Y2K), which is expected to strike when computers fail to differentiate between the years 2000 and 1900. The extent to which companies are prepared to deal with this problem varies radically from country to country and industry to industry. (Leading market intelligence supplier The Gartner Group estimates that worldwide compliance might reach only 50 percent, with Asia, Latin America, and the Middle East being hardest hit.)

The Rough Guide to the Millennium by Nick Hanna (Rough Guides, 1999) reports on things that might go haywire that day: Air conditioners, airplanes, air traffic controllers, automatic doors, bar code readers, cafeteria equipment, cameras, cars, cash registers, clocks, credit-card scanners, electronic vaults, emergency lighting, escalators, fax machines, fire alarms, fridge/freezers, heating systems, helicopters, hospital equipment, elevators, lighting systems, medical equipment, microwaves, military hardware, missile systems, motorized wheelchairs, optical readers, pagers, photocopiers, postage meters, power management systems, printers, satellite receivers, scanners, security gates, telephones, thermostats, time clocks, traffic lights, vending machines, video recorders, and water heaters.

How bad will it really be? Let's put it this way: According to *Wired*, some software programmers assigned to deal with the Y2K bug are building bomb-shelterlike compounds and stocking nonperishable foods. Even the CIA is advising agents abroad to keep cash on hand and stockpile extra blankets.

Deutsche Bank economist Edward Yardeni says there's a 70 percent chance Y2K will trigger a global recession, according to a July 1998 report in *Industry Standard Intelligencer*. All told, analysts predict the worldwide bill for Y2K repairs will reach $300-$500 billion. In anticipation of cash-hoarding before Y2K, the Federal Reserve has announced plans to store an extra $50 billion in government vaults.

Of the 93 percent of people who have heard of the Y2K problem, 66 percent believe it will be solved before 2000, according the Fox News/Opinion Dynamics. While 61 percent plan to leave their money where it is is, 31 percent will take at least some of their money out of the bank by December 31, 1999.

A British government study predicted there will be 600 to 1,500 Y2K-related deaths throughout the United Kingdom. (If we assume the same ratio of incidents to citizens in the United States, that means between 3,000 and 7,500 Americans bite the dust come New Year's 2000.) "It's probably a very conservative prediction," says Mike Smith, author of the report and professor of medical technology at St. Bartholomew's, Royal London School of Medicine and Dentistry. The report notes that primary life-sustaining devices are likely to be fixed, but secondary systems such as computerized medical records and emergency systems are in jeopardy.

Especially in the United States, as Americans tend to be litigious, look for lots of money to be won in the aftermath of millennial mayhem. Where there are crises, lawsuits are sure to follow. The Gartner Group estimates that the cost of Y2K litigation will be more than $1 trillion.

EXPERIENCE GATHERING

This book records the changes we've noted in Europe, North America, and elsewhere over the past years and it cites the sources that helped us to identify key shifts and corroborate major patterns of life and work Next. Our approach is intended to empower readers by showing them how to interpret for themselves the information they consume via traditional news channels and on and off the Internet. By harnessing the power of the information you receive each day rather than being overwhelmed by it, you will be ready to manage the impending and the inevitable.

WATCHING THE FUTURE

McLuhan's repeated urging to "know the present" is even more pertinent today, for the present is the watchtower from which we view the future. Consider, if you will, the trends we—and, most likely, some of you as well—are already living. In addition to being bona-fide global villagers (as our frequent-flyer miles will attest!), Ira spearheaded Chiat/Day's New York office's conversion to the world's most virtual office in the summer of 1994. The purpose was simple: to adopt breakthroughs in office design that would enable us to accomplish even more effectively our mission of connecting people to brands. Marian invented focus groups in cyberspace in the early 1990s, and she and Ann and Christy were the first three people to conduct useful market research in a computer-mediated environment. More recently, as the Brand Futures Group, we've found ourselves inventing or, more accurately, defining the ideas of "blue marketing" and "blue mindsets" for the news media and the business communities in the Western Hemisphere.

Serve Them Blue

With the Industrial Revolution came air pollution, pesticides, excessive noise, and other environmental negatives. To counter these changes, citizens are looking for businesses to be more sensitive to the environment. Today, companies that give back to the planet at least as much as they take away are known as Green. Blue companies go one step further, giving *more* to the planet than they take away. They're post-Green.

Why blue? Blue is the color of air and water; it's the color associated with thoughtfulness—at a time when introspection is the yin and celebration is the yang—and an unlimited frontier.

Blue is also associated with maleness and crusades, and many see the journey into the millennium as a male-spearheaded journey.

Blue is suddenly the color of the hour, day, week, month, and year, as we count down toward the millennium. Motorola has introduced True Blue pagers for consumers of all ages and Blue E-Luma glow pagers and Blue Streak pagers for teens. Ice blue has become an important color for brides, who are choosing it for their own dresses, for their bridesmaids' dresses, and for dresses for their mothers. More relevant still, as Pepsi celebrated its Blue Centennial in 1998 and anticipated the coming millennium, its packaging, including the design of the cans, became markedly more blue. *Soap-Cosmetics Chemicals Specialties* reports that "hues of the earth and sea will be taking center stage this season." Ice blue is a hot makeup color. Cosmetics-maker Bioelements has even introduced a cooling blue ultraviolet lipstick. Lancome's new nail polish shades include dark blue.

Apple Computer, now on the rebound, has shifted to a bluer logo palette with the introduction of the iMac and the swift G3 Powerbook. As *Brandweek* reports, "iMac desktops sport a new modular design and a larger, quarter-size apple logo in a new color Apple calls Bondi Blue, a sea-green turquoise shade that complements the new color highlights on the iMac itself." As *The Houston Chronicle* noted, "Susan Iverson of the Color Marketing Group says that the baton has passed from green to blue as the dominant color influence." And a nationally syndicated report on fashion and style reads, "If the forecasts prove true, we're going to sail into the year 2000 on a sea of blue. And blue-green. And navy. And icy pale blue. No global warming ahead—it's a cool-down."

WHAT TO EXPECT NEXT

For the sake of making *Next: Trends for the Near Future* an easier read, we have created a few devices to highlight the key themes.

- **"Big Nexts"** are the megatrends that are so big they transcend place and point of view and touch almost everyone.

- **"Nexts"** are the key trends that are influencing the influencers—and that will shape life and work next, as we countdown into the next century.
- **"What's Nexts?"** are sprinkled throughout this book. It's a technique we've had in our toolbox ever since we joined Y&R, in order to give ourselves license to speculate thoughtfully on probable scenarios—the ultimate product of credible trend analysis.

POP GOES THE WORLD CULTURE

"America is not just interested in exporting its films. It is interested in exporting its way of life."

—GILES JACOB, head of the Cannes Film Festival, as quoted *The Economist*

Forget big-ticket items like computers and airplanes. America's "deep impact" export is its popular culture. For better or worse, American movies, television, music, food, and clothing are infiltrating every pocket of the globe.

According to a *Star-Tribune* report, the Blockbuster Entertainment Corp. video chain has opened two thousand outlets in twenty-six countries outside the U.S., and Tower Records has seventy stores in fifteen countries. Their contributions helped international sales of software and entertainment products rise to $60.2 billion in 1996, surpassing all other U.S. industries, according to the Commerce Department. And that doesn't include the untold billions of dollars lost to pirated copies.

But the U.S. isn't the only peddler of pop. As the world market becomes increasingly global and the Internet connects the antipodes of the earth, the people of far-flung countries are finding common cultural ground in movies, television, music, and sports.

Universal Pictures

U.S. distributors took in $5.85 billion at the international box office lin 1998. That number has placed Hollywood creative types in the clutches of the global marketplace, for the decision to green light a film is increasingly tied to its overseas potential. Two months before the release of *Armageddon*, according to a *Washington Post* report, Disney went so far as to spend an additional $3 million on explosions and reaction-to-the-asteroid shots in Morocco and Paris so as to give the movie a more global flavor.

The global box office is poised to grow dramatically in the near future. While there currently are just sixty-three thousand movie screens outside the U.S. (compared to about thirty-two thousand in the U.S.), that number will rise as more multiplexes are completed in movie-hungry countries such as Russia and the young democracies of Central Europe. China and India also promise to become major markets.

The small screen gives much of the world an additional window on American pop culture. In Cuba, illegal home satellite dishes along the northern coast are capturing U.S. sports, news, and entertainment signals. Hungary had no cable television at the start of the decade; now, 40 percent of its households can watch CNN and MTV. And in Greece, fifty unlicensed television stations play almost nothing but U.S. programming, much of it pirated.

World Beat

As with movies, countries separated by thousands of miles often recognize each other as cultural cousins through music. Cuban music, for example, has long enjoyed cult status in South Africa. But last year's South African release of the Grammy Award-winning "Buena Vista Social Club" made the love affair mutual. South Africans relate to Cuba's political strife, and to the ignominy of watching foreign-produced bands attempt to sell salsa music to Cubans in much the same way Paul Simon went to South Africa to sell mbaqanga.

Meanwhile, in Taiwan, where the music industry has long kept mainland Chinese bands at arm's length, some global warming is taking place as MTV and the Internet forge a cultural bridge between the two nations. While Taiwanese bands have long monopolized the Chinese airwaves, the mainland's counter-invasion has only just begun. The *Christian Science Monitor* notes this year a Chinese band called Qingxing has risen to the top of the charts, beating out the Taiwanese competition for the first time in MTV Asia's history.

Next: The Most Global Game

Soccer, the ultimate global sport, has found an enthusiastic fan base in China. During the World Cup playoffs last June, sales of color televisions more than doubled in Beijing, Shanghai, Tianjin, and Guangzhou. Analysts estimate that 57 percent of Beijing's residents watched the playoffs, despite the fact that China's team didn't qualify for the finals.

Soccer has started to catch on in the U.S., too, at least among kids. The American Youth Soccer Organization's Web site (www.soccer.org) tallies its membership at nearly six hundred and thirty thousand children ages four to eighteen. So mainstream is the sport today that the term "soccer mom" has even entered the lexicon of modern politics.

What's Next:
- The gross-out appeal of *There's Something About Mary* and the animated television show "South Park" will continue. Look also for the mainstreaming of World Wrestling.
- The next manifestation of the Western world's embrace of Eastern culture (yoga, tai chi, qi gong) will be the adoption of Thailand's muay thai boxing as a mind-body discipline. Look for it at a gym near you.

New Names and Faces

The names and the faces may be changing. But as we head into the new millennium, it's a safe bet that America will continue to export its way of life via popular culture, *and* from that culture will increasingly reflect the influences of other parts of the globe.

Let's get a better perspective on what the world—the *whole* world—really looks like. Last December, the World Village Project (www.worldvillage.org) published a study that described what our world would look like if it were reduced to a population of one thousand people, with all ratios left unchanged. Consider these realities:
- More than seven hundred of the one thousand people on the planet would live in Asia and Africa
- Two hundred people would possess 75 percent of the wealth
- Eight hundred people—presumably the eight hundred who share the remaining 25 percent of the wealth—would live in "substandard" housing

- Seventy people would own a car
- Three hundred and fifty people would be illiterate
- Fewer than four hundred people would have clean drinking water
- *One* person would own a computer—and it probably wouldn't be connected to the Internet

That picture doesn't look very much like the United States, does it?

Americans really are different from the rest of the world, for better and for worse. Until it ended its seven-year run, the most successful television show in America had been *Seinfeld*, a comedy in which "nothing happens." The empty plot line mirrors much of daily life in America. Perhaps the appeal of nothingness is a response to information overload: nitty-gritty details of current affairs routinely evolve into big stories and blend into little stories, all against a backdrop of analytical commentary that, naturally, is further balanced by so-called hard news. Perhaps Americans have shut down because life beyond the television screen is changing too fast. Then again, perhaps we're simply a nation that's become complacent with its success as an economic and cultural force.

For we realize that, for many, garnering insights into the future is as much a personal hobby as a business necessity. It is our hope that you will take the insights contained within this book and use them to live and work with the confidence that is gained from knowing you're prepared for the likely—and poised for the unexpected. We hope you will enjoy this travelogue to the near future.

—IRA MATATHIA, *Greenwich, CT*
—MARIAN SALZMAN, *New York, NY*
—ANN O'REILLY, *Lutz, FL*

CHAPTER 1:
Big Nexts

WE BEGIN WITH THE BIG NEXTS, the overarching factors that will define the near future. Many are expressed here as paradoxes. These apparent contradictions suggest that, in the near future, making things work will require a more expansive worldview.

THE EVER MORE DEMANDING CONSUMER

Imagine you're sitting at your desk, waiting for an important contract. You check your fax machine, your e-mail, and even for Fed Ex and courier deliveries. And then you call the person who drew up the contract, and he says, "Don't worry; you'll get it. I dropped it in the mail slot yesterday." Fifteen years ago, that response wouldn't have raised an eyebrow. But today, who has time to wait for snail mail? We want everything yesterday, and we grow frustrated with people who waste our time with antiquated means of communication.

Well, that's exactly how today's consumers feel. Having made new technologies a part of our lives, we want everything faster than ever before. Anything that's not *immediate* is s-l-o-w. Same-day delivery. Instant news. Nuked meals. DirecTV. PC banking. Increasingly, we have no patience for products and services we can't access *right now*. In addition, our satisfaction with brands is defined increasingly by immediacy rather than quality of service, a point of great commercial significance. In North America in particular, retailers are discovering that customers aren't willing to wait until their local store reopens at 9 A.M. to buy a quart of milk. They want it now—and they'll get it, whether from a competitor that stays open late or at a twenty-four-hour convenience store. The result is a burgeoning number of twenty-four-hour retail establishments, from bookstores to restaurants to copy shops.

Not only do we want it faster, we want it *customized*. Consumers around the world are rejecting the notion that one size fits all. A popular T-shirt we've seen reads, I ASK ONLY THAT YOU TREAT ME NO DIFFERENTLY THAN YOU WOULD THE QUEEN. The T-shirt is a joke, but the attitude is pure reality. As new technologies have made it easier for companies to target individuals, consumers have grown accustomed to white-glove treatment. *Time* magazine comes with a printout showing how the subscribers' local representatives voted on critical issues. Levi Strauss lets us order computerized-fit jeans. Parents can buy personalized storybooks that feature their children's names, the names of their pets, familiar places, and so on—videos and dolls can also be personalized. And customer service centers around the world are scrambling to put a touch of 1:1 marketing in their responses. GTE Telesystems in the United States, for example, rates each call coming into its customer service center with three graphic devices (calendar pages to indicate customer longevity, sticks of dynamite to indicate past service problems, and money bags to indicate volume). The system allows personnel to respond more appropriately to each caller's problem.

It's really very simple. As consumers, we're being led to expect products that meet our specific needs. Why should I sit through world forecasts on the Weather Channel when I can have my particular city's weather report e-mailed to me each morning? We want to access products via distribution mechanisms that are convenient to us, whether through one-stop shopping, twenty-four-hour superstores, home delivery, or some equally agreeable method. And we want an immediate and satisfactory customer service response when problems arise.

Our desire to remain in control in an uncertain world—combined with our insistence on having things when and how we want them—also translates into a demand for personalized marketing campaigns. Mass marketing is obsolete in high-tech cultures. Complex technology-based products, increased competition, and additional channels of communication, everything from the sides of delivery trucks to sponsored e-mails to customized couponing at point of purchase, result in declining advertising effectiveness.

In the near term, one can expect to see many more examples of increased interactivity between businesses and targets in the form of consumer-data collection and 1:1 marketing campaigns. In addressing the Public Relations Society of America at New York's Harvard Club, Larry Weber, who runs a national public-relations consultancy that bears his name, described one small example of a new communications channel. "Imagine you're at your local supermarket, buying a six-pack of Coca-Cola. The scanner that recognized the six-pack of Coke also triggers a software program, which spits out a fifty-cents-off coupon for a six-pack of Pepsi. Automatically. Let's say you ignore the coupon, or you take it home and lose it. The next time you buy Coke, the scanner recognizes the Coke on your debit card. The software looks up your record, knows you didn't respond to the last coupon, and spits out a $1-off coupon for Pepsi. Next time, it's a $1.50. If you don't switch in three tries, the software gives up on you for now. That's an actual system now being tested. Retailing is not about merchandise anymore. It's a war of information and communication."

Developments such as customized products and 1:1 marketing initiatives are creating in consumers an *expectation* that we will be catered to. In some parts of the world, mail-order goods take weeks to arrive. In the U.S. today—because we have grown accustomed to top-flight service—many of us get impatient if we can't have a product delivered overnight or if we're unable to have our customer service problem solved at 3 A.M. on a Sunday. This isn't going to go away. As new technologies are developed and as production and distribution methods are improved, consumers will continue to grow ever more demanding—not just in the U.S., but around the world. Any company that thinks the way it did business in 1970, 1980, even 1995, is going to cut it with today's consumer is going to be blown away.

SEEKING SECURITY

Just twenty years ago, most of us worked in offices without PCs, fax machines, and voice mail. Our homes were not equipped with VCRs; our phones were not equipped with caller ID. Many of us would have scoffed at the notion that computer technology would fundamentally alter the way we live and work in just two decades' time. And now, with the new millennium upon us, we are taking a peek into the future, imagining how our worlds will change in the *next* ten years.

One of the terms that has emerged in the past couple of years is *premillennial tension*. In the Western world the general population's anticipation of the year 2000 is tempered with concern, even fear. The novelist James Baldwin wrote, "Most of us are about as eager to be changed as we were to be born, and go through our changes in a similar state of shock." We know there will be changes in the coming years, but we don't know what exactly they'll be or how dramatic their impact. The result: an intensified search for security.

Trust No One

A key reason we've become so demanding as consumers is that we no longer trust businesses to be looking out for our best interests. This attitude has been honed by years of being lied to and misled—not just by big business but by government leaders, celebrities, and just about everyone else in the media spotlight. In our travels across Europe, we spoke with citizens who are no longer willing to tolerate corruption in any form; they are unbending in their desire to have only honest individuals govern them. Americans always wanted to believe their government was corruption-free; with the exception of the Watergate scandal, there was a perception that elected officials were essentially honorable public servants. This has all changed at the end of the 1990s, and Americans, too, are starting to demand accountability during campaigning and upon a candidate's election to public office. (Expect more term limits and campaign finance reform as yet another way to "check" the power of those who seek office.)

Whether it's hedge funds, the volatility of the stock market, corporate accounting practices, profit performance versus expectations, or continuing personal crisis in the lives of elected officials, Americans have a distinct sense of unease regarding the institutions that drive the nation's fortunes. One of the forces contributing to this anxiety is increased access to information. Whether from the Internet, cable or satellite television, or independent 'zines, today's consumers have more access to more news, and to more styles of news reporting, including the Matt Drudge-style of "expose."

Fear

As the new millennium approaches, fearful and cynical consumers are seeking trustworthy brands. Laurence Bernstein, an ad man in Toronto, gave us his view of how the premillennial tension we're describing is affecting Canadians: "The most significant trend in Canada right now," he says, "is a profound change in the Canadian worldview, moving people from a society with a therapeutic perspective ('We can do it now because everything can be fixed') to a society driven by a prophylactic sense of caution ('Whatever we do now, we must be careful because we may not be able to fix it in the future')." Bernstein contends that this shift "is evident in almost every aspect of life and can be viewed as the force behind such social phenomena as environmental concern (people actually recycling), the antismoking campaign, et cetera."

In our view, people in many parts of the world are undergoing a similar shift from a therapeutic to a prophylactic perspective. As we attempt to take advantage of the benefits of new technologies and other conveniences, we remain acutely aware of the potential pitfalls. And in a world traveling at hyperspeed, it's a brave (or delusional) person who never questions whether he or she will be able to keep up.

THE GLOBAL VERSUS
HYPERLOCAL PARADOX

As the world gets smaller, we aren't just becoming more globally aware, we're becoming increasingly focused on the hyperlocal
(think small and easy to master—hyperlocal communities can be
anything from the town of Sparta, New Jersey, to Jewish divorce
attorneys, to parents of Eagle Scouts) places and communities in
our lives. Our perspective, as businesspeople and marketers, is
decidedly global . . . Yet we are also decidedly hyperlocal. This very
Monday, Ira needs to race from a session with our publisher to a
school board meeting in the Connecticut town where he lives and
where two of his children attend the public schools. (School budget
cuts are a matter most Americans can relate to, especially if they
have kids in public schools. And the desire to raise smart kids is a
universal goal—we've seen it in quantitative data from Taiwan,
heard it during interviews with thirty-somethings in France, know
it about our fellow Americans, and lived it with Dutch neighbors
who put enormous emphasis on nurturing the academic skills of
their offspring.) Marian has a date with her university alumni club
penciled in for this week too, because that's the community that has
been one of the most important to her over the last decade. She also
has a Women in New Media breakfast to attend; networking is a
1980s buzzword that in the 1990s translates into forging hyperlocal ties. Ira too belongs to a number of committees—mainly ones
that do outreach involving the advertising community.

It seems to us that achieving a balance between the global and
the hyperlocal will be of increasing importance to both people—
and brands—in the years ahead. Hyperlocal ties help people par-
tition the world into manageable chunks. I might not know how
to solve the problems that will arise from Europe's new single currency, but I can create a workable budget for my homeowners'
association or chess club. I might feel overwhelmed when surfing
through Usenet newsgroups, but I feel very much at home when
"chatting" with people in my online birding group.

For brands, the push and pull of the global and hyperlocal continuum is somewhat different. Aided by their embrace of new technologies—which keep them plugged into world events and points of view—new consumers are beginning to develop a global outlook that infuses the way they think, act, and buy. A brand can invent desire in Milan using the same triggers that it uses to invent desire in Miami or Memphis or Melbourne, Australia. Transnational commerce is leading, in turn, toward the media globalization of MTV, CNN, Sony, and the magazines in the Condé Nast empire.

As consumers become more global, we're seeing a deepening sense that marketing messages can—and should—be transmitted across borders, sometimes even using the same (localized) vehicles to do so. The trick lies in providing messages that balance universal appeal with sufficient localization to attract and retain the interest of consumers in each market. Disney, Coke, Nikon, Apple, IBM, Levi's and Nike are just some of the brands already globally consistent. But if "Think Different" featured just one iconographic image it would have become "Think American"; instead, the advertising campaign used unique insights into who would be admired and emulated in each culture in which Apple sought to be reborn. But remember that hyperlocal advertising can mean reaching all the advertising creatives in a variety of nations, just as it can mean reaching Parisians.

Today's drive toward globalization means companies need to make hard decisions on everything from whether brand names need to be globally consistent to which brand messages translate across cultures to what logo or icon will best represent a brand around the world. Not every company can have a symbol as globally recognized as the Nike swoosh—but all of them would like to.

As brands consider the implications of going global, it's important that they also recognize the enormous draw of hyperlocal connections. Forging hyperlocal links with consumers is a must for tomorrow's brands, no matter how global the overall distribution and marketing goals and objectives. Brands need to be "just right for people like me" versus "just right for someone else." That requires intense connecting with the consumer, and messaging is a necessary step in cementing that connection. In fact, we can safely assume that tomorrow's mass-appeal brands will share three characteristics: global relevance, hyperlocal desirability, and strong ties to multiple niches.

How can a product have both global relevance and hyperlocal appeal? Some smart brands will take advantage of convergence opportunities. When done right, convergence is about brands bonding because their combined power is greater than the sum of their parts (what used to be called synergy). Moving forward, we can expect to see global champions such as Frito-Lay co-brand with local winners such as the Netherlands's Smith's chips, thereby ensuring that ubiquity and familiarity are in sync. Frito-Lay would be ill-advised, in our opinion, to distribute Smith's far beyond the Netherlands-Belgium borders but can easily cross-promote global Frito-Lay's snacks with local Smith's chips in Holland.

Smart marketers are also coming up with other ways to give mass-produced products local appeal. How many of us have been fooled by supposedly homegrown microbrews and specialty snack products in our grocery stores that are, in fact, manufactured by the very same conglomerates selling mass-marketed products a bit farther down the aisle? (Altoids is just the latest success story— would you believe it is brought to you by Kraft General Foods?) Companies slap on a local-sounding name or the colors of a local sports team knowing that consumers are not apt to read the fine print about the product's true origins. Häagen-Dazs, taking a similar tack, manufactures not only fresh, exotic flavors but also a name that sounds foreign and luxurious. In fact, it is a product brought to you by a local American ice creamery. Somehow Häagen-Dazs turned all its consumers into special affluents, buyers of Godiva versus Hershey's, travelers to the Gold Coast of Australia versus the Gold Coast of Florida, and all for just a small premium over the standard cost of a pint of chocolate, vanilla, or strawberry.

McDonald's has managed to reinvent itself, depending upon the customs and traditions of the countries in which it establishes itself, according to *The Chicago Tribune*. (The company earns 59 percent of its profits outside the United States, which isn't too surprising but is testimony to the brand's universality.) In Japan it serves sausage patties with teriyaki sauce. In Norway, one favorite is the McLox (a salmon sandwich), and Manila gets noodles. In India, the Maharaja Mac is the cultural representation of America's Big Mac, using lamb instead of beef out of respect for

Hindu beliefs. McDonald's success in foreign markets proves it must be doing something right globally.

One successful strategy is that McDonald's sells more fish where consumers want fish—think Japan—and more burgers where consumers want burgers—think England. But in countries like India, where more vegetarians live than anywhere else in the world, menus reflect that preference. The idea is global branding, global menus, and local highlights and modifications.

On a city level, one can see how global and hyperlocal approaches can not only coexist, but even enrich one another. Amsterdam, for instance, despite being a comfortable participant on the world stage, has the feel of a village. When Adidas, one of the most on-trend brands of sports apparel in the world, relocated many of its creative, marketing, promotions, and sales functions to Amsterdam, the Dutch press explained it this way: Amsterdam is chosen as second head-quarters for its international cosmopolitan feel, in a village setting.

Contrast June 1997's European Union summit (a.k.a. Eurotop) in Amsterdam with the Olympic Games at Nagano, Japan. The Amsterdam event felt as though the world had been invited to a New Age picnic (BYOB) and musical celebration of the future (there were many performances during the celebratory moments and plenty of respites from the meetings). In contrast, the sleepy, isolated village of Nagano seemed determined to resist the exhortations of CBS to "spend a moment with the world." Amid reports that local businesses were turning away foreigners, the prevailing view of the townsfolk was that this intrusion from the outside world was simply to be suffered through as they eagerly awaited a return to anonymity.

NOSTALGIA AND FUTURISM: A WINNING YIN AND YANG

Throughout our global village, residents are being asked to accommodate change at an unprecedented pace. The *new world order*—one characterized by real interdependence (based on con-nected social, political, and economic systems) and by networks

based on new technologies that create legitimate global media—
dictates that "change is the only constant."

In the West, as we discussed earlier in this chapter, anxiety
about this change is exacerbated by premillennial tension. As
observed by *Megatrends* author John Naisbitt, the millennium is a
metaphor for the future. Wrapped up in it are our greatest hopes—
and our greatest fears. We're uncertain how the changes to come
will affect us personally. The result has been an oscillation between
optimism and anxiety. Indeed, we have been struck by how much
of society's "future view" is caught up in such paradoxes. Today's
trends include a push toward both risk and safety, indulgence and
cost-consciousness. But no paradox is as interesting, or as marketable, as that of nostalgia and futurism. As marketing consultant
James Rosenfield says, "People seem to be trying on both the past
and the future for size."

Given these circumstances, coexisting tendencies toward nostalgia and futurism are not so surprising. When confronted with
accelerated change, people often gravitate to the familiar and comfortable—an accustomed food brand, an old TV show or a retro
fashion. But because swearing off the changes of the future simply
is not an option, we alleviate our anxieties by finding a balance
between what has been, what is now, and what is to come. The
exact comfort equation among the three is as unique to each individual as his or her fingerprints, but most involve creating a sturdy
bridge that spans past, present, and future.

Marketers and product developers must take this consumer
ambivalence into account to strike a balance that's appropriate for
their target. Chanel's last ready-to-wear collection rose to the
challenge by featuring both long skirts (a nod to the attire of
Coco's youth) and a new bag designed for the millennium and
called "2005."

When we consider brands for the future (sometimes called "millennium brands"), it's clear to us that, whether classic or newly minted,
these brands will share a capacity to be reinvented, reinterpreted, and
reoriented at an extraordinary rate. Rather than be motivated by a
chameleonlike hypocrisy, such change will be an extension of the
brand's guiding force. Authenticity also is important. Worn down by
an unceasing barrage of questionable product claims and an unre-

lenting need to read the fine print, consumers gravitate toward—and seek out—people and products that deliver honesty and integrity.

Smart marketers have been quick to take advantage of consumers' nostalgic leanings. Microsoft launched Windows 95 with help from the Rolling Stones; Nissan reconnected to its history with the aid of rock group Van Halen and toy soldier G.I. Joe. Around the world we're seeing a rise in companies setting out to "stake-claim" their legacies (asserting their histories and their authenticity, versus being "me too" follower) as businesses work to ensure that tomorrow is familiar. Going forward, we'll see that the most effective marketing strategies meld the essence of nostalgia (reliability, quality, beauty, familiarity) with the positive elements of futurism (functionality, convenience, versatility).

• NEXT: ENTHUSIASM FOR RELIGION

Attention citizens scanning the horizon of the twenty-first century: You'd be well advised to tune your radar to religion. Quite simply, God is back.

For many years, adherence to organized religion has been on the decline across much of the industrialized world. Witness the dramatically reduced birthrates in former bastions of Catholicism Italy and Spain—despite the church's ban on contraception. Yet figures indicate that the ebbing tide of religious interest is turning. In the most recent wave of data from Y&R's global consumer survey, 54.2 percent of the almost six thousand U.S. respondents expressed strong or moderate agreement with the statement "Religion plays an important part in my life." Even more significant is that this figure is higher among trendsetters.

Using our TrendTracker segmentation, Brand Futures Group identified the leading 10 percent of the Y&R sample. Among those respondents, 59.4 percent agreed with the above statement. Of course, this doesn't necessarily equate to a rise in conventional religious belief—except that 41.5 percent of U.S. trendsetters agreed strongly or moderately that "The world literally was created in six days just as the Bible says." That's in line with the overall U.S. figure of 40.9 percent. In looking at the sample of fifteen hundred from the notoriously freewheeling Netherlands, we saw similar results: 26.5 percent of trendsetters said religion is strongly or moderately important in their lives, compared with just 23 percent of the total sample. As in the U.S., belief in the six days of creation also is higher among trendsetters (17.5 percent agree strongly or moderately) than among the population as a whole (14.8 percent).

A study conducted for the Center for Gender Equality, cited by the Herman Group's *Trend Alert*, points in the same direction, with findings that 75 percent of U.S. women feel religion is very important in their lives. This is up from 69 percent in 1996. Illinois-based Teenage Research Unlimited, which interviews two thousand U.S. teenagers every six months, confirms an increase in religious interest among teens.

• NEXT: WEAR IT WITH PRIDE

For most of the rock 'n roll era, displays of religious faith have been deeply uncool in much of the Western world. U.S. President Jimmy Carter's piousness arguably was more damaging to his public image than President Bill Clinton's sexual misadventures were to his own. Yet in the late 1990s, it's perfectly possible for a public figure to be both religious and trendy. One case in point is the ever-trendy British Prime Minister Tony Blair who won by a landslide in 1997 despite his religious avowals.

Of course, how uncool could religion be if it's showing up in tattoos (praying hands, sacred hearts, angels, crosses) and teen apparel? The popular WWJD (What Would Jesus Do?) bracelet worn by seventeen-year-old Cassie Bernall during the Columbine High School massacre attracted the attention of one of the gunmen. Holding a gun to the girl's head, he asked her if she believed in God. She said yes, and he killed her. If the history of the early Christian church is anything to go by, Bernall's martyrdom is likely to spur many more public professions of faith.

• NEXT: RECONCILING FAITH AND SCIENCE

The upsurge in religious interest begs the question: What about science? For most of the 20th century, education in scientific method, with its insistence on objectively measurable results, has been at the expense of religious faith. Applied science has delivered the goods with seemingly miraculous innovations in virtually every area from medicine to agriculture. And now rapid developments in

genetics are allowing scientists to "play God" not only by pro-
longing life, but also by actually creating new life forms.

Yet on the threshold of the next century, there are signs of a
growing desire to somehow reconcile science and religion. Y&R's
survey data shows that trendsetters who express an interest in religion also tend to have an above-average interest in reading about
scientific subjects—47.1 percent versus 9.6 percent of regular folk.
It seems science and religion, to many people, are not so incom-
patible after all.

That's hardly surprising given that, for nonspecialists, contemplating the further reaches of science—black holes, quarks, anti-
matter, and so on—requires no less faith than believing in God and
an afterlife. Science popularizers such as Fritjof Capra (author of
The Tao of Physics) laid the groundwork, drawing parallels
between Eastern religious thinking and the cutting edge of physics.
In the words of Australian Margaret Wertheim (author of *The
Pearly Gates of Cyberspace* and the recent television documentary
"Faith and Reason") in the *Tampa Tribune*, "We need to correct
the idea that a person can't believe in science and religion at once.
This is important because at the beginning of this century many
people thought religion would die out, but the opposite has happened. We're going through a new wave of religious belief in this
century, and it affects science."

PERPETUAL YOUTH AND
OUR AGING WORLD

It used to be that people over fifty were old and people under
thirty were young. Then people like Mick Jagger began to turn
fifty and continued to strut their stuff, and our theory of aging had
to be revamped. Today midlife crises occur not on one's thirty-fifth
birthday but on the forty-fifth or fifty-fifth, or even later. Men and
women in their seventies and eighties are remaining physically
(even sexually) active, are traveling the world, and sometimes are
even still running companies—and countries.

Throughout Europe and North America, women are delaying
childbirth until their thirties or even forties. Adults are running

around in tennis shoes and short shorts. They're working out at the gym in an attempt to delay some of the normal processes of aging, and they're having plastic surgery to mask others. The fashion industry has been forced to redesign its youth fashions to fit the bodies of the middle-aged men and women who continue to wear them rather than adopting more "grown-up" fashions.

In the years ahead, expect the world's "elders" (whether aging boomers or their parents) to command unprecedented attention from marketers and the media and to have an enormous impact on the rest of the population. We're entering an era in which the elderly will make up a larger proportion of the global population than ever before. Already the most rapidly growing age group is eighty-five-plus. In the United States this age group will double by 2025 and increase fivefold by 2050. Consider the implications: By the year 2030, approximately 20 percent of the U.S. population will be over age sixty-five. That's sixty-nine million people. Around the world, half of all people aged sixty-five and over who have ever lived are alive today.

Our aging population promises to influence everything from financial planning to home design to the way products are made and sold. Likely developments include everything from "adult friendly" caps on medicine bottles to wider car doors to foods that compensate for changing tastes and dietary needs. We'll see even greater changes in our attitudes toward aging. As seniors increase in number, so will they increase in power. Images of the elderly as victims will become history. Their favor is already being curried by all the major institutions. We'll see seniors who grow more active in politics and who maintain and even increase their economic power as they move fully into their second half century of life. Socially, politically—and certainly economically—we will all feel the implications of this Big Next.

THE EXPERIENCE ECONOMY

Welcome to the Experience Economy, where it's no longer enough to provide goods and services. To be competitive, companies are finding it pays to stage experiences, turning something as ordinary as a meal or plane ride into an adventure. It's all part of catering to consumers' increased appetite for fulfillment of the senses.

Driving this quest for experiences is an intensified focus on creating full, flexible, diverse lives. We're seeing a growing number of people take an à la carte approach to life, seeking thrills by taking on adventure vacations, grazing for cheap luxuries, such as storefront massages, and buying "memberships" in exclusive coteries, even if the purchase entails a mere hour at an upscale salon. Our mission: to drink in as much as possible—multitasking (doing several things simultaneously—watching TV, reading, and talking on the telephone all at once) to ensure that not one moment is wasted.

Conversational Value as a Form of Wealth

Permanence used to be the quality of greatest value ("Diamonds are forever"). Today, experience value is becoming for many the ultimate form of wealth: For many, an African safari is far more compelling than a "big rock." The result is a rise in everything from ecotourism to kickboxing to classes in Kente cloth design. Not sure what to get your little one this holiday season? You could shell out thirty-five thousand dollars for FAO Schwarz's Castle Bed, but for a mere twenty thousand dollars, why not buy one of the two available "Barbie Experiences"? Your two-day visit to New York will include a private meeting with a Barbie doll designer and a custom-designed doll, created to your child's specifications. (How can one customize Barbie? Use your imagination.) Now, that's something for a kid to brag about when school's back in session!

Selling Memories

Experience collectors want to sample as many things as possible, so portions must be manageable. Products and services—whether a piece of furniture or dinner for two—need to deliver rich and memorable stories. Virgin Atlantic doesn't just sell a ride across the Atlantic. It sells a hip, fun travel experience. On TWA, a vacation begins at your destination; on Virgin, a holiday begins when you board the plane. From the personal video players in economy class (with a first-rate selection of movies), to menus that excite (decent steaks, pasta Bolognese), to a free goodie bag with items from the Body Shop and other British "high street" boutiques, to comfy socks, Virgin salutes its passengers. Two major ingredients are required to create memorable experience: surprise and indulgence. Without the unexpected, there's little reason for most people to repeat an experience.

Companies expert at turning an experience into a memory understand the value of keepsakes. Theme restaurants (from the Hard Rock Café to Planet Hollywood to Boogie's Diner in Aspen, Colorado) have been particularly adept at selling such merchandise, ranging from boxer shorts to beach towels. The National Restaurant Association reports that more than a third of table-service restaurants in the United States sell merchandise, with customers spending well over five billion dollars a year on T-shirts alone.

Collecting

Collecting isn't just about accumulating goods. It's about tying yourself into something larger and enjoying the experience of hunting down that priceless (to the collector, anyway) print or autographed playbill. For many collectors, the hobby is less about a financial investment than about belonging to an exclusive club— preferably one with a reputation for discerning taste and an air of scholarly or artistic refinement. *Worth* magazine reports that in the United States alone, retail sales of figurines, toys, plates, and other collectibles topped ten billion dollars last year. Also growing are sales through collector clubs—up almost 25 percent since 1995. In addition to gaining access to members-only pieces, club members can socialize with "others like them" at special events, whether in person or on line.

Raising the Ante

As consumers clamor for better and bigger and more memorable experiences, companies are forced to go to further extremes.

In the case of movies, we're not just seeing skyrocketing budgets and special effects, we're also seeing changes in the venues in which people watch. Today's megaplex theaters feature stadium seating, premium sound systems, plush seats, and enormous concession stands (or even full-service restaurants).

So how can a company, an organization or an individual maintain an edge in a world in which the bar of entertainment keeps being lifted? In "Welcome to the Experience Economy," an article in the *Harvard Business Review* (July/August 1998), B. Joseph Pine II and James H. Gilmor lay out the following five principles for success: First, create a consistent theme, one that resonates throughout the entire experience. Second, layer the theme with positive cues (e.g., easy-to-follow signs). Third, eliminate negative cues, those visual or aural messages that distract or contradict the theme. Fourth, offer memorabilia that commemorate the experience for the user. Finally, engage all five senses to heighten the experience. Consider, as an example, the promotion of a film, especially to its prime audience—often kids and teens—where the marketing program will include not only conventional advertising, but also an exhaustive media tour of its stars on the talk show circuit, prerelease and active promotion of the soundtrack, including a title song from a "name" artist, which will ensure its active radio play, and the requisite fast food chain tie-in for collectable toys.

We've chosen to place our final two Big Nexts—the United States of Europe and an Independent Asia—in separate chapters. These Big Nexts differ from our usual stock in trade in that they focus on geopolitics and regional economics rather than on consumerism, popular culture, and the like. Whether you live in one of the regions in question or in the Americas, Africa, or elsewhere, the implications of what's to come in Europe and Asia will be enormous.

CHAPTER 2:
United States
of Europe

*F*OR MANY OF EUROPE'S 350-plus million citizens, the next five to ten years will be the most exciting, promising, and possibly disturbing era of their lives.

The quarrelsome patchwork of nations, peoples, cultures, economies, climates, and topographies loosely known as Europe is facing the next millennium more united—or at least more closely bound together by external factors—than anyone could have dreamed just fifty years ago.

Take a bow, Brussels—you're in the spotlight, at least for now.

The capital of Belgium has become shorthand for the ambitious project of European integration that started in the early 1950s. The changing names of the project over the decades reflect the broadening ambitions of the "Eurocrats" and the visionary politicians who have driven it: the European Coal and Steel Community (1952), the European Economic Community (1957), the European Community (1967), and now the European Union (1993).

What started out as a forum for collaboration among six countries in a limited area of industry has evolved into the creation of a virtual United States of Europe, with its own single currency and supranational legislature governing eleven countries, with more in the waiting room.

Not everybody in Europe is on board. Groups of people who used be known as "right wing"—typified by Britain's Conservative Party and its former leader Margaret Thatcher and her successor John Major—resent the political dimension. They think the project should stick to fostering trade and commerce and keep its hands off social policy, let alone political integration. (But current British Prime Minister Tony Blair has proven to be more open to his countrymen joining a unified Europe, in spite of the naysayers.) Some "left wing" Europeans see the whole thing as a vehicle for big business to have its wicked way with workers, playing off those in high-wage countries against those in lower-cost areas.

As the process grinds on through committees, white papers, debates and summits, it might seem like a typically European phenomenon—long-winded, ponderous, bureaucratic, short on star performers and sex appeal. But it's worth remembering that the Western Europeans who have grown up watching this process are the first in many generations who haven't taken time out from their lives for war. And as recent events in the former Yugoslavia have shown, Europe's capacity for ethnic violence can never be discounted. This is true even though every country in Europe—because of guest workers (inexpensive temporary labor from nearby third world countries, typically working menial jobs), and jobs that cross national boundaries—is a de facto multi-ethnic place.

We need to wonder, will ethnic integration continue? Perhaps a Next for some will be collecting globes and maps—with the names changing seemingly weekly, it's no wonder that such a hobby can be invigorating; already globes that feature the U.S.S.R. sell for a premium at flea markets in New York City and San Francisco.

Take another bow, Brussels.

Slowly but surely, nations across Europe are in the process of uniting their destinies with former foes, handing over strands of sovereignty previously held dearer than life itself. Broad-ranging cooperation between the French and the Germans would have been inconceivable early in this century. That the Dutch head of the European Central Bank is willingly headquartered in Frankfurt shows just how far old prejudices have melted away in the name of progress. But, even in the near term, what Brussels stands for is many Europeans living under common rules invented by other Europeans who don't even speak the same language. This sort of prospect used to lead to fighting in Europe, but so far it has sparked only a war of words between the "Europhiles" and the "Euroskeptics" within countries. Perhaps one reason for this willingness to unify is a desire to have genuine clout against a United States that has been the sole superpower for long enough to motivate many Europeans to mobilize.

With a fair wind, the early years of the next millennium should see the laborious but peaceful emergence of a true European Union, put together by committees rather than by combatants, but nevertheless a heroic achievement. What General Charles de Gaulle said of his native France is even more applicable to Europe as a whole today: My friend, you can't expect to unify overnight a country that boasts 257 different types of cheese.

Déjà History

One of Europe's big problems (and points of pride) is that the past is always getting in the way of the present and the future. For example, engineers trying to excavate tunnels for the city metro in Rome routinely came across ancient Roman relics—cues to stop digging and call in the archaeologists again. As far afield as London, developers in the financial district have faced similar problems with buried Roman relics.

Even the idea of unifying Europe goes back a long way. On the eve of the first millennium, the year 0, the Romans ruled an empire that covered much of the territory now in the European Union. A thousand years later, the German-speaking area of Europe was engaged in a long-running attempt to put together a second empire—the would-be Holy Roman Empire. And after Napoleon's short-lived conquest of most of Europe in the early 1800s, Hitler made his bid, which finally failed in 1945.

On a less grand scale, many of the European social and workplace attitudes prevalent for much of this century are steeped in a sense of the past—the dynamics of left-wing/right-wing class politics and the efforts of workers to protect their interests. Workers' struggles have lived on as heroic moments in many memories, and even today large numbers of Europeans are loath to give up hard-won privileges for the uncertain prospect of a continental future.

In short, Europeans' history, their perception of history, and the legacies of history have all too often served to keep them apart and stuck in the past. Progress may depend on quality-of-life issues. Europeans have greater expectations now about matters such as length of paid vacations, "free" health care, government support services, etc. While many Americans assume that Europeans are finally realizing they must become more American in terms of employee benefits, such as job security and four-plus weeks of vacation a year, Europeans, in fact, have a sense of superiority and believe that America doesn't motivate its workforce properly. (Given that The Netherlands, Finland, Norway, Switzerland, Denmark and Luxembourg, are with the United States, Singapore, Hong Kong, and Canada on the short list of the most competitive places to do business in the world, and given the enormous differences in employee benefits between the United States and The Netherlands, for example, perhaps competitiveness doesn't require stripping employees of their benefits. Dutch employees are guaranteed twenty-nine days of paid vacation each year, beyond the ten official holidays, and employees must provide an extra month's pay each May to ensure they have money for travel and relaxation. More shocking still is that a Dutch employee can get seventy percent disability pay for an unlimited period of time, with complete job security, if he can prove he's suffering from stress. And this is in the country that The Economist says is the most lucrative place in the world to be in business.)

Yin: Don't change. Yang: Change. History versus progress, tradition versus innovation. This is the Yin and Yang balancing act of the New Europe. There is a mounting awareness, particularly on the part of younger citizens who realize that things have to progress, that the future must be different from both what's gone before and what's happening now. And at present, it seems that the grip of history is loosening across the whole continent.

New generations of Europeans have grown up in times of peace and plenty, eating the same fast food, drinking many of the same soft drinks, driving similar cars, and increasingly sharing the same tastes in music, movies and TV shows. While it was originally exported from America, today's version of the good life is being localized. MTV was initially one feed; today it has local feeds, and a German station has one-upped MTV throughout Germany with its offer of "All Music, All German." While not nearly as materialistic as their American counterparts, these New Europeans display a "live for the moment" mindset that breaks with the thinking of previous generations. Compared with their parents, they're much more focused on the here and now, on themselves and on their own futures. They are much less interested in where they are from and much more concerned with where they are going. Their willingness to speak several languages, and to work in whatever country offers them the best quality of life and the fattest paycheck, makes them unique—and very different from Americans of the same generation. To paraphrase Francis Fukuyama (author of *The End of History*), we might well be witnessing something akin to the end of history in Europe—or at least the beginning of the end of Europe's obsession with history.

The Euro Nightmare

With the approach of the year 2000, computerized countries all over the world are facing the same Y2K millennium bug problems. But as Y2K fever heats up, Europe has added its own complication to the computer systems nightmare—a new currency, the euro, which is the flagship of an ambitious project of the European Monetary Union. Banks and businesses in Europe have historically dealt with transactions among the fifteen currencies of the European Union, whose exchange rates have constantly fluctuated within fairly narrow bands. To simplify cross-border business in the future, Europe has phased in this single currency, with some countries embracing the euro immediately and whole-heartedly. The euro is likely to make things much easier in the long term but a lot more complicated in the short term. In the words of *The Economist*, the whole undertaking promises to be "an awfully big adventure" and one that will play out for three to four years to come.

Europeans started using the euro in electronic transactions only on January 1, 1999, and for a three-year transition period it is primarily to be used in conjunction with existing national currencies. After that it will be goodbye franc, goodbye mark. In fact, these currencies will cease to be legal tender in the summer of 2002. During the transition period, the euro will be the cross-rate hub— exchange rates will be calculated on the basis of each currency's rate versus the euro rather than directly between the currencies.

It's not clear whether the European authorities were fully aware of the Y2K problem when they decided on the single European currency schedule. What is sure is that the timing is likely to keep legions of programmers very busy through January 1, 2000, and perhaps for a much longer time to come.

Phasing in the euro brings plenty of challenges. At present, many companies need only deal with their national currencies, but even small, locally focused companies will have to phase in or switch to euro systems sooner or later. And the systems range from cash tills and computer keyboards with euro symbols, all the way up to powerful number-crunching programs handling corporate accounts.

IBM calculates that the cost to companies doing business across the Continent will be in the range of one hundred seventy-five billion dollars. Fortunately, the banking industry is ahead of the pack in its preparations for the euro, which are thought to cost around a hundred million dollars for big banks.

And the euro shift won't only touch countries in the first wave of euro adopters. The European Union is the main trading partner for Britain, and while the British government is adhering to a "watch from the wings" philosophy, British companies doing business with the mainland will probably find that it pays to go euro sooner rather than later, since big Continental companies will be changing over. *Business Week* reports that Philips Electronics and Siemens are among the companies that began operating in euros at the birth of the new currency on the first day of January. They took legions of suppliers and customers along with them.

Nonetheless, a year before the beginning of the transition to the euro, a survey by the accounting firm Grant, Thornton of London indicated that some 37 percent of European companies had not even started thinking about the euro. It's a fair bet that a considerably higher proportion of the cash-wielding public was even further from incorporating the euro into their plans in 1999. But then again, how fast the future arrives, now that life, too, is progressing at hyperspeed.

The Euro Dream

It shouldn't take Europeans long to experience the benefits of the euro—which, among other things, will allow prices to be compared in different countries. The variations in price are sometimes vast, and with no border controls between many European Union (also referred to as EU) countries, we can expect a sharp increase in cross-border shopping trips.

Despite the darkest suspicions of diehard euroskeptics, the single currency wasn't introduced to confuse people and make life more difficult. It's part of a policy of removing the obstacles to doing business between European countries, with the hopes of creating a unified trading zone with a GDP to match that of the United States. One likely consequence, posits *The Economist*, is that the euro will become a real alternative to the U.S. dollar on a world scale, making it harder for the United States to run unlimited current-account deficits and exercise unchallenged leadership of the international financial system. Could it be that this will happen by 2002? Sooner? (For Americans especially, this shift in terms of real clout of the United States on a global scale is real food for thought—unless our brains are too preoccupied with the latest tabloid report of the Washington escapades that have been the focus during the final months of 1998 and early 1999.)

To qualify for entry into the European Monetary Union, countries had to fulfill some strict national budget conditions. Eleven members of the EU were accepted into the European Monetary Union. Greece missed its chance to gain entrance in 1999, but should qualify in 2001. Only Britain, Denmark, and Sweden have chosen not to join at this point. (These four countries explain why the unified Europe is sometimes referred to as the G15, although it is more commonly called the G11.)

In any event, the focus on the EMU entry criteria spurred countries to greater budgetary sobriety across Europe and subsequently helped drive interest rates down—all good news for investors, including foreigners. Furthermore, the increased merger activity in Europe spells windfalls for those who pick their investment holdings intelligently. With a large number of companies now traded as American Depository Reciepts (ADRs), it is even easier for a smart American to benefit from a solvent, well-managed European business environment.

Banks, insurers, and finance houses have been among the first companies to go regional with cross-border product offerings in the single currency, which makes for greater consumer choice and greater mobility within Europe. While in the late 1990s it was theoretically possible to take out a mortgage in one currency to buy a property in another, the foreign exchange risks were daunting for the average consumer. With the euro, that risk is eliminated. The increasing pace of preparations for Y2K and the euro is making software houses an irresistible investment opportunity, too.

As the zero hour approached, things fell into place for the euro. Maybe it had an appointment with destiny. Against expectations, European economies started picking up in 1998 after almost a decade of sluggish performance, which threatened to scupper the currency's introduction. What's more, *The Economist* reports that European commissioner for monetary affairs Yves-Thibault de Silguy noted that spending on preparations for the euro, coming on top of Y2K spending, gave Europe's economies a further boost. (Again, that's the Yin of "optimistic spin"; the Yang of "negativity" comes from forecasts of a global recession set off by Y2K failures and further exasperated by the cost of the 2000-2002 evolution from local currencies to the euro. Think about the fact that every vending machine in Europe needs to be switched.)

Russia Now and Next

When President Boris Yeltsin was checked yet again into a sanitarium to recover from a severe case of bronchitis, it seemed that little was being done to heal either his medical woes or his country's gravely ill economy. Though the I.M.F. sent 4.8 billion dollars to Russia in July 1998, *The New York Times* reports it has put a seventeen-billion-dollar financial bailout package on hold until the Kremlin publishes a budget and stops printing rubles—sending inflation through the roof—to pay off its staggering debts. Though recent reports from Russia have been nothing but doom and gloom, there are some indications that the foundation has been laid for a swift recovery. Energy Minister Sergei Generalov has said that Russia expects record exports this year of crude oil, its top foreign-currency earner, according to the Associated Press. And multinational companies are standing their ground, insisting that Russia remains as important a market now as it was when they first set up shop in the early '90s.

Should Generalov be wrong and Russia fall into total chaos, the consequences for Americans are so extensive that we'd all prefer to think nostalgically of the days when we needed bomb shelters in case Russians acted on their animosity toward us, or vice versa. At least on a financial scale, America's banks are already dealing with this pressure. And there is the sagging infrastructure that caused Chernobyl and that will never be repaired until there's some cash surplus. What's next for Russia? Here are a few nexts we're following.

Next: Importing Capitalism

Unlike in the United States, according to a States Statistics Committee report, a "Made in Russia" tag runs the risk of seriously damaging sales. In a country where 48 percent of all consumer goods are foreign-made, the term "import" translates as "luxury." It's not uncommon for middle-class families in Russia to eat American chicken on Chinese plates while watching a Mexican soap opera on their Japanese television set.

Such TV dinners are a fairly new occurrence. Until 1991, the few Russians who had TVs could watch a mere three (state-run) stations in black-and-white. Muscovites now enjoy dubbed American soaps such as "Dynasty," "Santa Barbara," and "Dallas" on six full-color channels, plus a twenty-station cable system. And there have been reports that Russian women are lifting their "Dallas-style" hairstyles and lavish weddings directly from the soaps.

The fashion industry, too, is betting that Russian aristocrats will still spend on minks and martinis. Christian Dior Couture has one multibrand shop in Russia already, and recently to opened a 3,300-square-foot Dior-exclusive store in Moscow. Neither the uncertainty in other markets such as Brazil (where another mega store is planned) nor the financial turbulence in Russia has changed Dior's overall international expansion strategy. *Women's Wear Daily* reports that the Escada Group, Guy Laroche, Cartier, Mila Schon, Fendi, Trussardi, Bennetton, Gianfranco Ferre, L'Oreal, and Yves Rocher also have a strong presence in Russia's major urban centers.

Due to a combination of poor healthcare and diet and heavy drinking, Russians have seen a six-year-drop in life expectancy (to fifty-eight) over the past decade. (Perhaps accompanying this fact is a recognition that the shift to capitalism and the subsequent unraveling of the status quo have been mighty stressful for your average Russian.) Seeking to reverse the trend, Bob Swan, President of the Corporation for Russian-American enterprise, has set up campaigns to fight heart disease and increase AIDS awareness. He called on foreign firms to give one percent of their sales in Russia to support the public health education drive. One company that has already agreed to this is cold remedy maker Quigley Corp.

Next: The Struggle to Modernize

The term "convenience store" does not yet exist in the Russian language. There are currently three ways to shop: at Western stores (bigger selection, higher prices), at Russian stores, and at open-air markets. Shopping at Russian stores is a prehistorically slow, three-tier process. There's no handling the merchandise— everything is behind the counter. Once you spy something you want, you pay the cashier, who sits in a cage-like structure at the other end of the store, and get a receipt to claim the item.

Ordering take-out is not an option for most Russians, whose telephone network is so outdated that thousands of people have been waiting for years to have a telephone installed in their homes. Frustrated by such vestiges of Soviet rule, Russians are ponying-up to buy cell phones. Companies such as Akos are going door to door signing up homeowners for its fixed-rate cellular or cordless phones. More desperate measures include smuggling in illegal radio telephones from China and Taiwan which are of such poor quality that phone conversations end up on neighbors' television sets or on airline radio frequencies, reported *The Moscow Times*.

Another reason to own a cell phone in Russia: the Y2K bug. *The Moscow Times* reported that, fearing the computer bug will cause an even greater financial and telecommunications melt-down, struggling former Soviet Republics have recently ordered their nuclear power plants to thoroughly examine all their computers and have asked all ministries, departments, and regional administrations to make similar checks and report their findings. In the Ukraine, where Chernobyl is located, the problem could turn deadly.

Russia's "new economy" has put hospitals at risk as well. Though alternative medicines are thriving, and Western-style medicine is available to those who can afford it (an entire cardiac center was sent straight from Iowa to a hospital near the Kremlin when President Boris Yeltsin suffered heart trouble), some doctors, nurses and other public health employees haven't been paid for eight months as of spring 1999, and are owed, in total, some three billion rubles (187 million dollars). That could be another factor, in addition to the shortage of medicine and equipment is making people sicker. Of the one hundred and fifty million people living in Russia, twenty-one and a half million were registered ill during eight months in 1998, reported Reuters.

Immigration Matters: Europe Without Borders

For cross-border travelers in Europe, the situation is finally returning to its status of a century ago, when it was possible to wander across the Continent without a passport. Only recently have border controls between many European countries been dropped (under the EU's Schengen agreement), but already some countries are wondering what they have gotten into.

Since October of 1997, flights between Italy and France, Germany, the Benelux countries (Belgium, the Netherlands and Luxembourg), Portugal, Spain, Denmark, Sweden, and Finland have had domestic status, while land border controls are virtually nonexistent. The big worry now is that there are no secondary lines of defense to pick up illegal or undesirable immigrants. Once such people make it into one of the countries, they can travel unimpeded to any of the others.

Europeans are already troubled by the prospect of innocent economic migrants and asylum-seekers turning up on their doorsteps from Africa and the near East. Many refugees are Iraqi or Turkish Kurds, who have been arriving in increasing numbers and applying for political asylum. EU countries are afraid things could get worse to their way of thinking, which can be xenophobic or even racist. Recent years have also seen sudden influxes from Albania and Bosnia. And the risk of mass migration from the countries of North Africa is ever present, particularly with Algeria virtually in a state of civil war.

But of much more concern are the activities of organized criminals, who now make big money smuggling illegal immigrants, as well as the more traditional contraband of drugs, guns, and money. According to Professor Ernesto Savona, director of Italy's Transcrime Research Institute, the Albanian Mafia has now grown so powerful that it has already chased the Italian Mafia, once its patron and big brother, right out of the lucrative business of trafficking migrants. *The Electronic Telegraph* (a Web site created by London's *The Telegraph*) reported, "Albanian-organized crime has its foot in the door, which is Italy, and this means people, prostitution, and drugs." It will be tough for EU countries to hold onto the Schengen ideal of free movement of people without more stringent immigration and asylum laws. (Schengen is the place where the original significant treaty creating the European Union was signed in 1993.)

Expect Europe's open-borders policy to come under a lot of pressure within the Schengen group, while the United Kingdom looks on smugly with a "told you so" expression.

If you're looking for a hot-button topic in Europe, immigration has long been a pretty reliable choice and is likely to stay that way well into the next millennium. Now-deceased British politician Enoch Powell made his name thirty years ago with his notorious "rivers of blood" speech on immigration, while in France, the National Front Party of Jean-Marie Le Pen has commanded around fifteen percent of French votes on an anti-immigrant platform of "France for the French" on more than one occasion in the last ten years.

The immigration conflict is primarily about culture (with a small *c*), jobs, and welfare. (That's not so different from similar conflicts in the United States at times when the economy has been lukewarm or worse and unemployment has been high.)

Small differences count big in much of Europe. It's not unusual to hear people from one town claim that people from the next town, just a few miles away, talk funny or eat strange food. So it's not surprising that the presence of immigrants who are really, seriously different allows plenty of opportunity for culture shock, especially when they arrive in large numbers and form their own self-contained communities. For instance, Germany, Europe's biggest receiver of immigrants, has around seven million immigrants out of a population of eighty-two million. Germany has also had to bring together two very diverse cultures: the well-educated Westerners, comfortable in service industries, and the poorly trained Easterners, who are unable to make a smooth transition into the marketplace of the future. Immigrants have made the unemployment issue even more volatile.

Gerhard Schroeder may have been elected in part because he pledged to bring to Germany the Dutch miracle—but good luck to Chancellor Schroeder, who needs to bring innovations and reforms to all eighty million Germans (in contrast, the entire population of the Netherlands is about fifteen million, which is slightly more than the state of Florida).

Each European country has a unique immigrant population profile, which itself begs the question of how many generations it takes for immigrants to be classified as locals. The United Kingdom, France, Belgium, and the Netherlands have people from their former colonies, Germany has Turks and Eastern Europeans, most Northern European countries have people from Southern Europe, and Southern Europe, which used to lose migrants to the north, is now having to deal with the unaccustomed problem of absorbing immigrants from Africa and the Balkans.

Apart from the smells of unfamiliar food and the sounds of strange languages, big fears are either that the immigrants will work, taking the jobs of local people and driving down pay levels, or that they won't work but instead will live on benefit payments from the government.

Slow-to-change communities are feeling the effects of the economic upheavals that are sweeping the world and devastating traditional industries, such as shipping and steel production, leaving legions of unemployed. It's easy for bewildered Europeans to point a finger at immigrants, who are often concentrated in areas where the hardest-hit local people live, too. And it's tempting for extremist parties to play on voters' fears, forcing even moderate politicians to take a harder line on immigration.

For example, the left-wing government of French Prime Minister Lionel Jospin caused a furor among its own supporters as it examined residency requests from 140,000 illegal immigrants. The government is aiming to modify tough immigration regulations passed by previous conservative governments under pressure from the far-right National Front, which wants to send all immigrants back to their country of origin. Jospin's law is easier on immigrants who have French-born children or who have been in the country for many years, but is tougher on recent arrivals and bachelors.

All across Europe, governments will have a tough job balancing countervailing factors—on one hand, staying true to their humanitarian traditions and tackling the practical task of integrating new arrivals, and on the other hand, being mindful of the risk of social conflict that is likely if they overstretch the capacity of local people to absorb newcomers.

So far the immigration debate has been conducted largely in terms of rights and responsibilities, economic burdens, and redistributing an economic cake that is assumed to be of fixed size. But in the early years of the coming millennium, expect to see the focus start to shift toward finding ways to help immigration contribute more to the economies of receiving countries.

The fact is, Europe needs immigrants. Birth rates across Europe are low, and the native populations of most European countries are aging. As people live longer and the demographic bulge of baby-boomers starts heading toward retirement, Europe will increasingly need the work and the taxes of immigrants to keep its economies humming along.

You Are What You Speak

So in the Europe of the year 2002, you'll be able to cross borders without noticing them, and you'll need to carry only one type of currency, the euro. But what language will you speak? It's likely to be English. Increasing numbers of Europeans are deciding that if they have to invest time and effort in learning a second language, it might as well be one that can be used as widely as possible in Europe and beyond.

There is a precedent for Europeans sharing a common tongue, otherwise known as a *lingua franca*. For well over a thousand years, into the early centuries of the present millennium, educated people across the Continent spoke variants of Latin, the language imposed by the Romans. Modern French, Italian, Spanish, Portuguese and Catalan are descendants of Latin.

For much of the current millennium, Europeans spoke a wide variety of local dialects. It was only with the establishment of modern nation-states and public schooling that the idea of standardized national languages took hold, enabling people in different parts of the same country to communicate. But language isn't only a means of communication, it's also a repository of national culture, identity, and pride.

French was the dominant language of the European Community until the United Kingdom joined in 1972, when English began to pose a threat. Since the admission of the Scandinavian countries in 1995, English has been even more widely used; an article in *Electronic Telegraph* noted a recent survey of more than a billion pages of EU documents that confirmed that English has taken the lead. Although there are eleven official EU languages, European Commission meetings (part of the bureaucracy of the New "unified" Europe) take place in just three tongues: English, French, and German.

The smaller EU nations, such as the Scandinavian countries and the Netherlands, take it for granted that their languages are only of domestic interest. Even Italy and Spain apparently have no international aspirations for their languages. Not so with Germany and France, where the national languages are seen as flagships of the national culture, deserving of government backing to stop what is perceived as the insidious slide toward English.

More than half of the German foreign ministry's cultural budget is devoted to promoting German language and culture abroad in 180 German schools with 2,200 teachers and specialists. Nearly 170 government-supported Goethe Institutes employ 750 people in seventy-eight countries to champion the cause.

France takes its language very seriously indeed and is trying its best to stem the tide of English. It has a highly respected organization, the Academie Française, to rule on correct usage and has placed legal restrictions on the use of English in public communications. France even runs an international forum of forty-nine Francophone countries, which held its seventh summit in Hanoi, Vietnam, last year.

Earlier this year, France lodged an official protest with the European Commission about the way English is supplanting French as Europe's prime working language. As part of its campaign, France has made clear that it will block the appointment of the next president of the EC if he or she is not fluent in French.

But for better or worse, English is becoming the industry standard, in much the same way that VHS became the videocassette standard and MS-DOS, Wintel, and TCP/IP have become computer standards. Perhaps it's the fact that English developed as a melting pot of the major European languages. Or maybe it's because it's an "open standards" language not owned by any one country.

The New York Times reports that young French people are flocking to Britain to improve their English-language skills, which are appreciated in much of Europe but considered a threat to the primacy of the French language back home. the Netherlands has successfully touted the English language skills of its people to promote itself as an ideal location for multinational companies to set up their European headquarters.

Paradoxically, even as Europeans adopt English as their trading language, many find themselves more able than ever to slip back into their minority languages and dialects back home. Linguistic biodiversity is thriving in Europe. In Spain young Catalans, Basques, and Galicians have grown up being encouraged to learn and speak in languages that were banned under General

Franco. In Italy it was recently discovered that Italian had not been officially registered as the national language. So, according to a BBC report, while amending this oversight, legislators took the opportunity to register eighteen regional dialects and languages.

Despite its reputation as being English-only, the Internet is providing a low-cost medium for minority-language speakers across Europe and beyond to network in languages ranging from Albanian to Welsh. Visit www.partal.com/ciemen/europe.html for hotlinks to the many "foreign language alternatives" available online.

In the coming millennium, expect Europeans to apply global-local thinking to language. For functional global communication, English is bound to emerge as the best option. For local, personal and cultural purposes, local languages will continue to be the entrance tickets to parallel worlds. The losers in this process will be those poor souls who speak *only* English.

What's Next in the U.K.?

U.K. stands for United Kingdom, and what's next even in terms of those two words begs a lot of questions. Namely, how far into the new millennium will the country still be a kingdom, and how much longer will it remain united?

But starting this section on a negative—or even a questioning—note would run counter to the spirit of the times for the United Kingdom. The country is on a roll; Cool Britannia, feted by feature writers the world over, is once again regarded as a world-class capital. And it's been lauded not only as a style leader, but also as being ahead of many other European countries in terms of its preparedness for the New Economy. "The United Kingdom is seen in some quarters as a model for a more commercial, entrepreneurial Europe," says Adrian Day, senior executive director of leading brand consultants Landor Associates, based in London.

The buzz has spread all over the world, but probably the sweetest satisfaction comes from changed perceptions close to home. France has tended to regard Britain with amused and slightly bemused hauteur—a trendy French tourist guide of the '80s was titled *London, 100 Years Behind and 10 Years Ahead*. But many French are now seriously wondering whether Britain is leaving *them* behind. Unprecedentedly large numbers of young French people are crossing the channel to find work in Britain and polish their English—some sixty thousand in London's financial district alone, according to the conservative French newspaper *Le Figaro*. Even the leader of the French parliament, Laurent Fabius, recently praised Britain's prime minister, according to a report in *The Financial Times*, saying, "We are curious about you, dear Tony Blair, your personality and style, which have made more than one of us feel old-fashioned."

Who would have expected it? Through the late 1980s and much of the 1990s, Britain seemed to be suffering through a hangover from the Thatcher Revolution. The '80s boom peaked in 1988 and was followed by gloomy years of waiting for the return of the elusive "Feel Good Factor," a phrase used by the Conservative government of John Major, who succeeded Thatcher. Real estate prices languished, homeless people were everywhere, and politicians faced incessant accusations of corruption and wrongdoing. Ironically, the Feel Good Factor did return—but not until May 1997, with the landslide victory of the reengineered "New" Labour Party under Tony Blair.

Britain in the postwar years has been characterized by boom-and-bust cycles, and time will tell whether the latest upswing will fall into the patterns of the past or break them. New Labour has certainly declared its intention to change the country. Much of the groundwork was laid by successive Thatcher governments in the 1980s; they were responsible for breaking the power of the labor unions, abolishing restrictive working practices, privatizing state monopolies, and forcing the notions of good accounting and profitability on both the public and private sectors. And New Labour's macroeconomic thinking is not a million miles from Thatcher's.

Blair's honeymoon period has extended well beyond a hundred days, although some of his high-profile showbiz supporters (e.g., the Gallagher brothers of pop band Oasis) have already turned against him to protest reforms of the welfare system. And there must be some doubts whether the Cool Britannia aura will survive untarnished until the new millennium. After all, fashion is fickle.

The British at large have a sense of optimism that the country is changing, and that New Labour is modernizing it. So Tony Blair and the British people might well still find themselves on an extended honeymoon when the millennium turns. In any event, with a landslide majority behind him, Blair is one of the few world leaders who can be confident of still being in his job when the year 2000 dawns. For Britain it's a fair bet that the years straddling the turn of the millennium will go down in history as the Blair years.

United? Kingdom?

"United Kingdom" isn't just a fancy way of saying England. The U.K. includes three other countries—Wales, Scotland, and Northern Ireland—in which the people are British but most definitely not English. The sense of difference they experience has nurtured long-running movements for various forms of autonomy—mostly peaceful, but bitter to the extreme in Northern Ireland.

For the first time in many years, there is a real prospect of London handing over, or "devolving," power to Wales, Scotland, and Northern Ireland, provided that mutually acceptable formulas can be devised. A monumental peace agreement was reached in April 1998 between Britain and Northern Ireland. British troops have been pulling out of the area since the agreement was signed. The outcome remains to be seen, but this will be a truly millennial achievement if it succeeds in leaving behind the violent civil conflict and creates a formula acceptable to both the "Republicans," who want the province to join the Republic of Ireland, and the "Unionists," or "Loyalists," who want it to remain part of the United Kingdom.

The early years of the next millennium are unlikely to see any substantial change in the sovereignty of Wales and Scotland (despite noise to the contrary), provided international sporting authorities continue to allow them to field their own national soccer and rugby teams. After all, national passions run highest for sports.

As for the monarchy, the death of Princess Diana triggered substantial debate about her former inlaws, the royal family, and the continuing loyalty of the British to the monarchy. Polls at the time showed a marked cooling of feeling toward the royals and increased question as to their relevance to modern British life. On a more progressive level, would-be constitutional reformers used the occasion of the death of Diana, the People's Princess, to renew debate about whether it is appropriate for the people of a modern, postindustrial nation to be "subjects" rather than "citizens."

Yet, the future of the monarchy, at least for the first half of the next century, is likely to be decided by emotional criteria. Public discussion of the royals tends to focus not on constitutional issues but on personalities and, occasionally, on money. Polls have indicated that Prince Charles has recovered a lot of the ground he lost in the years prior to Diana's death, and Prince William has inherited his mother's good looks and charm—to the delight of the British people. According to a report in the *San Francisco Examiner*, "About 60 percent of Britons want the monarchy to continue. In the aftermath of Diana's death, support for the monarchy dropped to between 40 and 50 percent, the lowest level in modern times. Analysts note that William's father, Prince Charles, has been able to take advantage of the public's affection for William and his younger brother, Harry, to restore at least a portion of his own image, heavily damaged by his stormy divorce from Diana and his admitted affair with Camilla Parker Bowles."

So, provided the royals perform well for the media and are discreet with their money, they can probably count on the sort of public goodwill that will keep the monarchy show running and the K in U.K. On the other hand, the media must be drooling for the day when the young prince starts dating and, inevitably, screening candidates for a wife. The precedents don't bode well.

Identity and Change

Some world powers are the product of revolution, of people taking charge of their own destiny—France, the United States, Russia, China, India. Others have recast themselves after the turmoil of war or civil conflict—Germany, Italy, and Japan being obvious examples. Almost alone among the world's great industrial nations, Britain has no Independence Day or Liberation Day to celebrate.

Modern Britain is the product of evolution, not revolution. The British have never had a violent break with their past, though many other peoples have had violent breaks with *them*, and they have never had to sit down together and write out a constitution or think up a completely new way of governing themselves. The legal system goes back centuries, with sedimentary layers of laws and modifications of laws. Historically, the British way of experiencing change has been back and tweak what has worked in the past rather than undertake a radical makeover.

This approach paid dividends for a long time. Over the centuries the country amassed an empire that spanned the globe. Older Brits still recall school atlases on which every continent had large areas of red to mark British possessions, an era when "the sun never set on the British Empire." But all that changed with World Wars I and II, which depleted the country and forever loosened its grip on its colonial possessions.

Over the last fifty years Britain has been forced to rethink itself, to abandon some cherished tenets of its self-mythology and to allow a new identity to emerge. The process has been long and painful, but seemingly welcome. It's also irreversible. In the mid 1990s, then-Prime Minister John Major tried to stem the tide with a call for a "Back to Basics" approach—along with a dewy-eyed evocation of old maids on bicycles and cricket on the village green. The country ridiculed his vision and voted him out at the next opportunity.

The British seem increasingly prepared, or perhaps resigned, to face a harsher future in which old maids won't ride around on bicycles and the state won't try to provide for all needs. "In the U.K., a sea change is occurring," reports Gavin Heron, an ex-Londoner who is strategic planning director at TBWA China. "People are moving from a dependency mindset to that of personal responsibility or control. They no longer believe the government will provide for them as it used to. The millennium is acting as a catalyst for a break with the past. It represents the future as now."

Embracing Foreigners

Britain is in the process of consciously becoming a multicultural country—an enormous change from the days of the empire.

The United States forges its nationhood in schools with the Pledge of Allegiance. In France, immigrants are expected to put aside their origins and assimilate, as happened in France's former colonies. But the British have never expected foreigners to become British, so they were pretty much left to carry on with their own ethnic traditions, as was the case in British colonies. And in Britain, immigrant groups have tended to retain their own ethnicity as they find their way into society.

Absorbing immigrants has gone against the grain for many British people. Racial issues have been debated for many years, and the anti-immigrant National Front enjoyed a brief spell of limited support in the 1980s. But an indication of the progress made can be seen in Mike Leigh's award-winning feature film *Secrets and Lies*, in which a working-class English woman is tracked down by the daughter who was taken from her at birth. The fact that the daughter is black and the mother is white is barely mentioned and has little relevance to the story, which is about family relationships. Had the film been made ten years earlier, it would probably have focused on race.

Much of Britain's self-mythology has centered on the notion of a plucky little country resisting foreign attempts to invade it—the Spanish in the sixteenth century, the French under Napoleon in the nineteenth century, and the Germans under Hitler. The country's history of military and imperial success bred a feeling that Britain had little to learn from foreigners.

This belief, described by a Cypriot psychologist residing in London (and passed along to us by our colleague Stuart Harris) as "effortless superiority" has been severely eroded and even turned on its head. Over the last fifty years, as Britain has slipped down world rankings in all sorts of areas—GDP, income, standard of living, nutrition, education, sports, and cultural output—many British people began to acknowledge that maybe foreigners knew a thing or two after all. Perhaps we could argue that after fifty years of slippage, they were virtually hit over the head by foreigners who seemed to have accomplished a great deal in spite of no affiliation with English aristocracy or arrogance. A willingness to learn from foreigners is perhaps what distinguishes New Brits most from previous generations.

One measure of this willingness is the fact that some of Britain's most chauvinistic and reactionary clubs have thrown their doors wide open to foreigners. Britain's soccer clubs—flush with cash from new TV deals—now field players from all over the world. Even more surprising is that some of the top clubs have hired foreign managers—a radical development for the country that claims to have invented the game.

CHAPTER 3:

An Independent Asia

A HUNDRED YEARS AGO, vast tracts of Asia were under colonial rule or foreign domination. Powerful industrialized countries controlled the destinies of many millions of Asians. In the region, for the most part, only Thailand and Japan could be regarded as sovereign nations. And so it continued for almost fifty years through and beyond the Second World War.

Now, as the twentieth century comes to a close, the continent can look back over several decades of extraordinary changes and rapid development. Many Asians enjoy levels of education and affluence that surpass even those of the old colonial masters. The last vestige of foreign dominion was removed at midnight, on June 30, 1997, when Britain returned Hong Kong to China, thereby ending what many Chinese described as "150 years of shame."

Asians now control their own destiny. The region's response to several big issues will be crucial in shaping that destiny and determining what sort of century the next one will be.

The Asian Crisis

It is a great pity for the region that the Hong Kong handover celebrations were almost immediately overshadowed by months of headlines about a regional economic crisis that grew and grew, just as forest fires in Indonesia burned out of control and blanketed much of Southeast Asia in choking smoke. The sobering effect of the crisis has led to widespread fears that the hard-won economic gains of the last decades might be lost in some countries and that the twenty-first century might not turn out to be "the Asian Century," as had been so widely predicted.

The ramifications of the regional economic crisis are still working themselves out. Many analysts have come to the conclusion that the crisis was caused by structural problems, which the region is now being forced to tackle. According to this analysis, a good shakeout will help the countries of the region to discard unproductive practices and get themselves into shape for the next stage in their development. For manufacturers in the region who ride out the storm, lower currencies will provide an extra edge in export markets, but these manufacturers like their countries, are facing massive debt with hard currency exposures.

The notion that the problems are "structural," however, might be too pat, and if accepted at face value, this view could deflect the deeper analysis and problem-solving necessary to restore a stable economy. Rampant overinvestment in icons such as office buildings, hotels, and airports soaked up billions of dollars that might have been better invested in future productivity. Overreliance in the business world on traditional relationships, including those with family and friends, at the expense of a truly open market, led to many poor decisions. Indonesia may be the best example of a self-interested government that increases the wealth of only a few families. From 1968, when General Suharto, then head of the Army, was named president, until he resigned in May 1998, the Suharto family and its closest allies, including Bacharuddin Jusuf Habibie, who followed Suharto as president, have had very close ties to the oil exports that spurred the country's growth. A natural business cycle was at play here too. Boom to bust, expansion followed by recession, has been the hallmark of the twentith century. No one should have believed Asia was immune.

Not all countries in the region were affected. The Philippines barely merited a mention in the frenzied media coverage. Perhaps it should have. Its growth period started later (having been held back by the Marcos family, another corrupt empire), so it didn't have as far to fall. But it did fall, and hard. Vietnam only recently hooked into the global economy (when the United States lifted its trade embargo in 1994), and its currency, the dong, isn't convertible, so its exposure to the storm was limited. As a highly placed resident Westerner put it, "We haven't seen much of the economic crisis here. (Communist) Vietnam is still trying to sort out a local problem—Stalinism."

China's experience of the economic storm was mainly through Hong Kong, exposed to regional economies through its finance sector. Unlike those in other countries in the region, Hong Kong bank authorities managed to defend the Hong Kong dollar against the pressure of the foreign exchange markets. Its peg against the U.S. dollar is widely expected to hold, thanks to the dollar reserves of the city and the pride that's at stake; for the Hong Kong dollar to weaken so soon after the departure of Britain would mean a terrible loss of face for Beijing.

Although it was thought that some countries might come through the Asian economic crisis nearly unscathed, recently even Hong Kong has been hit by the global instability of the current economy. Unfortunately, they could not hold it off permanently. In May of 1998 it was announced that Hong Kong's economy had hit a thirteen-year low. A Hong Kong casualty of the Asian crisis is Peregrine Investment Holdings, which collapsed largely as a result of its relatively enormous exposure in Indonesia.

As for other Asian countries, Taiwan appears confident it can continue its steady economic growth, and the effects of the Asian economic crisis have barely been felt in China, although the warnings have not gone unnoticed. A colleague of ours based in Guangzhou reports, "There is much fear in China given the recent drop in the economy in the region and the talk of devaluating the yuan or the renminbi." China gives the region cause to hold its collective breath. If the renminbi falls, it is likely to take the rest of the region's currencies down with it.

As many commentators have pointed out, the only foreseeable major threat to the region lies in the social consequences of the economic crisis and the lifestyle and working style adjustments the region is experiencing. For the last twenty years, Asia has been largely stable and peaceful. Only a very small minority of Asians has been concerned with political freedom and social inequality. South Koreans routinely take to the streets to do battle with the authorities, but the majority of Asians have been more interested in working hard for material prosperity. Setbacks to rising standards of living, however, could prompt social unrest, as was seen in Indonesia from late 1997 on.

In fact, Indonesia has emerged as one of the most deeply troubled economies, with authorities unwilling to take the kinds of action that had the potential to salvage the situation in other hard-hit countries, such as Thailand and South Korea. This situation came to a head in May of 1998, when riots broke out in Jakarta over the nation's extreme poverty. As we've noted, President Suharto was forced to step down, but this has not solved the ongoing economic problems plaguing Indonesia. (Most Americans don't realize the scale of the Indonesian problem—the country is home to 212.9 million people, compared to the United States, which is home to 270 million people.)

Koreans hope for a return to Korea's previous track of growth. South Korea is no stranger to the vested interests and cozy behind-the-scenes deal-making that have characterized Asian economies in recent years. But it has taken the IMF's (International Monetary Fund) strictures very seriously. With the country's recent economic achievements and its determination to out-do neighboring Japan, the economic crisis could end up strengthening South Korea.

Although China has been barely affected, there are fears that even the current process of economic change there could lead to problems. If the income gaps between rural and urban centers are not narrowed, there may be tremendous social upheaval. There are enormous environmental issues in China, too; the green movement there is generously described as "pale green." Very few environmental efforts have gained widespread attention, despite the fact that Beijing, to name just one city, has an enormous problem with air pollution.

The Journal of Business Ethics spelled out the issues as follows: In the transformation of the employment system and the opening of labor markets, there are nearly one hundred million potentially unemployed people in rural areas, and ten million in state-owned enterprises. If the enterprises continue to employ the latter, the reforms in the enterprises will fail and the new enterprises cannot bear such heavy burdens. Moreover, it is easier for rural workers to find jobs in cities because they are willing to accept lower wages than urban workers. . . Shanghai has two million unemployed workers but over four million jobs are offered only to the nonlocal workers.

The factors that were expected to lead to the Asian Century still apply for the most part: large, dynamic populations eager to work for prosperity (and to work for less than many of their "developed market" counterparts), belief in the power of education and training, support for market economic, collective values and social stability, growing self-confidence and huge, largely untapped markets for growth-minded multinationals. The region has already established a track record for realizing its potential, and there is clearly still a lot more potential to be realized in the twenty-first century.

Asian-Consciousness

National boundaries are internationally established, while names for places vary throughout the world. For example, what Westerners call the Middle East is called West Asia in Malaysia. For our purposes, the Asian countries covered in this section are those with shorelines washed by Pacific Ocean waters. Even within this definition, Asia is a vast and diverse region, stretching from the highly seasonal northern parts of Japan down to the equator and beyond, including the year-round tropical heat of Indonesia. The religious landscape is similarly varied, ranging from Confucianism in the north, Catholicism in the Philippines, many varieties of Buddhism and growing devotion to Islam in the south, to a recent overlay of Marxism in China and Vietnam.

Conversation with people in the region reveals little about what makes them "Asian." For some it's a certain gentleness and graciousness of manner that contrasts with the more abrupt, aggressive style of Westerners. For others it's the central place that rice-growing and -eating have had in their cultures. For still others it's a question of geographical proximity and unity, even though the vast majority of people in the region have never traveled abroad. Some cite the much-touted "Asian values," meaning respect for authority and age and a willingness to put the interests of the group before the interests of the individual.

In the final analysis, being Asian may be a question of choice, a question of identifying with the issues, interests, and sensibilities of other people in the region, of making common cause with them. A new Asian sensibility will spring from very modern history, as the national cultures, as well as daily life, have changed dramatically since World War II. The development of Asian-consciousness will come not just from trading goods, but also from sharing ideas and culture. While Asia is a powerhouse exporter of manufactured goods, it continues to be a big importer of entertainment and style products, including Hollywood films, popular music, designer fashions, computer software, and sports. The region has its own products in all of these areas, but the audience is barely regional, let alone global. Still, boxing from Thailand is now an occasional ESPN favorite.

As Steven Lyons, of public relations giant Burson-Marsteller's Hong Kong based operations in the Asian region said, "Lifestyles and values will continue to be altered by Western media and product developments. Asia will have to work hard at maintaining its cultural identities. Rural areas will be the last bastions of traditional cultural and family values."

The emergence of Asian-consciousness, and with it Asian confidence and creativity, will be a key factor in the maturing of the region. Consumers in Asia, and indeed around the world, would have no hesitation buying electronic goods or domestic appliances made in Asia, but the same cannot be said for "intellectual copyright" products. Until the world embraces the idea that innovations of all kinds can come from this continent, Asians are unlikely to lead the world in areas considered "creative." The turning point will come when Vietnamese soap operas top the TV ratings in Indonesia, when Indonesian pop stars play to packed stadiums in Thailand, when a Thai fashion designer sells clothes like hotcakes in Shanghai and when a Chinese feature film breaks box office records across Asia.

Getting Schooled

One of the cornerstones of "Asian values" is education. In societies without Social Security, children are a sort of pension plan. It used to be smart to have lots of children to spread the risk. These days, the emphasis has switched from having lots of pairs of hands to having just a few well-educated brains. Families are shrinking, and parents are investing in giving their children a higher education.

The pressure to get educated is being felt by children of all ages, all the way down to preschoolers. Steven Lyons says he expects "serious education to start at increasingly younger ages (three to four)." Stuart Harris once e-mailed us to report, "My son Ruben got his first school report in Kuala Lumpur at age twenty-one months!" And, as a Shanghai-based advertising industry executive observed of children there, "The pressures from their parents are tremendous, to the point where children are given little time to enjoy themselves—most of it is spent studying or learning new skills, such as computer, piano, painting, etc."

Rapidly expanding economies need skilled and educated people at every level, which has resulted in a severe labor crunch in some of the fast-growing economies of the region. This need has provided a bonanza for overseas universities, particularly in Australia, Britain, the United States, and Canada. But the sharp devaluation of some currencies in the region and the risk of devaluation hitting other currencies are making students look closer to home for their education. "There will be a major drop in Asian students being sent abroad," predicted Singapore-based Han van Dijk, Dentsu Young & Rubicam's account planning director for Asia. This story is already news fodder in Australia and New Zealand, where institutions have been hit hard by the loss of tuition dollars.

Two educational factors will be crucial in determining the shape and success of Asia in the twenty-first century. The first is how education is imparted. Obedience and respect for authority are deeply instilled in Asian children. Unquestioning rote learning is pretty much the norm, and not only for Chinese and Japanese children, who need to memorize hundreds of complex characters just to be able to read. While the top-down, memorizing approach produces socially responsible youngsters who apply themselves diligently to their studies, some people are beginning to worry that that it doesn't foster the personal qualities that Asia needs to make quantum leaps into the new economies of the next century.

Already Japanese employers are complaining that university graduates are not up to speed for today's workplace. *The Economist* reports that unemployment among graduates and drop-outs is two to three times higher than the national average. The government has introduced changes to take the emphasis off exhaustive examination. As *The Economist* reported, however, Japanese parents might welcome the idea of more liberal, creative education, but they fear that changes might damage their children's employment chances.

Nevertheless, our colleagues in Japan think Japan is likely to see greater emphasis on teaching analytical skills, with more attention paid to the personal development of children, while in China, our colleagues in the marketing communications industry forecast that education will become more focused on guiding children and bringing out their potential, instead of forcing them to memorize things they may not even understand. The whole examination system will be changed. Grades will still be important but not omnipotent. More students will be accepted at universities, as admissions policies will be based on potential and talent rather than just examination grades. In addition, there might also be more private universities available to students.

The second key factor will be the development of regional centers of educational excellence. High-quality establishments already exist, but they tend to draw students from their local markets. Ambitious students study either locally or overseas, with few considering study in another Asian country.

The common culture of television and the Internet will help build relations between young Asians, but there is no substitute for the bonds that are created when people from different countries meet face to face and study together.

Dealing With China

The question of how to deal with China is a common issue for all Asian countries—including China itself. The sheer size of the place, its 1.2 billion population, and its diaspora demand attention.

Chinese culture and thinking continue to impact all countries in the region. Over the centuries, Japan has been tremendously influenced by China. Japanese writing is based on the Chinese system, even though the languages are totally different. Countries sharing borders with China have felt the need to assert their own identity while developing strategies and policies for living with such a huge neighbor.

Chinese emigrants have established themselves throughout the region, often achieving great success in business and arousing local envy in the process. So-called overseas Chinese number some fifty-seven million worldwide, with an estimated fifty-three million of them in Asia Pacific, according to John Naisbitt in his book *Megatrends Asia*.

Since the beginning of history, China has been a massive presence in the Asia Pacific region, a country with a manifest belief in its status as the Middle Kingdom. As the century draws to a close, China has emerged from years of turmoil and hardship and is looking forward to taking its place among the wealthy superpowers. "Deng Xiao Ping created the blueprint of a brilliant future for Chinese people," says Shanghai resident Sharon Lee, who is employed in a senior capacity at an ad agency. "The next millennium will be a great era for China, a continuation of the new future that has been created."

China's pride and ambition have far-reaching implications. Being virtually shut off for much of the twentieth century has limited the impact of China's vast population on the rest of the world. But China has increasingly opened up with the reforms masterminded by Deng.

It used to be said that if all the people in China jumped up and down at the same time, the world would shake. This is obviously not literally true, but it's the sort of thought that naturally comes to mind when contemplating a population of

1.2 billion people, most of whom currently don't travel, don't own cars, don't have central heating or air conditioning and don't have a telephone or a life insurance policy. But those 1.2 billion potential customers don't all live within geographical or financial reach of consumer heaven; for the moment that privilege is enjoyed primarily by the one hundred million or so urban dwellers on the coast.

During the first decades of its existence, the People's Republic of China tended to exert its will by military means. The new economically liberal China under the guidance of President Jiang Zemin is finding a very effective lever in its economic power and the prospect of granting or denying access to China's vast and potentially lucrative market. For instance, the U.K. book publisher HarperCollins got into trouble with its owner, media magnate Rupert Murdoch, for contracting to publish a book by former Hong Kong governor Chris Patten. According to the *Sydney Morning Herald*, "Mr. Murdoch denied censoring Mr. Patten's book but said he had made clear to HarperCollins's management that it had negative aspects and should be dropped. Mr. Murdoch has extensive media interests in China and was accused of being worried about how criticism of Beijing published by parts of his media empire might affect his other businesses." The book may have been dropped by the Murdoch organization but was, of course, ultimately published by various first-rate publishers, including Times Books in America and Macmillan in the United Kingdom. *East and West* was a bestseller in Hong Kong (of course!), Australia, and in many other places, even if it did offend President Jiang Zemin.

Three of Asia Pacific's great success stories are Chinese: Singapore, Hong Kong, and the island of Taiwan, which the People's Republic officially regards as a renegade province. As China's economy grows and opens, the links between them will strengthen. Following an improved relationship with China, "The Great China Economic Circles" will gradually take shape.

The rise of these Chinese economies, and the prosperity of overseas Chinese, is likely to raise some serious questions in non-Chinese countries of the region, particularly with regard to their Chinese immigrant minorities.

In Indonesia, social tension always risks spilling over into anti-Chinese sentiment and even bloodletting. As many as 500,000 people were suspected of Communist sympathies and killed in the coup that brought Suharto to power in 1965, and anti-Chinese sentiment has been evident in Indonesia's latest troubles as well, wrote Simon Long in an article in *The Economist* entitled, "Suharto's End Game." In the end, as already noted, Suharto recently became a victim of the same violence that had brought him to power thirty years ago, when his people railed against his wealth and corruption to overthrow him.

In neighboring Malaysia, the government is very mindful of local resentment. It regards the large Chinese community—about 32 percent of the population—as economically advantaged and has implemented a pro-Malay "affirmative-action" program for the last twenty years.

In the future, will a powerful and prosperous China stand by if its overseas cousins are persecuted for just being Chinese? Will the huge and pervasive influence of China prompt non-Chinese (e.g., Malays in Malaysia) to assert their own culture and identity more vigorously? Will China be seen as a welcome Asian alternative to Americanization and Westernization? Or will Asians look even more to the West to counterbalance Chinese influence?

Japanification Meets Globalization

For a world grown used to the seemingly inexorable rise of Japan Inc., the country's current recession—the first since 1974—comes as a shock. In late twentieth century mythology, the media and academics have held up Japan as a model of a virtuous industrial society with a miraculously cohesive and purposeful population. All over the world, countries have measured themselves against Japan's low crime and high savings rates, educational standards, life expectancy of its people, and the extraordinary success of its corporations and their loyal, disciplined workforces.

Japan's rise from the ashes since 1945 has only added to the perception that the Japanese are special, somehow not the same as other peoples. Within the country itself, the mythology of Japanese differentness runs deep and wide. Books on "nihonjinron" (theories of *Japaneseness*) abound; Japanese readily cite instances of how they are physiologically different from other nationalities (their brains, digestive systems, immune systems, etc.), differences that are often used as justification for complicated regulations governing the import of foodstuffs and pharmaceutical products.

Over the centuries, the sense of being different has nurtured, and been nurtured by, Japan's tendency to regulate its contacts with the outside world, even to the extent of forbidding foreigners from setting foot on Japanese soil for two hundred years. That total isolation ended in 1854, when Commodore Perry forced Japan to concede trading rights, but its legacy persists in both positive and negative ways.

With few outsiders coming in, the Japanese have barely been troubled by the need to accommodate differences in their society. Novelties from the outside world are appreciated, but invariably are adapted to local tastes (Japanified). One unpleasant example occurs when the Japanese purchase pets that are readily abandoned when they outgrow their cuteness. On the plus side, being left to its own devices has produced a nation that prides itself on its homogeneity, where everybody knows and respects the rules and people expect to understand and agree with each other. On the minus side, it has left many Japanese ill-equipped to connect with people who differ from the Japanese norm—as the oft-quoted national saying has it, "The nail that sticks up gets knocked down." (Some of this solidarity has been breaking down slowly in recent years, revealing itself through less respect being shown the elderly as well as more professional opportunities for women. But by no means has there been widespread change in the basic Japanese contract with the community.)

The big questions for Japan in our increasingly globalized world are how it needs to change and whether it's actually capable of doing what needs to be done. What really needs to be decided is in what direction shifts should be made.

In today's global arena, Japan's heritage has proved a disadvantage. The Japanese place enormous emphasis on cultivating relationships with other Japanese and are ill-prepared to forge links with outsiders. Indeed, Japanese who spend any length of time outside Japan run the risk of finding themselves permanently on the outside when they go home. This is less a matter social ostracization and more a sheer lack of comfort with those who have broken the social contract of insulation and communal standards and values.

Some younger Japanese, women especially, have shown an appetite for exploring other cultures—flocking to flamenco classes in Madrid, trying on different personas in London. At present, these adventurous souls have put themselves outside the mainstream—Japanese corporations mostly recruit directly out of Japanese universities and shape their employees' life experiences for them. Whereas all Japanese men surveyed by Keio University were transferred to Hong Kong by employers, all women surveyed had moved there voluntarily in search of better jobs. In the future, Japan's ability to connect with the world will depend increasingly on its willingness to welcome back its adventurers and integrate their experiences into the fabric of mainstream life.

• NEXT: GOODBYE, "JOB FOR LIFE"

Japan's prolonged economic stagnation, sharpened by the crisis in Asia, has brought into question the country's famed "job for life" approach to employment. Bonds of mutual trust and loyalty, reminiscent of feudalism, have been the hallmark of Japan's workplace relations. In the past, employees unquestioningly dedicated most of their waking hours to their company, often to the detriment of family life. In return, companies looked after their employees, steadily moving them (females traditionally leave work on marrying) up the company hierarchy.

While the rest of the industrialized world has lived through a long and painful period of downsizing and restructuring, Japanese companies have done their utmost to avoid layoffs. But the continuation of this kind of job security started looking shaky with the unprecedented closure of Nissan's Zama plant in 1995. Three years later, when Prime Minister Keizo Obuchi took office, the government announced that the unemployment rate had hit a postwar high of 4.3 percent. (According to *Business Week*, informed estimates put the figure at double that or more. While 4.3 may be as low as the American unemployment rate has ever fallen, the Japanese way has been, and still is, that every man has a job always and forever.)

Western media, always alert to tales of weirdness and woe from Japan, are awash with accounts of bewildered unemployed lamenting the broken pact of loyalty. More tellingly, the Japanese are starting to question the system. As a senior salaryman noted, "Japanese are starting to go home earlier and have their own lives. They can't be sure their jobs will last, so they are less willing to give up their time for them."

• NEXT: MERIT OUTRANKING SENIORITY

Respect for seniority in business, but also in life, is one of the cornerstones of Japanese society, fostering stability, continuity and commitment. Expertise is accrued through patient apprenticeship over long years of practical experience under an older mentor. Whiz kids and high flyers are well advised to keep quiet and avoid rocking the boat.

But as Japan gradually opens up to foreign companies, adventurous young Japanese are finding that "slowly but surely" is no longer the only game in town. Nontraditional employers may not offer the "warm bath" appeal of a big, established Japanese corporation, but they do offer respect and responsibility on the basis of ability, not age—an important consideration in the absence of jobs for life.

• NEXT: LEADERSHIP, PLEASE

Although Japanese society is very hierarchical, strong leaders at the pinnacle of a hierarchy are the exception, not the rule. Power depends entirely on the consent and collaboration of those below you. This is clear from the revolving-door approach to government—Mr. Keizo Obuchi is Japan's ninth prime minister in as many years. Such a consensual, nonauthoritarian approach works well in stable times, but is proving inadequate in an era when new rules and clear direction are required.

The July 1998 selection of compromise candidate Obuchi— the least likely of the three runners to implement serious change—

was greeted with disappointment, both within and outside Japan. Signs that the country is ready to embrace a new approach are becoming evident: In *Lost Japan* (Lonely Planet, 1996), longtime resident Alex Kerr observed, ". . . the mid-levels of almost every Japanese institution are filled with people in their thirties and forties who are extremely dissatisfied . . . Above is the massive weight of decades of regulation by bureaucrats; below is rising desperation on the part of a generation that has some knowledge of the outside world and realizes that Japan is falling behind." Kerr's observations were confirmed by the recent *Economist*/Angus Reid World Poll, which gave "citizens' ratings of their quality of life and hope for the future across twnety-nine countries." In the "Hope Index" rating, Japan came in very low, with the majority of respondents expressing pessimism for the future.

POSTSCRIPT

As we were going to press, we realized that Latin America is also rising fast, maybe another Big Next. Though, for now, next.

• NEXT: WATCH LATIN AMERICA RISE

Despite major advances in democracy and economic stability, Latin America has yet to defeat serious problems related to drugs and crime. According to Eduardo Gamarra, a professor at Florida International University, personal security is "the No. 1 crisis in the entire region..." With an annual cost estimated at $168 billion, or 14 percent of the region's GDP, violent crime has been cited as the principal barrier to regional economic development.

While pension planners enthusiastically welcome a Latin American baby boom, educators anticipate problems in preparation for what's to come in the world. A communiqué from the second Summit of the Americas called for all governments in the region to provide universal access to elementary school education by 2010 and to provide high school education for 75 percent of the region's youngsters by the same year. Under a plan drawn up at the summit, the region will have access to $8.3 billion in new loans and grants, mainly from international lending organizations.

In a break from its traditional insularity, the Latin American business community is looking outside the region for ideas and investment opportunities. The Brazilian conglomerate Itausa, for instance, sent fifty managers from its Duratex subsidiary to study top companies in Japan. The company claims that by reorganizing decision-making, it reduced by 50 percent the time needed to get new products to market.

Latin America's strong sense of identity—fostered, in part, by a common religion (Catholicism) and only two major languages (Spanish and Portuguese)—means the region's influence will be felt far more strongly in the international community as global communication becomes a reality.

The Holy Grail of Economic Reform

Today, change is most often driven by a raging, metaphorical hunger—a voracious appetite for better, safer, richer, healthier, and easier lives. Much of the progress in Latin America can be attributed to this new appetite—one that has been spurred by economic reform. The more progressive governments have dismantled some of the trade barriers that shielded domestic companies from international competition. This shield, however, was not accompanied by the necessary sword, and companies were originally discouraged from investment and innovation. But under new government approaches, innovation is right around the corner, starting with the privatization of state monopolies.

The realization of economic reform in Latin America started with the formation of subregional trading blocks: Mercosur in the south, the Andean Community in the north, the Central American Common Market, and NAFTA in North America. Mercosur and the Andean Pact (its preliminary agreement was in March 1998) still hope to accomplish a free-trade zone spanning the entire continent by the dawn of the millennium. Trade among the four countries of Mercosur grew fivefold to $20.3 billion in the first seven years of this decade.

Mercosur has been an important economical and cultural amalgamating force. This economic plan is the hands-down winner as a key force to bringing Latin America forward into the 21st century. Additionally, it's a clear indication that there's a growing economic and cultural interdependence in the region.

It's not hard to imagine similar connections developing across Latin America as a whole; its nations are already clear leaders in this respect.

Overall, the IADB reckons that the reforms of the past decade, while incomplete, have lifted per capita income by 12 percent and GDP growth by 1.9 percent. It's believed that without the reforms this growth would not have been as high. The IADB calculates that with further reforms, annual growth could increase as much as 5.5 percent.

Current Economic Problems

Although current forecasts indicate that the economy is stabilizing in some regions, Latin Americans must forge ahead with plans to resolve current economic woes. Brazil and Argentina will play pivotal roles. In a macroeconomic sense, neither the balance of the world monetary powers, nor multinationals trading in Latin America, nor the world's banking institutions, can afford anything but a successful resolution of Brazil's current problems. Interestingly, those who have the most to gain may be the other Latin American nations, none more significantly than Argentina.

Until recently, rampant inflation and boom-and-bust economic cycles made chronic uncertainty a daily hazard for Latin American businesses, forcing them to focus on short-term survival at home rather than looking abroad or investing for the longer term. But growing economic stability is enabling Latin Americans to plan with greater confidence, especially in leading countries such as Brazil, the world's eighth-largest economy (at $800 billion).

Latin America Union and Leadership

So let's imagine at this point that a Latin American Union has been formed to ensure the expansion of economic and cultural growth in the region. Where would this new LAU be headquartered? And why?

After collecting and analyzing survey data from business people throughout Latin America—for an instant intelligence report we compiled for our company—the answer is overwhelmingly in favor of São Paolo, Brazil. Reasons include its centrality, its proximity to Latin American business, its wealth, its cultural diversity (influences from Europe, America, and Latin America, without any of them dominating), and its neutrality. One respondent even said, "Can you imagine a dispute between Argentina, Chile, and Colombia with a headquarters in Mexico?"

Other factors contributing to Brazil's leadership potential are the growth of its service sector, stronger industrial and agricultural sectors to increase the external economy, the augmentation of the per capita income, and the increased number of educated employees.

Runners Up

The closest contenders to Brazil for regional leadership include Buenos Aires (for its polyglot culture, as well as its economic stability) and Mexico City (mostly for its size, international visibility, cultural history, and regional clout). Mexico City is often felt to be "the most Latin American," with a long cultural history connecting it with Spain, and its own vibrant and active indigenous cultures, both Aztec and Mayan. Mexico City's "native" cultures successfully coexist and thrive alongside European and American influences.

The New Americas Equal Big Opportunity

Talk about feeling like a kid in a candy store: if you're a multinational corporation looking to expand your business, Latin America is *the* candy store. Latin America is a market with over four hundred eighty million consumers and $1 trillion in buying power. By the year 2025, the region will have six hundred seventy-four million consumers, with the vast majority of this population—80 percent—living in urban areas. Today, U.S.-based companies comprise 49 percent of the top two hundred fifty multinational companies in Latin America, while European-based multinational companies comprise 39 percent.

In the future, there will be plenty of fierce competition for the top-tier consumers, including competition within the region as well. There are now newly-formed Latin-owned multinationals poised to capture the hometown market. Getting a piece of the Latin American market will not be easy.

Over a decade ago, Latin America began to implement policies to sustain economic growth. Markets were open to foreign capital to increase competion. But all of the efforts were thwarted when Mexico's economy collapsed after an unsuccessful devaluation of the peso. Since that time, recession has torn through Latin America. The economy has become unstable, currency has been devalued, inflation is growing, and prices for consumer goods are getting higher.

What's Next? More Wealth Inequities

Mexico. Since 1989, the number of poor have risen by 9.6 million. The top 20 percent of wage earners command 55 percent of Mexico's wealth.

Brazil. Ten percent of Brazilians, the upper tier, retain 50 percent of the national income, while the poorest 50 percent have 10 percent. The government estimates a quarter of its 160 million people live below the poverty line.

Argentina. Last year, the richest 10 percent earned twenty-five times as much as the poorest 10 percent.

Poverty Perspective. According to a March 1999 Reuters report, if the economy in Latin America grows at a steady rate of three percent a year, it will take Chile thirty-seven years to wipe out extreme poverty; Mexico will need forty years; Peru seventy-two years; Brazil eighty-one years; and El Salvador will need ninety-eight years.

Two Nations Indivisible: United States and Latin America

It may seem an obvious connection but nevertheless it is a very important one: in the United States today, the Hispanic population is the fastest growing minority group, and by the year 2050, Hispanics will be the largest minority group in the United States. According to an Associated Press report, the Census Bureau finds that of the foreign-born U.S. residents counted in the last American census, 44.3 percent were from Latin America (including Mexico). This is by far the largest minority group. (Other non-foreign born totals include 26.3 percent from Asia; 22.9 percent from Europe; 4.0 from North America; 1.9 percent from Africa; 0.5 percent from the Pacific Islands.)

Understanding Latin culture and targeting this group, both in the United States and in Latin America, will become crucial to the future success of companies. It is more than mere coincidence that *Teen en Español* was launched in the U.S. and Latin America at the same time, and that other U.S. magazines such as *Latin Girl* are tapping into this market as well. Latin teens have a lot of spending power. They read magazines as much as they watch television. And it appears that many marketing experts are beginning to view Latin teens, along with urban and black teens, as trendsetters. Miami-based MTV Latin America is another example. Millions of teenagers in the U.S. and Latin America are avid viewers of this music channel. The Spanish-language service reaches 8.3 million households, and its Portuguese-language service in Brazil reaches 17 million.

CHAPTER 4:
Americans in a
Small World Next

COULD THE FACT THAT WE'RE REALLY a small world after all be the biggest Next—at least for Americans, and by extension for the world, as Americans wake up and react to this startling recognition? Isolationism won't work in the twenty-first century. The chairman of the board of governors of the Federal Reserve System said it most clearly just a few months after most financial geniuses pooh-poohed American vulnerabilities just because Asia and Latin America and then Russia started tanking, hard and fast. We repeating the following with emphasis, energy and in hopes of raising a big bright warning flag—*The New York Times* notes that Federal Reserve Board chairman Alan Greenspan said in September of 1998, "It is just not credible that the United States can remain an oasis of prosperity unaffected by a world that is experiencing greatly increased stress."

Completely separately, but in the wake of the domino effect of global capital markets, *The New York Times* also reported recently, "Ethnic shifts, though still small in most places, are subtly but broadly altering American perspectives. . . . The ability to interact directly with distant cultures is more within reach, largely because airline deregulation in the late 1970s triggered expanded flight schedules and lower ticket prices. In 1997, United States citizens flew 52.1 million international flights, up from 14.3 million in 1975, according to industry research firm BACK Associates Inc. of Stamford, Connecticut."

How Big is Small?

We're often confounded by the disinclination of many of our fellow countrymen and women to embrace anything new—that is, beyond trendy, disposable, wear-outable products and popular fashions. Globalization is one of those concepts most Americans would prefer to ignore. And beta launches and vaporware seem to have taken a toll on the American psyche, exhausting our capacity to become thrilled about newness. Instead, we are content to put our excitement on hold until presented with a personal opportunity to see and believe. While the media's tendency to overhype invites (some say demands) a skeptical reaction, the undercurrent of hesitation and pessimism betrays our history as the nation that courageously took "one giant step for mankind" back in the '60s.

NOTHING HAPPENS

Until it ended its seven-year run in 1998, the most successful TV show in America had been *Seinfeld*, a comedy that charmed viewers partially because "nothing happens." The empty plotlines mirrored much of daily life in America, specifically in New York City. Perhaps the appeal of nothingness is a response to information overload: In the world outside of *Seinfeld*, nitty-gritty details of current affairs routinely evolve into big stories and blend into little stories, all against a backdrop of analytical commentary that, naturally, is further balanced by so-called hard news. It's a case of life according to *Geraldo* or *Dateline* or *Larry King Live*. Conceivably, Americans have become numb because life beyond the TV screen is changing too fast. Then again, maybe we're simply a nation that's become complacent with its success as an economic and cultural force.

* * *

Isolationism has been a genuine part of the twentieth century in America. Today, the majority of Americans just don't get globalization. Their version of going global is to Americanize—delivering McDonald's, Burger King, and Pizza Hut to the world, not helping strengthen local businesses in marketplaces as diverse as Capetown, Caracas, Copenhagen, Larnaca, Lima, and Lisbon.

The last time we checked, only 23 percent (less than sixty-five million people) of Americans have ever had a passport. In the fiscal year of 1998, there were 6.5 million passports issued by the U.S. State Department, up from 6.3 million in the fiscal year of 1997. If growth continues at this rate, by 2005, nearly 40 percent of Americans should have a passport. *Why do Paris if we can do Parris Island, South Carolina, instead?* The French take a lot of heat for being jingoistic, but the truth is that we Americans are much worse. At least the French are more apt than we are to speak a second language. (In 1998 half of all Europeans aged fifteen to twenty-four could converse in English, according to the European Union. This was up from one in three in 1987.) Both of the authors knows well-off Americans who have never been abroad, and countless others who consider Paris truly exotic and the thought of a trip to the Acropolis or the Parthenon completely over the top. The simplistic explanation is that Americans don't have the proximity of foreign locales or ease of traveling that Europeans enjoy. But there are other, more complicated reasons for our complacency.

What's It Got to do With Us?

A striking example of Americans' head-in-the-sand mentality is our reaction (or lack thereof) to the Asian economic crisis, which threw our financial markets into turmoil as the 1990s wound down. "Who's wringing their hands over the fallout from Asia and other potential economic problems?" queried *Business Week*. "Not the average American. . . . Personally, Americans believe that they are doing very well (despite analysts' predictions of an economic slowdown)."

America Next probably won't be marked by blind faith. But will our facade of optimism crack apart when some act of fate, or a series of them, reminds us that we're not as isolated from economic problems in other parts of the world as the huge expanses of water separating us from other continents would lead us to believe? Almost two thirds (65 percent) of Americans rated economic conditions in this country as excellent or good, compared to about half (49 percent) in 1997. This was at the time of the peak of media coverage about an Asian meltdown, the demise of the Brazilian financial infrastructure, and Russia being just plain broke.

Given that change in America often is motivated by financial self-interest, we predict that, as the world shrinks and as the United States of Europe pulls together to provide the kind of economic challenge to United States hegemony heretofore unseen, Americans will be forced to abandon the modern-day "isolationism" (a blur of cultural, economic and political separation) that would have made Woodrow Wilson proud. Today's kids and teens (who, thanks to the Internet, are growing up with an electronic but fundamentally unreal window on the world) might prove to be the first generation to fully embrace the opportunities of the global stage.

We've often been asked if we resent having to spend so much time in countries where few people speak English fluently. In our travels around the world, the only thing we have resented are our own limitations as linguists. In the face of changing global realities, it is our fervent hope that more United States schools will grasp the importance of introducing students to other languages and cultures at an age when students can most readily absorb those lessons. As futurists, we recognize that a more globally oriented and inclusive America is an inevitable; as Americans, we hope the United States wakes up to this reality sooner rather than later.

Show Me the Money

The economic reconstruction of Asia must finally impact our Yankee fortunes, especially as we adjust to the realities that came by way of the devaluation of the currencies in Thailand, Japan, Indonesia, and other countries. For a near-term American Next, look for reduced domestic demand as either higher interest rates take their toll or softer equity prices (caused by increased price competition thanks to cheap imports and rising wages) and general slowdown in the "tradeables" sector accomplish the same thing.

Despite the fact that we have seen the Dow hit 10,000 and then 11,000, in rapid succession, look for tougher economic times in America, and when they come, for a new sensibility to emerge that says balancing budgets, whether personal budgets, business budgets, or even the local, state, and federal budgets, is a necessity. The biggest change, then, could well be an evolution away from spending with credit cards. In fact, watch for new interest in cash debit cards as more and more Americans start to contemplate retrenchment. Private consumption won't fall precipitously by any means, but the current consumer credit ratio of 17.4 percent of personal income may well not be sustained.

Thus, it's not surprising that we're forecasting that the economy will slow down while inflation accelerates, in part due to higher health-care costs and a somewhat weaker dollar. What we also know is that events in Asia and Latin America and the financial angst in Russia will keep the Federal Reserve bankers busy fiddling with interest rates so that the American economy doesn't land hard, and that there is a reasonable foundation for growth through 2002 and beyond. The Fed has already intervened to support the Japanese yen. The Japanese finance industry is being overhauled, and with this shift comes instability in their financial markets; to compound matters, the growing bilateral trade surplus Japan runs with the United States should slow down, in part due to the aging of the American population and our increased interest in cheaper Japanese imports.

The American dollar remains reasonably strong against the euro. But while a unified but fledgling euro will be subject to conflicting forces in its first few years, the new struggle of Dollarland versus Euroland versus Yenland spells lots of Nexts for Americans. Let's start with an increasing awareness that our superpower status is finally debatable—or will be when the United States of Europe gets fully organized from an economic standpoint.

Second, America's GDP will be significantly worse in the next few years, and gaps between exports and imports will remain significant. *The Economist* Intelligence Unit forecasts that "with the gap between exports and imports so large, export growth would have to outpace import growth by a significant margin in order to close the deficit. In the absence of a recession or a major collapse in the dollar this seems unlikely. We therefore expect the current-account deficit to widen further, reaching $338 billion by 2002 (3.3 percent of GDP)."

So what does the man behind the money, or rather the man who sets American monetary policy, have to say about what's next? Is isolation finally going to end? *Business Week* offered "Greenspan's Take on Today's Economy" as part of its special report called "The 21st Century Economy: The Big Picture." We paraphrase here his point of view about productivity, globalization, and the anxious worker.

- **Productivity:** Productivity growth is well above trends of recent years due to America's heavy corporate investment in computers and in other technologies that are labor savers.
- **Globalization:** Technological advances, coupled with the growth of the global economy, facilitate companies easily shifting production around the world; therefore, capacity shortages won't cause inflationary bottlenecks.
- **The Anxious Worker:** Employees are well aware that corporate downsizing combined with globalization means less job security—something on which they place great importance. The risk of wage inflation falls away as employees pick pay tied to performance as a means to secure their positions.

Is Isolation Finally Winding Down?

We noted a curious story in the *Wall Street Journal* in September of 1998, which in some ways captured our queries, concerns and consternation about America's future as a melting pot. It begins by introducing the idea that America's rural areas are becoming increasingly urbane and sophisticated.

There has been a partial reversal of the mass merchandising and production that characterized the U.S. economy for much of the century. The rise of uniformity-driven chain restaurants and retailers over the past several decades suffocated legions of coffee shops, cafes, single-screen cinemas, and small-town stores. But in today's saturated consumer economy, chain outlets of every stripe increasingly offer a broad range of niche products aimed at exploiting the very individuality of tastes that those neighborhood stores once fostered.

New bookstore chains, with their coffee bars and cafes, convey a sense of eclectic intimacy (in outlets that are nonetheless almost identical in every city). Grocery chains aggressively promote a diverse range of ethnic, regional and once-uncommon specialties: Tony Chachere's Creole Seasoning, long available only in the southernmost parishes of Louisiana, now sits on store shelves in Nebraska.

Outlet malls at rural interstate exits have become the purveyors of designers Liz Claiborne, Geoffrey Beene, and Jones New York to the distant masses. Pottery Barn units in regional malls re-introduce craftsman-style furniture at middle-class prices. The newest units of Wal-Mart Stores Inc. dedicate significant shelf space to more fashionable clothing, cutting-edge kitchen appliances, 230-thread-count sheets and newly released books.

"Take some new fashion from Milan, Italy, those things that used to take some extensive period of time to be translated to the mass channel. Everything is accelerated now. All of a sudden our customers are able to buy something very quickly that has gotten hot," says H. Lee Scott, president of Wal-Mart Stores, a unit of the retailing giant. "The girls in Princeton, New Jersey, are buying exactly the same products as the girls in Berryville, Arkansas, the same silhouette, the same colors, the same styles."

Educational, Ethnic Changes: Beyond the economic engine, significant cultural shifts are changing America's tastes. Despite concern about the poor showing of U.S. students as compared to pupils in other countries and laments about illiteracy, the educational attainment of Americans actually has risen sharply. Nearly 82 percent had a high-school diploma in 1996, compared with just over one third in 1950, according to the Census Bureau. Adult Americans with college degrees increased to 23.6 percent from 6.2 percent over the same period.

Ethnic shifts, though still small in most places, are subtly but broadly altering American perspectives. Chinese eateries, exotic to most Americans as recently as the 1970s, today appear in thousands of small towns, often as the only full-service restaurant. Similarly, Hispanic populations showed increases in 3,002 of the country's 3,143 counties between 1990 and 1996, according to University of Michigan researcher William H. Frey.

Still, we worry that the move toward genuine globalization may only encompass a small minority. We're concerned that it's the same global citizens living the future, doing the cross-cultural fertilization gig, while most Americans sip Starbucks coffee as they contemplate Martha Stewart's advice about fine living or debate who most deserves to win the World Series this year. Or is this just experience collection by another name?

THEM AND US

In this post–Cold War era, morality has become the new battleground. Enemies at home—those who would seek to lead our nations astray, politically, socially or morally—are deemed far more dangerous than those who would seek to do us harm from abroad. Whether you define such enemies as immigrants, gays, blacks, Jews, Muslims, liberals, or reactionaries, we'll see nations and communities become increasingly stratified over such issues. People—and companies—will wear their beliefs on their sleeves and pay to advertise them in the media (witness the ads in *The New York Times* by the Exodus organization, claiming the ability the change gays into straights.).

Despite the recent ethical vacuum that has shown itself in places such as the former Yugoslavia and Rwanda, government-imposed moral dogma and censure are still very much with us. In one glaring example, Greece recently banned what may be the most innocuous book in existence: the dictionary. The ban is due to definitions that contain racial slurs and stereotypes. For countries in the business of preserving a strict moral and political agenda, the Internet has been a wholesale disaster. In China, where Internet service providers are state-controlled, Web sites are subject to being banned without notice. According to Western experts, authorities simply submit a list of banned sites to Chinese ISPs, which then must refuse to provide hosting services. (The Chinese government denies blocking access to sites.) Moreover, Internet users in China must register with the police and can be punished for retrieving information deemed pornographic or harmful to social order. Notable examples of blocked Web sites include the BBC's non-commercial web service, which provides access to most of the BBC's publicly funded material, including *BBC News*.

Middle Eastern countries are among the most strident when it comes to proscribing freedoms that much of the Western world takes for granted. The death sentence (or fatwa) placed upon Salman Rushdie after the publication of *The Satanic Verses* has only recently been repudiated in Iran (and has been reinstated by other parties). And in Kuwait, an Islamic committee has suggested that the government set up a facility to censor foreign satellite broadcasts. As vice president for the committee, Adel al-Falah explained to *BBC Worldwide* this past September, "Every country has the option to protect its values and morals."

Expect to see even more stake claiming of the moral high ground (however you define it), as people on either side of hot-button issues become ever more vocal (even violent) about expressing their views. From murders of abortion providers to destructive acts of "animal liberation," we in the U.S. will see extremists wrest control of issues away from those who would tend toward moderation and compromise.

FEAR, FEAR EVERYWHERE

Big brother on steroids: There are some Americans who practically consider Bill Gates the anti-Christ. Not because of Microsoft's allegedly unfair business practices, but because Gates embodies all that we fear about technology. In the opening chapter of this book, we talked about global technofears—concerns that new technologies increasingly will invade our private lives and our businesses. In the United States some of these fears might well become realities before they hit much of the rest of the world. The degree to which we welcome technological innovations into our lives and homes makes us vulnerable to those who would choose to monitor our interests, our purchases—even our thoughts (via Internet postings).

Legislative action might restrict some prying digital eyes, but we've already lost much of the privacy we once took for granted. With satellites overhead and databases filled with our financial, medical, and other personal details, true anonymity is no longer possible.

Lock the gates, load the guns!: Already shaken by the World Trade

Center explosion two years before, Americans were jolted awake by the 1995 bombing of the Alfred P. Murrah Federal Building in Oklahoma City, in which 168 people lost their lives. The fact that this terrorist act was committed by Americans, took place in what the media love to call "America's Heartland," and involved the deaths of small children combined to make this event an almost unimaginable horror. Subsequent news stories about America's militias (who function outside the community and the law) further fueled our fears and feelings of insecurity.

There was a time when Americans feared acts of terrorism only while traveling abroad. That was before the World Trade Center bombing, before Oklahoma City, before the deadly explosion at the Atlanta Olympic Games in 1996. Fears of foreign (typically Islamic) terrorists are real, but many of us now feel even more acutely the threat posed by America's paramilitary groups armed with high-tech weapons and heightened paranoia. After all, they're already in the country, they're already armed, and, for the most part, they look just like the rest of us. While Americans feared fellow Americans who rioted and bombed during the 1960s too, these terrorists are that much more different—and particularly threatening since their commitment to ideology is unimaginable to the average Joe or Jane Public.

Not surprisingly, the result of increased violence (terrorist, random, and other) is that Americans no longer feel safe at home or on the street. We watch news reports about drive-by shootings and in-school massacres; we see kids die of drug overdoses and drunk-driving accidents; we follow trial coverage of alleged murderers on TV and via the Internet. Many of us react to this bombardment of violent images by clinging to the feelings of security afforded by familiar faces, places, and products. Others of us engage in extreme sports or other high-risk behaviors, getting a rush out of facing our mortality head-on. Others of us take steps to help ensure our own safety, perhaps by enrolling in a martial arts class, advocating gun control, or moving into a gated community.

In the years to come, expect increased efforts to bolster security, particularly among the wealthy. "In the next millennium the chasm between rich and poor is bound to grow even wider," forecast an article in *Maclean's*, the Canadian news magazine. The United States alone has reached a record number of billionaires at 189, according to *Forbes*. Of the top ten billionaires in America, all but two earned their fortunes from Microsoft and Wal-Mart. As Canada's *Maclean's* noted, "At the moment, the world's 358 billionaires, according to the United Nations, control more wealth than 45 percent of the earth's population. As this imbalance becomes even greater, social unrest will increase. In response, the upper class could share its wealth—but more likely its members will retreat behind guarded and gated fortress enclaves, where they will live in safety—and perpetual fear." The security trend does apply to everyone, not just the super rich, despite the media images of billionaires trapped behind fancy, golden gates.

Personal security will be a growth industry to watch, featuring everything from stylish bulletproof vests to trained attack dogs to sophisticated aerial surveillance. *Maclean's* also reports that the newest gadgets will include satellite images and helicopters with infrared cameras that can detect the heat from a burning cigarette. "The proving ground for such equipment is the Los Angeles Police Department," the magazine says, "which already operates four Aerospatiale helicopters with thirty-million candle-power spotlights to turn night into day, and a separate fleet of Bell Jet Ranger whirlybirds that can ferry SWAT teams into action at a moment's notice. It is only a matter of time, in the corporate world of tomorrow, before such services are privatized and offered to the highest bidders."

CHAPTER 5:

Globally Speaking, What's Next?

Eight Great Expectations of Global Citizens

*W*E OFFER THESE PREDICTIONS, our visions of what's likely to come, as an explanation and a backdrop for some of the turmoil we're forecasting for the near future.

1. An information revolution will drive productivity throughout the economy. And industries that are information-dependent or information-rich will change the most over the next decade. Watch for new business mores and practices to evolve in finance, media, and retail and wholesale trade. For example, content repurposing will be the norm (the *Harvard Business Review* predicts this will be the money-making side of the knowledge industry and calls it "versioning"), and so will contextual commerce—retail opportunities embedded in the written word. (For example, we imagine in the very near future that you'll be reading a www.rollingstone.com profile of Aerosmith and have the option to click on Steven Tyler's name and buy a poster, or a downloadable screensaver of

him; at another place in the profile, where his daughter Liv is mentioned, you will be able to click on her name and order video cassettes of her recent movies.)

2. Life will become more sci-fi than we're expecting over the next decade. Imagine coming home in the evening and deciding you want to turn your living room into a seduction scene. You flick a scent button, and musk filters into the air; the wallpaper goes from preppy checks to a romantic purple. You pop a pill to ensure sexual fulfillment, put on "intensity glasses" to maximize the thrill, and then log on using voice activation to your computer with its flatscreen monitor, supersized of course. There you liaise with your ideal lover, his or her voice pumped out of speakers built into the walls.

    Besides these lifestyle shifts, other technology breakthroughs will accelerate, especially in the fields of biotechnology and medicine. Whole new industries will be born. For example, tomorrow's plastic surgery clinics will feel much more approachable than ever before. Watch for doctors with private clinics, focused now on serving the middle and wealthier classes, to become as accessible as gas stations are today. There will be one every couple of miles, or closer, and they'll feature lots of special promotions to urge consumers to visit them instead of the competition.

3. Going global will be unavoidable—even for the isolationists who abound in the United States. Byproducts of globalization will include much larger markets and tougher competitive marketplaces as foreign competitors jump into our home turf, which has been the territory of American companies for decades. Think of Aussie Rupert Murdoch, whose empire includes newspapers, the Fox Network, a sports franchise, and much, much more. The "Made in America" machine spent millions of dollars trying to keep him from becoming a tycoon on our soil. What's next? Innovation and cost-cutting, as Americans learn to become lean, mean, globally competitive machines. This will translate into more layoffs. While jobs will also be created, the people being laid off rarely have the skill sets (analytical and technical) to fulfill

these more thoughtful, less physical positions that are being conceived in our new experience economy.

4. Everything is getting faster, and this includes the rate at which the economy will grow; most economists aren't predicting it, but the economy could accelerate—perhaps to 3 percent or more per year—spurred by the massive boom in the high-technology sector.

5. Change is inevitable, but those changes won't necessarily be bad. While it's true that we may experience some PMT—premillennial tension—and Y2K fears, such as planes falling out of the sky and bank accounts disappearing a minute after midnight on December 31, 1999, we'll also be likely to enjoy a higher standard of living and become even less tolerant of such phenomena as large budget deficits.

6. The competitive edge will go to countries that manage to master the change game and in which the political climate fosters innovation, free trade, and, especially, open financial systems that provide the necessary flexibility for companies to ride the waves of change with confidence. Businesses that master new technologies will stake claim to increased market share and bigger profits. But for the first time in history, small may be better, if small means adaptable.

7. Not all the news is good. Dislocations and uncertainty, even chaos, will be a millennial reality, and businesses (and individuals) that cannot adapt quickly will find themselves victims of the revolution that is driving us from the here and now into a full-fledged experience economy, where we will pay premiums for quality experiences, as described previously. (The subtle transition here is the emerging value we place on services and sensory fulfilment as opposed to material acquistion. In the experience economy, less may be more, if more equals more senses engaged and enraptured.)

8. Technoshock is now. And technoshocks will increase in frequency and strength in the United States and around the world as we get hyped up and begin to absorb the full benefits of years of scientific breakthroughs—breakthroughs that will make the Jetsons seem like the Flintstones.

MILLENNIUM COUNTDOWN

Living in this time of enormous change—a period that spans the second and third millennia—fosters a sense of historical importance that leads to an increased desire to leave a mark on the world. Individuals will assess their lives in the twentieth century, making pacts with themselves for changes that will be brought about in the twenty-first—the ultimate New Year's resolutions. For the eve of December 31, 1999, reservations already have been made to ring in the new year on the *QE2*, on the international dateline and in New York City. (Times Square will be millennium central for many.)

Cause for Celebration?

"The actual celebration of the arrival of the next millennium isn't as important in the East as it is in the West. While looking forward to the onset of the next millennium, the current economic situation has put a damper on expectations. The overall attitude is one of hope," reports Yoshitaka Abe, a high-ranking marketing executive in Tokyo. But, he points out, this business climate spells angst. "The economic downturn is at the forefront of businessmen's minds. The millennium bug is a worry for computerized companies. New Year's Eve (of 1999) is looked forward to, but not being made as big a deal as in the West."

Stuart Harris, our colleague, and a British market research practitioner who has been based in Kuala Lumpur, Malaysia and Amsterdam, explains: "Overall, the millennium is a European milestone (including honorary Europeans in the Americas) and is an imported concept in much of Asia. The Chinese think of their history in terms of six thousand years. Buddha's followers might well have his birth time (around 500 B.C.) as their reference point, and Muslims (most of Indonesia and half of Malaysia) haven't yet reached fifteen hundred years since the birth of the prophet. So although they're all counting our years too, I would suspect that they don't feel it so deeply."

While part of what's *Next* is definitely experiencing a sense of globalness, local reactions to change, including the change of centuries in the West, are deeply personal. Millennial angst isn't the same everywhere—at all. "In Canada, consumers' concerns about changes in the new millennium tend to center on changes to their personal situation," reports Toronto-based Laurence Bernstein. He goes on to note that, like Americans, "Canadians will be older and, therefore, more dependent on government assistance in the form of pensions (which they believe won't be available) and health care (which they believe will be severely cut). Younger people are concerned that when they enter the workforce, they will not be able to find employment or that their chances for advancement will be limited due to people working well into old age. Therefore, there is some concern and darkness in their view of the postmillennium society."

"People in interactive entertainment see the next millennium as a golden Digital Age," says Sven Meyer, a managing director at Psygnosis Germany, formerly Sony's electronic publishing division. "Most people in this industry see the year 2000 and beyond as an almost unlimited hunting ground for business opportunities." Around the world, businesses have rushed to register names associated with the changing century. Companies got creative, coming up with catchy names such as "nu.millennia inc.," the moniker chosen by a San Diego-based publishing house. In cyberspace, a host of millennium-oriented Web sites have been constructed, and many more are in development. When we ran a search for millennium, the total number that came back was 499,489. Now that's what we call overused!

A Mixed Reaction

In the popular square in front of Paris's Georges Pompidou Center, a digital clock has been counting down the millennium since 1987. Yet just months from the turn of the millennium, the mood across most of Europe falls a long way short of eager anticipation. Going by the response of people we've queried over the course of our trend treks, only the United Kingdom and Denmark (and possibly the increasingly wealthy Netherlands) are looking forward to the big click-over with optimism. (In the United Kingdom, the Blair spin machine has done everything it can to promote good will towards millennium partying and programs.)

The remaining countries are certainly anticipating change, but for many it's the kind of change that has to be endured rather than embraced. Even the changes countries have pursued, such as the single currency and the European Union, are viewed with less optimism than they were just a few years ago. In short, many Europeans fear that life won't be as good for them in the next century.

Unemployment continues to be the big headache for Germans, who have been accustomed to steadily rising living standards. Before they turn their minds to the millennium, they've already ensured that Gerhard Schroeder rather than Helmut Kohl leads them into the next century. This vote for change, despite all the noise about Germany's dangerous next Right, signals that this European Union leader will be an essential addition to the Blair-Clinton school of optimism.

Citizens of Sweden and Switzerland fear that their cozy prosperity will not last into the new millennium. Our trend scouts in Stockholm anticipate the collapse of Sweden's comprehensive social security system, while our scouts in Zurich report widespread consternation in Switzerland, which is located in the middle of the European Union, but is not a member. "The overall attitude at the moment is fear, uncertainty and instability, caused especially by the explosive rise of unemployment, which nobody was aware of a few years ago," says Sonja Huerlimann, of Y&R Advico in Zurich. "Also globalization worries the Swiss people, since it challenges their style of privacy and closed-deal dealmaking."

France is also entering a period of self-doubt, although some say that's always the French way. The centralized structure of authority in France since Napoleon, and a widespread sympathy with socialist principles, have led the French to expect the state to sort out their problems and provide for the future. Yet the state has proved powerless in the face of stubborn unemployment. Our French trend scouts report a depressed social climate, a sense that things are stuck, and increasing numbers of people looking for individual (custom) solutions and individual (personal) autonomy. The big question for many is whether the country will get behind these reforms and the trend towards self-help and self-centeredness, and celebrate it in time to use the turn of the millennium as an emotional springboard into globalness.

The Spanish are famed for their capacity to celebrate a good fiesta, which they did for many years following the death of General Franco in 1975 and the restoration of democracy. But as Lola Gonzalez, our source in Madrid reports, anticipation of the new millennium is "contaminated" by the fact that in 2002 Spain will enter the EMU, with consequent economic, social, and labor-market effects. There is fear that European Union subsidies will dry up as the EU switches development resources from Southern European to Eastern European countries.

Italians have long been enthusiastic supporters of the European project, partly out of gratitude for development funds and partly in the hope that Brussels would give them better government than their own politicians. Our Italian trend scouts (based in Milan) report that the country is approaching the millennium with a mixture of fear and optimism. Italians feel poorer than in the recent past and fear that the future will not be better, as technology and cheap labor abroad threaten jobs in Italy. But these fears are balanced by some positive developments that few would have imagined possible even just a few years ago—low inflation, public debt under control, a stable government comprised of two coalitions, agreement on institutional reform, and some healthy, big companies, including Fiat Group, ENI Generali Group, Telecom Italia, and Montedison Group. At the time we finished writing, it looks like the German telecom giant, not surprisingly named Deutsche Telecom, may swallow Telecom Italia, which fell into play after Olivetti attempted to acquire it. What better proof of a new European sensibility than Germany's techie telecom leader assuming responsibility for a phone company that's long been the butt of global jokes?

All in all, the mood of Europe at the turn of the millennium is likely to depend very much on economic news and the progress of the single currency project. If all goes well, it could be party time across the Continent, with optimism and millennial energy spilling over into the next century and driving forward Europe's essential reforms and restructuring.

The Biggest New Year's Celebration?

In contrast to its Continental cousins, the United Kingdom is one of the places in the world in which the dawn of the new millennium is most eagerly and anxiously anticipated.

The Scots are famed for their boisterous celebration of New Year's Eve—Hogmannay—and over the years, the rest of the United Kingdom has absorbed their traditions and enthusiasm for the occasion. If it's important to celebrate properly on a normal New Year's Eve, then for many it will be vitally important to celebrate the turn of the millennium with unparalleled panache. The big concern, according to Jim Williams, director of strategy and research in the European headquarters of Young & Rubicam, is to avoid being left out, one of the sad souls living through the great moment at home, alone.

Preparations for a truly memorable event are underway, especially on the site of the Millennium Dome, a vast and controversial celebratory edifice being constructed in the heart of London's Docklands. The structure is controversial because it cost Britain so much money at a time when its infrastructure might have been better served by a genuine boost versus a millennial answer to the Tower of London's tourist mystique.)There is also a big question about whether or not London's Jubilee Line will finish its extension to the Dome; if public transport doesn't get there by Millennium Eve, Cool Brittania may implode.

WHAT'S ON THE HORIZON

Whatever you claim to think of the impending millennium, those of us in the West can't help but be at least somewhat curious. We've grown up with futuristic novels and movies set in 2001 and beyond, and are curious as to how our lives will be altered by the period of rapid change we're currently experiencing.

Now that we've laid out the Big Nexts that will help shape life Next, we'd like to share with you our sense of what other key trends are lying in wait. The implications of these trends will not be quite so broad as those of the Big Nexts, but in combination they speak to the direction in which today's trendsetters are moving our worlds.

• NEXT: A DIN OF SMALL— AND NOT SO SMALL—VOICES

Think of Drudge—as in Matt Drudge, creator of *The Drudge Report*—as the proverbial mouse with a lion's roar. This is a man who, armed only with a computer and modem, has managed to build himself into a media mogul online. While his online report hasn't yet reaped major profits, it has provided a daily audience for his views and news reports—an audience far larger than would have been possible for anyone outside the major media before the birth of the Internet. We started "watching" Drudge in 1997—long before he made a name for himself in the big leagues with the story of the President and the cigar! By now, Matt Drudge has his television show on Fox and celebrity status on a par with pundits Geraldo Rivera and Chris Matthews, both of whom are virtual dailies on CNBC on topics from who killed JonBenet to who insulted O. J. last, or how the families of the Colorado school shooting victims are coping.

As is true of any form of mass media, the Internet wields great power. The difference between the Internet and TV or radio is that the Internet allows two-way communication and gives as much potential power to a thirteen-year-old computer geek as to a corporate CEO or government leader. Power online is based solely on the ability to draw in an audience and communicate with it in a persuasive manner. This power could be utilized to bolster the ranks of a political party, form a fan club for a favorite celebrity, or sell products and build a brand.

Voices outside of traditional news organizations are being heard in other media as well. A most interesting development in recent years has been the video news release (VNR), which routinely is substituted for "hard news," without warning to viewers that the footage was created by, for, and about a brand, company, or organization—by anyone with the money to make and distribute the videocassettes. Clearly this is a consequence of the proliferation of 24/7 news services and of the subsequent hunger for programming. (Imagine how much more programming is demanded by the Internet.)

To get an idea of who uses VNR's, following is the first ten of Medialink's "Top 20 Video News Releases" of last year:

1. Six Flags Magic Mountain: Superman
2. Pepsi Cola Super Bowl Advertising
3. Burger King "Free Fry Day"
4. Nasal Spray Influenza Vaccine
5. Pizza Hut Gorbachev Commercial
6. United Parcel Service Response to the Teamsters' Strike
7. Neiman Marcus Christmas Catalog
8. FDA Approval of Meridia
9. Deep Blue Challenge—Rematch
10. MacWorld–Boston Keynote Speech

As brands make themselves heard at news stations worldwide, you don't have to take a very large step to consider the viability of branded news on TV. With iconography that has come to serve as a universal language (think of the American Express Centurion), many global brands are well on their way to creating the credibility they need to offer up believable "news" and feature coverage. Try "Sony, Coca-Cola and Nike Present *Entertainment This Week.*"

• NEXT: FIGHTING FOR THE SPOTLIGHT

Opting not to go quietly into that good night, and taking our television culture into the surreal, disgraced American sportscaster Marv Albert hit the talk show circuit to explain his sexual misconduct, his "treatment" and why his fiance and family stood by him in the courtroom and afterward. (In effect, Albert kept his face out there during the period he was off the air calling sporting events; suffice it to say, he was hired back the moment he became available for employment as opposed to doing unpaid guest appearances talking about his legal problems.)

The ever-so-private McCaughey family of Iowa thought nothing of inviting NBC's *Dateline* into their prayer circles and even into the delivery room to witness the birth of their septuplets. Today's promoter personalities know that celebrity is international currency. Being a personality has become a bona fide business, bringing with it the prospect of spokesperson's gigs, broadcast opportunities, and the cachet of being deemed a "winner"—no matter how many "loser" traits are exposed along the way.

• NEXT: ARM'S-LENGTH COMMUNION

Caucuses, coalitions, militias, networks. By any name, such groups are all the rage. But the last year before the millennium is not the time for joiners. It's a year in which followers sign on for brief respites of participation for the sole purpose of being recharged by the power of community. Join a church for the monthly potluck supper. Sign up for a half-day of volunteering, rather than committing to a long-term project. Tuck a membership card from a political action committee into your wallet—no need to attend a second meeting. Informal networks are in; rigid institutions are out. We want to believe we have no obligations and on one is watching us. Life is too stressed for the added angst.

• NEXT: BRANDS 2000

As a number of twentieth century powerhouse brands battle to retain market share, new industries are springing up as if out of nowhere to create power brands for the next millennium. Examples include Starbucks, which turned coffee into a retail experience; and America Online, which made the proverbial back fence a 24/7 opportunity for neighborly chat and captured a share of couch potatoes' minds and eyes from the television networks.

Three *Next*-related trends to watch: First, convergence, as manufacturers and programmers of the boxes that run home and office create ever-more-indispensable products. Convergence means blurring—and in this case it means business opportunities where change redefines business and lifestyle possiblities. Home PC means we want cookbooks on CD-ROM; online services mean we need cyberaddress books; VCR libraries mean we want software to chronicle our tapes. Second, look for more edutainment, which combines education with entertainment—think Carmen Sandiego for kids and any Quicken program for adults. Anything that teaches us while we play is edutainment; and it will only be more important in the years ahead as we strive to make the next generation (and ourselves) more competitive. Finally, take note of relaxation, as we pursue relief from the stresses of modern-day life.

• NEXT: A BRANDED EXISTENCE (NOWHERE TO RUN, NOWHERE TO HIDE.)

We will soon have an all-too-clear understanding of the adage "Everything communicates," as marketers stage a full-court press to extend their reach beyond the usual platforms. Already in the testing phase: advertisements delivered via automatic teller machine and product samples given out based on smart-card purchasing patterns. Just as urban infill is reclaiming the land of the city and will eventually lay claim to every vacant parcel in the urban landscape, so will "brand infill" ensure that the world's every experience, thought, place, and product is marketed to its utmost potential. Some of this infill will be brief but still productive, while other advertising unions will last a lifetime. The unstoppable James Bond branding machine—the marketing success story begun in 1997, which gave high-speed visibility to BMW, Ericsson, and Heineken, among others—is a reminder of the various highways now open to brand travel.

• NEXT: IN PRAISE OF PARENTHOOD

The death of eight-month-old Matthew Eappen while in the care of his British au pair sparked heated debate about his mother's choice to continue her professional career—albeit in a part-time capacity—rather than stay home to care for her children. The debate over "choice" will no longer revolve solely around abortion; instead, more and more women will be faced with the need to defend their decision to work outside the home, particularly when that home is in an upscale community. Parenting will be touted as the most important profession of the next decade.

• NEXT: REDEFINING DESIRABILITY

The new age of heightened desirability is thirty-six—the age at which Marilyn Monroe and Princess Diana will forever rest, frozen in time at the height of their popularity. The fashion industry will continue to push parallel images of the ultra-thin and chic sixteen-year-old model, mature beyond her years, and her counterpart, the youthful and innocent coquette. But the older, wiser, and that much more sexy Diana archetype will prove a compelling alternative. Mature woman–young stud relationships will make headline news, supplanting the Jennifer Phenomenon of the '80s, when twenty-something trophy wives were hunted and mounted by fifty-something tycoons. Look for Leonardo DiCaprio to partner with a Sharon Stone-type, for the Francesca Annis–Ralph Fiennes romance to be duplicated again and again. Mid-youth now runs until the onset of menopause, with thirty-six marking the absolute age of power and those age forty-two and over still regarded as "hot," bringing to relationships experience, enthusiasm, and—thanks to new fertility tricks—even the prospect of children.

• NEXT: GREENER APPROACHES

As this planet gets just a bit cozier (so much for population control), consumers are recognizing their impact on the world, the world's impact on them and our communal responsibility to future generations. Thus far the "pure consumer" has embraced Green products such as natural cosmetics, eco-friendly fabrics, and organic food. Interest in "sustainable architecture"—building that emphasizes energy conservation, long-life materials, and environmentally friendly building techniques—is on the rise. And electric vehicles and their gas-and-electric-powered cousins, the hybrids, are poised to usher in an era of Green automobiles. As Green thinking migrates from left to center, consumers increasingly will demand environmental accountability from product and service providers.

• NEXT: THEM AND US—LEFT VERSES RIGHT

In these next few years expect a major global clash between the Left/liberals and the Right/conservatives, akin to the one between capitalism and communism/socialism. This new civil Cold War will be fought with particular intensity over family values issues. The superwoman of the 1980s has been killed by innuendo, a backlash against feminism and the gains of the women's movement. Next on the Right's seek-and-destroy list: Those who want abortion available on demand. The overarching goal: to return religion to the center of public life.

Throughout the Western world, where family life has been less a priority than issues such as economic expansion and taxation and even education, expect social clashes to erupt, with women—particularly working women—bearing the brunt of the blows. Immigrants and minorities also will be the subject of increasingly violent debate, as global fears pertaining to everything from job shortages to the loss of national identity fuel the fears of those who face an uncertain future in the new millennium. Fundamentalist Christians and Muslims, ultra-Orthodox Jews, and other factions of the Religious Right have gathered force as the millennium approaches, many of them using the Internet as a tool for recruiting and proselytizing and denouncing the sins of the world.

• NEXT: DESPERATELY SEEKING PEOPLE LIKE ME

As a byproduct of this schism between Left and Right, expect more and more investors and businesses to seek partners with compatible political and social (even religious) points of view. Whether it's Shell Oil being scrutinized by potential investors, or home contractors incorporating scripture into their advertisements, business relationships will be based on far more than the bottom line.

The same sentiment holds true for people who simply are looking for a network, a club, a connection to others like them. In the coming years, geography will become far less important than shared attitudes, beliefs, experiences, and values. The Internet ensures that whoever we are and whatever our passion, we have a very good chance of connecting with "virtual neighbors" who will support and sustain us. This trend can be benign (at-home dads forming support networks, for instance) or it can be truly dangerous (already White Power activists, conspiracy theorists, and Holocaust revisionists are connecting on the Internet). As people become more adept at harnessing the power of cyberspace, these unions will have the potential to change the world, for good or evil.

- ## NEXT: PRIVACY IS DEAD

Of all the premillennial fears we face, loss of privacy is perhaps the most common. Privacy is dead. It's been taken away by a little thing called a microchip, and it's not coming back. One interesting side effect of our newly omniscient Big Brother is that our lack of privacy will spell freedom for many people. Instead of being ashamed of what we might consider our perversions or "unnatural" impulses, we'll see more and more just how many people think and behave the way we do. And once we realize that our indiscretions, big and small, are never secret for very long, we'll be encouraged to let our wild sides out of the closet a lot more often.

So while the right will grow stronger and more outspoken, we'll also see an increased indifference to the so-called scandals (how scandalous can something be when everyone is doing it?). From infidelity to bondage, foot fetishes to businessmen wearing women's undergarments, we'll see an "assumed blindness" develop to one another's underbellies, along with a sense of futility regarding efforts to keep humans from being human.

- ## NEXT: AM I NORMAL?

Getting inside the heads of ordinary people is an international craze. We now expect every guest who appears on a talk show to bare his or her dirty laundry—and very soul. And the fascinating thing is, just about all of them oblige us! There's even a family in Sweden that has mounted a camera inside their refrigerator so visitors to their Web site can monitor the family's noshing habits.

Is this trend simply a movement toward exhibitionism? We think it's much more than that. What we're seeing is a deep-seated desire for confirmation. We want to know that what we're doing, thinking and feeling is normal, and we're looking to an audience of strangers to reassure us that no matter how bizarre our actions or attitudes, there's someone else who's stranger. And as a result of our own loosened tongues, we're angrily rejecting everyone else's rights to be discreet. (Just consider the backlash against Britain's royal family when their mourning of the loss of Princess Diana didn't meet the public's standards of grief.)

A surge in online support groups and discussion forums will be one of the more obvious offshoots of this trend. In the political forum, we'll be willing to forgive every mistake, indiscretion, even crime—as long as we are privy to a detailed and heartfelt public confession or even an angry denial of wrongdoing. Consider the Clinton-Lewinsky scandal. A CNN and *USA Today* opinion poll taken the day after Clinton's grand jury testimony aired on national television showed that his approval rating was 66 percent. That was six points higher than the week before. What we won't forgive is the sin of silence.

WHAT'S NEXT?
TREND BYTES FOR TOMORROW

The remainder of this chapter is filled with trend bytes, our prognostications regarding new products/services and ways of working and living that we'll see develop in the next few years. Some of the ideas might strike you as unfeasible or ill-conceived; others might be exactly in line with your vision of the future. Some may even already be part of your life! Even we disagree as to which of these observations and postulations are most significant. What we do agree on, however, is that each of the following entries makes for intriguing fodder in our continued effort to discern the possibilities—and, ultimately, the probabilities—of life in the next millennium.

Lifestyle

Simple pleasures: Sewing, quilting bees, and other simple pleasures from times past will emerge as an antidote to today's chaotic lifestyles. Look for a revival of crafts such as candle making, wood carving, and paper making.

Hobbyist cooking: Staying at home to prepare a full meal will no longer be a customary practice in many households; instead, cooking will be seen as more of a hobby, a way to entertain friends or spend time with family.

Dinner clubs: In some families, dinners will become a bigger priority, as parents struggle to connect with their kids and busy days leave no time to enjoy a relaxed breakfast or lunch. Groups of neighbors will form "dinner clubs," in which each household is responsible for providing one dinner a week to all five participating families.

Silicon sex: In an age in which real-world sex has become risky, to say the least, many are turning to the relatively safe and frequently anonymous world of silicon sex. Options range from cybersex (in which partners—or groups—engage in explicit, real-time online communication, including chat and/or video) to online pornography, from computerized sex toys to the forthcoming "sexbot." (What's a sexbot, you wonder? A robot for bedroom fun and games.) Tomorrow's schools will incorporate cybersex and online sexual content into their sex-education lessons.

Coparenting: Working moms and dads will seek more assistance in raising their children from childless (or "child-free," depending on one's point of view) relatives and friends. Gay couples unable to adopt children will be among those who coparent. Retirees will serve a greater role in the lives of young children, not just as caretakers for their own grandchildren, but—on a paid or unpaid basis—as surrogate grandparents and field-trip organizers for kids whose own relatives live too far away.

VRTV: Virtual reality headsets will let viewers "walk through" TV shows—that is, see and sense the same things the main characters do.

Health cults: New tribes of kindred spirits (e.g., parents who homeschool, organic gardeners, mothers who perform community service, upwardly mobile professionals who bowl) will become the health cults of the twenty-first century. Cataloging these hyperlocal associations will allow marketers to target these groups with products and pitches designed especially for them.

Easing up: As the true costs of stress (physical, financial, and emotional) become more commonly known, look for companies to monitor and attempt to reduce the stress levels of employees. We'll see everything from on-site aromatherapy centers to healthful cooking classes to all-expenses-paid, company-planned vacations.

Surroundings

Rebirth of the big city: We'll see a backlash against country living as word gets out that the rural lifestyle is actually less healthful than living in metropolitan areas partly because of the physical inactivity that often goes with it. A Center for Disease Control study shows that while 27 percent of those living in metropolitan areas with a population of more than a million are physically inactive, 37 percent of people living in rural areas with populations of less than 2,500 are physically inactive. Nearly a quarter of all deaths from major chronic diseases are attributed to physical inactivity. Telecommuters especially will stay in or return to cities in an effort to retain a sense of connectedness to the world at large.

Members only: Parents concerned about their children's safety will buy memberships in local "safe havens" for kids. Look for an increase in members-only beaches and parks, zoo groups, and museum clubs. Small neighborhood parks will increasingly require electronic-passcard entrance.

Appliances smarter than you: Intelligent refrigerators will track consumption of staples, printing a shopping list on demand or transmitting it electronically to a home-delivery service; smart stoves will "know" how you like your eggs; energy-management systems will supervise the activities of major home appliances, enabling homeowners to take advantage of off-hour pricing. Look for off-hour pricing for electricity and water.

Wide world of walls: Intelligent fabrics, including wallpapers, will turn every flat surface into an art gallery one moment, a TV/computer screen the next. Virtual aquariums or scenic views on flat screens will add interest to the family room wall.

High-tech homes: We will control lights, phones, drapes, alarms, media units, climate and more with the touch of a button—and we'll soon take it all for granted. What's coming in the very near term are central control panels and computer systems to synchronize the whole nine yards!

Custom living: Homebuilders will see an increase in requests for special-purpose rooms, from sewing rooms and hobby shops to wine cellars and prayer rooms.

Tea parlors: Hot and cold, caffeine-laden and herbal, medicinal and simply comforting, tea will stake its claim as the all-purpose beverage of the millennium. Tea parlors will challenge coffeehouses in popularity.

Services

Nutrition on wheels: Companies will deliver an assortment of nutritious frozen meals to busy households once a week. Meal trucks will travel through neighborhoods at dinnertime each day to offer a selection of entrees and extras.

Community PAs: Harried homeowners will pool resources to hire community personal assistants to do the things they no longer have time to do for themselves (e.g., dry cleaning drop-off and pick-up, grocery shopping, pool maintenance, handyman repairs).

Mail-order genetics: With the rise in infertility and with more older couples wanting to have children, mail-order catalogs will provide details about egg and sperm donors, allowing prospective parents to shop for genetics in the comfort of their homes.

It-ain't-my-fault insurance: Look for insurance policies that cover the cost of divorce and others that protect parents from financial responsibilities caused by their children's misbehavior.

Media menus: Not satisfied with one-hundred-plus cable channels and pay-per-view options? Look for on-demand movies and TV episodes, downloadable via your computer or PC/TV.

Friendship finders: Computer-generated friendship circles will identify those around the world with whom you have the most in common. On the face-to-face level, paid agents will unite people interested in forming friendships with other like-minded individuals. While this might sound like old-fashioned matchmaking, its emphasis on platonic bonding gives it a fresh twist.

Four-legged security: In our increasingly security-conscious world, we'll see the growth of a rental market for trained dogs: bomb-sniffing attack dogs patrolling corporations, guard dogs for homeowners on vacation, and security dogs for people jogging alone or working late at night.

Vacation-in-a-box: Busy families will turn to packaged vacations and other celebrations to cut down on stress. Even middle-class consumers will hire entrepreneurs to decorate their homes for Christmas, using their own decor or rental decor from the company. Also expect to see an increase in packaged holiday meals, either delivered to the door or picked up at high-end hotels, restaurants, or supermarkets.

If you can't beat 'em, employ 'em: Soon after mourning the loss of their personal privacy, consumers will begin using Big Brother's arsenal to their advantage. After all, he is part of the family. Internet-based private eyes will be employed to check the criminal and financial background and medical records of a potential mate or employee; satellite technology will enable anyone to purchase a photo of a celebrity wedding, a competitor's top-secret facility, or a spouse's indiscretions. Parents of young children will insist on having visual access to their little darlings at day care, and parents of latchkey kids may install camera-surveillance systems in their own homes.

Automatic gift transmission: A growing number of companies (florists, wine merchants, specialty food stores) will offer personal shopping—in advance. Once a year, customers will fill out a form indicating what should be sent to whom. The process will be carried out automatically at the appropriate times, with shipments billed to customers' credit cards.

Digital signatures: Unique to the individual, digital signatures will be as important in the coming decade as PIN numbers are today in promoting security on the Internet.

Dial-a-geek: The increase in home offices will escalate demand for on-site emergency computer diagnostics and repair.

Gene screen: We can expect an increase in genetic discrimination, as dates, job applicants, and club members are screened by intelligence aptitude.

Triple play: Day-care/elder-care initiatives increasingly will bring together three groups in need of companionship: children, the elderly, and pets.

Personal shoppers: Migrating from department stores to supermarkets, personal shoppers will be retained by busy consumers to plan a week's worth of meals and deliver the necessary combination of raw ingredients, frozen foods, and prepared meals. Menus will be tailored to family preferences, dietary needs, lifestyle, and weekly schedules.

Gadgets and Gizmos

Sleep channels: Sleeping machines will be used either to produce restful sleep or provoke intense dreams. In development: Nova-Dreamers, a technology that combines eye masks and circuitry to promote dreaming. Alarms awaken the user moments after the dream has ended so he or she can make a record of the dream.

Robotic lawn mowers: Mowing grass within a specified boundary and programmed to avoid obstacles such as bushes and children's playthings, these timesavers will be an increasingly common sight in suburban backyards.

Digital nutrition-analysis kiosks: Plug in information such as age, family medical history, and lifestyle for a printout of recommended vitamins, herbs, supplements, and food choices—plus discount coupons.

Personal Appearance

Insta-makeovers: Inspired by TV talk shows, makeovers will be an increasingly popular form of self-indulgence. Full-day sessions will incorporate hair redesign, makeup lessons, clothing consultation and a complete new outfit, teeth whitening, and, as an option, makeup tattooing (such as permanent eyeliner). Longer stays at spa facilities will include things such as outpatient plastic surgery and etiquette courses.

Big as you wanna be: The fat-acceptance movement is growing and will only increase as baby-boomers head into their fifties and sixties. Results will include better fashion options for larger women, as well as continued growth of publications such as *Mode*, designed to help women live healthfully and happily, regardless of size.

Functional fashion: Allowing for the ultimate personalization of the wardrobe, fabrics of tomorrow might include stress-relieving, massaging fabrics; fabrics emitting favorite or aromatherapeutic scents; and fabrics containing personalized, printed messages and wearer-created designs. Nanotechnology will allow fabrics to be embedded with tiny computers, sensors, and micromachines; possible applications include cooling and heating systems, periodic self-cleaning, and self-repair.

Embracing one look: Twin movements toward customization and simplification will lead consumers to purchase a few essential, coordinating items of clothing rather than waste money on extensive wardrobes that take up precious storage space and rarely see the light of day.

Male beauty: An increasing number of all-male beauty salons (already common in Paris) will provide a variety of head-to-toe treatments, including manicures (complete with application of colored polish), chest-hair dying and eyelash tinting, body-shaping, anti-stress sessions, facials, and waxing.

Mindset

Big brother in the sky: An antisatellite backlash will grow as consumers and businesses become more concerned about invasions of privacy.

Smart stays sexy: Don't be surprised to hear about a new unisex fragrance called Brainy or Intellect or of orgasms grounded in mind fucking, with no physical contact, just the power of the mind to lead us beyond cybersex (i.e., mutual masturbation) into something more heady and esoteric. The elusive G-spot is above the shoulders.

Brains over brawn: An extension of the current trend of geek chic, modern-day heroes in popular culture will rely less on muscles than on brains—and computer know-how.

Global gung-ho: International realities have made us more aware not only of each other's fashions and preferences, but also of each other's passions and plights. Accompanying this awareness—as already evinced by worldwide organizations such as Amnesty International and Greenpeace—will be a deepening sense that you can truly "think globally" and "act globally."

Glocal citizens: Those who travel the world and cherry pick best practices, carry them home with them, and integrate them into their lives. Glocal citizens are often very familiar with foreign places, but home is still sweetest for them!\

New traditionalists: Jordan's Queen Noor is the ultimate new traditionalist—she attended the funeral of her late husband, respectfully, and distanced, because women are not welcome at such events. New traditionalists update existing customs; while they can seem inflexible at times, in fact, they are rewriting the rules of fundamentalism into more modern and liveable dictates, personalized to a man (or a woman).

CHAPTER 6:

Global Culture Swap

*I*N TODAY'S GLOBAL SOCIETY, consumers can't help but be aware of cultural icons and influences from other nations. Countries are swapping products and fads in a cross-cultural frenzy. Who has graced the cover of *People* magazine more times than any other? Why Diana, the late Princess of Wales, of course. A year or so ago, the United States club scene was in a frenzy over "foam parties," events in which people spray each other with creamy foam. This novel form of entertainment—equal parts sexy, playful, and faddish—was brought over from London after originating on the island of Ibiza, Spain. America's slacker grunge craze even gave way to a new United Kingdom invasion: Mod's third wave, a movement marked by British pop artists such as Blur, Elastica, Oasis, and Sleeper, and by fashion designers such as Alexandra McQueen and Vivienne Westwood.

To the dismay of many, trends and icons emanating from the United States are also leaving their mark around the world. And the results can be incongruous, to say the least! What's the biggest tourist attraction in Romania today? The painted monasteries of Bukovina? Dracula's castle? Guess again. The biggest attraction is Southfork Ranch, a million dollar replica of the homestead made famous by TV's eighties night-time soap opera *Dallas*. The center-piece of the Hermes Vacation Park in the city of Slobozia, Southfork drew more than two million visitors in its first year of operation. Explaining the Texas-based TV show's popularity in his country, owner Ilie Alexandrov told the *St. Petersburg Times* (Florida), "[*Dallas*] was a bridge to the West for us. The average Romanian could only fantasize about such beautiful cars, a ranch, nice clothes. It was a kind of paradise."

Trends emanating from the United States (courtesy of MTV, global marketing efforts, the Internet, and the like) range from hip-hop to snowboarding to gun culture. In addition to buying hundred-dollar plastic replicas of guns, some Japanese have traveled to the United States for "gun tours," featuring opportunities to hold and shoot a variety of firearms. "It's become a fad, a cool thing, to like guns," security company employee Michiko Nagashima told *The Washington Post*. "This is a bad import from the West."

Another enduring rage among Japanese youth is *chapatsu*, or tea hair. Dying one's hair is considered an act of individuality and rebellion, akin to the statement made by American and European hippies growing their hair long during the '60s. Japanese schools have responded by banning dyed hair, and many major companies are refusing to hire brown-haired (as opposed to black-haired) applicants.

Trend Filters

Although many of today's trends get their start in the United States and Western Europe, the way they get translated around the world varies. Important to the evolution of trends are the gate-keeping cities in each country, those places through which trends enter and are then spread throughout a nation.

The key cities of Guangzhou, Shanghai, and Beijing are where trends start in China. Typically, these trends are brought about by an influx of Western influence—media penetration and tourists. A colleague of ours, based in Guangzhou, writes: "Guangzhou in the southern part of China is heavily influenced by Hong Kong because of its proximity. This is also the seat of the yearly China

Trade Commodities Fair, so a lot of European, Japanese, and American traders pass through. Most of the multinational companies have their marketing and manufacturing offices in Hong Kong, so the presence of expats dictates the fast development or evolution of people and culture. Going forward, Hong Kong's influence will continue to be evident in fashion, music, and lifestyle. Beijing will remain the seat of politics, while Shanghai will be the fashion/lifestyle trendsetter—more sophisticated and the center of finance."

In China, parents of "little emperors"—the often-spoiled offspring created by China's one-child policy—were recently found to spend more money on imported goods than domestic products. More than 26 percent of parents like foreign food better, and more than 21 percent like foreign toys better—so much better, in fact, that they spend 1.2 billion dollars a year buying imported goods, according to a survey in the *Japan Economic Newswire*.

Sachin Talwar, a senior executive with Burson-Marsteller Roger Pereira Communications in Mumbai, tells us that trends in India also tend to originate in the United States, but they don't spread throughout the country until they've been filtered through gatekeeping cities such as Bombay (now Mumbai), New Delhi, and Bangalore. "All three cities share several characteristics," notes Talwar. "They are relatively more Westernized, they are cosmopolitan, they host many more foreigners and foreign enterprises, Indians educated abroad are more likely to find jobs there, and these cities have better schools and colleges—particularly among those that teach through the medium of English."

With teens and twenty-somethings in India, anything American— from DKNY and Nike to Pizza Hut and McDonald's—is "cool," according to *India Today*. *Teens Today*, a newly launched magazine in India, takes a very American viewpoint. Editor Ameena Jayal says, "It's how the kids are. They are Indian, but the slant is very American." Anshul Pathania, twenty, a college student in Bombay, puts it simply: "America is happening."

The role the English language plays in trend adoption is particularly evident in India. "The trendsetters in this country are not necessarily the rich," explains Talwar. "In fact, Bombay and New Delhi have vast numbers of the nouveau riche, but those people do not set trends. The trends are set by people the industry calls the 'English medium types' (EMTs). They are persons whose schooling has been at elite schools—both day and boarding—that teach in English. Traditionally, the sons of professionals, executives, and bureaucrats have been to these elite institutions of learning. All of them are not wealthy; most belong to the upper middle class. On the other hand, there are the 'Hindi medium types' (HMTs). At school, they have been educated in one of the Indian languages. Many of them would have also learned English but . . . their familiarity with the language would be more limited. Many of them in the big cities belong to the trading classes and are wealthy. Yet they are looked down upon by the EMTs. Worse, the HMTs often display an inferiority complex. While they are wealthy, they wish to emulate the EMTs in their social behavior. They tend to wait for the EMTs to adopt a trend before feeling confident about adopting it themselves. HMTs often send their children to elite schools to climb the 'emulation' ladder. While this is often successful as far as the child is concerned, it does lead to strains within the family, as the elders often find it difficult to accept the changed lifestyle of their child."

Talwar continues, "The trendsetters, in the main, emulate whatever is happening in the United States. Thus, most trends in the United States appear in India after an interval of time—in some cases the time is short; in some cases, it can be quite long. In areas such as music and clothing, the trends come to Bombay very fast indeed. Yet in areas to do with sexual mores, trends take a very long time to travel to India."

NEW WORLD CAPITALS

How long will the United States continue to drive trends around the world? Toronto-based Laurence Bernstein doesn't see this course changing anytime soon, ". . . unless the next stage of the development of the European Community is a cultural unification—which is unlikely given traditional language and cultural differences—major trends will probably continue to emanate from the United States," he says. "It takes a monumental, culturally homogenous society to lead deep-seated trends (ideas and fads can come from anywhere; trends tend to rise up from the essence of the people). Asian developing countries, some of which may have the size and cultural strength needed to be leaders, are too focused currently on American values to explore themselves and develop their own cultural progress in the near to mid-term. Furthermore, until such time as the American stranglehold on the media is replaced, it is hard to see how non-American cultural values will permeate the world."

Lucinda Sherborne, an Auckland, New Zealand-based adwoman, has a somewhat different take on the situation: "The next few years will continue to see key lifestyle trends being filtered out of the United Kingdom and the United States," she says. "However, we see these trends and the uptake of these trends speeding up as the world gets smaller and smaller, due to the increasing effectiveness of technology and the breakdown of global boundaries. The increasing ease of travel, immigration, technology/ Internet, and mass media communications will drive these trends, also providing different channels for different ones. I believe the opening up of the world will also allow other countries to generate trends, possibly bypassing traditional trendsetting countries."

We too believe that we'll see the increased influence of trendsetters from other countries in coming years. The Internet will have a big hand in this (a topic we cover more thoroughly in chapter 7). The simple fact is that as the world grows more interconnected, the influence of any one sector will be felt more readily by the others. This global interconnectedness levels the playing field in many respects, because it affords those outside today's trend centers access to a broader forum.

Another colleague, a Colombian based in California, sent us a note recently that said, "Trends develop more and more in less commercial economies where newness is creative expression versus a reaction to a new product that enters the marketplace with a large budget." She pointed to student enclaves and market towns as two likely sources for trendsetting *Next*. We think she's right!

Already we've seen shifts in centers of cultural influence around the globe as baby-boomers have regained their position at front and center (edging out those upstart media darlings, the Generation Xers). And they bring with them, their kids, sometimes called echo boomers, and whom we consider "Why" and "Z". They brought with them a renewed emphasis on the biggest cities, the cultural centers. Following are our predictions for trend centers *Next*, those cities that will dictate what we wear, watch, and listen to in the decade to come.

- ## DESTINATION NEXT: *GEMÜTLICH* PLACES ARE GLOBAL VILLAGES

"Genuine" people are more desirable today than those who are arrogant or aloof (think Chelsea Clinton versus Kate Moss), as are "genuine" places. They embody *gemütlich*, a German term that conveys a combination of all that's hospitable, homey and sane. Antwerp, a mini-Paris home to designers such as Dries Van Noten is in; Brussels is out. Capetown is in; Johannesburg is out. Cities that are global villages are trendiest, because they afford the ultimate combination of cozy lifestyle against a backdrop of blended world cultures.

In the West, two *gemütlich* cities, both global villages, are Amsterdam and San Francisco. Interestingly, these are also the digital capitals of Europe and North America, respectively. San Francisco has long been a melting pot of alternative lifestyles and creative expression; in the past decade it's also emerged as a center of digital creativity. Across the Atlantic, thanks to the Channel Tunnel, IT (meaning information technology and computing) hotshots and Web designers can ply their trade in London during the week, then hop on a train to Amsterdam on Friday evening and enjoy a weekend of laid-back vice and virtue—recreational drug use and parties all within easy walking or bicycling distance, no language problems, prices for every pocket, no pretensions, just come as you are and do your own thing.

As the world becomes increasingly wired, the cybersavvy duo of Amsterdam and San Francisco will command an even greater share of the spotlight. Expect *gemütlich* positioning—"cozy marketing"—to be the successful strategy for products ranging from consumer electronics to home meal replacements to remote banking.

• DESTINATION NEXT: GATEWAYS

Berlin and Prague, gateways to the East, will be very much global villages in the near future. Although they belong to generation Xers at the moment, these cities bear the mark of older generations who, throughout Central and Eastern Europe, preserved traditions in the face of cultural oppression. Prague was the setting of the 1989 Velvet Revolution, the romantic transition that restored democracy to Soviet-controlled Czechoslovakia. It also was home to a hipper, rock-music-influenced counterculture that venerated anarchy and produced playwright-as-president Vaclav Havel. The most untrendy aspect of modern Prague: American expatriate culture and its rampant commercialism. While the first post-revolution invasion brought art-seeking, anti-materialistic young Yanks, Prague now is global in the truest sense, down to its multiplex cinemas. And yet the city sustains a quirky balance; its ancient culture coexists, even blends, with the sense of perpetual newness, a strong wind that blows across Central Europe.

Back in the heart of Germany and therefore the heart of Europe, Berlin has been in the limelight before—think Christopher Isherwood and *Cabaret*. It has everything—fine buildings, huge public spaces, a romantic-tragic past, more than a hint of low life, status as a gateway to the East or West (depending on where you're coming from), and now the nation's decision to make it the crowning glory of a country reunited at tremendous cost. The former Eastern Bloc countries still tend to see Germany as their partner in the West, which makes Berlin a natural for all those Easterners keen to brush up on their German. And Sony's decision to build a film center in the new city center is certain to attract trend leaders. On top of that, Berlin's "love parades" are an attraction, sometimes pulling in more than a million people. The message: love, peace, happiness. Drugs such as ecstasy are an important part of the scene.

The most threatening cloud on Germany's horizon is the rise of the new Right (a.k.a. neo-Nazis), whose surprisingly strong showing (despite the ultimate election of Gerhard Schroeder) in the last election reflects a populace increasingly dissatisfied with the byproducts of their new democratic order: namely, the record levels of unemployment that result when a state-controlled industrial economy enters the free market. The new enemy: everyone not German (*all* foreigners replace Jews as the neo-Nazi target).

• DESTINATION NEXT: MUSIC MECCAS

Because innovative musicians find a following in places that support creativity, we look to music meccas for signs of what's next. Chicago's Wicker Park boasts a music scene that includes Liz Phair, Urge Overkill, and Veruca Salt. Clubs and studios in this once downtrodden neighborhood thrive alongside megalabels such as Drag City, Touch and Go, and Wax Trax. In England, the small port city of Bristol is the birthplace of three influential bands: Massive Attack, Tricky, and Portishead. It was Portishead, creator of "trip-hop," that landed Bristol on the places-to-watch list. (Trip-hop, an underground dance style, draws on reggae sounds and incorporates torch singing and even nostalgic film scores.)

• DESTINATION NEXT: PORT CITIES

Sydney has long been the trendsetter capital of Australia, but its role as Olympic host in the year 2000 will ensure that its influence is felt far beyond Australian shores. Increased tourism means more "messengers" will visit Sydney, returning home with a catalog of experiences from a city in which styles are set by the gay community, a highly educated creative community, and new-money entrepreneurs. Other ports to watch: Genoa, Marseilles, Rotterdam, and Hamburg. The latter two are among the hippest cities around, each with a noteworthy fashion and music scene.

• DESTINATION NEXT: CITIES WITH AN EDGE

For hardier souls who like their trends a little edgier, there are alternatives, most notably, Moscow, St. Petersburg, and Naples.

Moscow/St. Petersburg: In a Europe where everything is coming together, Russia will give adventurous Europeans the chance to experience something very different—an advanced, industrialized European country living in the raw, close to the edge. As Zoya Ivanova, our colleague in Moscow, sees it, life in Russia will get harder but more interesting; citizens fight with their brains rather than guns. This will be a thrilling and disturbing experience for cosseted young Europeans, far more exotic than trips to more distant destinations. It will also give them some new angles on things they take for granted.

Naples: For adventurous Europeans who can't face the chill of Russia, Naples offers the experience of managing chaos under azure skies. Without the tourist hordes and self-consciousness of many Italian cities, Naples will be the place to observe old Italy head-to-head with the twenty-first century—rapier-sharp native wit and invention devising strategies to handle high-tech and regulations. Marco Lombardi, our colleague in Milan, notes that Naples is today a dramatization of both Italy's good qualities and its faults. "When you are there," Lombardi says, "you can feel in the air a positive tension, which is best expressed through the music of the people coming from *centri sociali* [self-managed young communities]."

• DESTINATION NEXT: NEW ASIAN HUBS

After centuries of bigger-is-better nationalism around the world, it's easy to forget that historically some of the most influential and successful human enterprises have not been huge countries, but rather city-states—Athens, Florence, and Venice, to name but three of note. In Asia, Hong Kong and Singapore have proved the value of small, concentrated units, and these two cities increasingly rival each other as regional hubs—metacapitals acting as magnets both for their hinterland and for overseas entrepreneurs looking to do business in the region.

The scene is set for other influential hubs to emerge. Shanghai already has a glorious heritage from its prerevolutionary days and will act as a focus for talent to rival Hong Kong/Guangzhou. In a recent America Online interview, Pete Engardio, a *Business Week* staffer covering the region, said that China's coastal provinces are so economically dynamic that they could absorb about five cities like Hong Kong, although Hong Kong is likely to retain the unique advantages of a legal system, a free press and a corruption-free society.

Shanghai is home to thirteen million people, which makes it the largest city in the fastest growing nation in the world. *Time International* describes the niche that Shanghai is carving for itself as "the Manhattan of twenty-first century Asia." Since 1990 Shanghai has erected more than one thousand new buildings and is in the process of building another five hundred, a far cry from the fishing village it once was. The question remains: Will Shanghai get a chance to show off its new makeover in the face of current economic woes? The people of Shanghai give themselves ten years before they beat out Hong Kong.

Meanwhile, emerging nations such as Singapore, Malaysia, and Vietnam are jockeying for position in the regional and international community. Malaysia, which aims to oust Singapore as the cornerstone of Southeast Asia, is busy developing a vast high-tech enterprise zone, the Multimedia Super Corridor, with the aim of leap-frogging Malaysia into the Information Age. Vietnam is focusing less on technology and more on its unique cultural heritage. Our colleague in Ho Chi Minh City predicts great things for Vietnamese artists and creators, both in the field of plastic arts and in TV and advertising, and foresees an international style based on Vietnam's traditional womenswear. According to this manager, "Western women will start to wear the Vietnamese national dress, the *ao dai*. Or Western fashion designers will adapt it for Western women to wear. The dress is too feminine, too sexy for designers to pass up."

One form of this cultural heritage is water puppetry, which is unique to Vietnam. It began in villages all over Vietnam, but recently the government has taken charge to popularize it as an art form around the world by building the Thang Long Water Puppet Theatre in Hanoi. Water Puppet shows are done with mechanized wooden puppets. They are set in lakes or ponds so the audience cannot see the mechanisms or the puppeteers, and the stories typically revolve around different aspects of village life. There is even a school in Hanoi that teaches this art form. The theater also has a troupe that tours around the world, so others may know of this incredible cultural heritage. The troupe recently returned from a trip to France and Belgium. The government hopes to use such examples of Vietnam's cultural uniqueness to attract tourists.

TREND FOOD FOR THOUGHT

When thinking about where trends will take off, consider the population patterns of the coming decade. In 2010, the five largest populations will be China (1,388.47 million), India (1,189.08 million), the United States (297.49 million), Indonesia (239.60 million), and Pakistan (210.10 million). The next five largest populations will be Brazil (199.33 million), Nigeria (168.37 million), Bangladesh (162.50 million), Russia (143.13 million), and Japan (127.15 million). And finally, eleven to twenty will be Mexico, Vietnam, Iran, Philippines, Ethiopia, Egypt, Germany, Turkey, Zaire, and Thailand. (Thailand's population in 2010 will be 67.13 million, up from 44.28 million.) It's with these shifts in mind that we suggest a look at the following places, which have category and/or regional influence now and in the near future.

CULTURE CAPITALS

• Stockholm was 1998's Culture Capital of Europe. The fifteen-nation European Union chooses a different city each year. In 1997, it was Thessalonika in Greece; in 1999 it's Weimar, Germany. More than one thousand exhibitions and events mark this year-long program, ranging from venues for the performing arts to food festivals, from the merry to the magnificent.

• Throughout the United States, museums are coming into their own as big-time destinations, economic engines, and gathering places. Baby boomers are driving the trend. They're settling into middle age and looking for slower, more intellectual adventures for themselves, their children, and their grandchildren, researchers say. The resulting surge in museum popularity is easing some of the perpetual money problems facing cultural institutions at a time when federal funding has been cut back, allowing curators to augment their collections and add attractions. According to estimates from museum specialists, $4–$5 billion has been spent on museum capital programs nationwide. Expert marketing seems to be the key to survival. Many museums are entering partnerships with such marketing successes as Disney and Children's Television Workshop; the Smithsonian has begun setting up affiliation agreements with cultural planners around the country. And, as Boston Museum of Fine Arts Director Malcolm Rogers said in the *Times-Union* (Albany, NY), "If you can get the message out that you aren't a dowager, people will make that first visit and find they are welcome."

The New York State Museum partnered with the Metropolitan Museum of Art for two shows, most recently "Still Life." Chicago's Office of Tourism has become part of the Department of Cultural Affairs. In Seattle, the Museum of Flight had its best numbers in its fifteen-year history when it added the first presidential jet, a modified Boeing 707 that carried Dwight D. Eisenhower. Boston's Museum of Fine Arts spruced up its buildings, restored two gardens, instituted a Friday night happy hour and tried some nontraditional programming, including a show by fashion photographer Herb Ritts and an animation festival by Nick Park creator of the popular Wallace and Gromit characters. Finally, the Strong Museum in Rochester, New York added a 10,000-square-foot atrium that houses a 1918 carousel and a 1956 diner; in a year, attendance rose by 45 percent, and membership was up by 109 percent. In addition, the museum signed an agreement with the Children's Television Workshop to do a permanent exhibit on *Sesame Street* and sent its guides to a Disney school for instruction.

• The Atlanta Convention and Visitors Bureau's cultural tourism initiative got a big shot in the arm with the announcement of a three-year, $300,000 corporate sponsorship from Visa USA. The Visa sponsorship means that the bureau's initiative to sell the city as an arts and culture capital has met its corporate underwriting goal and can proceed with creating programs to promote the seventy nonprofit Atlanta arts groups under its umbrella. The Atlanta *Journal-Constitution* reported, "The bureau inaugurated its cultural tourism program last year with seed money from

BellSouth and Coca-Cola. BellSouth also committed $300,000 for three years; Coca-Cola has pledged $100,000 for three years."

• According to the *Ladies Home Journal*, the most spiritual cities in the United States are Charleston, West Virginia; Salt Lake City, Utah; Abilene, Texas, Birmingham, Alabama; and Sioux Falls, South Dakota. Several factors were weighed in the survey, including houses of worship per capita, parks and cultural institutions available, and the percentage of women that vote.

HIGH TECH CAPITALS

• South Korean officials are looking to the creation of an information-technology complex in the port city of Inchon to help fuel their depressed nation's recovery. The commercial zone will include a massive international airport, due to open in 2001, industrial zones with duty-free status and an enclave known as Media Valley, for budding technologies. *The Washington Times* reported what Yun Seok–Yun, a top official in the city's Development Planning Agency, sees as Korea's future, "Media Valley is the best choice for Korea to become one the world's great economic powers in the twenty-first century." The complex, Yun Seok–Yun says, "will provide cheap land and lucrative tax breaks for so–called 'information technology' companies that provide software, telecommunications and computer related services. The first phase, to be completed in 2005, will cost more than eight billion dollars, with nearly 90 percent of the money put up by a consortium of private companies such as Daewoo Telecom and Hyundai Electronics. The remainder will come from the city of Inchon."

• *Newsweek* named Tel Aviv as one of the top ten high tech sectors in the world. The sector has become arguably the largest technology incubator outside the United States. The number of start-ups per capita is by far the largest, approaching the number in the United States in absolute terms. Six factors were cited that typify high tech capitals of the world: a prominent success story, a major research institution, the quality of the work force, availability of venture capital, modern infrastructure, and a risk-taking attitude. Only one does not apply to the Israel experience—the model of a single or small group of major companies leading the way, such as Seattle's Microsoft or Helsinki's Nokia.

• Atlanta's growing high tech sector is wooing computer geeks from all over, including those who left the South for higher paying jobs elsewhere. Entrepreneurs are hatching start-up companies by the hundreds in university incubators, and private investors are putting their money where their word-of-mouth is. Metro Atlanta snagged $340 million in venture capital—money investors stake to fledgling companies or even just to good ideas—in 1997 alone, catapulting Georgia into the top ten states in an annual survey by the accounting firm Price Waterhouse. This put them ahead of Florida and North Carolina for the first time. The migration of people and money to Atlanta is a byproduct of the 1996 Summer Olympics, which left the city wired with more fiberoptic cable than any other in the world. As the Austin *American Statesman* reported, Atlanta, like other Southeastern cities, is concentrating on high tech niches—telecommunications and start-ups.

• *Newsweek* has noted that across America and around the world, many other hot spots are challenging Silicon Valley, including these seven:

1. Austin, Texas, used to be famous for Willie Nelson, but it's now known as the home of gazillionaire Michael Dell and Origin Systems, the software company who made your computer into an astral war zone with Wing Commander. Almost two thousand high tech companies employ 20 percent of the region's work force.

2. Salt Lake City has more high tech companies than fast food restaurants.

3. Seattle's roster of billion-dollar software giants (Microsoft, of course, leads the pack) has officially geekified the Northwest.

4. Boston has enjoyed a full recovery from the extinction of its minicomputer empire. It's now a hip hotbed of exotic start-ups and is the second biggest recipient of venture capital

funding. According to a 1997 BankBoston study, MIT has spawned four thousand companies employing more than a million people.

5. England's hope lies in Cambridge. A developmental plan of the future of the city actually superimposed a geographical outline of the Valley over a map of East Anglia. After eight hundred years of perching above the commercial fray, Cambridge University is now actively leading an effort to Valley-ize its surroundings. Graduates and faculty members are encouraged to go into business, and two of its colleges have opened up science parks to incubate start-ups.

6. At Taiwan's Hsinchu Science-Based Industrial Park, the engineers are almost indistinguishable from the nerds who park their Volvos in Santa Clara parking lots. Most cut their programming teeth at United States universities. Revenues from the two hundred fifty companies in the park alone are expected to account for a tenth of Taiwan's GNP.

7. Bangalore, India, has evolved into a hotbed of programmers.

FINANCIAL CAPITALS

• According to *The Economist*, there will be fewer financial centers in the future. Today's mainly national finance centers will be replaced by just a handful of international centers. As the planet goes global and the forces that produced financial centers are ignoring national boundaries, these international sites are gathering up ever more financial businesses than power shifts are beginning. While New York's domestic market beats the field by a wide margin, only Tokyo's stock and government bond markets get anywhere near it. But add up the markets of all of the countries that have just adopted Europe's single currency, and Europe's financial markets turn out to be nearly as big as America's.

• Some believe that the Euro will create new financial markets and remove the need for some of the old ones, and that London, which will start off outside the single currency area, will lose out. Frankfurt, Germany, is New Europe's Financial Capital, charged with the mission of setting monetary policy for Europe. It will have custody of the Euro, the currency that will help centralize European commerce when it is introduced into member nations in January.

• One of the world's three great financial centers is now under new ownership, if not new management. Hong Kong was returned to China last July. But China has its own fast-growing financial centers, including Shanghai and Shenzhen.

• The Africa News Service reported that The Tigray Dedebit micro-financing institution established in 1994 and modeled after Bangladesh's Grameen Bank, is now being increasingly looked at as a model for similar institutions throughout Ethiopia. The beneficiaries of the company are poor farmers and those with low incomes engaged in micro-enterprises. Borrowers must be organized into primary groups of five to seven who are then eligible for credit and financing. Credit repayments are reported to be very high and are largely contingent on peer pressure.

• Finally, the New South's financial capital, Charlotte, North Carolina, hosted the Trans-Atlantic Business Dialogue in fall 1998 bringing United States and European leaders together. The Queen City edged out larger rivals such as San Francisco and Philadelphia, joining an impressive list of former host cities: Rome, Chicago, and Seville, Spain. Participants, including dozens of United States executives and their counterparts from European companies, as well as senior government officials from both sides of the Atlantic, discussed topics such as global economic turmoil and other international trade issues—electronic commerce, Mutual Recognition Agreements in such industries as telecommunications and pharmaceuticals, and reducing bribery and corruption in world trade. In addition, Charlotte—home to two of the country's largest banks, more than five hundred international firms, and a long tradition of welcoming foreign investment—is poised to showcase itself as one of the nation's emerging business centers, reported the Greensboro *News-Record*.

CHAPTER 7:
Living in the
Digital Age

"There is no reason for any individual to have a computer in their home." —KEN OLSON, then chairman of Digital Equipment, in an address to the World Future Society, Boston, 1977

A couple of years ago, Richard Eastman of Billerica, Massachusetts, who managed a genealogy forum on online access provider CompuServe, noticed some odd messages from one of about twenty computer users during a regular weekly gathering of their cybercommunity. A message from the Reverend Kenneth Walker indicated that he wasn't feeling terribly well, and Walker soon began transmitting messages with gross typographical errors. Another member of the cybercommunity, a nurse from Long Island, New York, immediately began asking Reverend Walker for his symptoms. At one point, according to a report from Reuters, Walker wrote, "By keyboatd it melting. . . . I jest nuut." Minutes later, he typed, "Helo . . . have broblemd , , , thimk I am waying stroke." Eastman then started asking him for his phone number. After six attempts, he finally got the number, called a telephone operator, and found himself talking to a police officer in Scotland. The police forced their way into Walker's home minutes after Eastman called and took Walker to a hospital.

Walker, who says doctors believe he might have suffered an

epileptic attack, called Eastman to thank him. "This wasn't any great heroism," Eastman said. "The only thing different in this case is that it was online." Eastman, who has written a book about genealogy, and Walker, an expert on Scottish records and archives, have since found they have many things in common. "It's kind of an interesting thing how two lives three thousand miles apart get wrapped up," Eastman said. "Obviously, we share a common interest. There is a kinship, if you will."

Welcome to the global neighborhood.

THE HUMAN FACES OF CHANGE

As we mentioned earlier, we didn't grow up with computers. If anything, Marian long considered them the province of geeks and couldn't have been more surprised to find herself labeled an "Internet guru" by the media only a couple of years after she got hooked on America Online. As the father of three (one born in the mid-1970s and two a decade later), Ira has had an opportunity to watch as computers became fundamental in the lives of each of his children. His oldest son, David, was considering a career as an advertising copywriter through college (in fact, over the strenuous objections of his father, David majored in advertising). Having had the advantage of student internships, he determined that copywriting was not his ideal career, yet he was looking for an outlet for his creativity, combined with a self-taught acumen for harnessing the intelligence of the Internet. David's first job was as a global product manager at Shadwick Communications in New York, where his principal charge was to use the Internet as a tool to generate insights for new business development. Lily (at age eleven) was published years before her dad, collaborating with Robert Pondiscio and Marian on *Going to the Net: A Girl's Guide to Cyberspace* (Camelot, 1996). The book grew out of Marian's interest in the medium and Lily's typical prepubescent understanding that the Internet was both "cool"—source of information about celebrities and "stuff girls are interested in"—and in many ways a better communication Interface than the phone. At age ten, Ira's youngest child, Nicky, who started by wanting to emulate everything his big sister could do, has grown from a hunt-and-peck typist into an avid game player, to the kind of Web-surfer who is able to figure out how to find the myth of Scorpius online for a school report.

For those who have become "plugged in," the Internet offers a world of new people, new ideas, and new information. It opens up avenues of communication that allow us access to places we otherwise might never have gone. It's becoming increasingly evident that the Internet also will alter the paths trends take around the world. Today, online communication is taking place primarily in English (an estimated three-quarters of all Internet sites are located in English-speaking countries). As the Internet attracts a more global audience, however, there is a mounting effort to broaden its appeal and usefulness by enabling and encouraging people to communicate and collaborate in their native languages.

Although English remains the lingua franca of the Internet, the number of multilingual Web sites is growing. The Internet Society and Montreal-based Alis Technologies have established Babel (babel.alis.com:8080/), a site aimed at internationalizing the Web by promoting the use of languages other than English. Babel eventually will be available in approximately ten languages. Dynalab (www.dynalab.com), a Taiwanese font manufacturer, is marketing GlobalSurf, a utility that provides fonts in twenty-three languages, including Arabic, Chinese, Japanese, Korean, Thai, Hebrew, and most European languages. The product solves the common problem of garbled type resulting from double-byte Asian characters by using fonts that support Unicode. Web pages can now correctly display these foreign-language characters on any browser that supports Unicode.

As the online population gradually falls more closely in line with global realities, we can be sure that cross-cultural influences will no longer emanate primarily from Western trend capitals. In the past few years, the online community has evolved beyond technogeeks to encompass the thought and opinion leaders who—with close, smart tracking—can serve as important barometers of how, when, and whether particular fads, trends, and styles will evolve from the "mindspace" of the Internet to the "marketplace" of the face-to-face world. It's these pioneers of *Next* who will reshape the world of marketing communications and commerce for the future.

Cybercommunication

In watching the evolution of communication online, it's been interesting to note how cybernauts have resolved the problem of the lack of body language in this medium. As any Internet user can tell you, an entire code has been developed to convey the human emotions that one cannot see in cyberspace. These typed symbols—called emoticons or smileys—give a degree of life and individuality to online expression.

• To view a Western smiley, tilt your head to the left. Among the most common examples:

:-)	Basic smiley (shows humor or happiness)
;-)	A wink (shows you're being a flirt or sarcastic)
:-(	A frown (means you're sad, depressed, or have hurt feelings)
:'-(	Crying
:-D	Laughter, or a really big grin
:-*	A kiss
:-P	Sticking out your tongue
:-x	"My lips are sealed."
:-0	Astonished

• In contrast, here's a sampling of Japanese *kao maaku* (face marks), which are meant to be viewed straight-on:

(^_^)	Happy face
(;_;)	Weeping face
\(^_^)/	Banzai smiley (arms raised in a traditional cheer)
(*^o^*)	Excited face
(^^;)	Cold sweat
(_o_)	"I'm sorry."

The Internet is also creating its very own language, one that steals from everyone from stenographers to street kids. Many of us have become adept at the standard abbreviations of the Internet—using BTW instead of writing out "by the way" and IMHO for "in my humble opinion." We've also usurped shorthand made popular by urban black youth in the United States: dis as a stand-in for "disrespect"; 24/7 to mean "twenty-four hours a day, seven days a week." As Europeans and Asians establish more of a presence in Internet chatrooms and newsgroups, we suspect that Euro and Asian slang will infiltrate cyberlingo. At the same time, we'll be seeing cyberlingo begin to infiltrate language offline. Already our former Dutch colleagues are using BTW and ITRW (short for "in the real world") in everyday conversation. And just as African-American slang has pervaded American language in the 1990s (courtesy of rap music), geekspeak has pervaded the jargon of business life in the United States.

WIRED WORLD?

Europe Online

The Internet is still dominated by North Americans. So how long until it becomes a global medium? Western Europe is an affluent, educated place with a high penetration of high-tech appliances and good telecommunications infrastructure. So why is it so far behind the United States with regard to Internet adoption?

To be fair, there are exceptions. Northern Europe has many more computer and Internet users than does Southern Europe. In fact, the faraway Icelanders, famous for being people of few words, boast the world's highest per capita ratio of Internet servers and users, and "greater Scandinavia" is easily the world's best-connected region, according to a new compendium of Internet-related statistics called "The Internet Industry Almanac."

In contrast to the Scandinavians, not even 5 percent of the loquacious Italians use the Internet. Italian marketing consultant Giancarlo Livraghi (gandalf.it/netmark/) blames this poor showing on technophobia and fears about the dangers of the Internet: "Families (as well as politicians and teachers) are bombarded *off* the Internet every day with sensationalism and misinformation that make them uncomfortable and scare them away." In other words, why log on for more of the same nuisances?

Climate and social customs probably play a part too. Long, dark, hard winters force Northern Europeans to spend many months of the year indoors—ideal for developing computer skills and networking online. As Katarina Varenius, a marketing strategist in Stockholm, puts it, "The trend is that we will see less of these people out in the garden, since they will be sitting in front of the computer. The computer is a fully legitimate place to be. You don't have to explain to anybody whether you do something useful or not." By the same token, the long, fine summers of Southern Europe make pavement cafe and beach life irresistible. Why shut yourself away with a computer and modem when you can go out and socialize in the sun?

Language is cited as an obstacle to non-English speakers using the Internet. The vast majority of Web sites are American, and many non-United States sites have English-language versions. Yet the Internet hasn't caught on big time in the United Kingdom, which obviously has no language problem. Some analysts speculate that the British predisposition for tradition has in some ways hampered their embrace of this new medium. It will be interesting to see whether Richard Branson's Internet venture, Virgin Net, will succeed in galvanizing Britain into becoming more of a force in cyberspace. Judging from the success of past Branson ventures, such a scenario is likely.

In some respects, France was ahead of the European pack with France Telecom's Minitel system, a sort of screen-based dial-up information and communication system launched in 1984. The equipment was provided free on demand, and as many as 6.5 million subscribers used it. Yet some industry analysts think that having Minitel might have inclined many French to dismiss the Internet as unnecessary for their needs. Minitel is certainly well entrenched. France's major national daily papers *Le Monde* and *Le Figaro* are on the Web and even offer search facilities, but their archives cannot be accessed through the Internet; it's Minitel-only for them.

Nevertheless, in the late 1990s, Prime Minister Lionel Jospin became the first French leader ever to appear on a podium with a cyberguru when he welcomed Microsoft founder William H. Gates III at a technology conference. Jospin's government has vowed to embrace the Internet, even if its primary language is English.

Part of Europe's problem is that the use of computers is a lot lower in Europe than in the United States, and it's growing at a less rapid pace in Europe than in North America and Asia. Sweden has developed an innovative socialist-capitalist approach to address this situation: Lands Organisationen (LO), the country's largest labor union, has negotiated a special bulk lease-purchase deal for its members, resulting in a huge increase in business for PC-makers. Just four months after it was struck in 1997, the LO deal with PC manufacturer Hewlett-Packard accounted for more than thirty percent of all home PCs sold in Sweden that year. Swedish tax breaks also are making it easier for employers to supply their workers with cheap PCs. Expect more deals of these types to drive higher computer sales in other countries over the coming years.

But even for computer owners with Internet access, relatively high telephone charges discourage the sort of long online sessions that enable users to develop Internet interest and skills. The deregulation of European telecoms markets that took place in January 1998 is likely to increase competition and drive down prices. But the case of British Telecom in Britain shows that entrenched monopolies aren't dislodged overnight—it takes quite a while for serious competition to be established.

The feedback on the Internet from around Europe, except Holland and the Nordic countries, is pretty consistent, along the lines of "There's lots of hype, it hasn't had much impact here yet, but people are very interested and expect it to change the way they do business."

Some Europeans have concrete expectations; our Swedish colleague, Katarina Varenius says, "The changes to expect, I would think, would be closing down retailer branches of all sorts, due to the shift from visiting a physical location to visiting it on the Internet. Post offices, banks, and grocery stores will close down their 'bread and butter' stores and focus their competence and one-on-one service on flagship stores. . . . The number of smaller businesses has increased. The high unemployment level has caused a need for creating jobs, and one way is to start your own business. But the Internet has made it much easier to succeed, due to the low costs involved in presenting your idea and your business to the market."

Our Danish trend scout told us: "The Internet is not only for technology freaks anymore. A lot of Danish institutions and cultural organizations are on the Internet. The Ministry of Culture in Denmark sponsors Kulturnet Danmark (www.kulturnet.dk), a site with links to all cultural institutions on the Internet. Kulturnet also helps cultural organizations to get on the Internet by helping them program their homepage. Even the Royal Danish Theatre is online, and so is the Danish Royal Family."

There's little risk in predicting that Western Europe is not going to take the world lead in cyberspace in the foreseeable future. The old continent has its share of "digerati," but Europe looks to be a long way from reaching the critical mass of popular usage that will encourage and sustain a real range of local Internet initiatives. The United States will lead the race well into the next millennium.

Within Europe, it's hard to imagine the southern countries doing anything other than playing catch-up—at best—for years to come. For European leads on the Internet, it's probably worth watching the Nordic countries. They've been on the Internet for some time now, and the Swedes in particular have proved that they can put together marketing concepts that cross borders easily—the pop band Abba, home furnishings manufacturer and retailer IKEA, and two distinctive car marquees (Volvo and Saab).

Watch out for the Netherlands, too—the Dutch are rapidly adding to their Internet server count which, per capita in Europe, lags behind only the Scandinavian countries and Switzerland. Given their great talent for languages, the Dutch are having no problem jumping into the Internet mainstream and holding their own. And because they have astute trading bred in their bones, the Internet is just the thing to stimulate Dutch commercial use, with everyone from Royal Dutch Airlines to porn merchants offering their services.

Asia Online

For most Asians, the Internet is more of a promise than a reality. Cybercafés are springing up all over the region, making the Internet more accessible, but usage is generally limited by the low level of overall computer ownership and tight government restrictions in China and Vietnam.

Asian governments are pretty bullish about promoting the Internet. Even Vietnam, with one of the most censorious and information-restrictive governments in the region, celebrated an official "Vietnam Internet Day" in November of 1997. The occasion marked the awarding of licenses for four Internet service providers (ISP). Signing up costs around thirty-six dollars, with four dollars monthly access charges—not for everyone in a country in which the average annual wage is three hundred dollars.

In the face of economic crisis, Asia is banking on the Internet to help them through the recession. Visa International just released the results of a recent survey stating that 68 percent of respondents believe that e-commerce will help their businesses remain competitive. Sixty percent say that it will help them sell more of a range of products than actual stores, according to a *New Strait Times* report. The Ministry of Foreign Trade and Economic Cooperation has unveiled its attempt to increase exports from China with China Market (www.chinamarket.com.cn), a Web site that links users to Chinese companies selling more than eight thousand industrial products. The site is in Chinese and English and also has a chat room in which people can conduct business. During a trial run, the site received 62,000 hits on its first day and more than a half million hits in the first week.

Surprisingly, the most technologically advanced country in the region, Japan, has been slow to use the Internet. MIT Media Lab chief Nicholas Negroponte has posited that the adoption of personal computers, and hence e-mail, by the Japanese was held up by the invention of the fax, which permitted handwritten telecommunication. Using a standard QWERTY keyboard (so named for the order of the uppermost row of letters) to input Japanese characters is certainly less convenient.

On the other hand, Chinese characters are equally difficult to input, yet Taiwan has 1.26 million Internet users, according to a 1997 survey by Internet Information and Intelligence, a market research entity. And that number is expected to climb to three million by the year 2000. The popularity of the Internet has boosted consumer acceptance and usage of Web shopping sites. Taiwanese consumers can even pay their taxes over the Internet.

A survey by www.research shows that online shopping in Asia

has not suffered. Forty percent of users in Thailand have shopped online in the last twelve months. Twenty-five percent of Indonesian users have shopped online, one-third of whom spent more than a thousand dollars. For Singapore the percentage is twenty, and the spending dropped to around a hundred and fifty dollars, as reported in *Business Times* in 1998.

Several years ago, Singapore declared its intention to become a fully wired state, with a connection in every household. Initially, the government tried to control its citizens' Internet usage by routing traffic through an official gateway and barring access to sites deemed unsuitable. It quickly realized, though, that controlling even Singapore's bit of the Internet was a losing game.

Neighboring Malaysia, as mentioned earlier, is determined to become the IT center of the region, with its Multimedia Super Corridor enterprise zone and cyberlaws guaranteeing digital freedom—a U-turn from the government's previous stance. News broadcasts routinely show government ministers consulting the World Wide Web, and approximately a million ordinary citizens are thought to do likewise. Ad industry employees in Kuala Lumpur report that the Internet has had a tremendous impact on the working and personal lives of its users. It has meant better access to information and connectivity, allowing users "to be in touch with the world anytime [they] want."

India announced in November of 1997 that it would privatize its ISP (Internet Service Providers) industry. Until that time there was only one government-controlled company. Recently it was reported in *Techserver*, a trade publication in the region, that the government still has a monopoly on the industry, but that AT&T, Microsoft, and Compuserve have shown interest in getting into the ISP market in India once pricing issues have been resolved. A selection of Indian software companies looked far from out of place at the 1998 CeBIT, the world's biggest IT trade fair, in Hannover, Germany. (For much more about Asian cyberbiz, see Chapter 16.)

Thanks to modems and satellite links, big foreign companies can call on the talents of highly qualified Indian IT specialists in cities such as Bangalore and Pune for data processing, programming, and other skilled work. Many Indian software houses are focusing on helping overseas companies deal with the millennium bug problem—a labor-intensive and therefore costly process of auditing codes, fixing date-compliance problems and then verifying the fixes in a dry run.

INTERNET 2010

At present, the world's widely disparate rates for adoption of the Internet have to do with a number of factors, ranging from limited phone lines to repressive governments, from excessive telephone charges to cultural separations between work and home. All of these barriers to adoption will fall as the Internet continues to invade our lives at work and home. Why are we so convinced of this? Perhaps the most compelling reason is that computers are no longer about technology. They're about something far more important: community and communicating.

Computers = Community + Communicating

When the telephone was invented, it was initially a tool of commerce, controlled by men in the workplace. Gradually, its value as a means of connecting with friends and family was discovered, and it found its way into the home. Like most "intrusions" into our personal domains, the telephone first was relegated to the home's "public space," most likely on a "conversation bench" in the reception area of the foyer. Today, who among us sleeps without a phone within reach? And when was the last time you thought about the technology associated with the device? All we know is that with the right number combination, we can access our party of choice on the other end of the line. How does it work? Who cares?

Thanks to the Internet, computers currently are making a similar transition from technology to communications tool, although the transition has been far simpler in North America than in other parts of the world. One reason for the apparent reluctance of consumers to log on in many countries is the much firmer line that's drawn between work and home. In the United States, the workforce sees no problem with the notion of being "on call." From the telephone to the answering machine to the beeper to PCs, we are using new technologies to blur the line between work and home, allowing us to merge our two lives. We've even developed entirely new workstyles—including home offices, telecommuting, and virtual offices—to take better advantage of new technologies.

In most parts of Europe and Latin America, by contrast, when you close your office door behind you, you're closed for business. There is no expectation that you should be able or willing to conduct commerce beyond traditional work hours. This sharp delineation between work and home makes it far easier to understand why home PCs fall way down on the list of must-haves in some parts of the world. In fact, research shows that in many countries the home computer market is driven by a focus on raising competitive children rather than a desire to extend professional productivity or connect to new media.

Like other barriers—including today's near monopoly of English-language content online—consumer reluctance to in-home computers will decline. In tradition-bound Latin America, we're seeing significant growth in online access, with users in Colombia, for instance, quadrupling during 1997. Our colleagues in offices in that region tell us that the ultimate use for most Latin Americans won't be online research or shopping or gaming; instead, it will be online chat—a natural outlet for cultures that stress social interaction.

In a recent survey done by the Nazca Satchi and Satchi advertising agency, the online population in Latin America is expected to reach thirty-four million by the turn of the century. Between 1995 and 1997, Internet use increased by 788 percent. Brazilians bought 2.5 million PCs in 1997, and there is an online population in Brazil of more than a million.

Technology and Tradition

Since a meaningful component of our thoughts about change revolves around new media and emerging technologies, it's not surprising that when we were working together within the TBWA advertising agency, our unit decided to conduct a global study of consumers' attitudes toward the technologies that are changing their lives, which we dubbed the Technology + Tradition study.

Once, over cocktails in Milan, the two of us hypothesized that people living in more "traditional" cultures—for instance, Italy and Spain—would be more fearful of new technologies than those living in "modern" cultures, such as the United States, the Netherlands, and Sweden, where digital convergence is a reality for the average professional. We couldn't have been more mistaken. Responses to our study—from more than two thousand households in thirty countries in Europe, North America, Asia, and Africa—indicated that it is, in fact, people who are already "plugged in" to the Internet and other technologies who are most wary of what the future might hold (including information overload and loss of privacy). Consumers who are not yet plugged in are far less likely to express such concerns.

Among the findings of the "Technology + Tradition" study:

• Consumers are future-oriented, but the past remains extremely relevant

56% agree: "I look ahead to the future, but I derive a good deal of comfort from looking back at the past."

39% agree: "I'm a very modern, future-oriented person; I look ahead, not back."

2% agree: "I'm much more interested in the past than the future."

• Traditionals seem divided between wholehearted futurism and the draw of the past, while Moderns are decidedly more likely to look ahead while deriving comfort from the past.

	Traditionals		Moderns	
Attitude/% agree	Italy	Spain	United States	Denmark
Very modern	45%	50%	29%	11%
Look ahead/comfort from past	40%	50%	71%	89%
Past-oriented	15%	0%	0%	0%

But despite growing reliance, technology is not considered all-important: 83 percent agreed that "composing music will always be more important than writing great computer software," and

20 percent agreed with the statement "I'm excited by new technologies." The excitement of both Traditionals and Moderns is hampered by concerns about technology's impact:

	Traditionals	Moderns
Concerned that technology will dehumanize us	89%	81%
Concerned that new technologies will invade our privacy	84%	72%

But Moderns are made far more nervous by new technologies (30 percent) than are Traditionals (18 percent), and Moderns are more concerned (60 percent) than are Traditionals (50 percent) that they won't be able to keep up with technology's pace of change. The nervousness expressed by Moderns is likely rooted in experience (marketplace shifts, digital convergence), as well as the fact that Moderns are more apt to be on call all the time. No wonder they're more cautious about endorsing high-tech lifestyles.

	Traditionals	Moderns
Own telephone answering machine	51%	76%
Own personal pager/beeper	51%	68%
Own cellular phone	15%	20%
Own cordless phone	45%	54%

	Traditionals	Moderns
Very interested in telecommuting	50%	31%
Somewhat interested in telecommuting	33%	42%
Not at all interested in telecommuting	11%	19%
Telecommute (part- or full-time basis)	2%	5%

The Internet was rated the most impressive modern-day technological device/advancement (26 percent agree):

- "Global communications available cheaply for all." (Australia)
- "It's accessible to everybody—it's like inventing the telephone all over again." (Chile)

– "It has leveled the world playing field." (United Arab Emirates)
– "It connects all parts of the world, whether for business or pleasure." (Lebanon)

There's No Pulling the Plug

Despite fears about things such as information overload, slow rates of in-home PC adoption in some parts of the world, and the cost of connecting people in remote corners of the globe, we are convinced that Internet usage will become commonplace in virtually every part of the world within the next decade. For those of us whose lives are already deeply embedded in the Internet, there simply is no going back. And in our global economy, when corporate leaders in North America and parts of Asia and Europe are connected to the Internet, you can be sure would-be customers, suppliers, and competitors will come online too—and they'll bring consumers in their countries along with them.

Once that happens—and the Internet becomes truly global— fads and trends from Latin America, Africa, Australasia, and Europe will make their way onto the computer screens of fad-hungry early adopters across North America, and vice versa. We'll see a trend-swapping free-for-all that will forever change the cultural power bases around the world.

CHAPTER 8:
Rites of Purification: Body and Soul

---

*N*EW BEGINNINGS BRING OUT the human urge to clean up and start fresh—spring cleaning. With the start of the next millennium just around the corner, it's a fair bet that this urge will become pretty strong in societies that measure time by the Western calendar.

Major religions have their own ways of body/mind/spirit purification, often involving fasting or abstaining from certain types of food. Muslims observe the fasting month of Ramadan, when they can't eat or drink between sunrise and sunset. Hindus don't eat meat on prayer days and festivals. For Christians, the pre-Easter forty days of Lent have traditionally been a time of frugality, preceded by the excesses of Mardi Gras or Carnival.

Early industrial man had purgatives to eliminate unwanted substances from the body. For late-twentieth-century man, purification means detoxification. In the last quarter-century or so, the urge to purify has grown stronger due to a rise in the number of harmful substances, a growing inclination to worry about them, and—fortunately—more ways for concerned individuals to take action for themselves.

Approaches to purification vary, but the underlying belief is that the combination of faith, goodness and perhaps a few well-chosen commercial products and services will enable the individual to restore him- or herself to a natural, pristine state in time for the new beginning of the year 2000. This final stretch before the next millennium will give new meaning and impetus to the spirituality and health trends of the last couple of decades.

• NEXT: AGGRESSIVE HEALTH MAINTENANCE

Technology is coming that will ensure less invasive, more civilized, and more humane ways to prevent, detect, and treat disease. Ten years ago, magnetic resonance imaging (MRI) was a Next, providing a radiation-free alternative to scanning. The potential of this innovation will be extended far beyond testing for neurological disorders. MRI scanners will become ubiquitous, and even primary-care practitioners will have access to such machines, enabling them to do everything from detecting mammography abnormalities to determining the extent of knee and spinal injuries. At the same time, CT scans—which produce cross-sectional images by computing, using small doses of radiation—will facilitate virtual examinations of the lungs, the bowels, and other organs, without the need for painful and dangerous invasive procedures.

There is a yin and a yang to most trends, though, and this one is not without a flip side. As disease screening becomes more prevalent and more sophisticated, people determined to be predisposed to particular diseases might be subjected to unnecessary medical procedures. Already we're seeing healthy women submit to radical mastectomies simply out of the fear a "high risk" label engenders in them.

As the health field grows more technical, and as patient choices continue to expand, expect to see a growing cadre of "medical advocates"—professionals hired to guide individuals through the jumble of medical literature, "alternative" medicines, and available medical options. These people will become the new family doctors, although they are not practicing physicians.

• NEXT: ALTERNATIVE (HOLISTIC) MEDICAL SOLUTIONS

Like so many of our observations and forecasts, the counter-trend to aggressive health maintenance is as important as the initial movement towards it. Frustrated by managed care plans and dissatisfied with modern medical treatments, more and more Americans are opting for less expensive and less intrusive alternatives. While there were only two hundred homeopaths in the United States in 1970, there are three thousand this year. Forty-two percent of American adults have used some kind of alternative health care during the last year, according to a study commissioned by the Landmark Healthcare HMO. More importantly, four out of five of those who used alternative health care say that their medical doctors supported this choice.

In a national poll, those who pursued alternative treatments were more likely to agree with the statement: The health of my body, mind and spirit are related, and whoever cares for my health should take that into account. The *Los Angeles Times* reported that alternative medicine is edging into the mainstream, with Californians leading the way. It's now an eighteen billion dollar industry in the United States, with consumers spending $3.65 billion last year on herbal remedies alone. The article noted the following examples of growth in holistic approaches to health and wellness, showing the degree to which the Left Coast is leading the way on this trend:

* **Drugstore Shelf Space** for Vitamin, Mineral, and Herb Supplements**
1995: 8 feet
1998: 22 feet
** Rite-Aid, store average

* **Alternative Care Use in U.S. in the Last Year**

Herbal products: 17%	High-dose vitamins: 13%
Chiropractic: 16%	Homeopathy: 5%
Massage: 14%	Acupuncture: 2%

* **Alternative Care Use in California in the Last Year**

High-dose vitamins: 35%	Homeopathy: 11%
Chiropractic: 32%	Acupuncture: 8%
Herbal products: 30%	Other: 11%

* **Changes in Opinion over Five Years Toward Alternative Health Care**
More positive: 40%
Remained same: 58%
More negative: 2%

• NEXT: DRUG-INDUCED SOLUTIONS

From Viagra to Prozac to "miracle" diet drugs, consumers are gulping down pills for just about anything and everything that ails them. It's all a part of our growing intolerance for anything but the quickest of fixes. In the coming year, we'll see an increase in self-directed medical care, as well as heightened media hype about the latest and greatest anti-aging drugs and "smart pills"—both designed to give us an edge in the new millennium.

The pharmaceutical industry, spurred on by best-selling "quality of life" drugs, is ushering in a second honeymoon in the marriage between medicine and commerce. And now that people are feeling more libidinous, happy, and virile than ever, there is a growing expectation that any ailment—whether sexual dysfunction or a lack of mental acuity—will be treatable with a miracle pill in the near future. So-called smart drugs, diet pills, and a slew of homeopathic nostrums are flying off the shelves. And with boomers turning fifty, the anti-aging department has become one of the hottest industries going. (We write more about Nexts impacting health and wellness in various places in the book, but urge you to remember that none other than Bill and Melinda Gates have declared that their non-Microsoft investing for the future will be in the category of biotechnology.) We assume that health-related innovations and new products will be to the next decade what high technology and Internet stocks have been to the '90s: a volatile joy ride offering a bonanza of new solutions.

Youth, inc.: DHEA, among the new crop of age busters, works to protect the body from some of the degenerative changes of old age. A naturally occurring hormone, DHEA—in supplement form—has been claimed to boost sex drive, increase muscle mass and bone density, improve memory, reduce obesity, and increase energy levels. Another runaway seller is ginkgo biloba, an extract from the maidenhair tree. The product is said to increase blood flow throughout the body and to restore cognitive skills. Insomniacs are driving the market for melatonin—another natural hormone and a soporific that has been reputed to stop the aging process. Green tea is the newest addition to the anti-aging (and anticarcinogen) arsenal. (The Japanese are now adding it to chewing gum.) And Linus Pauling disciples swear by antioxidants such as vitamins A, C, and E, which have been shown to help with age-related illnesses by ridding the body of waste.

The orgasm pill: Finally, a cure for Viagra-envy. The correlative for women, the Erogenex formula EX22 (www.erogenex.com)—touted by its manufacturers as the "orgasm pill"—has been a hot seller in parts of the world and is steadily making inroads in the United States. Since a third to half of all women don't experience orgasm during sex, any drug that claims to increase drive, stamina, and lubrication is virtually guaranteed a market. Moreover, by claiming to boost a woman's testosterone levels, Erogenex may even help women decrease fat by building muscle. (Erogenex does not require a prescription.)

Fat burners: Though there are more low-fat foods on the market than ever before, people just keep getting heavier. There are more than 350 million overweight people in the world today, and ten different fat-fighting drugs are in trials and pending approval, according to the Biotechnology Research Institute. Until mid-1997, fen-phen was touted as the holy grail of weight-loss products. Thousands of obese women were downing the Molotov of pill cocktails before potentially lethal heart valve side-effects were detected. The drug was recalled in September of 1997, and a class action lawsuit followed.

Though the fen-phen scare sent shock waves through both patients and providers, making them less willing to believe the hype about new fat burners, there was much anticipation over two more recently released drugs: Meridia and Xenical. Meridia acts as an appetite suppressant by slowing the absorption of serotonin, while Xenical purportedly blocks the absorption of one-third of fat intake.

Cancer cures: Though modern medicine has virtually extinguished many of man's most life-threatening diseases, a cure for cancer still eludes us. That's not to say that recent research into experimental treatments has not been promising. Indeed, initial trials of angiostatin and endostatin (two drugs that shrink tumors by cutting off their blood supply) have been so positive that doctors are receiving thousands of calls a week from patients who want to try the drugs.

Another drug, tamoxifen, has been shown to reduce the risk for breast cancer by 45 percent in women who are at high risk for the disease. And in Italy, scientists have achieved remission in ten thousand cancer patients through a combination of vitamins and hormones, including somatostatine. The therapy has not been licensed, but the Italian government recently passed a bill allowing terminal patients to be treated free of charge until all tests are completed.

Mixed smoke signals: Quitting smoking may reduce your risk of cancer, but don't expect it to make you happy. Dr. John Rosecrans, professor of pharmacology, toxicology and rehabilitation counseling at Virginia Commonwealth University, has written that depression, pain and neurological disease can all be kept at bay by a cigarette a day. He cites studies that have shown that nicotine acts as an analgesic in laboratory mice and may, in fact, work the same way for people. The theory is that nicotine may affect serotonin and dopamine levels in the brain, much as antidepressants do. Accordingly, nicotine patches have helped to diminish some symptoms of Tourette's syndrome and Parkinson's disease.

Noggin nostrum: "Smart drugs" aren't just for rave kids anymore. One of the newest noggin enhancers to hit the market is Cerebro-Gain, "an oxygenator and activator of cerebral metabolism." Though the data to support its claims are skimpy, CerebroGain is said to be twenty times more "active" than gingko.

Thanks for the memories: Alzheimer's may be the last stage, but from age twenty on, the average person loses six percent of his or her memory over each ten-year increment. How to stop the clock? Cortex Pharmaceuticals Inc. has created a new line of drugs called ampikines, which help brain cells communicate with each other more clearly (the more communication, the better the memory). Even more impressive is Piracetam (being marketed in South Africa as Nootropil), which purports to increase the flow of information between hemispheres of the brain. Some fifty other memory enhancers are currently being tested.

Other miscellaneous miracles: Celebrex (for the treatment of arthritis pain); Revia (to treat alcoholism); Rogaine (for hair replacement); Leptin (a weight-loss drug); "Andro" (the performance-enhancing substance that raised questions about Mark McGwire's home run record); NutriMan TNT (a kind of natural Viagra, said to both increase sex drive and enhance the experience).

WHAT'S NEXT?

Personalized pills: Customized formulas of vitamin and herbal supplements based on the purchaser's blood type, weight, health history (personal and family), ethnicity and lifestyle.

In-office healers: In a bid to keep workers happy and healthy, employers will hire naturopaths, nutritionists, personal trainers, and other health and fitness professionals to provide advice, training, and treatment.

Brain boosters for babies: Specially formulated supplements designed to give the next generation an edge in the new millennium.

Spirituality pills: Mood-enhancing pills designed to open up the mind to the wonders of spiritual enlightenment.

Functional foods: Leaders in medicine, nutrition, and high-tech fields are collaborating to create a new class of products known as "functional foods," "medical foods," or "nutraceuticals." By any name, these foods have been engineered to impart health benefits beyond basic nutrition, and the movement is far from a fringe one. Dr. Stephen DeFelice of the United States-based Foundation for Innovation in Medicine recently told *The Guardian* that "every major food and pharmaceutical company out there has a nutraceutical task force."

Dr. DeFelice predicts that consumers soon will be equally likely to seek cures for what ails them at the supermarket as at the pharmacy. "The main advantage of medical foods over drugs is that they contain naturally occurring products—even if they weren't made naturally," said DeFelice. "Their main medical effect will be to shift emphasis from curing illness to preventing illness."

"Enhanced foods" are modified and/or fortified to promote health benefits. In Japan, drinks with added "polyols" have been introduced to reduce the risk of dental cavities, and Coca-Cola has launched a controversial adolescent soft drink containing DHA, an essential fatty acid said to promote learning ability. Sales of the fermented milk drink Yakult, available in Japan since 1935, now total more than twenty-three million units a day in some sixteen countries worldwide. The product contains 6.5 billion lactobacillus casei shirota bacteria, which, consumed daily, are said to promote "positive intestinal flora." Since 1992, Japan has approved more than seventy-five products as "Foods for Specialized Health Use," including protein-modified rice for people with allergies and phosphate milk for those with kidney disorders. Labels on these products include a recommendation from a Japanese nutritional foods association and a reminder to eat a balanced diet.

At Sainsbury's, the magnificent and profitable supermarket chain in the United Kingdom, women considering pregnancy can purchase bread fortified with folic acid (known to prevent spina bifida in babies). Those concerned with cholesterol levels can purchase loaves with oat fiber, and the "omega loaf" adds fish oil for a healthy heart. European scientists have also bred a tomato with about four times the normal level of beta-carotene, which the body uses to make vitamin A, and twice the level of lycopene, which might reduce the risk of some cancers.

The Finnish margarine Benecol was such a success in Europe that it has made its way to the United States. This "healing" margarine gains its powers from a natural ingredient found in pine trees, and it prevents the body from absorbing cholesterol. With the growing popularity of "enhanced foods" and the ninety-eight million Americans who suffer from high cholesterol, this product is sure to sell well, even if it costs six times more than the average margarine.

In the United States, there are products such as Brain Gum, which contains phospholipids, a type of fat that helps the nervous system function. The gum claims to reduce memory loss due to age by up to twelve years. You can buy chips fortified with herbs such as ginkgo biloba and ginseng. Market intelligence source Datamonitor says sales of such nutraceuticals hit $8.8 billion in 1996. Thirty percent of functional food sales comes from fortified juices and sodas.

Although there are ongoing debates about whether herbs should have to withstand the same rigorous testing as man-made or synthetic drugs, they have not affected sales at all. These products tend to fall into four categories. Nineteen percent are "green." These are herbal products that have gone through and passed testing on humans. Nine percent are "yellow," which means that when tested they provided health benefits, although more tests must be done. Thirty percent are "orange," which means they have been tested only on animals or in a limited way on humans. The rest of the products, 41 percent, have scant evidence to support claims. (These percentages add up to 99 percent.)

Certain natural foods, free of alterations and additives, are also being recognized and promoted for their functional qualities. Bruce Ames, professor of biochemistry at the University of California at Berkeley, reports that dietary antioxidants slow down or limit the metabolic processes that damage cells, thus reducing the risk of disease and helping people live longer and healthier lives. Ames's example: The quarter of the United States population that eats the least fruits and vegetables—rich in antioxidants—are deficient in folic acid, vitamin C, and carotenoids. Rates "for virtually every kind of cancer" in this group are double those for the quarter of the population that eats the most fruits and vegetables. In the United States oatmeal is one of the few foods that can claim official government sanction for health benefits. This all-natural, low-fat food has been proven to lower cholesterol and might reduce the risk of heart disease; it soon will carry a label of approval by the Food and Drug Administration. Scientists are studying garlic, soy, cranberries, broccoli, and red wine to determine if similar FDA health-benefits labels are deserved.

When genetic research succeeds in pinpointing each individual's predisposition to specific illnesses, people will be able to consume an appropriate combination of functional foods to ward off illness. Parents will be among the first true believers, using food profiles to plan their children's diets.

Supplements: Vitamins and herbs increasingly are being added to the arsenals of those intent on keeping their bodies pure and healthy through natural means. Vitamin C, in particular, is touted as a combatant of free radicals (highly reactive chemicals suspected of being carcinogenic), but vitamin E is fast gaining prominence. Citing recent information that it fights certain cancers, cardiovascular disease and even Alzheimer's disease, *Food Processing* magazine labeled vitamin E "the nutrient of the year."

The market for herbal products is skyrocketing in the United States, having grown from five hundred million dollars in 1992 to more than three billion dollars in 1998. Consumer interest in alternative medicine has fueled this growth, as did passage of the Dietary Supplement Health and Education Act of 1994, which defined herbs as food supplements and set limits of government regulation far below that required of pharmaceuticals. According to a Gallup survey, Americans' use of herbs increased nearly 70 percent last year.

According to The Atlanta *Journal-Constitution*, these are the herbs (and their reputed effects) that Americans bought the most last year:
1. Ginseng (relieves fatigue)
2. Garlic (reduces blood cholesterol)
3. Ginkgo Biloba (might improve circulation, memory)
4. Echinacea (helps maintain immune system)
5. St. John's Wort (antidepressant)
6. Saw Palmetto (helps maintain urinary tract function in older men)
7. Echinacea/Goldenseal (might boost immune system)
8. Pycnogenol/Grape Seed (antioxidant)
9. Goldenseal (antibacterial)
10. Evening Primrose (relieves PMS, arthritis, breast pain)

READYING THE SOUL:
IN SEARCH OF SPIRITUALITY

- ### NEXT: SOMETHING TO BELIEVE IN

In response to an increased sense of isolation, a disconnected-ness from the natural world, and even fears related to the millennium, Westerners (particularly baby-boomers) are turning for solace and insights to the mysticism and spirituality of Eastern and New Age religions.

The United States has recently seen a large increase in the scope of religions that inhabit the continent. There are two hundred different religious denominations in America today. There are at least five million Muslims, three-quarters of a million Buddhists, one million Hindus and ten million Pentecostals.

Although only 20,000 Americans claim New Age as their religion, 23 percent believe in reincarnation, and 12 percent believe in astrology. And gurus such as Marianne Williamson and Deepak Chopra are raking in followers and cash at a dizzying pace. Chopra estimates his annual gross at fifteen million dollars; his nineteen books have been translated into twenty-five languages. More than ten million books were sold in the New Age category last year.

The ancient tradition of Kabbalah, a form of Jewish mysticism, is also attracting enthusiastic students around the world, including American celebrities such as Madonna, Sandra Bernhard, Roseanne and Barbra Streisand. Mysticism is the answer to "a hungry, thirsty, bottle-of-water-in-the-desert need for connection with transcendent meanings," United Jewish Appeal officer Alan Bayer told *Time* magazine.

The Hindu population in the United States has grown from about 70,000 in 1977 to 800,000 today. And Buddhism, the fastest-growing Eastern religion in the United States, has an estimated 750,000 adherents. In the United Kingdom, while the number of monks and nuns in traditional Catholic orders is in steady decline, there is now a six-month waiting list to join the Buddhist sangha (community) of monks and nuns at a popular monastery called Samye Ling in Scotland, according to *Telegraph* magazine.

Seeing ancient religion employed by modern-day icons can be discordant, to say the least. While sitting in a cafe in Berlin, Germany, we noted how small our world has become: The waiters were Milanese, the bartender Albanian, and the music was supplied by none other than Barbra Streisand, singing the most holy Jewish prayer. What was intriguing is that the music was piped through this space as nothing more than song: as entertainment. Will religion become universally edutainment Next, as it already is for so many? Could this be a mass global movement, conceivably even a Big Next in the making?

There is already evidence that a diverse spiritual culture will become more common in our daily lives. Greeting card lines, for example, will expand to incorporate New Age sentiments, interfaith celebrations, and "alternative" holidays such as the winter solstice. Interfaith households will come to represent an important niche market, driving increased demand for products and services geared to their specific needs. (A survey at the beginning of this decade found that one in three American Jews was living in an interfaith household, as were 21 percent of Catholics, 30 percent of Mormons, and 40 percent of Muslims.)

Spirituality's increased prominence in daily life will be reflected in things such as summer spirituality camps for kids and weeklong retreats for adults, both intended to infuse participants with spiritual rejuvenation and growth.

While not only about spirituality, the following examples illustrate why religious sentiments are making the world that much more charged as we accelerate into the future ever more connected than yesterday. In the wake of the recent bombings of two United States embassies and a Planet Hollywood in Africa by Muslim extremists, terrorism has gripped the United States, and Hollywood is playing it up. As stereotypes about the Islamic faith abound, *The Siege*, a movie starring Bruce Willis, has come under attack by Muslims around the nation. The movie depicts a bombing campaign by fictional Muslims that leads to the mass arrest and imprisonment of Muslims and Arabs, much like the WWII internment camps for Japanese-Americans in the 1940s. According to the Council on American-Islamic Relations (CAIR), as reported by the *Toronto Star*, 280 cases of anti-Muslim violence, discrimination, stereotyping, bias, and harassment were reported in the United States in 1997.

Consider that people of Islamic faith already outnumber both Presbyterians and Episcopalians and might very well overtake the number of Jews by the year 2000. The irony is that America is the only country where Muslims have their freedom. As reported by the *Rocky Mountain News*, Charles Kimball, a world-renowned Middle Eastern scholar from Wake Forest University, believes Americans have "got to get to know each other, break through stereotypes and history. Not that we will agree or develop a theology that is a mishmash of everything. But we've got to go beyond tolerating to respecting our diversity. And certainly, as Americans, we've got to affirm the rights of others to worship freely."

Islamic Europe

An increasing majority of Europeans no longer practice any religion other than consumerism. Not so for the followers of Islam, Europe's fastest growing religion. The scene is set for Islam to become a major factor in Europe's political and social life in the coming millennium, as second-generation Muslim immigrants figure out how they relate to their host cultures and as more Muslim immigrants arrive.

The Muslim population has risen to around three million in Germany (mainly Turkish), more than two million in France (mostly North African), and around 1.5 million in the United Kingdom (mainly from Pakistan and Bangladesh), with sizable Muslim communities also in the Netherlands and Sweden. Fresh legal and illegal arrivals, especially from nearby trouble spots Algeria and the Balkans, are likely to swell the numbers and make Muslims an even more visible part of Europe's patchwork. Already, according to the *Electronic Telegraph*, Britain has around three thousand makeshift places of Islamic worship, with 160 purpose-built mosques and another eighty to 100 scheduled for completion by the millennium.

Prince Charles has made a point of getting close to Muslim community leaders, but for many Europeans, having large numbers of Muslims in their midst is taking a lot of adjustment. Muslims in Europe are, in fact, far from being a new phenomenon. Muslim Moors ruled Spain for seven hundred years, until 1492, developing one of the most advanced cultures in Europe—the Spanish language still bears a strong Arabic imprint. The Turkish Ottoman Empire ruled Greece for four hundred years, until the early nineteenth century, and twice narrowly missed conquering Vienna (1529 and 1683). In former Yugoslavia, Muslims lived alongside Catholics and Orthodox Christians until just a few years ago. Conversely, France ruled Algeria for one hundred thirty years, until 1962.

Unfortunately, Europe's dealings with Muslims have left a legacy of mistrust that will be difficult to overcome. Both Christianity and Islam have been militant, proselytizing religions fighting each other for territory and converts, and most Muslim immigrants in Europe come from countries that were colonized or militarily defeated by European powers. Resentments linger.

Europe's support for Israel since its foundation, for Salman Rushdie's book *The Satanic Verses*, and for the Gulf War, and its failure to stop the massacre of Bosnians, have all been interpreted by some Muslims as confirmation that Europeans are anti-Islam. Insecurity is further exacerbated by the rhetoric of anti-immigrant parties such as France's National Front, by arson and other attacks on immigrants, and by media coverage that tends to play up the stereotypical wild-eyed fanatic elements of Islamic fundamentalists.

Flare-ups will no doubt continue on both sides, but new developments are likely in the early years of the new millennium:

• More Euro-Muslims will achieve wealth;
• The Internet will encourage more networking and solidarity between different Muslim communities across borders;
• Euro-Muslims will increasingly use their numbers to exercise political pressure on governments in matters of concern, such as Middle East policy;
• Islam will become a cultural heritage rather than a religious practice for many second-, third-, and fourth-generation Muslims —much as Christianity is for many Europeans today as well as for secular Jews; and
• Elements of Muslim culture will be adopted as counter-culture platforms by rebellious and spiritually thirsty Europeans.

A little further into the century, Europe will become a cradle for progressive Islamic thinking, as educated young Euro-Muslims reevaluate their beliefs and culture from a Westernized standpoint, a process that would be difficult in Islamic states, where questioning of religious orthodoxy can be life-threatening.

Home as spiritual sanctuary: In North America, an increasing number of homeowners are requesting amenities tailored to specific religious and cultural practices. As reported in the *Wall Street Journal*, the movement includes the Chinese practice of feng shui (the Taoist art and science of living in harmony with the environment), Zen gardens for Buddhists, side-by-side kosher kitchens for Orthodox Jewish families, and homes oriented toward Mecca for Muslims.

Suntosh Village, a 130-home retirement community near Orlando, Florida, features an optional prayer room for Hindus. The rooms, built on the eastern sides of houses to take advantage of the rising sun, feature arched and ceramic-tiled walls, a marble floor, and storage cabinets for prayer items. "Almost all people of East Indian origin will have a space, if not a room, designated for prayer," says project spokesperson Vince Desai. "What we're doing is preparing a room for this use from the beginning." Loosely translated from old Sanskrit, suntosh means contentment.

Pilgrimage 2000: Travel that fulfills a spiritual quest also is on the rise. A decade ago, according to a report in the *Utne Reader*, fewer than four thousand people annually followed El Camino de Santiago, Spain's fabled pilgrimage route. In the summer of 1996, ninety-five thousand made the trek. In Taize, France, Generation Xers from around the world converge each week to pray and sing repetitive chants, known as the songs of Taize. In 1994, the Taize monks' trek to Paris attracted one hundred thousand-plus pilgrims. As many as twenty-five to thirty million Christians are expected to make a pilgrimage to Nazareth by next year.

Spiritual healing: Once derided by practitioners of modern medicine, faith healing is gaining legitimacy. Ninety-nine percent of 269 doctors interviewed at a meeting of the American Academy of Family Physicians said they're convinced religious belief can help heal. Three-quarters believe the prayers of others can help a patient's recovery, and 38 percent think faith healers can make people well. Recent studies linking faith and healing have led an increasing number of doctors to prescribe prayer and meditation as a complement to regular medical care. In fact, some HMOs have begun incorporating prayer into their treatments. In a recent survey conducted at a Harvard Medical School conference on "Spirituality and Healing in Medicine," it was determined that 74 percent of HMO professionals believe that spiritual healing will help contain medical costs in the future. Doctors will prescribe meditation rather than medication, positive thinking rather than Percocet. In a backlash against the daily rigors of a twenty-drug breakfast cocktail, patients are turning to the simple comfort of spirituality for support—and a cure.

Spirituality-based spending: Entrepreneurs catering to religious sensibilities will offer an expanded range of products and services. For example, Oklahoma-based long-distance phone service provider Lifeline, founded in 1990 as an "alternative that stands for biblical values," has more than 900,000 customers, with billings in excess of $14 million a month.

• NEXT: BODIES AS TEMPLES

The urge to detoxify and "purify" our bodies (and our environment) has been widespread ever since Rachel Carson's book *Silent Spring* sounded the alarm in 1962. In the past few years, though, the alarm has rung far louder, as news headlines warn us of everything from mad cow disease to mysteriously falling male fertility rates to the possible dangers of electromagnetic emissions.

In the popular lexicon, *chemicals* used to be the catch-all word for man-made substances perceived as undesirable or dangerous. The term of choice is now *toxins*, a far more powerful concept that covers not only man-made but also naturally occurring substances ranging from snake venom to bacterial and fungal byproducts. Confirming their place in modern demonology, toxins are featured as one of the hazards in Doom, one of the world's best-selling shoot-'em-up computer games.

In the past, eco-health concerns stirred high-profile collective action in the form of pressure groups such as Greenpeace. But the self-help, take-charge-of-your-life spirit of the late 1990s is now prompting millions of ordinary individuals around the world to develop their own eco-health strategies via combinations of avoidance, combatance, and elimination.

Body beautiful: Modern consumers do not distinguish among wellness and health and fitness; the tendency is to equate feeling good with looking good and vice versa. In Japan, for example, wellness and fitness blur together in terms of consumer perceptions of the gym or fitness club. Similarly, today's beauty-selling industry has seen lust and sensuality pushed into a corner as elements of "allure," while "total wellness"—encompassing mind, body and spirit—has taken center stage as the more powerful and more convincing modern-day aphrodisiac.

Alternative therapies: As alternative medicine makes it way into the mainstream, it generated an estimated thirteen billion dollars in 1998. *The Landmark Report on Public Perceptions of Alternative Care* (Landmark Healthcare, 1998) reported that 42 percent of people in the United States turned to nonconventional treatment in 1997 as a result of dissatisfaction with conventional medical treatments. Seventy-four percent used alternative therapy in conjunction with traditional treatments. The most common treatments of that 42 percent of the population were the following: herbal therapy (17 percent), chiropractic (16 percent), massage therapy (14 percent), and vitamin therapy (13 percent).

Asia Inc., a newsmagazine focused on Asia, reports that after years of turning to modern medicine, Asian executives are returning to ancient healing techniques, including massage and acupuncture. "We're in the unusual position of reintroducing old techniques to young Asians," commented Nancy Bekhor, managing director of Hong Kong's Vital Life Centre. Rather than psychological stress, Asians tend to complain about a loss of physical and emotional energy. One popular healer who caters to the business crowd offers $45 sessions that include soft music, vigorous rubbing—both on and above the body—and a lecture on channel-healing and the spiritual world.

Workers with tension-filled necks and shoulders are keeping masseuses busy. In the United States the number of massage therapists has increased 8 to 15 percent in each of the past ten years, reports the American Massage Therapy Association. This organization also estimates that Americans make seventy-five million visits to massage therapists each year. What used to be considered an indulgence is increasingly seen as a form of therapy. In response to survey results from its 1.5 million members, Oxford Health Plans, an HMO, has added to its New York regional network approximately one thousand alternative medicine practitioners, including massage therapists, yoga instructors, acupuncturists, nutritionists, and chiropractors.

To fight back against toxins, consumers are turning to a variety of methods and products aimed at assisting the body's natural cleansing systems. Fasting diets, for instance—which can range from water-only fasts to a diet made up solely of whole foods—support detoxification by releasing into the body stored, fat-soluble toxins, which are then broken down by cleansing organs and excreted. For those who want faster results, health-food stores sell a variety of herbs reputed to aid detox efforts. Gaia's Supreme Cleanse Internal Cleansing Program ($34.95), for example, is billed as a four-part, two-week program that yields a full-body cleanse.

In the future, expect to see a greater number of artificial environments dedicated to "natural healing." The Alpha Health Environment Capsule, which premiered in 1990 in Tokyo, is one such example. As reported in *Business Daily*, the capsule, which is equipped with a dry heat sauna, massage vibration, aromatherapy, germicidal lamp, ionized face air, calorie indicator, ultraviolet light, brain wave therapy, and stereophonic sounds (New Age music or nature sounds), is intended to make users "look, feel and live better." The capsule's "passenger" relaxes on the machine's contour comfort bed while wearing special lightshield glasses designed to put his or her mind "in meditative ease." Already very popular in Korea, Japan and China, Alpha Capsules are beginning to make their way west. Two new machines from Sybaritic Inc. that promise to be equally popular are the Sunspectra (featuring a domed hood and special color light effects to enhance treatments) and the Weitrol 123 (targeted for weight loss through natural metabolic stimulation).

Day spas: Once upon a time, a trip to the spa meant a week or ten days of relaxation and rejuvenation. Such an investment (in time and money) is too much for many of today's consumers, who opt for some quick R&R at a day spa. In 1992, according to the International Spa and Fitness Association, there were approximately thirty day spas in the United States, representing a fifty-million-dollar industry. Today, more than six hundred spas bring in a total of $250 million a year. The best spas manage to provide a taste of the destination spa experience at a fraction of the cost. The *Los Angeles Times* reports that the Yamaguchi Salon and Coastal Day Spa in Ventura, California, for example, evokes a Zenlike mood with scented candles, steaming cups of herbal tea, and mini-sculptures of water falling on stones. The spa's Day of Beauty ($265) includes a light organic breakfast, massage, facial, pedicure, manicure, scalp massage, color consultation, hairstyling, makeup, lunch, and spa gifts.

Shopping malls are becoming particularly popular sites for day spas, whether as stand-alone units or as part of upscale department stores. Harried shoppers can choose from an assortment of beauty and relaxation treatments. A six-hour package offered by Maximus Total Beauty Day Spa Deluxe in Long Island, New York, for instance, consists of a facial, full-body massage, spa manicure and pedicure, and lunch. Priced at $300, it's the perfect way to finish off a day of credit-overload.

Gentle exercise: Endorphins earned over twenty miles of serious running are rarely worth the effort, not to mention the surgery later in life to replace damaged ligaments and cartilage. For a more beneficial "high," a growing number of stressed-out Westerners are opting for the Eastern practice of yoga and t'ai chi.

The general aim of yoga is to increase oxygenation of the blood, stretch muscles, and increase suppleness. This, in turn, increases concentration and helps reduce toxin levels, a key source of skin problems and stress-compounding mood swings. Yoga is also reputed to stimulate internal organs, particularly the heart and lungs, and slow the aging process. In the United Kingdom, yoga is regularly practiced by a quarter of a million people and is expected to grow by 20 percent in the next year. Roper estimates that six million Americans currently are regular yoga practitioners.

In addition to using yoga to stay fit (half an hour of power yoga uses the same number of calories, 300 to 350, as jogging for the same length of time), adherents are turning to yoga as an alternative medical technique. Jon Kabat-Zinn, Ph.D., founder of the Stress Reduction Clinic at the University of Massachusetts Medical Center, combines yoga and meditation in his standard eight-week program. *Business Daily* reported that Columbia-Presbyterian Hospital, in an effort to reduce post-surgical stress and depression, speed up recovery, and prevent further heart problems, is experimenting with a battery of alternative healing methods, including yoga, hypnotherapy, Swedish massage, and therapeutic touch. Companies with stressed-out workers are also taking note of yoga's healing benefits. *Newsweek* reports that CMP Media Inc. in Manhasset, New York, sets aside a conference room for one hour each week for yoga. An instructor conducts a class that's been modified for the varied ages and conditions of participating employees.

In recent years, the centuries-old art of t'ai chi has made its way from China to many parts of Europe and North America. A growing body of scientific evidence has found that this "internal" martial art—intended to build body strength and *qi* (pronounced "chee"), your energy or life force—can decrease blood pressure, increase muscle mass, lower levels of body chemicals related to stress, and even reverse the frailty of old age. T'ai chi classes can now be found in many Western cities, in places such as senior centers, neighborhood parks, and rehabilitative programs. Gannett News Services reported recently that some companies are even getting in on the action. European American Bank, for instance, hired Jesse "Two Owls" Teasley, a poet and medicine man, to teach employees the principles of t'ai chi.

A breath of fresh air: Among products seeing increased sales are home air-filtration systems and vacuum cleaners that use a water-filtration system rather than a bag for collecting house dust. Also available at premium prices are microfiltration dust bags intended to limit dust dispersion. The enemy: airborne allergens such as dust-mite particles.

Residents of smog-ridden cities such as Mexico City, Tokyo, and Beijing turn to oxygen booths for a respite from those cities' high pollution levels. As reported by the digital news source alt.culture.daily (www.altculture.com), a more upscale version of this fad, the oxygen bar, has taken hold among health-conscious Americans and Europeans. In 1996, former competitive swimmer Lissa Charron opened the first North American oxygen bar in Toronto, the O2 Spa Bar, where masked patrons "gas up" on pure or flavored oxygen. Spinoffs soon followed in Reno, Los Angeles, and New York. True believers insist that regular shots of oxygen not only increase one's energy, but can also relieve maladies ranging from allergies to hangovers. Although professional athletes inhale oxygen before competition to boost energy, there is little scientific evidence to substantiate benefits claims (and some doctors warn that too many trips to the oxygen bar could result in oxygen toxicity and/or cellular abnormalities). Oxygen has also become a staple at day spas and health resorts, where the range of treatments now includes oxygen pills, oxygen-enhanced drinks, and oxygenated skin creams. Oxygen-snorting celebrities are said to include Jeff Goldblum, Ben Stiller, Kirstie Alley, and Woody Harrelson, who opened a Los Angeles yoga center with an adjoining oxygen bar in 1997.

Water, water everywhere: Consumers turned off by artificial colors and flavors in soft drinks are opting for more healthful beverages. Fruit beverages, ready-to-drink teas and sports drinks are growing in popularity, but the number-one seller in an estimated 1.4 million hotel mini-bars worldwide is none other than bottled water.

At the height of the Southeast Asian haze scare throughout the late '90s, authorities advised citizens to stay indoors and drink plenty of water to flush out the toxins contained in the smoke, which was caused by widespread forest fires in Indonesia. The idea of flushing out harmful substances seems to be intuitively right to the human psyche. Although plain water does the job, there will be increased opportunities for products that offer enhanced cleansing action. A number of French mineral waters have long claimed to promote action of the kidneys, and in West Africa, where many people believe that malaria can be flushed from the body, beer drinkers value brands that are reputed to cause increased urination.

Bottled water infused with nutrition supplements such as ginkgo biloba, ginseng, or multivitamins is a certain Next. Watch for the development of special-use water, bottled and marketed for specific environments. For instance, a particular brand's Type A might be perfect for everyday use, Type B for après-exercise and Type C for entertaining. For consumers taking baby steps toward better health, there's already Water Joe, a caffeinated water product promoted as "a caffeine alternative in a healthier format." A half-liter bottle packs the caffeine equivalent of one cup of coffee.

Look for more consumers to invest in in-home water-purification systems. According to *Time*, American homeowners bought more than $450 million worth of water-treatment systems in a recent year. At least 12 percent of United States households treat their water in some manner, even though the United States has one of the best water-supply systems in the world. Consumers' primary concerns are to remove lead, bacteria, arsenic, and other contaminants that influence the water's taste and safety.

Organic eats: "Give me spots on my apples, but leave me the birds and the bees," Joni Mitchell sang in "Big Yellow Taxi" thirty years ago. The song was one of the earliest pop laments for ecology. Consumer demand for organic fare has since grown steadily in the developed world. Organic food is grown without pesticides, hormones, antibiotics, or herbicides; meat is reared without additives, and animals are kept in humane conditions.

Despite a cost that's typically 10 to 15 percent more than conventionally produced food (due to higher production costs), United States demand for organic food was estimated in 1996 to be growing at a rate of 20 percent per year. Sales of organic foods have skyrocketed from one hundred and seventy-eight million dollars in 1980 to more than four billion dollars today, and sales of "natural products" are over twelve billion dollars. Whole Foods, which started in 1980 in Austin, Texas, is now one of the nation's largest organic food chains, with seventy-eight stores in seventeen states. Whole Foods has seen a 900 percent growth during the 1990s.

Currently the federal government is trying to set nationwide standards for what foods are deemed "organic." Standards were announced, but a wave of protest caused United States Senator Dan Glickman to rethink the definition. His first proposal was to allow genetically altered food to carry an organic label. Facing what seemed to be the largest public response the Department of Agriculture has ever seen, the labels are being modified.

In Britain, business increased 55 percent a couple of years ago for Organic Farm Foods, Britain's largest organic food supplier, with sales of more than six hundred tons to supermarkets each week. Managing director Peter Segger told *The Observer*, "Until last year there was a steady growth in interest in organic foods, but since BSE [bovine spongiform encephalopy], there has been a fundamental change. People are thinking a lot more about where their food comes from." BSE is the killer disease known as "mad cow" since it is contracted from eating cattle fed meat and bone meal made from the diseased carcasses of sheep and other cattle. To date, a total of thirty-five people have died from BSE.

On the European continent, organic food is becoming a priority for a growing number of companies and governments. As reported in *The Guardian* (London), ten percent of all food sold in Denmark in 1997 was expected to be organic, ". . . and the government is revising its goal upward to 20 percent; ditto Finland, Sweden, and many German provinces." Thus far, in the fifteen member states of the European Union, 63,000 farmers have gone organic, representing 0.75 percent of all farmers and 1.1 percent of farmed land, reports *The Times* (London). Top performers are Sweden and Austria, with 8.6 and 8 percent of their land, respectively, now organically farmed. Swedish policy is to convert 10 percent of all farms within three years. In France, the organic-food market is set to double by the year 2000. In hopes of claiming a 10 percent market share, French retailer Carrefour has launched forty-eight organic products, ranging from flour and oil to chocolate and jam. *Eurofood*—the trade publication—reports that products in the Carrefour Bio line cost 10 to 30 percent more than nonorganic products but 20 to 30 percent less than branded organics.

Consumers' hearts might warm to the idea of fruit and vegetables grown "the natural way," but the less-than-perfect appearance of much organic produce is a turnoff for many. Now, choices are being introduced for consumers in search of produce that is pleasing to the eye *and* palate. Two pesticide-free alternatives: hydroponic and aeroponic products, which are grown in controlled, enclosed conditions that don't require pesticides, and genetically manipulated plants, with an in-bred resistance to pests that renders chemicals unnecessary.

Vegetarianism: While people adopt vegetarian lifestyles for many reasons—ethical and environmental, among them—the current surge in vegetarianism seems most closely linked to the desire to live more healthfully. As early as 1993, *Beef Improvement News* of Australia noted "widespread vegetarianism" among teenage girls aged fourteen to seventeen. And a single mention of the United States-based Vegetarian Resource Group in America's *Parade* magazine a few years ago generated an estimated three to four thousand inquiries.

According to *Vegetarian Times* magazine, there are 12.4 million practicing vegetarians in the United States today. A Gallup Poll offered further evidence when it published the information that thirteen thousand people stop eating red meat each week. Marketing Intelligence, a market research business, estimates that nearly 100 new vegetarian or meatless products were introduced in 1998 alone.

In response to the demand for meatless food, manufacturers have introduced "meat analog products" with names such as "Foney Baloney" and "Fakin' Bacon." McDonald's recently introduced a soy-based sandwich in some of its New York locations. Anticipate increased vegetarian fare at mainstream fast-food venues, as well as the development of more vegetarian-only establishments.

Lite/low-fat/no-fat: As consumers take a more active role in monitoring their health, lite/low-fat/no-fat products will take up more and more space in grocery stores worldwide. Importantly, qualifying products are apt to be marketed to consumers as "healthful choices" rather than weight-loss products. A recent, heavily publicized manufacturer-sponsored study indicates that when

American consumers look at the nutrition label on a food product, 74 percent are looking for fat-content information. This exceeds the percentage looking for the number of calories (58 percent), cholesterol content (56 percent), sodium content (51 percent) and serving size (41 percent).

As expressed by Steven C. Anderson, president of the American Frozen Food Institute, "The frozen food industry has led the rest of the food industry in making not only convenient and high quality products, but products that are low in fat, which is what consumers are looking for today." Currently the $3.3 billion frozen-entree category is dominated by ConAgra's Healthy Choice. To avoid being pushed out of the market, H.J. Heinz is repositioning its Weight Watchers frozen dinners, emphasizing health first, vanity second. Among other steps, the company has signed deals with insurers such as Independence Blue Cross Inc. of Philadelphia to give rebates on life-insurance premiums to members of the Weight Watchers program. Celentano's Great Choice line of reduced-fat entrees appeals to the same market as Healthy Choice.

Culinary freshness: Consumers are also placing renewed emphasis on quality and freshness, and manufacturers and governments are responding. Nissin Gourmet Beef of Osaka, Japan, has patented a method to quick-freeze fish and meat, keeping it fresher longer. This has important implications for restaurants, which often serve "fresh" fish that is six to ten days old, rather than its frozen counterpart, which is generally soft and tasteless as a result of cell membranes having been broken by ice crystals. The new process uses an alternative freezing method that is so fast, ice crystals don't have a chance to form. The result is a product, "Trufresh," that tastes fresher than most never-frozen fish. Trufresh fish isn't sold in supermarkets, since the daily defrost cycle most freezer cases have would cause the fish to thaw out and refreeze the slow way. In the future, expiration dates might become obsolete.

LifeLines Technology of New Jersey has developed "smart" labels that change color to indicate when the food may have gone bad by keeping tabs on the temperatures to which the product is exposed. A frozen-food package that had been left unrefrigerated for too long, for example, would alert the consumer that the food might have spoiled despite its not having reached its expiration date. To emphasize the quality of their products, frozen food manufacturers have taken to referring to them as "temperature controlled" or "fresh frozen." Until recently, United States inspectors only looked at, touched, and smelled animal carcasses when inspecting meat. Under new rules, inspectors will scientifically test samples.

The Malaysian company Halim Mazmin Bhd is targeting thirteen countries for distribution of frozen halal (sanctioned by Islam) food. In addition to Islamic countries, target markets include Britain, China, South Korea, Taiwan, and the United States. "There is a high demand for halal food from various countries regardless of religion, as halal food is known to be clean and safe and is widely consumed even by non-Muslims," claims Executive Chairman Halim Mohammad. Similarly, non-Jews are taking greater interest in kosher food due to the perception that it is somehow "cleaner" than non-kosher products.

The field is wide open for a food manufacturer to establish its identity as the "safety" brand, providing a nonreligious seal of cleanliness and safety.

• NEXT: PURE PRODUCTS

Consumer interest in natural products stems from simultaneous desires to minimize our impact on the environment and limit the impact of the environment on us. Although Crystal Pepsi was a failure when it was launched in the early 1990s, the trend toward clear products—another outgrowth of the Green movement—has moved well beyond New Age beverages to encompass deodorants, shampoos, dishwashing liquids, and toiletries. Regardless of the actual ingredients used, consumers continue to regard these products as somehow purer, more natural, and more healthful.

Going natural: In the health and beauty industry, the appeal of natural (versus synthetic) cosmetics ingredients is reaping profits for makers of everything from botanical shampoo to herbal toothpaste. For example, since 1978, when it began selling plant-based shampoos, Aveda has grown into an international, hundred-million-dollar industry powerhouse, now owned by Estée Lauder.

Today, more than thirty thousand salons stock several hundred items bearing the Aveda name. Taking some cues from the United Kingdoms' Body Shop, Origins Natural Resources, an environmentally friendly line of cosmetics and aromatherapy products, has grown into a forty-five-million-dollar business in only six years. The fastest growing division of industry giant Estée Lauder, Origins has nineteen freestanding stores and forty "stores within stores" in the United States, Denmark, England, Germany and Japan. And Tom's of Maine, long a staple of health-food stores, has begun to win shelf space in drugstores and supermarkets in the United States. Its all-natural (no additives, dyes, or sugars), herbal toothpaste now accounts for annual sales of approximately twenty million dollars. The company sells approximately 250 all-natural products, including deodorant, shampoo, and mouthwash (www.toms-of-maine.com). Purity sells, so even manufacturers unable to make claims of being "all natural" might instead point to "pure" characteristics, such as being "hypo-allergenic" or "not tested on animals."

Chemical-free kids: Keeping our babies chemical-free is a fast-growing industry. Baby clothes made from organically grown cotton, for example, are being touted as healthier for babies because there are no pesticides or chemical residues to be absorbed through the skin. Likewise, companies that sell organic baby foods, such as Earth's Best Baby Food in the United States, are beginning to win shelf space from industry giants such as Heinz, Gerber, and Beechtree. Also in response to parents' concerns, Hasbro's Playskool toy line has launched a line of children's products and toys featuring Microban antibacterial protection. The intent is to protect the toys—and by extension, the children who use them—from the growth of germs and bacteria. Older children and adults can also purchase a new product called "No Sweat," a sweatband that adheres to the inside of a baseball cap. The charcoal-activated hat liner with a bactericide absorbs moisture when the user sweats.

• NEXT: ONE-WORLD CONSUMERISM

In an effort to ensure that the healthful life continues to be a choice, people are embracing one-world consumerism—the vote-with-your-dollars acknowledgment that "what goes around, comes around." As we live the results of our centuries-long promiscuous waste of planet resources, the environmental mantra "reduce, reuse, recycle" becomes that much more meaningful.

Although consumers in Europe and North America generally stress quality and price over environmental concerns, more large retailers are beginning to stock Green items and make Green decisions. The U.S. company Patagonia, known for its upscale outdoor clothing, has announced plans to use only organically grown cotton. One of its recent catalogs pointed to the fact that "the process of growing conventional cotton involves the heavy use of chemicals that toxify the soil, air and ground water." (In the United States alone, twenty million pounds of pesticides are used to grow cotton every year.) In Germany, the central travel agency removed short-trip Concorde flights from its program, acknowledging undue pressure on the environment. (The Concorde uses five times the energy required by a normal jet.)

As recently as 1985, less than 1 percent of all merchandise produced in the United States was marketed as environmentally friendly. By 1995, that percentage had increased to 20. In Germany, the Green movement is so strong that Hans Tietmeyer, president of Deutsche Bundesbank, has predicted, "[In the long run,] only those companies that consider environmental protection to be an integrated and natural component of management, development, production, and even the products themselves—rather than viewing it as a bothersome appendage—will be successful and have a chance at surviving on the market."

Renewals: Consumption in the near future will be about reusable, multipurpose items that limit strain on the environment. A study conducted at the Milan Furniture Fair points to a growing interest in upgradeable furnishings, flexible pieces that can be added to or adjusted as your needs change and your finances permit. IKEA, for instance, now offers modular kitchen cabinets set into wood frames that can sit on the floor or be fastened to a wall. The idea is that young people can invest in a few simple pieces at first and then add more units as their families and incomes grow.

Already in demand is everything from America's modestly

priced Castro Convertible couches (sofas that double as beds) to roller skates that convert to in-line skates when Johnny is ready to move from bumps and scratches onto more serious injuries. Parents fed up with shelling out money for every age and stage of their children's lives are fueling the demand for all manner of children's products that "grow" with their kids. You can now purchase nursery mobiles that turn into toddler activity centers and then art units for older children. Also popular are bassinets that become cribs, then toddler beds, and, finally, glider benches. Some furniture-makers are even producing tables with multiple sets of removable legs so parents can adjust the height as their children grow.

CHAPTER 9:

Loving
and Lusting

SEXUAL HARASSMENT. Sexual addiction. Homosexuality. Cybersex. In one form or another, the once taboo subject of sex has emerged as a leading topic of conversation—and debate. Why all the interest in what's happening in the world's bedrooms? For many people, sex and sexuality are moral issues. Some perceive the rise in out-of-wedlock births, the fight for gay rights, and the depiction of sexual acts on television and in the movies as evidence of the steady decline of society. Others consider this view to be small-minded intolerance that has turned acts of love and/or passion into something "dirty."

We are interested in sex for a slightly different reason. We are students of the art of the sexy sell and find it intriguing that sex is used to market everything from lingerie to automobiles, perfume to CDs. And we understand that society's ever-evolving sexual attitudes have a tremendous impact on how products are sold.

Among marketers, it's common knowledge that sexual messages can be far more explicit in Europe than in the United States. America's puritanical bent very often becomes a factor when advertising and television and movie content attempts to cross the Atlantic. Witness the fact that Adrian Lyne's *Lolita*, depicting a man's sexual interest in a twelve-year-old girl, ran successfully across Europe, but it took a year to bring the film to America. In fact, its original United States release was via the pay cable service Showtime. It made its theatrical debut some five months later, in limited release. A similar situation developed when TV star Roseanne announced plans to produce a United States version of British TV's *Absolutely Fabulous*. Her network decreed that the producers would need to tone down the characters' sexual promiscuity (and alcohol and drug use) in order to meet network standards and attract advertisers.

In past decades, differing standards have not posed a major problem for advertisers. In today's global market, however, some analysts are warning companies such as McDonald's and Pepsi that if they want to attract consumers in overseas markets, they'll need to inject more sexy sizzle into their ad campaigns. At the same time, European multinationals must heed social—and sometimes even legal—constraints in other parts of the world. The success of cross-border marketing efforts continues to be contingent on satisfying each market's desire for excitement and stimulation without offending the sensibilities of consumers in other targeted countries. Not an easy task given the widely variant attitudes toward sex in Europe, the United States, Asia, and Islamic countries.

And it's not just differing moral standards that must be taken into account. That which is deemed sexy, erotic, or romantic also differs from country to country and culture to culture. Harlequin, the prolific publisher of romance novels, recently conducted a survey to determine what women around the world do to make themselves feel more romantic. In analyzing the responses of some 6,200 women in twenty-one countries, Harlequin found the following:

- Women in France, Germany, Greece, Turkey, and Norway are most likely to listen to romantic music.
- Women in Argentina, Finland, and Holland prefer to watch a romantic movie.
- Respondents in Canada and the United States are most likely to opt for a bubble bath.
- Women in Russia and Hungary are most apt to read a love story.

As you review the global Nexts that follow, keep in mind the existence of such regional distinctions. For when it comes to matters of the heart (and libido), cultural differences can spell opportunity—or disaster.

• NEXT: SEX REDEFINED

To a certain degree, sex is sex. The act itself hasn't changed over time. Sure, there are interesting variations, but you can be certain that everything that can be done in the sex department has already been done. Nonetheless, we're seeing a redefinition of sex today, as new attitudes and new technologies begin to alter how we look at—and even engage in—sexual acts.

The new intimacy: Those who prefer to couch conversations about sex in euphemisms sometimes refer to sex as "being intimate." But just what does it mean to "be intimate" these days? Does intimacy involve bodily contact or simply personal knowledge? Can you be intimate with someone you've never seen? The definition of sex appears to be changing: The new understanding of adultery, as defined in *Newsweek*, is that it's "a sin of the heart and mind as much as—or even more than—the body." The essence of an affair, according to American psychiatrist Dr. Frank Pittman, is the secret intimacy between two people that must be defended with dishonesty. "Infidelity isn't about whom you lie with," he says. "It's whom you lie to." Proponents contend that "emotional adultery" is committed when a person other than your spouse becomes more central to your thoughts and fantasies than your partner.

In the Digital Age, you don't always need to meet a partner in person (much less have sex with him or her) to be intimate by Pittman's definition. In an age in which real-world sex has become risky, to say the least, the relatively safe and frequently anonymous world of cybersex has proven to be a viable alternative. The real-time communication supported by online services and Internet Relay Chat enables people to live out their sexual fantasies with virtual strangers, online. On America Online, the most chat-friendly online service, people can engage in group conversations in sexually oriented public chat rooms, create private chat rooms for a little one-on-one, and get down and dirty via instant messages. Switching genders online is a popular activity among members of both sexes, as is a tendency to lie about any and all other personal information.

In an interesting trend, electronic intimacy—whether via online chat services, e-mail, or phone—increasingly is becoming as legitimate and powerful as the real thing. In a letter to American advice columnist Ann Landers, one cyberlover wrote, "I met my girlfriend on the Internet. She is Canadian. I live in Illinois. We have gotten together face-to-face only once, but over the last few months, we have . . . fallen in love." Another American, from New Jersey, sued his wife for divorce, alleging that her racy computer messages to a man she had never met constituted adultery. A judge didn't agree—this time. Any remaining doubts about the true nature of an electronic relationship were dispelled by a sensational case that unfolded not too long ago in the United States. An enraged man killed his wife upon learning that she had received flowers from a man she had "met" online.

Silicon sex: New technologies aren't being used just for cybersex; they're also playing a role in bringing couples together, spicing up sex lives, even providing "alternative" partners.

Philips Electronics plans to introduce a "singles chip" that's designed to unite compatible lovers. The chip, which is small enough to be concealed in an earring or tie pin, can be programmed with information such as likes, dislikes, and personality traits. To be used in a singles bar, nightclub, or other social arena, the chip is designed to scan the room for other chips and beep if it locates a compatible profile.

People who prefer computer screens to the real-world singles scene can employ online personal-ad services such as Match.com. In addition to being convenient and open twenty-four hours a day, these sites have the added advantage (according to some of their operators) of having a clientele—simply by virtue of being on the Internet—that is more affluent and better educated than the average population.

In the software realm, a new genre of sexy titles—including

Interactive Sex Therapy, Anne Hooper's Ultimate Sex Guide, The Joy of Sex and *Dr. Ruth's Encyclopedia of Sex*—is being promoted as self-help for those hoping to improve their sex lives. As might be expected, much of the content focuses on sexual enhancement (making sex last longer and better). Searching for entertainment rather than enlightenment? There's always *Virtual Valerie* and *The Penthouse Photo Shoot.*

Online sex has been around since the infancy of computer bulletin boards in the early 1980s, when entrepreneurs discovered people would pay to download suggestive pictures and engage in lewd talk on electronic message boards. Modern offerings are much more diverse. In Britain, when the Adam and Eve film channel found it difficult to gain permission to broadcast on television throughout the day, it sidestepped this regulation by running its erotic films around the clock on the Internet. And Adam and Eve aren't alone: At present there are more than ten thousand sex-related Web sites.

A range of adult products also are available to cybershoppers, including everything from sexy lingerie to instructional videos. The most recent estimate of Forrester Research is that online sales of adult merchandise in the United States are about 10 percent of all consumer goods sold over the Internet. That number doesn't include revenue from subscriptions or per-minute video sex charges, which account for the majority of many online sex companies' sales.

Speaking of video sex: Leading search engine Yahoo now lists more than three hundred Web sites that offer an interactive service, which is the equivalent of phone sex with pictures. Customers of virtual strip shows pay up to ten dollars a minute to talk to a stripper via computer and watch a live video performance. Customers of Las Vegas-based Virtual Dreams, which claims to be grossing close to one million dollars each month, pay $5.99 a minute to watch and direct a personal stripper, or as little as $2.99 a minute to tune into other customers' fantasies. The average call lasts twelve minutes, but some customers run up tabs of several hundred dollars or more. Of those dialing Virtual Dreams' video-conferencing service, 75 percent are in the United States. The company is in the process of setting up deals with independent studios in places such as Amsterdam, Stockholm, and London to create a global network of interactive strip shows. Seattle-based Internet Entertainment Group, which operates one of the largest sex businesses on the Internet, runs at least a dozen Web sites that sell subscriptions, digital phones, adult videos and other merchandise. But IEG is best known as one of America's biggest proprietors of video phone sex. All told, company revenue was about twenty million dollars in 1998.

It seems that recently everyone has been trying to come up with some way to shock the world with the most outrageous production via the Internet. First, there was the woman who gave birth on the Internet; next came the young couple who was going to lose their virginity on the Internet, which turned out to be a scam. Now, Calypso Productions is organizing a new Internet first: a sexchange operation that would take place online. For a small fee, anyone could log on to see the event.

The Futurist, a magazine published by the World Future Society, predicts the availability in coming years of a broader array of e-pleasure alternatives. According to the magaziane, robots that provide sexual companionship will become common in the future, and prototype models already have been reported in Japan. The so-called sexbots will have human features and will be soft and pliant, like the latest dolls for children. Vibrators will provide tactile stimulation, and sound systems will provide "love talk."

• NEXT: NEW STANDARDS OF DESIRABILITY

The definition of what's sexy also is undergoing change. As we discussed previously, today's optimum age of desirability is much higher than Lolita's. Today it's Ivanka Trump versus Ivana Trump, and (at age 50) Ivana is closer to her peak. In the United States and Europe, forty-plus celebrity women are posing in the buff, inspiring both desire and curiosity. There's no question that such pictorials sell magazines: The December 1995 issue of *Playboy*, which featured fifty-year-old covermate Farrah Fawcett, sold 2.5 times the average—and the actress appeared in the magazine again in June of 1997. (Fifty-two isn't fifty-two anymore, to paraphrase a quip feminist Gloria Steinem made several years ago, when her

desirability was toasted as she turned fifty.) But such layouts successfully sell something else, as well: the image of middle-aged
women as not only beautiful, but sexy. While this is hardly news
to Europeans—consider the long-standing appeal of Catherine
Deneuve, Simone Signoret and others—America has long been
home to the so-called cult of youth. (Remember the Big Next we
noted on youth and aging, and the Next we cited about the new
age of desirability.)

Slimness is another beauty standard being called into question.
Egypt's top sex symbol, Laila Alwi, admits to 140 pounds, but the
public estimates her weight as high as 220 pounds. Egypt's *Radio
and TV Magazine* recently noted that the country's film and TV
stars "fluctuate between obesity and plumpness" and suggested
they adopt the slogan "Down with slimness!" Local advertisers
acknowledge they now seek a decidedly full look in their mass
marketing.

Although thin is still the beauty ideal in the United States, there's
evidence that Americans are beginning to accept the larger woman:
Ms. Average American stands 5'4" and weighs 144 pounds. A growing number of magazines that target large-size women, including *Big
Beautiful Women*, *Radiance* and *Mode*, are growing in popularity.
Their message: You don't have to be thin to have great clothes and
an exciting, fulfilling lifestyle. A plethora of books advancing the
"don't diet" message has hit the shelves, including Glenn Gaessner's
Big Fat Lies, Richard Klein's *Eat Fat* and Barbara Altman Bruno's
Worth Your Weight. And recognizable and respected fashion
designers finally have added larger sizes to their lines to accommo-
date the clothing needs of the estimated sixty-five million women
who wear size twelve-plus. The list includes Ellen Tracy, Emanuel
Ungaro (under the label Emanuel), Dana Buchman, MaxMara
(Marina Rinaldi), David Dart, Carole Little, Liz Claiborne
(Elisabeth), and Tamotsu. The Ford Models twelve-plus division
has some fifty women on its roster, including Emme (named one of
People magazine's 50 most beautiful people).

Extending the redefinition of physical beauty even further, a
North American marketing campaign for high-tech wheelchair
company Colours broke with the traditional advertising tendency
to portray the disabled as asexual and passive. With the intent of

drawing attention to the disabled as sexual beings, the People of Colours campaign included images such as a near-naked, quadri-plegic pregnant woman in a wheelchair and a couple embracing on a bed with a wheelchair off to the side. The ads are credited with sparking an openness among the disabled and society in general. "The disabled community is coming of age," Tony Coelho, chairman of the United States President's Committee on Employment of People with Disabilities, told the *Toronto Star*, "A lot of folks in advertising and the media continue to portray us as being incapable of having these feelings. This has been very educational. It shows everyone that the disabled have sexual feelings, they're sensuous and they have an interest in their bodies, just like anybody who isn't disabled."

• NEXT: REEMPHASIS ON THE ART OF SEDUCTION

Old yin and yang are at in again. In the area of love and lust, we're seeing both a rise in silicon sex and a return to the romantic gestures of a slower time.

Romantic revival: In *Last Night in Paradise: Sex and Morals at the Century's End*, American author Katie Roiphe argues that young people are floundering in their attempts to give sex meaning again. "We have all this freedom and an unprecedented amount of equality between the sexes, and we aren't happy," she explained to a *New York Times* interviewer. Roiphe attributes the popularity of nineteenth century British author Jane Austen, whose novels *Emma* and *Sense and Sensibility* have been adapted for recent big-budget films, to a nostalgia for romance and a world in which the rules of courtship are clear.

Today, romance novels are responsible for close to 55 percent of mass-market paperback sales, generating annual revenues of approximately one billion dollars, according to the Romance Writers of America. African-American, Asian and Hispanic women make up about one-third of romance readers, making multicultural romances one of the fastest-growing subsets of the genre. As the market has broadened, so too have the plot lines; only a fraction of the romance market is composed of the historical or period bodice-rippers of years past. In line with movies and television, romance novels have turned to the nitty-gritty of modern-day life, focusing on subjects such as alcoholism and illiteracy.

The genre also is moving away from violent images, such as maidens being ravaged by swarthy pirates and other rogues. In the '90s, romance heroines are rarely brutalized. As noted by *U.S. News & World Report,* "Long attacked by feminists as mind candy for oppressed housewives, [romance novels] now are being hailed as happily and unapologetically subversive by a growing group of women scholars." Typical modern romance heroines have satisfying jobs and find wonderful men with whom they have consensual and pleasurable sex. They sometimes struggle, but the women always win.

Harlequin Enterprises has also introduced a new line of Christian romance novels. The Steeple Hill division will publish novels in which the heroine is portrayed as "virginal," and God is involved in every romance. The contact in the books goes no further than a passionate kiss. According to Lisa Miles, special promotions manager for Harlequin, sales of inspirational novels will exceed one hundred thirty million dollars in the year 2000.

In the fashion world, romance emerged as the overall theme of both haute couture and ready-to-wear collections last year—and is still popular. The romantic revival included ruffles, flounces and florals. Period films have fed the frills trend, from empire-waisted *Emma* dresses to the gauzy, ethereal gowns and scarves worn by Kristen Scott Thomas in *The English Patient.* "It's a little nostalgic," French designer Agnes Trouble told the *Chicago Tribune.* "Fear of the twenty-first century" has inspired lovely fantasies of the past as an alternative to the uncertainty ahead, Trouble contends. "We may do the Gap and Banana Republic every day," says Richard Martin, curator of The Costume Institute at the Metropolitan Museum of Art in New York, "but we occasionally want something special, some element of fantasy and distinction. Romance is it."

Mainstream erotica: Erotica is all the rage these days, as erotic products are being embraced by couples turned off by hard-core pornography but whose sex lives need a bit of a jump-start. Products range from videos (*The Voyeur, Cabin Fever*) to audiotapes (*The Ten Commandments of Pleasure: Erotic Keys to a Healthy Sexual Life*) to books (*The Erotic Edge: Erotica for Couples*, *Real Moments for Lovers*, Anne Rice's *Sleeping Beauty* trilogy). In fact, the number of erotica books published increased 324 percent in the first six years of this decade, according to *Subject Guide to Books in Print*, while the overall number of books published increased only 83 percent. The genre has subdivided itself into everything from first sexual experience erotica to sadomasochistic erotica to vampire erotica. A clear sign that erotica is gaining mainstream acceptance: Collections of women's erotica are now available from the Book of the Month Club catalog.

In an article in the *San Jose Mercury News*, writer Melinda Sacks called erotica "all part of the move toward what is being called 'hot monogamy'—the idea that people can stay in one relationship for years and still have passionate sex." Susan Page, author of *Now That I'm Married, Why Isn't Everything Perfect?*, explains, "Since the sexual revolution, there's been a tremendous increase in our expectations about pleasure. We know it's possible, and we have been given permission to seek it out. The alternative to that is to say, 'Too bad, I'll never have really good sex again once the infatuation wears off.'"

By indulging in erotica, couples open doors of communication that allow them to share their sexual fantasies and preferences. The genre also serves as a sort of instruction manual, giving couples ideas for new or improved techniques. "Instead of just groping our way along," Los Angeles sex therapist and psychologist Dr. Susan Block told the *Mercury News*, "this gives us a chance to observe and learn."

Sexually speaking, Germany is in the lead. As the United Kingdom's the *Daily Telegraph* put it, "Leather, rubber, bondage, homosexuality, bisexuality or sado-masochism: You'll never feel like the odd one out in Germany—unless you happen to have a wife and two children and are into straight sex." Theresa Orlowsky and Dolly Buster, Germany's top hard-core porn stars, are household names and appear regularly on TV talk shows. One of Germany's leading public television networks recently commissioned twelve top leading film directors, including Nic Roeg, Ken

Russell and Susan Seidelman, to make half-hour erotic films and showed them to large audiences on weekend evenings. And nearly every German city and large town has a branch of the now publicly-traded Beate Uhse chain selling an array of pornography, sex toys and lingerie. Owned by Germany's seventy-seven-year-old millionaire of the same name, the stores have sprouted up in other countries across Europe, racking up annual sales of more than eighty million dollars. In January 1996, in celebration of her fiftieth anniversary in business, Uhse opened the Erotic Museum in Berlin. Located on a prime piece of downtown real estate, the museum fills three floors and contains more than three thousand items.

What used to be called porn has hit the mainstream. Nearly fourteen percent of all video sales and rentals come from adult videos. Jenna Jameson, a porn star, is quitting the business to become a mainstream actress after landing a role in Howard Stern's *Private Parts*. Porn shops have become less sleazy than they were a few years ago. The "Adam & Eve" catalog is mailed out to more than 2.5 million people each month. Tower Records has had signings with stars from *Vivid*, an adult film production company. Castle Superstores, by losing the peep shows and strippers, has managed to turn its clientele into almost 50 percent couples. The World Pornography Conference's keynote speaker was Nadine Strossen, who is president of the ACLU. With movies such as *The People vs. Larry Flint* and *Boogie Nights*, there has been an onslaught of producers wanting to make movies about the porn industry. By contrast, New York Mayor Rudolph Giuliani, as part of his ongoing effort to "clean up New York," has waged a successful battle to revoke the licenses of live sex clubs. This, on the heels of the total makeover of Times Square, once the vice capital of New York, has been seen as part of the effort to make the city cleaner and safer than ever before. There are those, however, who argue that a "white bread" New York will be severely lacking in character.

Sexy skivvies: Challenging every woman to seduce herself first, companies such as Victoria's Secret have convinced the female population to upgrade its utilitarian "underwear" to "lingerie." What used to be received as a gift is today a purchase made for yourself.

The United Kingdom, long a bastion of sensible undergarments, is among the countries experiencing an explosion of interest in lascivious skivvies. According to the *Daily Telegraph*, even that standard-bearer of respectability, Marks and Spencer, "cannot fight the commercial invasion of sexy underwear, nor the consequent awakening sensuality of British women." The hottest lingerie colors in Europe? The shock-value palette: scarlet, deep purple and black.

And Americans are catching onto the European trend of neighborhood lingerie shops. These types of shops are more refined than a Victoria's Secret—and a large part of sales come from bras. Women are looking for something that fits, and the chain lingerie stores don't always cut it. These boutiques feature better service, better fit, higher quality merchandise and higher prices than your average lingerie chain.

Sexy skivvies aren't confined to the West. In China, where advertising of lingerie was banned until recently, items once considered decadent are now welcomed. Demand for lingerie has been increasing 20 percent a year in Shanghai and Beijing and even faster in smaller cities. While many women are used to paying as little as two dollars for a cheaply made bra, German undergarment-maker Triumph International estimates that a twelve-dollar bra should be affordable to women making a hundred dollars a month, about an average worker's salary. The market potential is vast: China is home to nearly 400 million women aged fifteen to fifty-five.

In India, the latest fad is the designer bra. Munish Tangri, who runs a thirty-year-old family business in undergarments, told *India Today* that until five years ago, having twenty bra designs in stock was "more than enough." Today, even seventy styles is "too little." A bra boom occurs in the summers, says Tangri, when young girls seek strapless, deep-cut and well-designed bras to wear under off-shoulder or transparent dresses.

"Silk teddies, satin nightgowns and lacy two-piece wonders are taking the Arab world by storm," according to an article in *Business Monthly*, the journal of the American Chamber of Commerce in Egypt. As elsewhere in the Muslim world, an Egyptian woman's daytime fashions are conservative. But in the privacy of her bedroom, a married woman can wear whatever she chooses in front of her husband. Sevel, one of Egypt's best-known companies, began making lingerie in 1986 under license to the French company Valisère. *The Washington Post* reports that the company saw annual sales climb from $177,000 to $3.26 million over the course of last year.

Evidence of lingerie's crossover to daytime fashion is seen in the slip dress phenomena. With its slinky suggestion of lingerie, the silhouette has become the profile of the late '90s. Consider what is perhaps the most famous and most photographed dress of this decade: Carolyn Bessette-Kennedy's wedding gown. Even sexier and more wispy is a definite Next.

Seductive scents: *Elle Decoration* recently reported that getting in touch with your sensual side is imperative for maintaining physical and mental health. An article entitled "Fifty Ways to Make Your Home a Sensual Haven" notes that humans can identify more than ten thousand different smells. After seven hours of sensory deprivation, the mind slows down and begins to generate its own stimulus: anxiety. In extreme cases, hallucinations and delusions result. The relationship between sexuality and sensuality and scent is being exploited at a record pace.

While scented candles have long been a mainstay in homes, those said to have aromatherapeutic properties are grabbing an increasing share of the market. Proponents believe the essential oils (plant extracts) found in such candles alleviate a variety of ailments, from headaches to tension. Some, with names such as Seduction and Sensuality, are even touted as aphrodisiacs and "mood-setters." "It's part of the growing trend toward pampering [ourselves]," says Susan Rogers of home and beauty products retailer Crabtree & Evelyn. "People want to be able to indulge themselves in a way that's healthy and stress-free." Also growing in popularity are fragrances claiming to "center the body and mind." Chakras, for example, is a collection of unisex fragrances said to adjust to an individual's body chemistry and induce the various sensations for which the scents are named. Available scents include Attraction, Bliss and Fulfillment.

In coming months, expect mainstream status for aromatherapy

for men. Already marketed in the United Kingdom, according to the newspaper *The Independent*, are such manly mood mixes as Aahhh!, Brrr! and Woah!, male-oriented treatments designed to tackle stress, promote relaxation or create a positive attitude. In the men's fragrance market, anticipate the migration of sampling efforts from the department store into places such as high-traffic commuter venues and sports events.

Which leads us to another Next . . . .

• NEXT: THE NEW MAN

Meet the new man. He works out. He's attentive to his wardrobe. And he might well patronize a beauty salon, makeup counter or plastic surgeon's office. Make no mistake, this is no girly-man. He simply enjoys looking good and feeling sexy, and he appreciates the very tangible rewards that come with his efforts. Increasingly, he feels no need to apologize for his commitment to self-preservation, pampering and perfection. Narcissus is pleased.

"Men's fashion is coming up in the world," says model Malcolm Kelly, seen in a prestigious recent campaign for Armani. "There's now much more emphasis on the whole culture of vanity for men," reported Reuters. "Sex and the modern male are on the agenda of the fall menswear season," reported the *International Herald-Tribune*, adding that "After a period of Plain John fashion—minimalist sportswear cut on straight lines—the peacock male is back. But designers who catch the spirit have a fresh take on sexuality, which is absorbed into the cut of the strokeable fabrics. 'It's buttoned-up sex—quite classical,' said [Gucci designer] Tom Ford." To help men achieve their desired look, Under Wears, a New York store devoted to men's undergarments, sells a variety of shapewear. Customers can achieve faux firming through girdle-like briefs or augment their form with built-in "bottoms" in the rear or "endowment panels" in the front.

For modern men, clothing is just part of the picture. At Joseph's, a London men's shop, proprietor Joseph Ettedgui promotes "conceptual living." *The Independent* reports that Joseph's clientele is urged to "pick an attitude and a lifestyle and go for it." For each segment of Joseph's broad target market—encompassing ad execs, yuppies, pop stars and soccer players—the store sells not only clothing but also the requisite props: furniture, accessories, books and luggage. Expect a variety of style programming to speak to this rapt male audience via drivetime radio shows, Web sites with fashion sense and twenty-four-hour direct TV channels.

Makeup is also bridging the gender gap. (Two famous examples: rocker Marilyn Manson sporting eyeliner—and much more—and basketball star Dennis Rodman's eye shadow.) In the United States, nail polish manufacturers are courting the male market with promotions and products. Urban Decay advertises its unisex colors in *Rolling Stone* and *Spin*, Hard Candy has launched Candy Man and OPI features men in its ads for colorless Matte Nail Envy. As Urban Decay creative director Wende Zomnir explained to the *Los Angeles Times*, "Guys these days are really breaking out into their own. You can see it with fashion, and now you're seeing it with their grooming habits, which isn't just about getting a haircut."

And where there's makeup, there's skin care. Men are hydrating, cleansing, exfoliating and self-tanning at a record pace. Estée Lauder's Lab Series for Men, Clinique Skin Supplies for Men and Technique Pour Homme from Chanel are but a few of the prestige lines of skin-care products for men. The Average Joe is contributing to a decided boom in men's cosmetics and toiletries. Market researcher Euromonitor estimated last year's sales values for select men's markets as follows: United States, $3.5 billion; Japan, $1.9 billion; Germany, $1.6 billion; France, $1.5 billion; United Kingdom, $1.1 billion; Italy, $.9 billion; and Spain, $.6 billion.

In Japan, research by Japanese cosmetic giant Shiseido indicates that 65 percent of men under age thirty have bleached their hair, 38 percent have had their eyebrows shaped and 32 percent have applied a facial pack. When Shiseido introduced the market's first eyebrow-shaping kit for men (complete with eyebrow pencil) in 1996, the first-year sales target was surpassed in just six months.

For guys in need of a total overhaul, male beauty salons now deliver head-to-toe treatment. Services offered by Marc Delacre in Paris, for instance, range from the traditional manicure to the decidedly nontraditional dyeing of chest hair. Initially intended as a sideline, beauty treatments now account for 60 percent of turnover. A salon in Madrid offers five-hour courses on discreet makeup for men. Look for high-end men's stores to create in-store facilities to manicure and beautify those who aren't quite secure enough in their new-manhood to visit a vanity parlor.

In recent years, men's interest in looking and feeling younger has also accelerated. At the most basic level, this translates into a maintaining of health. (Monthly readership of *Men's Health*, a magazine offering health and beauty tips, now approaches 500,000.) On a superficial level, the cosmetic surgery industry is appealing not only to male boomers' vanity but also to their concerns about job performance. "If you are the head of a company, you are supposed to be on top of things, and part of that, for better or for worse, is your appearance," wrote William J. Wolfenden, Jr. in *Forbes FYI*. "For men plastic surgery is an investment that pays a pretty good dividend." According to the American Academy of Cosmetic Surgery, men accounted for about 21 percent of aesthetic surgery patients in 1996, up from 14 percent in 1992. Men's most common reasons for choosing cosmetic surgery are: 1) to improve self-image, 2) to enhance career, 3) to keep up with peers who have had cosmetic surgery, 4) because they recently have become single, and 5) strong influence from spouse or significant other.

WHAT'S NEXT?

A new kind of fatherhood: Men who wonder what it feels like to be pregnant might someday get a chance to find out. London's *Independent* reported on British fertility expert Professor Lord Robert Winston's announcement that it is now technically possible for men to bear children. The still-theoretical scenario calls for the embryo to be implanted in a man's abdomen, with the placenta attached to an internal organ (the bowel, for example), and delivery by Cesarean section. Treatment with female hormones also would be necessary.

Other experts have come out against the treatment, on the grounds that its chances of succeeding are small—"thousands to one against," in the words of one doctor—and any benefits might be out-weighed by risks to the man's health. Lord Winston, who describes the technique in his book *The IVF Revolution*, admits that the process could be dangerous to the expectant father due to the risk of bleeding. Given the odds and the risks, most men will probably opt to become fathers the old-fashioned way, at least for now.

• NEXT: COURTING THE HOMOSEXUAL CONSUMER

One of the big sex-related stories this decade has, of course, been the gay-rights movement. As homosexuality makes its way out of the closet, big business (particularly in North America and Europe) is responding to what the British press has called "the power of the pink pound."

Worldwide, images associated with gay men and lesbians have become increasingly prevalent in print advertisements for products ranging from Absolut vodka to American Express travelers checks, Subaru automobiles to Gardenburger vegetable patties. In 1997, IBM and United Airlines advertised in gay magazines for the first time. In a study conducted by Simmons Market Research for the National Gay Newspaper Guild, it was found that people who read gay newspapers have more than twice the average income of the rest of the population. *Out* magazine, which has recenty been redesigned, saw its last year's circulation increase by 12 percent. Television spots feature same-sex couples, celebrities known to be homosexuals, drag queens and even a transsexual or two. Michael Wilke, a reporter for *Advertising Age*, has collected close to 100 commercials from around the world that feature or evoke homo-sexual imagery. Some were spotlighted in *The New York Times*. Among them:

  • An Australian commercial for Domestos, a spray cleaner sold by Unilever PLC, features a character who resembles the transsexual in the film *Priscilla, Queen of the Desert*. The spot ends with the character declaring a bathroom cleaned with Domestos as "fit for a queen." (Ad agency: Ammirati Puris Lintas; Sydney, Australia)

  • A commercial for Diesel jeans focuses on a training class at a fictional Scout camp. As a handsome young man performs mouth-to-mouth resuscitation on his older, bearded Scout-master, images of a pretty young woman flash on the screen. The spot ends, however, with the Scout and the Scoutmaster galloping off together on horses—and the older man winking at the camera. (Ad agency: Paradiset DDB; Stockholm)

• A spot for Imperial Car Hire, a South African auto-rental company, depicts two men driving along a highway. One exclaims, "I love you. I need you. I have to have you." The other man looks askance. Then these words appear on screen: "Hands-free phones, soon in all our cars." (Ad agency: Hunt Lascaris/TBWA; Sandton, South Africa)

• A Bailey's Original Irish Cream print ad shows two coffee cups that are winking at each other, both with a little bow on the handle. The tag line reads "Our limited-edition coffee cups are available nationwide, though only recognized as a set in Hawaii."

• American Airlines has just added five members to its marketing staff who will focus on marketing to the gay consumer, yet the company does not offer benefits for gay or lesbian partners of employees. The island getaway of St. Maarten is looking to start courting gay consumers based on the simple fact that they have a great deal of disposable income. In contrast, however, the island of Grand Cayman recently turned away a cruise ship carrying 850 homosexual men, claiming that they were unsure whether they would behave appropriately.

Gay Meccas: San Francisco has long been considered a haven for the gay community in the United States. The Castro, in the heart of San Francisco's gay district, has been a gathering place for twenty years. "Cruisin' The Castro," a walking tour that explains the history of gay and lesbian people in San Francisco, has become a tradition in the city. More recently South Beach, Florida, has made its name known in the gay community. And again, in the effort to "homogenize" New York, we note the attempts to cancel the annual Christopher Street Halloween Parade, a major gay event for many years, as a response to the recent increase in violence perpetrated on the New York homosexual community. Many are arguing that the cancellation is a wrong-headed response to the issue.

Marketing Gay Lifestyles: London, which some consider the

gay capital of Europe, now offers a vibrant social life, a cohesive gay community and newfound business and marketing opportunities. *Wall Street Journal Europe* reports that the number of gay bars in London has grown to 107, from just thirty-eight in 1981. And Bass Taverns, the retail unit of United Kingdom drinks-and-lodging giant Bass PLC, has created an entire unit to spearhead efforts to reach the gay market. Of the 2,800 pubs it owns nationwide, Bass now has twenty-eight gay pubs, which it attempts to staff with gay managers and bartenders.

As boomers head into retirement, so do many people in the gay and lesbian communities. Currently under consideration are retirement homes for elderly gays and lesbians. Variations on this seniors theme include mobile home parks and other types of community living that have already opened or are in the works in Washington, Arizona, Florida, Georgia, Massachusetts and North Carolina.

The travel industry has also zeroed in on gays and lesbians as a lucrative niche market. The International Gay Travel Association, which has grown to include 1,200 members from just twenty-five in 1983, estimates that its member travel agents book approximately one billion travel dollars a year. Fodor recently published *Gay Guide to the USA*. The publication follows research in the U.S. that found that gays and lesbians spend more money on tourism than does any other consumer group. Fodor is also considering publishing gay guides to European cities.

On the other side of the coin, a new campaign has just been launched in the United States attempting to convince homosexuals to convert to heterosexuality. A conservative Christian organization called the Center for Reclaiming America, along with fourteen other groups, took out ads in *The New York Times*, *The Washington Post*, and *USA Today*. One ad was a photo of "former homosexuals" with the copy-line, "Homosexuals Can Change." This has launched yet another battle of sex between gays and religious activists.

• NEXT: PURITANICAL BACKLASH

As sexual images become more blatant and homosexuality more "mainstream," we've seen the expected resistance from those who prefer that sex—and sexuality—remain behind closed doors. We expect these forces to gather even more strength in the months and years ahead.

Them versus us—battle lines are drawn: Although an increasing number of United States employers (including IBM, ABC, Coors Brewing Company, and Levi Strauss) are extending benefits to gay and lesbian live-ins, overall the United States is far from ready to embrace homosexuality. According to recently released results of the periodic "National Health and Social Life Survey" (regarded by many as the most extensive study of American sexuality), homosexuality is still viewed as "always wrong" by 67 percent of American adults. Same-sex marriages—permitted in Denmark, Norway, and Sweden—were banned by the United States in 1996. The United States Defense of Marriage Act defines marriage as a legal union between a man and a women and allows states to refuse to honor same-sex marriages performed outside their boundaries. While states can legalize gay marriages, such unions will not be recognized by the United States government for taxation or other purposes.

The battle is being waged on the consumer front as well. Delegates at the Southern Baptist Convention in 1997 voted to boycott the Walt Disney Company because of its alleged "anti-Christian and anti-family direction." Complaints brought against Disney by the fifteen-million-member group include Disney's provision of health benefits to partners of its gay employees, its refusal to block gay and lesbian groups from holding events at Disney theme parks and the fact that it allowed the title character of the ABC sitcom *Ellen* to come out of the closet (ABC is owned by Disney). Southern Baptists are the largest Protestant religious denomination in the United States. (ABC canceled *Ellen* the following season, citing its low ratings.)

Naughty's not nice: While upscale lingerie is entering a new era of desirability, advertisers must be careful that messages don't conflict with public conservatism. The tales of woe are many: An advertising slogan used in the United Kingdom for Gossard's underwear (U.K.) queried, "Who said a woman can't get pleasure from something soft?" Critics termed the slogan "lewd and inappropriate." United States television networks banned lingerie ads featuring model Claudia Schiffer because they deemed them too sexy. Franchisers of the Holiday Inn hotel chain forced the parent company to cancel a commercial featuring a busty transsexual; the ad ran only once, during the 1997 Super Bowl. In Mexico, a billboard for the Playtex Wonderbra found itself at the center of a national controversy about public morality. The ad, which drew no criticism in Europe and the United States, featured a blonde whose ample bosom is barely contained in a satin brassiere. The caption: "I like what you're thinking." Citizen complaints led to an ad overhaul.

For many critics, advertising is a matter of morality. In 1996, Bruce Gyngell, one of Britain's senior-most broadcasters and the managing director of Yorkshire-Tyne Tees Television, told an audience of TV executives that they should not be afraid to censor. "We broadcasters have that duty—to consider what we put out, to ensure that it does not undermine society as a whole," said Gyngell, who has banned programs such as *The Good Sex Guide* and *God's Gift*, a late-night dating game, from the Yorkshire region.

Even in "private matters," people are increasingly expected to display a certain amount of reserve. Chicago psychiatrist Jennifer Knopf told *Newsweek* that she has observed a "renewed commitment to conservatism and family values" among her patients, adding, "I'm seeing less of the kind of affairs or flings that are wild and unpredictable. . . . They're appearing to be more thoughtful. If there is such a thing." And Silicon Valley family therapist Jean Hollands reported that for a man to be caught with a female colleague or hooker "is not a sign of virility anymore, but a sign of stupidity." A few years ago, writer Adam Gopnik noted in *The New Yorker*, "[The French] are in the midst of a nicely turned sex-and-power scandal . . . centering on Princess Stephanie of Monaco, who wants to divorce her husband because he was photographed in the nude embracing a strip-teaseuse. . . . What troubles people, though, apparently including Stephanie, about this matter isn't the strip-teaseuse but the recklessness. 'Didn't you think it was imprudent to make love at the edge of a swimming pool?' a tabloid reporter asked Fili."

Those who successfully walk the line between desirability and conservatism can realize a significant upside. When Frederick's of Hollywood—once the purveyor of all things tawdry—threw out the see-through synthetics and peek-a-boo nighties, it opened the door to the mass market. "Women in the United States wanted sexy lingerie, but they were intimidated by Frederick's," said spokesperson Ellen Appel. After the company dropped "everything a basically conservative public might consider offensive," its sales soared from forty-nine million dollars in 1986 to one hundred million in 1996.

Campaigning for premarital abstinence: A growing number of groups are spreading the word that it's okay to preserve your virginity. In 1993, conservative Christians responded to the rise in teenage pregnancy and promiscuity in North America with a major chastity drive called True Love Waits. Hundreds of thousands of young people in the United States and Canada signed the organization's agreement, pledging to refrain from intercourse until marriage. The Canadian Challenge Team, an unrelated drive, uses trained university-age volunteers who spend about six weeks each year talking with Canadian teens about chastity. Funded by private donations, the team visits approximately four hundred schools each year and has had requests to appear in California, England and Ireland. The presentation asks teens to wait until marriage before they have sex not because God says so but because it's what's best for relationships. And last year the administration of President Clinton announced a $250 million program aimed at telling Americans that sex before marriage is "likely to have harmful psychological and physical effects." The primary target of the program is minority and low-income communities, in which women are likely to have children before marriage.

The high-profile push for premarital abstinence might be paying off. Surveys reveal that in recent years sexual activity among American teens has declined for the first time since 1970. Two federal studies show that among girls aged fifteen to nineteen, the number who had "gone all the way" fell from 55 percent in 1990 to 50 percent five years later, and the number dropped from 60 to 50 percent among boys. These studies were followed by a national survey for *USA Today* of more than 200,000 teens in which a majority said that a teenager should be eigteen years old before becoming sexually active. Thousands contended that sex should wait for marriage.

Teens around the world who *are* having sex are, however, having it earlier than ever before. The survey, commissioned by The London International Group (Durex condoms), found that the average age at which teens (sixteen to nineteen) reported first having had sex was 15.7 years. When sixteen to forty-five year olds were surveyed, the age increased to 17.6 years. Teens in the United States are the youngest to have sex, at 16.3 years. Canada and France came in second at 16.6 years, and Thai teens waited the longest, at 19.6 years.

Ronan Keating, the twenty-year-old lead singer of Irish boy band Boyzone, has endeared himself to young female fans by going on record as a virgin. "I'm waiting for the right person," he told *The Daily Telegraph*, "and I would like to think that I would only sleep with the woman I marry." Keating is not the only virgin of celebrity status. In recent years, rocker Juliana Hatfield and MTV veejay Kennedy have come out as virgins, as has NBA star A. C. Green, founder of an athletes-for-abstinence campaign.

In Seattle, Laura Kate Van Hollebeke, a self-proclaimed former party girl, has started the Born-Again Virgins of America Movement (BAVAM), a nonreligious support group for what she jokingly refers to as "recovering sluts." Any celibate person, even one who has had sex, can now declare him- or herself a virgin— or, in keeping with the terminology of the movement, a "recycled virgin." Since making its debut in 1996, BAVAM has received thousands of letters thanking Van Hollebeke for making abstinence cool. And in the born-again crusader category, perhaps there is none more interesting than Donna Rice-Hughes, whose involvement with Senator Gary Hart bought down his presidential campaign a decade ago. Rice-Hughes now heads the Campaign for Internet Decency.

Interestingly, in this age of explicit sexual messages, abstinence is more fashionable these days than it has been in decades. In the United Kingdom, four out of ten single women aged sixteen to forty-nine are not having sexual relations, according to a General

Household Survey from the Office for National Statistics. "The idea, ten or twenty years ago, that you met someone in a pub and then hopped into bed is not so common now," commented Michele Misgala, spokeswoman for the United Kingdom's Family Planning Association, in *The Daily Telegraph*. "There are safety considerations, not just because of sexually transmitted diseases. Women are saying, 'Do I know this person well enough to want to take this further?'" says Julie Cole, a spokeswoman for counseling organization Relate. Cole adds, "There has been a great change in women's lives from the 1950s, when the expectation was that you would marry and have children. In the 1990s, when there is a great range of choice—careers, marriage, relationships, children, part-time work, in every permutation—there is a multiplicity of choice for women. Not having sex is one of those choices."

A decrease in intercourse does not, however, necessarily spell the end of sexual relations. Oral sex—perceived by some as less intimate and less risky than intercourse—has become common-place initiation into sexual activity among American teens. And thanks to our president's escapades, there are no teens now or next lacking in a sense of who does what to whom to guarantee plea-sure. Pregnancy is avoided, virginity is preserved and many teens (incorrectly) believe they don't have to take any precautions against AIDS with oral sex. One study among Los Angeles high-school students found that 10 percent of those who were still virgins had engaged in oral sex, and boys and girls were equally likely to be the receiving partner.

CHAPTER 10:
Family Styles

_W_HAT CONSTITUTES A FAMILY? A couple of decades ago, that might have seemed like a trick question. Everyone knew that a family was made up of a man, his lawfully wedded woman and one or more legitimate children. Today, that traditional nuclear family is becoming less and less common. We're seeing a rise in single parenting and in "blended" families, with "his kids" and "her kids" shuttling between two or more households. And these trends are felt throughout the developed world. Unwed motherhood has become a bona fide option. More than one in three French babies are now born out of wedlock, one of the highest rates in Europe and equal to that of the United States. Outside traditionalist Catholic circles, illegitimacy no longer carries a stigma. In Scandinavia, in particular, we note an acceptance of unwed couples with children. It doesn't appear at all uncommon for couples to cohabitate and to have and raise children together without bothering to marry. In the case of some couples, it would seem that marriage is greater cause for concern than parenthood.

In some ways, we're seeing a new flexibility in family life. Today, many people consider it perfectly acceptable for a lesbian to have a child via in-vitro fertilization or for a single man to adopt an infant. Surrogate parenting is becoming more common, and the upper limits of a woman's childbearing years appear to extend with each passing year. We're also seeing some flexibility in sex roles, as reflected by the growing number of stay-at-home dads.

At the same time, today's families are facing new demands. In addition to the career and household pressures they feel, parents are raising children in a time when drugs and youth violence are commonplace. With increased evidence that the youth of the world are in dire straits (or at least that they are maturing at hyperspeed), politicians, sociologists, and others point fingers of blame in any number of directions—violent TV programs, sexual content on the Internet and explicit song lyrics, among them. But there is one segment of the population upon which the ultimate responsibility for children most often is placed: parents.

Why is it so difficult to raise children these days? Some criticize dual-career couples who entrust others to care for their children instead of taking on the responsibility themselves. In the United States, for instance, about one-third of the estimated ten million preschool children are in some type of organized day-care facility, up from a quarter of the preschool population just a few years ago. An additional one-fifth of kids are cared for either in the home of a nonrelative or by a babysitter, and about half of United States preschoolers are cared for by relatives.

The issue of how we are raising our children will be a hot topic well into the next millennium. The remainder of this chapter outlines some of the other trends we're seeing among families today.

• NEXT: WOMEN DIVIDED

On the homefront, women are facing potentially overwhelming pressure to succeed as wives and mothers and as wage earners. In the '80s, the media played up the idea that women could do it all. They could run a corporation, be perfect mothers and keep their men begging for more (whether "more" meant sex or chicken and dumplings). But now, it seems, the jig is up. Few women believe they can be the ultimate both at home and on the job; life is simply about juggling, attempting to find some sort of balance they and their families can live with.

Think-tank Demos recently released findings from two national surveys of more than 3,000 British women. The results point to one of the major consequences of the demands facing modern-day women. Demos's "Tomorrow's Women" report cites a widening gap, not between men and women, but between women of varying lifestyles. According to the report, conflicting needs and opinions will drive a wedge between women with children and those without, between single women and those who are married, between the highly educated and the less educated and between women of various generations. Helen Wilkinson, co-author of the report, commented, "If women's expectations are not met, if new opportunities are not matched by policies to enable women to balance careers and family, and if the barriers to less skilled women are not overcome . . . then the gaps in pay and opportunities could widen once again, the frustration experienced by less-skilled women could explode and a return of traditional values could push women back into the home."

It's a dramatic scenario, but it represents just one of many possibilities that might alter the shape of families in the years to come. As women and men adjust to the the future, they're establishing new parameters for relationships, families and parenting.

• NEXT: CHILD-FREE BY CHOICE

The awareness that it might not be possible to have it all is leading a growing number of women to opt for career over family. More than 25 percent of American women aged thirty to thirty-four were childless in 1990, compared with only 16 percent in 1976. And it's been estimated that fully 22 percent of women born between 1956 and 1972 will never have kids, a higher rate than at any other time in United States history. In 1996, the number of women between the ages of thirty-five to thirty-nine who chose to remain childless nearly doubled, to be 19.7 percent. Fighting the so-called "tyranny of parentism" is the ChildFree Network, a nationwide support group of about two thousand adults committed to the proposition that it's possible to have a perfectly fulfilling life even if you don't have children.

According to the National Center for Health Statistics, women who choose to remain child-free are usually highly educated, less traditional, less religious, white, urban and professional. They also tend to be in more egalitarian marriages.

In her book *Pride and Joy: The Lives and Passions of Women Without Children*, Terri Casey talks to twenty-five women who chose to be child-free. The women were chosen from around the country, their ages range from twenties to eighties and they have diverse lifestyles. According to Casey, the women who chose to remain childless generally tend to be independent and high achievers. They knew early on that they did not want to have children and were either firstborn or only children. They also have fulfilling pursuits and need time for themselves. It is a misconception that women who do not have kids don't like them. One benefit to not having children is increased marital satisfaction.

In Western Europe, decreased childbirth rates already are cause for concern, particularly because a shrinking population will exacerbate the economic burden caused by the rising proportion of elderly citizens. Demographer Jean-Claude Chesnais, in an article in *Population and Development Review*, suggests that raising the status of women in affected countries might be a precondition to increasing childbirth rates. He notes that Italy, where benefits for children have been slashed in the past couple of decades and women continue to struggle to gain equality at work and at home, has seen its fertility rate fall from 2.4 children per woman in the early '70s to 1.2 in the late '90s. In Sweden, where some 85 percent of working-age women are employed and women account for 40 percent of the seats in parliament, fertility rates have held steadily at 2.0 children per woman, the highest rate in Western Europe. Social benefits in Sweden include child-care services and paid parental leave for both parents.

• NEXT: BUILDING A HOUSEHOLD "STAFF"

One result of parents struggling to juggle responsibilities at work and home is increased dependence on outside helpers. Around the world, all manner of businesses are popping up to provide a vast array of family-oriented services. In the United States, for example, some day-care centers offer the convenience of dry-cleaning drop-off and dinners to go. Our co-author Ann O'Reilly reports that in Tampa, Florida, a service agency called The Perfect Task offers house sitting, pet sitting, shopping, errand running, gift wrapping, home organization, check writing, bill paying, and computer work, among other services. Also in Tampa is a business called Rent-a-Husband, which offers handyman services and household repairs.

A growing number of parents are also taking to heart the African proverb that Hilary made famous: "It takes a village to raise a child." In an era in which a decreasing proportion of families remain in one place from generation to generation, there can be far less reliance on assistance from grandparents, aunts and uncles, and other relatives. As a result, some parents are creating their own networks of helpers and nurturers. The following is an excerpt from an open letter that ran in the Dutch daily newspaper *de Volkskrant*.

We had children and they didn't. Such was destiny's decision and it was OK. Our friends, who lived around the corner, obviously enjoyed our children and cared for them as well. We shared the joys and the burdens, and soon enough they were our co-parents. Which we liked very much, considering the big responsibility with which one must cope—having children— from one day to the other, twenty-four hours a day. Whenever the children were at their place, our friends were the parents and we were visitors. The children were comfortable with it; on those occasions they did a whole lot of fun things, had their own rules, their own friends, toys and rituals.

When we moved to Haarlem, our co-parents demanded arrangements concerning parental access—obviously. Now they lease our children one weekend a month, whether it does or doesn't suit us. The children are used to it and like it. For us it's lovely to have the weekend to ourselves. Except for the occasional weekend that coincides with such family things as Sinterklaas (Santa Claus). We bite our lip, to be honest . . .

• NEXT: CORPORATE COOPERATION— FLEXTIME AND OTHER FAMILY-FRIENDLY POLICIES

Parents haven't yet figured out how to add more hours to the day, but they are taking a proactive role in determining how their waking moments are divvied up, and more of them are expecting their employers to cooperate. Sus Røedgaard, a marketer in Copenhagen, notes that "one of the most important changes we're seeing in the workplace in Denmark is a tendency toward more flexible hours. Telecommuting will be more normal. According to a study by Andersen Consulting, there are already 10,000 telecommuters in Denmark, and the forecast is to have 250,000 telecommuting jobs in the year 2000. The possibilities for flexible hours will also be growing."

Røedgaard reports that retail businesses are also chipping in: "In Denmark we have a very strict law for closing time in the stores. One of the large supermarkets is at the moment breaking the law on purpose to influence decision-makers to change the law. I expect the law to be changed in the next few years, so people can shop whenever they like. One of the large supermarket chains has just launched Internet shopping, and it is already a success. People want to have more time with their families and friends and for personal interests, and therefore they welcome initiatives that can make time more flexible."

In the United States, companies are scrambling to be considered family friendly—and the results are often as good for the business as they are for employees. For example, the highest-rated family-friendly company in a study conducted by *Business Week* in conjunction with the Center on Work and Family at Boston University was First Tennessee National Corporation, which began treating family issues as strategic business questions a few years ago. The bank decreased its number of work rules, let employees schedule their own work hours and instituted a number of family-oriented programs. The result: Supervisors rated by their subordinates as supportive of work–family balance retained employees twice as long as the bank average and attracted 7 percent more retail customers. According to First Tennessee, these higher retention rates contributed to a 55 percent profit gain over two years. Other family-friendly companies have reported increased employee loyalty and reductions in absenteeism and turnover.

In the "Business Work-Life Study" conducted by the Families and Work Institute, it was found that United States companies cannot truly be called family friendly. Of the thousand companies surveyed, 90 percent allow parents time off for school events. Half allow parents to stay home with sick kids without cutting into their vacation time. Two-thirds allow flextime for employees who must alter their work hours. Only 9 percent have company day-care facilities, though, and only 33 percent allow more than thirteen weeks for maternity leave. Forty percent of human-resources people said that their companies did not make the company family policies known to their employees.

Acknowledging the dearth of quality child care, the American Business Collaboration for Quality Dependent Care (ABC)—a consortium of twenty-one major corporations, including Kodak, Chevron, Johnson & Johnson and IBM—initiated a six-year, $100 million investment in sixty-six communities around the United States. The money is being used to build on-site child-care centers, train child-care workers and expand services for infant care and elder care. This initiative reflects a growing recognition among businesses that providing assistance with employees' family issues boosts the bottom line.

• NEXT: RETHINKING FATHERHOOD

Debate over the role of fathers continues to be heated on both sides of the Atlantic and don't forget the new birthing techniques we introduced on page 196. Recent studies blame absentee or "disengaged" fathers for numerous problems among children, including substance abuse, high dropout rates and criminality. "Deadbeat Dads" (those not paying child support) are a hot topic in the United States at present, although we're also seeing a countermovement among men who contend that child support and custody laws are biased in favor of mothers. One result of Americans' reexamination of the role and responsibilities of fathers has been the creation of the right-wing Christian organization Promise Keepers, which preaches that men must be the heads of their households and assume the economic, spiritual, and other responsibilities inherent in that role. Similarly, African-American leaders staged 1996's Million Man March in Washington, DC, to educate and energize potential male role models (fathers and others) among African-Americans.

A Whirlpool Foundation study by the Families and Work Institute with Louis Harris and Associates looked into what makes men and women feel successful at home. The results of this study indicate that despite the prevalence of women working outside the home, men continue to define their level of success in terms of how much money they bring home, while women look to healthy and well-adjusted children as a sign that they have been successful.

A recent series of polls conducted by *The Washington Post*, Harvard University and the Henry J. Kaiser Family Foundation emphasized the conflicting roles that men and women must play in their daily lives. Overall, men are doing more around the house and with their children than before, but 38 percent of women have a problem with the amount of housework their husbands do, compared with 24 percent of the men. Sixty-nine percent of women feel too much pressure to have it all, compared with 50 percent of men.

This shows what those polled blamed for causing stress in their lives "very often" or "somewhat often":

	Women	Men
Work-related pressure	57	60
Juggling commitments between work and family	56	53
Not having enough money	52	49
Caring for children	54	42
Conflicts in your marriage/relationship	40	39

Recent anecdotal evidence, however, points to a growing willingness on the part of some fathers to make sacrifices at work to devote more time to their families. Former U.S. Labor Secretary Robert Reich, American Express President Jeffrey Stiefler, and actor Mandy Patinkin (of *Chicago Hope*) are just three of the high-profile men who have cited a desire to spend more time with their children as a primary reason for leaving prestigious jobs.

• NEXT: WOMEN RETURN TO THE HOME?

We're also seeing increased calls for a return of mothers to the home full time. In the United States, at least, women are listening. Recent surveys by the Bureau of Labor Statistics show that a smaller percentage of young mothers are working today than in

1987. A study by investment banking firm Donaldson, Lufkin, and Jenrette found that between 1990 and 1995, the number of United States families with only one wage earner grew at a rate of approximately 1.8 percent a year, reversing the trend from the 1980s, when the number of dual-income families rose. Factors contributing to this trend include a stronger economy (meaning more job security for the working spouse and increased confidence that the nonworking spouse can find a job once the children are older) and a desire on the part of younger women whose own mothers worked not to put their own children in day care. A number of surveys show that young women today are more likely than those a decade ago to indicate an interest in staying home once their children are born. Being an at-home mom is beginning to imply a choice to place your children before your career. It's not necessarily that these couples are in a better position financially to keep one parent at home, it's that they're no longer willing to have their children pay the price for their economic success.

These findings are somewhat inconclusive, however, with regard to women today. Studies have found that today's working women are here to stay, but the future generations are more likely to stay home. A recent study by The Whirlpool Foundation (noted above) found that only 18 percent of working mothers are planning to quit their jobs to stay home with their kids. Forty-eight percent of mothers who currently stay home with their children are planning to go back to work in the future, with the main reason being financial. Since most salaries of working mothers cover at least half of the household expenses, it might be difficult to give up that kind of stability. Ninety-two percent of respondents say that by working they are able to provide their kids with more opportunities, and 83 percent get a sense of fulfillment from working. Women who stay at home do so for two reasons. The first is concern with their kids' education. The second is the belief that women should be home with their children. All mothers, working or not, want what is best for their children.

The Whirlpool Foundation interviewed not only mothers, but children as well—and the findings were fascinating. Children are still much more likely to turn to their mothers for emotional support, and fathers continue to play a financial role. Half of the girls interviewed said that they would stay home with their children rather than go to work. Sixty percent of boys want their wives to stay home and raise the children. This is in clear contrast to the realities of work today: 67.7 percent of women with kids worked outside the home in 1997.

• NEXT: PARENTING FOR THE MILLENNIUM

In addition to coping with changing family structures, today's parents are faced with the unique pressures—and conveniences—of raising children in the Digital Age. Expectations are high. Resources are plentiful. Time (as always) is limited. And the race is on.

Preparing children for life "Next": In our increasingly competitive world, many parents worry that they are not providing the essential skills their kids need to have an edge in work and life. One result is that more and more parents are turning to products that promise to help their offspring reach their full potential as quickly as possible. The Glenn Doman Baby's Reading Kit, from a company called Love to Learn Inc., promises to "provide the vital stimulation essential to increase your baby's intellectual potential." Parents are encouraged to buy the kit to help their babies "learn to read as early and as naturally" as they learn to speak. Concerned that your unborn child is already lagging behind his peers? Enroll your unborn baby in Prenatal University, a nonprofit organization founded in California in 1979. The course, which is based on the concept that interaction with the fetus "stimulates brain development and fosters learning in infancy," has had more than three thousand graduates.

A dedication to maximizing potential extends well into childhood. In the United States, sales of children's books soared from $336 million in 1985 to $1.36 billion in 1995. The newest craze is children's books that are written by celebrities. Shaquille O'Neal is one of the latest celebs to hit the publishing houses, signing a contract with Scholastic. Jamie Lee Curtis published her third children's book; all of them have been bestsellers. Singer Michael Bolton was honored with *Publishers Weekly*'s "Most Objectionable Book" for children in 1997, but *The Secret of the Lost Kingdom* (Disney) still sold 65,000 copies.

In China, the first parent-financed school has opened in Beijing. In a country in which 260 million children face what child psychologist Feng Quihua terms "killing competition" in school, parents are eager to give their children the sort of edge a private school can provide. To make up for inadequacies in their children's education (China currently spends just three percent of its GNP—approximately $0.60 per child—on education), parents spend, on average, 40 percent of their income on educating their children, including cultural excursions.

Children's museums have become increasingly popular in the United States and Europe. Based on the learning theories of child psychologist Jean Piaget—that children learn by interacting with their environment in developmentally appropriate ways—over 150 dedicated museums for children already exist in the United States, and more are in the works, according to the Association of Youth Museums. Since 1991, there are sixty-two new museums, and attendance in 1998 reached twenty-two million. According to Michael Spock, son of Dr. Benjamin Spock, in an article in *The New York Times*, "Many kids these days have very heavily managed lives. They're from families that organize the pants off them. So a very rich educational environment, a place of free exploration and learning, becomes very important to them."

Between academics, karate, piano lessons and the like, it's not at all unusual for today's youngsters to be scheduled for sixty-plus hours a week. The result: Hurried Child Syndrome, a term first coined by Tufts University professor David Elkind in the early eighties. A prime example was seven-year-old pilot Jessica Dubroff, who died while attempting to fly a light aircraft across the United States. Concerned parents can now order a six-part audiocassette collection entitled *Helping Your Child Manage Stress, Pressure and Anxiety* (Bettie B. Youngs, Ph.D., Family First Network).

The desire to prepare your child to succeed has also fueled the tendency to label children academically and developmentally. In the United States, programs for the "gifted" have multiplied rapidly, as have special classes and programs for children diagnosed with learning disabilities such as Attention Deficit Disorder (ADD) and Attention Deficit Hyperactivity Disorder (ADHD). There has also been what some people consider an alarming increase in the use of drugs such as Ritalin to help kids focus on schoolwork and behave in a more controllable fashion in a classroom. Parents and educators are also paying more attention to various learning styles, such as auditory, visual and kinesthetic, the last of which encourages learning through movement.

Raising techies: One factor contributing to the premillennial pressures some parents feel is the perceived need to prepare kids for an increasingly high-tech world. To make sure their children receive every educational advantage, more and more parents are purchasing so-called "edutainment" products that combine learning and fun. Often such products are high-tech in nature. Shipments of electronic learning toys, for example, are growing at a rate of approximately 28 percent a year in the United States and sales reached nearly $290 million in 1995, according to the Toy Manufacturers Association.

Nearly 40 percent of families in the United States with children under age eighteen now own a desktop PC, according to information reseller Find/SVP (also a market research leader in its own right), and an estimated eight million Americans under age fifteen have Internet access either at school or at home. Among PC owners, parents in 90 percent of households report that their children actively use the PC—usually instead of watching TV. Although households in most other countries are not yet quite so high tech, manufacturers are taking steps to ensure that their products become more appealing to the global family market. Examples include low-priced color inkjet printers (suitable for printing kids' digital artwork) and computers designed for preschoolers. IBM and the Little Tikes division of Rubbermaid, for instance, have created Young Explorer ($2,400), a computer housed in a tamper-proof, kid-sized desk with an attached bench. A three-year warranty and Edmark educational software are included. For now, the product is being offered only to preschools, day-care centers and libraries.

Educational software for kids is a booming business, with parents snapping up sophisticated graphics programs, math and spelling tutors (Ira's younger son learned his multiplication tables through a computer game), encyclopedias on CD-ROM and many other types of edutainment software. Today, Microsoft's hottest growth area is entertainment and reference titles on CD-ROM. The company's goal, according to vice-president Patty Stonesifer, is to provide "hands-on experiences with engaging sights, sounds and words [that] will inspire kids to discover their world and become lifelong learners."

The virtual parent: The very advances that once paved the way for the "virtual executive"—pagers, fax machines, cellular phones, voice mail and so on—are now helping to create the "virtual parent." "By keeping you accessible to your family and loved ones," in the words of a brochure from Motorola, "pagers free you to go virtually anywhere without fear of being out of touch." Analysts estimate that more than half of the purchasers of pagers are primarily for personal use rather than business. Also growing in popularity are personal toll-free numbers (allowing kids to call home for free) and "follow-me, find-me" numbers that let family members track each other down no matter where they are.

In addition to communications related to daily household life, new technologies also enable long-distance parents to stay in touch with their children. A divorced father who keeps in touch with his son in another state through e-mail, fax and phone even set up a Web site (no longer available) in which families could share ideas about long-distance parenting.

Some child-development experts are concerned that new technologies aid and abet parents with workaholic tendencies and allow their employers to increase workloads while still considering themselves family friendly. Our experience has been very different. This book's co-author, Ann is the mother of two young children and works at home. She is available to monitor her children and their nanny's activities, help with crises that might arise during the day (especially during teething!) and simply be a presence in the daily lives of her children despite holding down full-time jobs. Working at home gives her the added flexibility of being able to complete assignments in the evening after the children are in bed or during naptime on weekends.

- ## NEXT: KEEPING BABY SAFE

In an increasingly violent and insecure world, new parents are doing everything they can to protect their young ones from harm. And manufacturers are more than happy to provide the products that will help them do just that. In addition to car seats, baby monitors and cabinet locks, first-time parents are purchasing things such as antibacterial high chairs to ward off *E. coli*, salmonella and other germs; heat-sensitive bath mats that indicate when the water is too hot; cushion strips for the hard edges of fireplaces and coffee tables; carbon monoxide detectors; plexiglas barricades for staircases; burner covers; and latches to prevent curious toddlers from opening ovens, toilet seats, and clothes dryers. This heightened safety-consciousness appears to be paying off. According to the National Safe Kids Campaign in Washington, DC, the number of children under fourteen who die in the United States each year from accidents dropped 26 percent since the campaign's inception in 1988.

Today's new consumers in Europe and North America are renewing their efforts to keep violence-oriented toys and games out of their homes. Toy guns and destruction-based video games are giving way to a growing market in socially acceptable edutainment products. In the Netherlands, a controversy erupted over the 1996 introduction of a computer game called *Carmageddon*. The goal of the game: for the driver to run over as many animals and people as possible. Outraged parents worked to outlaw the game, but the Minister of Justice ruled that the game, however distasteful, could not be prohibited under Dutch law. Nevertheless, *Carmageddon* achieved huge sales, prompting its makers to produce *Carmageddon II: Carpocalypse Now*. In the U.S. *Carmageddon* was recommended by *Network Computing* magazine as a great Christmas gift idea.

- ## NEXT: PERMAKIDS

In the end, parents might discover that their window of opportunity for having a direct influence on their offspring is somewhat wider than originally thought. According to the *Journal of Family*

Issues, the majority of men aged twenty to twenty-four in Southern Europe (Greece, Italy, Spain), Western Europe (France, Germany, the United Kingdom), and the United States live at home. The number of women living with their parents is lower because women tend to marry at a younger age.

In Greece, Italy and Spain, 91 percent of men and 81 percent of women aged twenty to twenty-four are living in their parents' homes; in France, Germany and the United Kingdom, those numbers drop to 61 percent of men and 41 percent of women. In the United States, 52 percent of men and 37 percent of women aged twenty to twenty-four are living in their parents' homes.

Pets Make Family

Today's American family can be just a single person and his or her pet—and pets make American houses homes. They climb onto your dinner table, make confetti out of your furniture, take advantage of your hospitality and leave little "treats" on your favorite rug. And what do they have to say for themselves? Not a word. Of course not; they're pets, and they can't talk.

• NEXT: MAKE ROOM FOR FIFI AND FIDO

Pets enjoy one of the most privileged positions in human society. The world market for pet food is forecast to reach $24.7 billion by the year 2000. According to the American Veterinary Medical Association, there are 58.2 million pets in the United States, which means that almost 60 percent of households have some type of pet. People own 59.1 million cats, 52.9 million dogs, 12.6 million birds and more than thirteen million ferrets, rabbits and reptiles.

Why are we so devoted to pets? Everyone knows they're fun to play with (usually), and provide companionship and security and that owning a pet can teach children responsibility. But the motivations for having a pet around might go much deeper.

Many anthropologists and sociologists believe that love and respect for animals is an integral part of the human psyche, the result of a shared heritage and sense of community that reaches far back into our ancestral past. St. Francis of Assisi believed that this heritage was an essential source of life for humans. Perhaps Chief Sealth of Washington state's Duwamish tribe put it best when he said in 1855, "What is man without animals? If all the animals were gone, men would die from great loneliness of spirit, for whatever happens to the beast also happens to man. All things are connected. Whatever befalls the earth befalls the sons of earth."

This sense of connection might indeed be a remnant of *Homo sapiens'* survival instincts and origins. Because the flight of an animal with more acute senses than ours is a sure signal of danger, the presence of an undisturbed, friendly animal signals safety. Animals also have the ability to attract our attention outward, allowing us to shift from thinking or processing data to simply listening and looking. According to Dr. Aaron Katcher, the co-editor with Alan M. Beck of *New Perspectives on Our Lives With Companion Animals* (University of Pennsylvania Press, 1983), the authoritative text on human-animal relations, contemplating animals produces benefits similar to "the descriptions of the healing effected when people go out alone into nature away from contact with people, away from the familiar round of social activities."

Humans also enjoy the fact that their pets aren't constrained by human rules. That's one of the reasons they're so much fun. Hedonism might come and go in human eras, but it's a constant among animals. Pet owners "take secret delight in their pets' capacity to express greed, lust, gluttony, anger, jealousy, dependence, dominance, and sexuality, which they themselves are forbidden," notes Katcher. Put another way, the pet represents the id or inner demon of the owner, allowing us to keep in touch with our "human side," which we learn to suppress as we grow into adulthood.

On the other hand, domesticated animals are pretty tame. Most have a strong commitment to predictable daily routines and pursue the simple life with a vigor that has us bipeds wishing we could hang up our hats and run with the wind—or just curl up in a sunny spot. Pets help maintain a sense of constancy by engaging their owners in repetitive cyclical activities. When a human is presented with significant and disruptive change, a pet can provide continuity between the past and the present. In today's high-tech, rapidly changing world, it's a comfort to know that Spot will still be scratching to get out the front door at three in the morning because of a full bladder.

Can pets really be considered a part of the modern family? There's no question that most pet owners consider them just that. According to a recent survey of pet owners by the American Animal Hospital Association, 61 percent of pet owners go on car trips and run errands with their pets; 48 percent take their pets to visit friends; 35 percent take their pets with them on vacation; 76 percent say they feel guilty about leaving their pets home alone; 48 percent say they frequently rearrange their plans, staying home for the sake of their pets; and 37 percent think they share personality traits with their pets (although only five percent believe they look like their pets).

The pampered pet: Just as parents are increasingly willing to pamper their kids, so too are pet owners more inclined to pamper their pets. It's no wonder that boarding options for pets now extend beyond the standard cage/food/water to include luxurious pet resorts. According to the American Boarding Kennels Association, there are about 9,000 kennels in the United States, and of those 5 percent are "high class." The Malibu Pet Hotel, in metropolitan New York, for example, has individual apartments for its furry guests. The apartments include bedrooms, bathrooms and kitchens, and they are equipped with cable television. In Los Angeles, one pet resort even plays videotapes of movies starring the dog's owner.

Pet gear: As owners increasingly regard their pets (particularly their dogs) as one of the family, niche marketers are providing products and services that allow pets to participate in family-oriented activities outside the home. For example, outdoors adventurers can now purchase life preservers, snowshoes, helmets and other equipment for their dogs. Dog owners in parts of North America and Europe also can attend a human–canine summer camp, where owners and their pets spend a week or more together, swimming in a lake, hiking, playing Frisbee and generally enjoying a bit of fun in the company of other dogs and their owners.

Pet owners who refuse to leave their little ones at home have also created a market for pet carrying cases. These range from a basic nylon or denim model from Pet Pouch of Dallas to a très chic version from Fendi. And by the way, these items are priced Fendi-style—they are not cheap.

We can also expect to see continued growth in the overall gift market for pets, including mementos, photographs, videotapes, edible treats, personalized bedding and clothing and the like. In the United States, major greeting card companies are expanding their selection of pet cards, a trend that's not surprising given that 67 percent of United States pet owners sign cards and letters from their animals, according to an American Animal Hospital Association study. Hallmark's collection of approximately one hundred pet-related cards include pet birthday and holiday cards, sympathy cards for bereaved pet owners and birth announcements for dog and cat litters.

Canine cuisine: Canines bored with their daily fare can now head over to one of the growing number of dining establishments catering exclusively to their kind: At Poochie Parties, for $39.95 for six dogs, the partygoers will get an appetizer, entree and dessert along with party hats and balloons. For an extra $25, they can have a cake made out of peanut butter or liver. Pet owners in New Orleans can take their dogs to Three Dog Bakery, an establishment in the French Quarter that handles dog parties, weddings and other chic canine affairs. A full-time pastry chef ensures that all of the low-fat goodies are up to snuff—and sniff.

Elderpet care: It's not just the human population that's aging. A million-dollar retirement home is being built on a sixty-acre site in the posh Hamptons of Long Island, New York. It will feature around-the-clock medical care, sun rooms, recreation areas and on-site companions to care for the one hundred residents. Why is this newsworthy? The residents will be dogs and cats. For a one-time fee of $10,000, pet owners can reserve a place at the Bide-A-Wee retirement home for their pets, who will live in pampered comfort until they go to that great kennel in the sky. "The home is for animals whose owners die," said Julia Maucci, a spokeswoman for the Bide-A-Wee Association, a charity that runs three animal rescue shelters in Manhattan and Long Island. "Many people are worried about what will happen to their dogs and cats. Our home guarantees the cats and dogs will be cared for and loved for the rest of their lives." According to the *Daily Telegraph*, the retirement home has already received more than two thousand queries.

The healthy pet: It's not at all unusual these days to hear of dogs and cats having open-heart surgery, kidney transplants—even orthodontic braces to correct overbites. And for the depressed pooch? Why, Prozac, of course. In the United States alone, consumers spend in excess of seven billion dollars a year on medical care for cats and dogs. Pet medical specialists include dentists, cardiologists, neurologists and chiropractors. Not surprisingly, this increased care has opened up a new market for medical insurance. VPI Insurance Group, the leading pet health-care insurer in the United States, has sold 750,000 policies since 1982. Annual premiums range from $89 to $795, but owners can buy up to $12,500 in coverage for their pets. If this type of insurance doesn't fit the bill, there is Pet Assure, a pet HMO that guarantees 25 percent off products and services from participating vets. Another option for owners are health-care credit cards for pets. These high-interest cards provide a line of credit and long-term payment options for owners faced with unmanageable veterinary bills.

As improved health care leads to a longer life expectancy for household pets, we can expect to see an increased population of older dogs and cats. This, in turn, will lead to a growing market for specialized foods, medications and pet care services. The market for nutraceuticals and homeopathic and other "alternative" health-care products for pets also is likely to grow.

Pet owners concerned for their pets' health are also taking preventative measures to keep their cats and dogs fit. Whereas table scraps were once a mainstay of most pets' diets, consumers are now aware of the need to feed their pets food that is nutritionally sound. Health food has been among the fastest growing sectors of the pet food market. Its popularity mirrors a similar trend in the human food market and is likely spurred by the same concerns for health. Two areas to watch: low-sodium pet food with no preservatives and vegetarian food marketed for pets with either dietary restrictions or vegetarian owners opposed to living with a carnivore.

In fitness-crazed Los Angeles, pet owners have gone one step further. At Total Dog, corpulent canines can work out on specially designed treadmills, swim laps in the pool or take a turn at the obstacle course. And for après-exercise? A full-body massage, of course. It all costs owners as much as $800 a year.

WHAT'S NEXT?

Marriage-preservationists: Given society's growing concerns over the erosion of family values, it's no surprise that a marriage-preservation movement is cropping up in many parts of the world. Countering the prevailing attitude of the '70s and '80s that divorce is often in the best interest of the children, current research indicates that divorce can have far-reaching and devastating consequences for children. Increasingly common are programs geared toward helping parents and children cope with divorce. In the United States, programs such as Kids' Turn and Sandcastles use art, role playing and other creative means to encourage kids to talk about their emotions. In some cases, the programs are mandated by law. Judges in Dade Country, Florida, for example, will not grant a divorce involving children until the family has completed the Sandcastles program.

Active parenting: After the "me" decade and the glitz and glamour of the '80s, many parents are focusing on family values. The desire to be proactive in bringing up children can be seen in things such as the growing popularity of parenting magazines (e.g., *Child, Parent, Parenting, American Baby, Family PC,* and *Family Fun*) and the high traffic being experienced by cybersites such as Moms Online (www.momsonline.com) and ParentSoup (www.parentsoup.com).

We're also seeing a call for a return to disciplinarianism, a reaction to the permissive parenting of the '70s and '80s. Among books on the market are *Spoiled Rotten: Today's Children and How to Change Them* (Fred Gosman, Bashford and O'Neill, 1990) and *Raising a Responsible Child: How Parents Can Avoid Indulging Too Much and Rescuing Too Often* (Elizabeth Ellis, Carol Pulishing, 1996).

Health "insurance": Advances in science and technology are making it possible for parents to have their children screened for potential illnesses and other physical problems. Children who are susceptible to depression, for example, can now be identified through specially adapted brain-imaging techniques. Using MRI (magnetic resonance imaging) and PET (positron emission tomography) scans, researchers look for a distinctive pattern of metabolic activity in the section of the brain that registers strong emotions. Scientists also have developed a new vision-screening technology that can help ophthalmologists detect eye disorders in children as young as six months.

Morality markers: As society continues to debate issues such as abortion, working women and gay rights, consumers will call upon companies to declare their loyalties and leanings. Some brands will discard images of traditional family life; others will embrace them. And companies will create new methods of delivering messages that reflect society's move away from traditional patterns.

Pets by prescription: Pets can do more than distract us from our everyday stresses; they can help us fight serious physical illness. Doctors have known for years that companion animals have the power to help us recover from illness or depression. This potential was demonstrated by numerous studies in the 1980s, including one that proved that the one-year survival rate of coronary care unit patients who owned pets was significantly greater than for those who did not. Expect doctors to prescribe pets rather than pills to patients who need to relax.

CHAPTER 11:
Home

*T*HE CHANGING LIFESTYLES AND preferences of modern consumers are having an evolutionary effect on the home environment. Not long ago, builders and architects could comfortably make certain assumptions about family size (mother, father and 2.5 kids) and home function (a dwelling for sleeping, eating and entertaining). But the '90s family is a testament to diversity, and such categorizations might well no longer apply. The function of the modern home is expanding as well. In a wired world, it serves as both home and office. In an uncertain world, it has become a haven. On the macro level, an attempt to cultivate community has resulted in a unique blend of reaching out (new urbanism) and walling off (gated communities).

In 1923, Zelda Fitzgerald said, "The home is the place to do the things you want to do." Today, home also is the place to do the things you *have* to do. In this chapter, we present an overview of trends currently affecting the home environment. If you're looking for a rundown of preferred color schemes in modern kitchens, we respectfully refer you to the nearest magazine rack. We've opted instead to focus on trends that show promise of staying with us well into the coming millennium, not just the coming season.

• NEXT: NEW APPROACHES TO HOME DESIGN AND COMMUNITY DEVELOPMENT

New urbanism: In our work with clients, one of the dominant themes we've stressed these past couple of years has been consumers' search for community. As we lose the sense of belonging that used to come with place-based communities, we are increasingly taking steps to create our own specialized communities, be they cultural, based on a special interest or even developed in cyberspace. Some developers—known as new urbanists—are even trying to replicate the sense of community inherent in yesterday's small towns and villages, albeit with some premillennial touches.

Addressing a new urbanism conference in Austin, Texas, keynote speaker Neal Peirce, author of *Citistates*, observed that new urbanism "says to me that people do want some kind of association and that they're not really happy with the disjointed nature of their lives and contacts. So what does new urbanism have to do with it? It's permitting us for the first time in decades to think about community as geography—as a physical place. It's reminding us that for all our talk of communities, we've managed to let slip away what may be the most basic community of all: geographic, place-based community, where people have what matters to them most: personal contact made possible through friendlier streets and walkability and variety and personalism."

Several core principles distinguish the village-style approach of new-urbanist planning: design for density versus sprawl; design for pedestrians as well as cars by providing sidewalks and mixed-use development within walking distance, supported by a network of narrow streets; design with borders, beyond which wilderness or agricultural uses are preserved; design for ritualized public space, such as pocket parks and town squares fronted by formalized public buildings (town halls, churches and post offices); design for an integrated mix of income types and land uses—such as low-income housing above retail stores and design to minimize energy waste from needless car travel, thereby reducing air pollution and time lost in transit and traffic jams.

Green building: We have already cited the trends of pure consumerism and Green buying. This desire to protect the planet is gaining momentum within the building industry too. Proponents of Green building, also known as environmentally responsible or sustainable architecture, utilize strategies such as informed materials selection, energy planning, and construction-waste management to ensure minimal harm to the environment. As explained in *Architectural Record*, Green builders advocate the analysis of building components that considers the acquisition of raw materials; the processing and manufacturing process; the packaging and distribution impacts; installation, use, and maintenance issues; and the potential for disposal, reuse or recycling. At the heart of the Green building movement is an understanding that the world's resources are limited and that utilizing available resources to their maximum efficiency is in society's best interest.

Energy conservation is one of the hallmarks of the movement. Although energy-efficient construction techniques can cost more than traditional alternatives up front, many have the advantage of saving money over the long run. A home that uses less energy and costs less to operate is appealing to most homeowners, regardless of their environmental stance. Techniques used to facilitate low-energy consumption include passive-solar design, which pays careful attention to building orientation, direct heat gain, daylighting, shading and well-insulated construction; high thermal mass construction, which retains heat in winter and remains cool in summer; high-efficiency windows, heating and cooling systems; low-energy light bulbs and sensors that switch off lights if no one is present; and the reduction of water waste through use of low-flow and water-conserving plumbing fixtures, xeriscaping (use of indigenous plants in landscaping to reduce watering needs), subsurface irrigation to reduce water loss from evaporation, rainwater-collection systems and cisterns and gray-water recycling (a system that collects, stores, and filters water from baths, sinks, and showers before using it for flushing toilets or irrigation).

In addition to promoting techniques that result in lower electricity and gas bills, Green builders also attempt to reduce "embodied energy," which includes the power used to manufacture a building's components and to transport them to the building site. In Britain, for example, it's estimated that embodied energy might account for nearly a sixth of national energy consumption. Products and techniques that involve less manufacturing (e.g., reused roof tiles or demolition brick) or are locally available (e.g., earthen construction) require much less energy, so their use reduces the strain on the environment.

Green products are likely to become more affordable as the demand for them increases. Some building-materials retailers already specialize in used and/or environmentally sound products. In Boulder, Colorado, two Green stores generate a million dollars in sales each year: Planetary Solutions is a decor-oriented show-room for flooring, painting and wallcovering products; its sister company, Eco-Products, is a lumberyard.

As more of the earth's resources are depleted, the sustainable approach to building and development increasingly is viewed not only as possible but necessary. Commitment to sustainable build-ing is evident on many levels, from government agencies to non-profit groups, products manufacturers to architects.

• In Dallas, Texas, a new type of home has been built. The Earth House has been built underground, and the energy sav-ings are incredible. There are four feet (about 800 tons) of soil on top of this home. It cost $750,000 to build, but it greatly reduces the impact of building on the environment. The house stays cool in the summer and warm in the winter, resulting in about half the energy costs of the average home. Although the house is underground, the back wall is a bank of windows that looks out onto a backyard, allowing light in and alleviating the claustrophobia factor.

• To aid prospective buyers in the assessment of a Green home, Austin, Texas, founded the United States' first city-funded Green builder certification program in 1992. Builders partici-pate voluntarily. Last year the program certified 471 of the 2,821 new homes in the city.

• There is a new campaign in Denver to build $2 billion dol-lars' worth of Green homes in Colorado by 2002. The goal is to build ten thousand Green homes! The Green Builder Program of Metro Denver and the Home Builders Association of Metro Denver have launched a marketing blitz to increase the numbers of structures "build green."

- Washington state boasts at least fifty straw-bale structures. The technique involves stacking and shaping bales of hay (five hundred for a 2,200 square-foot home), then shaping the hay and covering it with wire mesh. The final step is to stucco the outside of the home. The only telltale sign of the building materials is the "truth window," which exposes the straw and other materials. Straw-bale homes have become chic in parts of New Mexico, where some straw homes are upwards of 7,700 square feet and worth a million dollars.

Flexible housing: As noted by Andrea Saveri, director of the Institute for the Future in Menlo Park, California, "A lot of [home] purchasing in the past has been based on an old paradigm of what constitutes a traditional household and traditional jobs. All of that is breaking down. If you get multiple people in the house doing different things, the reality of day-to-day life is very different than it was twenty years ago." Perhaps stemming from a belated recognition that change (in needs, lifestyle, and preferences) is the only constant, modern buyers seek flexible and adaptable home designs that allow them to live in a given home as long as they like, without incurring costly renovations each time they go through a major (or minor) life change.

The demographics associated with home ownership are changing as the traditional nuclear family becomes less common. By the year 2000, the mother-father-two-kids family will represent less than twenty-five percent of total American households, reports John Schleimer, a market researcher from California. Housing expert Avi Friedman, a professor of architecture at McGill University, in Montreal, notes that "the number of what we call traditional families is now lower than 50 percent in Canada. It's the first time in home buying that marginal groups combined form the majority."

Tomorrow's homeowners promise to include greater numbers of single women, single parents, empty-nesters and couples with only one child who are looking for small, affordable homes. Conversely, multigenerational families will want larger homes that can be easily renovated to house family members and visiting friends or relatives.

As we've already noted, families have been redefined since the 1970s. A recent report released by the Census Bureau states that 18 percent of households are headed by a single mother. Twenty-six million Americans live alone. Elderly women make up the largest proportion of this group.

There is also growing demand for homes that can be altered to meet the needs of the elderly. Not only are the realities of aging catching up with the baby-boomers, but a distinct category of people, known as the "oldest old" (men and women over eighty), is now one of the fastest growing population segments worldwide. Design trends already common in planned retirement communities are becoming evident in mass-market residential construction. Among them: shorter stair-risers, one-story or two-story homes with a master bedroom suite on the first floor, maximization of natural lighting (helpful to aging eyes), use of levers in place of doorknobs and showers equipped with built-in seats. "Hidden" accommodations also are being made. For example, negotiating stairwells and narrow doorways are just two of the challenges facing those with restricted mobility. To increase flexibility in current floor plans, some homes are being designed with "bump out" floor plans (openings that easily can be enlarged to add more space) or with closets above one another in multistory homes, making it possible to retrofit an elevator. Other provisions include shelving and counters that are adjustable to a variety of heights; reinforced interior walls, which allow for later installation of handrails; prewiring for home automation of security, heating, lighting and electrical outlets; and the inclusion of space that one day can be used by a live-in caregiver.

The advent of the home office has also drawn attention to the need for flexible design. Partitions that can be taken down or moved to suit homeowners' needs and preferences are seen as one possibility. Also being considered in advance of construction are communications needs (existing and prospective). "I think we will soon get panel floors in houses, as we do in offices," Chris Westhead of Gordon Lindsay Design told *The Times* (London). "Then we can bring out cables at any point or change floor spaces whenever we want." Westhead completed a house in London with a fiber-optic backbone running through its six floors, in anticipation of the wireless house.

Planning for the future, a team of professionals at McGill University has proposed the Next Home, a three-story house in which people can choose to buy only the space they need and can afford. Once buyers decide how many stories they want, they choose a layout design from a catalogue. "Homes can be sold the way cars are sold," says McGill's Avi Friedman. "In other words, there's no reason to require a single person who rarely eats at home to buy a large, expensive kitchen." The Next Home also is designed to make moving walls and even plumbing a simple matter.

The Home of the Future, a collaboration betweem Centex Corporation, B3 Architects & Planners, and *Builder* and *Home* magazines opened for tours in Dallas in 1997. It includes walls that can be moved to accommodate the occupants' needs. In the front of the house are dual *casitas* (Spanish for "little houses") that can be used as home offices or workout rooms, and maintenance and upkeep requirements have been minimized since most home buyers lack time for these upkeep measures.

V. R. "Pete" Halter, president of V. R. Halter & Associates in Atlanta, Georgia, predicts that "builders who offer design flexibility will command a very strong competitive advantage. I'm talking about production customization, not true customization—taking the basic plan and allowing consumers some flexibility to adapt it to their lifestyles."

• NEXT: THE WIRED HOME

Home automation: From humble beginnings such as The Clapper, a device that allows you to turn your lights on and off by simply clapping your hands, home automation has transformed into a burgeoning industry. Installation of home-automation systems has grown exponentially in the United States in the past few years, reports the Washington, DC-based Home Automation Association. And smart homes are by no means just an American phenomenon. Puri Casablanca, a development of four condominium towers in South Jakarta, is equipped with an Australian-designed system that lets residents operate their lighting and electrical appliances through their telephone. The passive infra-red sensory system turns lights on when movement is detected in a room.

In basic terms, home automation enables people to control monotonous, repetitive events by either time or situation. Consumers typically choose to automate their homes for one or more of four reasons: convenience, energy savings, security or comfort. A survey of 750 affluent American households on behalf of the Consumer Electronics Manufacturers Association found that security was the primary interest of 38 percent of participants, followed by convenience (23 percent), energy-saving (22 percent) and home entertainment (nine percent).

As reported in *HFN*, the weekly newspaper of the Home Furnishings Network, modern consumers can expect to pay upwards of $10,000 for home automation that ties together security, lighting, communications, home office, entertainment, environmental controls and appliance operations. Large systems are often electronically programmed with "modes" or groups of functions. A professional dealer–installer does the programming, but homeowners can create or design their own modes. At the chosen time, for example, a typical "good morning" mode might turn on designated lights, adjust the thermostat, activate the hot water heater and start brewing coffee. Systems are accessed through the telephone, video remotes, home computers and/or keypads. There is even technology available to "weigh" each room in the house to determine how many people are in it, just in case you wanted to know if anyone was home without getting off the couch.

One of the most affordable dealer-installed home automation systems is Honeywell's TotalHome Control System, which integrates security, temperature, lighting and appliance controls into one wall-mounted keypad for both new and existing homes. The basic system, which costs $4,000, includes ten points of lighting, ten security points (doors, windows, or motion sensors), a smart thermostat, two touchpads, and a voice module that allows users to control the system from any touch-tone phone.

Because most homeowners cannot afford to install a comprehensive home automation system all at once, manufacturers now offer simplified systems that perform only a few functions. This retail approach reduces the upfront cost and allows consumers to expand systems as their finances allow and interests dictate. Already, do-it-yourselfers can purchase software and hardware systems that enable personal computers to program lighting, heating and cooling systems, and appliances for daily, weekly or one-time events. While some systems are limited to on/off controls, others support macro capabilities, which enable users to program in a series of events based on conditions (for example, if no one is home and it's dark outside, the system might turn on the light in the den).

According to the Home Automation Association, sales of home automation equipment have the potential to increase to $7.1 billion by the year 2000. And while home automation is elective in the late '90s, it might well become a necessity in some parts of the world in the years ahead. As energy resources become less plentiful and more expensive, utility companies are experimenting with peak and off-peak usage plans that resemble the day/ evening/night rates made popular by phone companies. When such plans are implemented, utility bills will reflect the advantage of running major appliances during off-peak hours (typically 10 P.M. to 6 A.M.). Home automation technology supervises the turning on and off of appliances, enabling homeowners to sleep undisturbed. Trials of so-called energy management systems already are under way in the United States.

Plugging in: For many of today's wired consumers, home automation is a nicety. Being connected to the Internet is a near necessity. Already family members keep in touch with long-distance relatives with e-mail, and children utilize the Web to conduct research for school. Frank Feather, president of Ontario, Canada-based Global Marketing, reports that multimedia technology/information highway compatibility is the predominant request in many new subdivisions. In south London, the developer Thirlstone Homes has tapped this interest by wiring several new housing developments with computer systems. The developer provides multimedia equipment and half a day's computer training for each new resident. In the United States, many consumers who custom-build their homes also are taking advantage of opportunities to design an integrated computer network.

Lucent Technologies markets HomeStar, a home automation wiring system that provides 128K Internet access from any room in the house and integrates home appliances such as VCRs, fax machines, PCs and phones. The system runs anywhere from $700 to $2,000. To keep up on any new advances in the home automation field, you may want to view the HTI Home Toys online newsletter (www.hometoys.com).

• NEXT: HOME AS HAVEN

Speaking at a design forum in the Philippines, Ilse Crawford of *Elle Decor* offered the following insights into the modern consumer at home: "Today's modernity is softer and more sensual; it is tolerant—mixing past with present, personal with practical, handmade with mass-produced. In short, the late '90s consumer wants easy modern living, a home that looks good, feels good, and works. . . . As an antidote to the stresses of working life, the home has become a place to recharge rather than show off. There is a greater interest in the things that make a home feel good physically, sensually, and emotionally—from fantastic bed linen to feng shui, tactile flooring to aromatherapy."

Increased space is a common goal in new dwellings. Jeremy Myerson, writing for *The Times* (London), recently observed that "accommodation pressures at work, particularly new office arrangements that force employees into crowded open-plan setups, make the spacious oasis at home all the more alluring. Conversely, the generous proportions of so many new public environments— shopping malls, the giant scale of the new designer restaurants— remind people of what they are missing when they live in properties comprising a series of cubbyholes." Myerson interviewed architect David Adjaye, who believes the trend toward openness is "all about creating a breathing space in which people can be inspired."

As the trend in home design moves to a more open plan—large living and kitchen spaces instead of distinct rooms—private spaces such as the bedroom and bathroom take on particular importance. "While the kitchen is a place of gatherings, a social room, the bed and bath are an area of solitude, of escape," observes Irene Wilson, divisional vice-president and fashion director for catalog retailer Spiegel. "It is the place where you can be alone, to exercise, to eat, to watch TV, to read, to do office work or just to enjoy beautiful bed linens and bath items and pamper yourself." It seems that looking good might be taking a back seat to living well. According to *Barnard's Retail Trend Report*, home merchandise spending has overtaken the apparel market in the United States. For example, in the last three months of 1997, Americans spent $304.4 billion on furnishings, compared with $279.3 billion on apparel. The *Cincinnati Enquirer* reported that in the last seven years, spending on household items has increased 71 percent.

Over the past few years, flowers have gone from being a special-occasion purchase to a regular feature of home decor. According to the Floral Index, a market research monitor, approximately forty-five million United States households now purchase flowers at least once a month, up from thirty-one million a decade ago. The *Commercial Appeal* reports that the Floral Index also found that sales of flowers in supermarkets have increased 183 percent over the past ten years.

High-tech items, which initially contributed to the cocooning trend simply by allowing us to be home more often, now help make home a nicer place to be. From the automatic breadmakers of recent years that deliver freshness on demand to online shopping that delivers practically everything else, consumers are becoming accustomed to the idea that high-tech can go a long way toward making a house feel like home. Barbara Caplan, of Connecticut-based marketing research gurus Yankelovich Partners, predicts that "lifestyle fit" will emerge as one of the leading drivers in consumers' new-home purchase decisions. "Status is becoming more personal," she notes. "Instead of ROI (return on investment), people are looking for ROE (return on enjoyment)."

One thing about which consumers are increasingly certain: A high-maintenance home is not a haven. Consumers want low-maintenance, easy-to-clean homes that utilize space efficiently. Functional items, including candle snuffers, pitchers, bookends and tray tables, have replaced curios as important decorative accents. And maintenance-free exteriors and interiors, achieved through use of materials that afford years of durability and require little or no upkeep, are growing in popularity. Home storage also is key. Done well, it facilitates organization and enables people to stock up on supplies, thereby reducing the number of necessary shopping trips. Smaller lawns, which require far less maintenance than expansive spreads, are a selling point among young, busy professionals and older homeowners.

A recent survey commissioned by America's National Association of Home Builders found that features formerly considered luxuries in new homes—high ceilings, pantries, great rooms with bars, and media centers—are now regarded as desirables in homes built for average-income buyers. Current trends among the affluent that demonstrate trickle-down promise: old-world moldings, home laundries with professional equipment such as pressing machines and kitchens equipped with stainless steel counters, a commercial range, and an outsize freezer and refrigerator.

Finally: What is a haven, if not safe? Motion sensors, alarms, and panic buttons will become increasingly important, as will hidden closets, bulletproof hideouts, and disappearing barricades. The growing obsession with home security has led some to equate modern homes with armored cocoons. Gated communities, commonplace in the United Kingdom and Brazil, have found a market in the United States as well. Many of these multifamily walled estates employ private security guards.

Until a few years ago, home-security systems carried price tags of $1,500 to $50,000 and were bought mainly by affluent households. Today, alarms start at $99 or less. Security companies have come to understand that the cost associated with a contract to monitor the system is more valuable than the cost of the system itself, which is now highly subsidized.

In the United States, more than one in five single family homes has some form of crime deterrent today. There are more than twelve thousand companies selling security systems nationwide. One problem that has grown as much as the industry is false alarms. The average is 2.2 false alarms per security system each year.

Over-the-top security systems have even become something of a fashion statement. Los Angeles homes designed by Washington, DC, architect Hugh Newell Jacobsen, for example, are intended to be as secure as nuclear-bomb shelters. He notes in a widely syndicated news article, "The second an alarm goes off . . . an entire family can get to a room protected by a steel door, rely on their own generator and water supply, and use an unlisted number to call for help."

• NEXT: DOING IT OURSELVES

The modern consumer, with more than a little encouragement from profiting parties, has come to believe that he or she can accomplish almost anything, regardless of experience or talent. Having visualized their ideal space, homeowners set out to create it—by buying it in bits and pieces, building it from the ground up or, in the case of gardens and houseplants, growing it.

The pervasiveness of the do-it-yourself spirit is reflected in the volume and variety of books targeting do-it-yourselfers. British designer Sir Terence Conran, founder of the Habitat furniture chain, offers tips on how to achieve a cool, chic look in *The Essential House Book* (Crown). *Updating Your Home* (Reader's Digest) recommends thirty ways to improve the way your home looks and works, from changing a doorway into an arch to ensuring proper roof ventilation. Those with larger projects in mind can choose one of two spiral-bound step-by-step guides from Canadian residential designer-consultant David Caldwell: *Contracting Your Own Home* and *Renovating Your Own Home* (Stoddart).

When it comes to interior design, do-it-yourself is so trendy that even those who don't do it themselves want everyone else to think they did. As noted in *The Wall Street Journal*, hiring a decorator is still "in" among those who can afford such luxuries—but admitting to it is not. The solution? A "ghost" decorator who designs interiors so subtle and casual that the client can claim credit. "It's much more 'in' to seem to have done it yourself," observed a real estate broker in the resort community of East Hampton, New York.

According to the *American Express Retail Index*, 39 percent of United States homeowners will take on home projects this year (up 8 percent from last year), with an average budget of $2,929 (up 10 percent). Here's a breakdown of the projects homeowners intend to tackle this year: refurnish/decorate: 59 percent, renovate/remodel: 32 percent, landscaping: 29 percent, gardening: 27 percent, mandatory maintenance: 24 percent, exterior decorating: 22 percent, expansion: 14 percent, and restoration: 13 percent. The boom has spawned one of the great successes in recent American retailing,

Home Depot. While this major national chain has brought price, service and standardization to the United States's do-it-yourself industry, its detractors bemoan the demise of the local hardware, paint and wood stores, which cannot compete with Home Depot's selection and prices.

Although the implementation of do-it-yourself home improvements often remains decidedly low-tech, the planning stage has entered the Digital Age. A range of software packages enables computerized do-it-yourselfers to design their own homes and gardens. Titles include *3D Home & Office Design*, *3D Virtual Reality Room Planner*, and *Garden Architect*. Home-design programs enable you to make onscreen decisions about everything from furniture placement to knocking down walls without having to actually go through the motions. Some software programs enable you to take a virtual walk through the home, while others estimate the cost of selected home improvements. Gardeners benefit from detailed information about caring for particular plants and also gain assistance in creating an overall landscape design. Through a computer software program called *ModaVISION*, for example, Sears's The Great Indoors offers customers a chance to see how a remodeled room in their home would look. The HouseNet Web site (www.housenet.com) offers visitors a chance to do everything from researching a future project to calculating and designing the plans to conversing with fellow do-it-yourselfers in chat rooms. The site also features an online shopping center in which you can purchase products for home and garden.

Large building-supply and home-finishings retailers, who have the most to gain from the trend, are doing everything they can think of to inspire the do-it-yourselfer lurking in every consumer. With its popular in-store, how-to seminars and knowledgeable sales staff, industry leader Home Depot has built its reputation on the belief that even the most unlikely of consumers can make home improvements such as building a deck, installing bifold doors and tiling a floor. Lowe's Companies, Inc. (www.lowes.com), America's number-two home-improvement retailer, publishes an e-zine filled with step-by-step how-to guides for projects ranging from hanging a door and installing vinyl flooring to finishing wood. New projects are added each month, contributing to an extensive online archive.

Sears is doing more than just offering products geared toward the do-it-yourself woman. It's created a one-stop shopping retail environment targeting the "chairman of the home" (the primary decision-maker with regard to purchases for the home—in most cases, a woman). The company opened its first The Great Indoors location in Denver, Colorado and plans to open an additional 200 to 250 locations around the United States within the next ten years. In a change from the warehouse-style format of many do-it-yourself chains, The Great Indoors is divided into "rooms," with merchandise categorized by bedroom, bathroom, kitchen and great room (family room/living room). A cafe will provide an inviting place in which customers can brainstorm and peruse reference books. This store is intended to target everyone from do-it-yourselfers to interior decorators to people just shopping for a gift.

Retail groups such as IKEA, John Lewis, Wickes, and MFI use a photo-realism system called PlanIt, which was developed by ICADS and can be used to design kitchens, bedrooms, bathrooms, living rooms and conservatories. Within minutes, PlanIt can design a room using a given retailer's stocked range of units. Initial drawings are of draft quality, which allows the system to work fast. PlanIt also will add up the cost of the furniture and produce an itemized quote. Once shoppers are happy with the draft price and picture, the system redraws the image using photo-realism.

WHAT'S NEXT?

Green thumbs: As gardening becomes an even greater preoccupation (more than 37 percent of United States households now have at least one serious gardener), expect to see increased efforts to prune the amount of time and energy it takes to pursue it. Product improvements and more options for online ordering will be available, as will a growing number of leaseable, family-sized plots for flower and vegetable gardening in urban settings.

Virtual communities: Via computer and modem, we'll see people forming more communities that cross geographic, social, cultural, and economic boundaries. For an evaluation of the possibilities and limitations of online communities, check out *The Virtual Community* by online guru Howard Rheingold. Rheingold has posted the book at www.well.com/user/hlr/vcbook/index.

Good noise: Noise pollution is an undeniable source of modern-day angst. The opposite of "bad noise" is "good noise," pumped throughout your haven to make you happier, healthier and more productive. According to *Science News*, a growing body of "acoustic ecologists"—individuals from disparate fields such as science, history, geography, technology and the arts—are beginning to focus attention on ways to preserve, encourage and multiply the sounds people enjoy. Acoustic ecologists study the effects of technology and human intervention on the acoustic environment while devising ways to enhance aural awareness and create balanced sonic environments. Can an application of this science to the home environment be far off?

Culture blending: Mixed ethnicity is in. As consumers work to create a truly personal space, we'll see them mix and match items from Africa, Asia, Europe—anywhere and everywhere that catches their fancy. In homes, you'll find reproductions of ancient Chinese sculpture on furniture of early American design but with traditional fabric patterns of Africa and prints of antique maps depicting the sea routes taken by European explorers of previous centuries.

CHAPTER 12:

Leisure and Entertainment

WITH ALL THE TALK ABOUT how new trends and technologies are changing the business world, it's easy to overlook the degree to which our personal lives have been affected. New technologies have reached into just about every aspect of personal entertainment, from the way we watch movies to how we buy our music CDs. They have also influenced our expectations regarding entertainment fare and products. No longer are we satisfied with just a few sources of programming or entertainment information. Rather than wait for the Sunday-night airing of Mutual of Omaha's *Wild Kingdom*, as many of us did in the '60s, we turn to the twenty-four-hour-a-day, seven-days-a-week Animal Planet expanded cable channel or pop a CD-ROM on animals into our multimedia PC. Children, who at one time were perfectly satisfied with a doll made of rags, now insist on animated playmates that can laugh, cry, yawn, and even urinate on demand. Even traditional board and card games such as Monopoly, Scrabble and Solitaire have been computerized.

Our movie consumption has changed drastically. Film fans over thirty remember when we had two choices: We could go see a movie at our local cinema (typically a single-screen venue) or we could wait a couple of years for an edited version to appear on network TV. Today, we can choose to watch a movie at our local multiplex or wait just a few months to purchase it on Pay-Per-View, rent it from a video store, watch it on one of the premium cable channels or purchase it on video, laser disc, or, most recently, DVD. Those of us who can't wait for a particular film to be released might also have the option of downloading clips from the Internet in advance of the film's opening night. In many cases, we can supplement our movie-watching experience by purchasing the film's soundtrack, buying related toys, clothing, books and other merchandise; or playing a game tied into the movie on our computer or video-game system.

The fact of the matter is, the Internet, satellite broadcasting, computer and video game technology, and other facets of our Digital Age are working together to change the very nature of entertainment around the world. Rather than remain passive witnesses, we are being invited into a world of interactivity. One result has been an escalating bid for the attention of members of the younger generations, who quickly grow bored in the absence of fast-paced action and stimulating visuals.

This chapter explores major entertainment and recreation trends that are developing as we begin the new millennium.

• NEXT: ENTERTAIN US!

They want us. They really, *really* want us. Retailers, movie studios, restaurants—you name it. They want our patronage (our money), and they'll do what it takes to get it, whether it means providing play options for our kids or creating special effects that'll blow our minds.

One-stop family entertainment centers: As new consumers increasingly demand entertainment options that are fun, high tech and convenient, a growing number of companies and entrepreneurs are developing sprawling entertainment centers that accommodate everyone from young children and their parents to teens and Generation-Xers out on a hot date. The high-tech arcade GameWorks (www.gameworks.com/), a joint venture of Steven

Spielberg's DreamWorks studio, Universal Studios, and Sega, debuted in Seattle in 1997. The thirty-thousand-square-foot complex is made up of a series of video arcades, virtual-reality rides, PCs linked to the Internet and performance arenas surrounded by walkways and restaurants on mezzanines. The standout feature of the complex is Vertical Reality, an interactive game designed by Spielberg, which revolves around three twenty-five-foot-high video screens representing a skyscraper. Twelve players, arranged in a circle, are strapped into seats that move up or down a pole, depending on the players' success at shooting cyborgs with their cyberguns. The winner gets a shot at Mr. Big and a full free fall to the floor. More than one-hundred GameWorks are scheduled to be constructed worldwide by 2002; all of the sites will be linked via the Internet, so game players can compete against others around the world.

In a Los Angeles suburb, Walt Disney Company has opened the first of a planned one hundred Club Disney centers. Aimed at families with young children, the centers include multimedia PCs with Internet access, a playground, maze, film studio, arts and crafts center, restaurant, retail shop, and birthday party rooms. In San Francisco, Sony has created an entertainment center that features a fifteen-screen movie theater, 3-D Sony IMAX theater, restaurant, live musical performances, Sony and Discovery Channel theme stores, and interactive arcades and play areas designed by children's author, Maurice Sendak.

High stakes: For many people, nothing is more entertaining than the thrill of risking it all—whether on a sporting event, a hand of cards or a horse race. Around the world, gambling is enjoying unprecedented popularity, both as an entertainment option and, increasingly, as an alternative avenue to working hard for financial success. We see this trend as having its roots in a number of social phenomena, among them our increasing demand for instant gratification (who wants to work hard at a dead-end job when a good day at the races could put us on Easy Street?) and the desire for thrill-seeking that is many people's reaction to the fears that come with the uncertainties of the impending millennium.

In the United States, some form of legal, regulated gambling is available in forty-eight of the fifty states. Options include state-run lotteries, instant scratch-off games, casinos, horse and dog tracks, video terminals and riverboat gambling. In 1996 Americans spent more than $550 billion on gambling, a figure, noted *Mother Jones* magazine, that exceeds the revenue from movies, spectator sports, theme parks, cruise ships, and recorded music—combined. *Annals of the American Academy of Political & Social Science* (March 1998) identifies gambling as one of the fastest growing sectors of the economy, accounting for approximately ten percent of leisure expenditures.

In Las Vegas, gambling reaches far beyond casinos and taverns. Records, according to *The Los Angeles Time*s, show that 2,465 slot machines operate in more than three hundred businesses, including convenience stores, groceries, drugstores, laundries, and even a few car washes and doughnut shops.

This is no surprise. Sin City has been reborn as family mecca, with new themed casinos and attractions aimed at making the once quintessentially adult destination a G-rated attraction. Within this overall trend, the latest addition is definitely adult. Steve Wynn's new casino/hotel/experience, Bellagio, takes its name from the tiny Lake Como, Italy, tourist village (the very same village where Ira lives). The reaction of the Italian locals is a combination of bemusement and anticipation over whether its newfound notoriety will set off a wave of tourism to the genuine article. If experience and Americans' lack of interest in world travel are any guide, we can expect that faux Bellagio will be more than enough for the Vegas pilgrim.

During the summer of 1998, the Powerball lottery, a joint lottery among twenty states, reached $295.7 million. The odds of winning were eighty million to one, yet people stood in line for hours. In the wake of Powerball fever, Greenwich, Connecticut, moved to outlaw sales of Powerball tickets because out-of-state residents were drawn by the thousands to this closest sales locale for New York and New Jersey residents, whose states do not participate in Powerball. The invasion of out-of-staters wreaked havoc on traffic, parking and local commerce for weeks.

As gambling takes off, a number of industries are trying to cash in on the trend. The travel industry, for example, is taking advantage of travelers with cash in their pockets and time to kill, both at the airport and in flight. Two examples: Singapore Airlines uses an interactive video system to allow passengers to gamble while in flight. Stakes will remain small, the airline says, since its objective is to entertain passengers, not to allow them to win or lose large sums of money. Amsterdam's Schipol Airport draws passengers into its on-site casino, featuring seventy-five slot machines, a roulette wheel, and cards.

Gamblers also are flocking to the Internet, leading to expectations that Internet gambling—called "nambling" or "Interbetting"—will be a $10 billion dollar industry by the year 2000. Nearly three hundred gambling-related Web sites are in operation, ranging from virtual casinos to magazines to discussion forums. Approximately forty Web sites allow gamblers to wager real money on games of chance, such as blackjack and roulette, as well as on sports events. Typically, an electronic line of credit is established before bets are placed. Winners are paid via check or deposit to credit-card accounts; losses show up on monthly credit-card bills. Interest is worldwide: According to *Newsday*, fans in England, Japan, the United States and Russia placed bets with World Sports Exchange (www.worldsportsexchange.com) during the NCAA basketball championships.

What's next? For a lot of people, not surprisingly, treatment for addiction. According to the Council on Compulsive Gambling, 5 percent of gamblers become compulsive, and 90 percent of these turn to crime to support their habit. Up to 80 percent of compulsive gamblers contemplate suicide, and 14 percent attempt it. A recently released study by Harvard University Medical School's Division on Addictions shows that 3.88 percent of American teenagers are addicted to gambling, and another 9.45 percent are problem gamblers. The number of visitors to American casinos has doubled in the past five years.

• NEXT: GREAT ESCAPES

As delighted as we are with our new and multiplying entertainment options, we can't help but note that our playtime, in general, is increasingly limited. While sitting in a seemingly endless meeting, waiting for a pubescent cashier to finish chatting with her friends, or picking up takeout for dinner, most of us experience a longing for something different. Blame it on anything you'd like— you'd probably be right. This discontent has its roots in everything from life-work imbalance to information-overload to premillennial tension. Most of us don't have the option of getting away from it all by taking a Grand Tour through Europe, renting a lakeside villa for a few months, or quitting our jobs and starting over in a new locale. Instead, we make do with short-term fixes, brief respites from the stresses of our everyday lives that allow us to recharge and begin anew. While these escapes often take the form of traditional entertainment—an engrossing movie or a day hike—they also incorporate a new breed of pursuits based on relaxation and rejuvenation.

Going retro: For many young Americans, getting away from it all now means turning the calendar back to what they perceive as a simpler time. Rather than adopting the electronic sound of techno music and other high-tech trends, nostalgic youth are embracing entertainment options made popular in their parents' and grandparents' youth. "Cocktail chic" is now all the rage in a number of cities, with twentysomethings heading to clubs to listen to Tony Bennett and Henry Mancini, dance to Vegas-style swing, sip oh-so-sophisticated martinis and soak up the lava-lamp atmosphere.

Swing-noir, made famous in the '30s and '40s, has also caught on big time. Young men and women are decking themselves out in the fashion of their grandparents' time (cocktail dresses, zoot suits, two-tone wingtips) and swinging the night away to the big-band sounds in the growing number of clubs catering to this hip crowd. Lee Bennett Sobel, publisher of *Lo-Fi*, a 'zine about the American retro scene, explained the swing phenomenon to *The New York Times* this way: People are frightened by the coming millennium, and retro culture brings a measure of comfort. Marc Campbell, owner of New York's Louisiana Bar and Grill, agrees. As he told the *Times*, "Swing offers a joyous alternative to a generation that came of age during the AIDS crisis and a time when sexuality was hidden under grunge. This is a return to elegance, to touch dancing and wearing your sexuality on your sleeve. Swing is definitely the thing."

Old pop and rock tunes also have been top-sellers of late. The nostalgia trend has sparked increased sales of boxed-set music CD anthologies, including top-sellers such as the three-volume *Beatles Anthology* and the two-CD *James Brown: 40th Anniversary Collection*. The retro trend is even having an impact on the instruments used in the music industry. Vintage guitars are in great demand, and manufacturers are scrambling to reissue the designs used on old Gibsons, Martins and Fenders. Digital keyboards, all the rage a decade ago, are now being replaced by "old-fashioned" analog synthesizers. Yamaha is billing its AN1x keyboard as a "virtual analog synthesizer, possessing the sound and feel of vintage instruments."

The 1970s revival, under way for some time among trendsetters, has also hit the mainstream. Today's retro fashion lineup includes polyester prints, flared denim jeans, navel-baring tops with zip fronts and v-necks, hip-huggers, platform shoes, super-short A-line skirts, and floppy collars. In the past couple of years, hit songs of the '70s have been heard in a slew of American TV ads: "Nacho Man"—based on the 1978 Village People tune "Macho Man"— danced his way through an advertisement for Old El Paso products; a KC and the Sunshine Band hit from 1975, "That's the Way (I Like It)," was among the '70s songs recently featured in Burger King ads; and '70s icon Barry White has been stumping for Anheuser-Busch's Bud Light and Prodigy. The new Volkswagen Beetle has helped increase VW's sales by 50 percent in the first quarter of 1998.

On the New York-based VH1 cable television network, reruns of *American Bandstand* that originally aired from 1975 through 1985 have earned a place among the most-watched programs. "I've been trying to figure out why the '70s are so appealing," said Joshua Katz, senior vice-president for marketing at VH1. "And believe it or not, it's because, despite all the craziness—all the drug use, all the casual sex—people find it a more innocent time."

Vacations redefined: Although escaping via movies and music continues to be popular, physical escapes are also a draw. The difference these days is that pressures of work rarely allow for a proper vacation. Instead many of us are making do with quick trips, sometimes without even leaving our desks.

Virtual travel: Anyone's who's plugged into new technologies knows how hard it can be to break away. In an interesting twist, workers are using that very same technology to leave behind their business routines, even if only for a ten-minute, mind-cleansing virtual vacation. An Internet itinerary affords the convenience of continent-hopping without the threat of jet lag. From the rowdiness of Munich Oktoberfest (www.oktoberfest-guides.com) to the adventure of an African safari (www.safaris.com/baobab), the limits of travel are dictated only by the speed of your modem.

Those seeking more surreal virtual surroundings can try their hand at fantasy computer games. The undisputed leader these days is Cyan Inc.'s *Riven*, the sequel to the record-breaking *Myst*; within two months of its release, more than half a million copies of the game had been sold. "*Riven*, like *Myst*, is . . . an indefatigable argument for distraction," wrote reviewer Tamara I. Hladik on the Sci-Fi Channel's website (www.scifi.com). The lush environments, high-resolution graphics, nonviolent puzzle-solving game play and stunning sound effects combine to immerse the player in an entirely new world. "We don't like to call it a game," explains *Riven* collaborator Richard Vander Wende. "It's a world, and it's a very real place to us." "It's a vacation, an immersive diversion," adds co-creator Rand Miller.

Combining business with pleasure: Business travelers frustrated by the amount of time they spend on the road are beginning to escape by squeezing family vacations into out-of-town business itineraries. With employers covering spousal travel, parents are able to maximize family time while minimizing expense. Today, more than forty-three million (more than 15 percent) of all business trips included a child, a 63 percent increase from 1990, according to the Travel Industry Association of America (TIAA). Catering to this market, fully 18 percent of the American Hotel and Motel Association's twelve thousand members now offer children's programs. Camp Hyatt (associated with the Hyatt Hotel chain), for example, offers a range of special activities for children, including educational offerings such as language classes and nature hikes.

Quick trips: Those of us who have a hard time taking even a long weekend are finding mini-escapes at local hotels and resorts. TIAA reports that the number of weekend jaunts has jumped seventy percent in the last decade, and getaways of one to five days now account for about half of all American travel. To capitalize on this trend, France's struggling Club Mediterranee will revamp its operations by focusing on mini-clubs—urban versions of its resort villages that you can visit for just a day or even a few hours. The mini-clubs will feature bistros, cafes, logo merchandise and fitness areas in which customers can rock-climb or snorkel.

For a quick weekend getaway without spending a fortune, Club Mud is just the place to go. Located at the foot of the Santa Ana Mountains in California, the Glen Ivy Hot Springs Spa boasts the only natural red clay bath in the area and fifteen springs-heated pools. Day-trippers can enjoy the clay bath and pools for $25, or you can check in for the full spa treatment.

Weekend trips are defined as one to five nights, including a Friday and/or a Saturday, according to the Travel Industry Association of America in its *Weekend Travel Report*. People in the United States took 604 million weekend trips last year, compared to 356.8 million ten years ago.

The *Independent on Sunday* (London) reports that young urbanites in London are forgoing jaunts to Paris in favor of weekend trips up the M4 to Longleat Center Parc, where an "executive" chalet, complete with maid service, runs just £88 (about $144.00) per person. In the United States, high-end hotels are luring customers not with images of romance, but with hard-core shopping, reports *The Wall Street Journal*. "Only so much romance can occur over a weekend," noted Richard Chambers of the New York Palace Hotel. "Shopping is something we can provide." And provide they do. Many hotels now offer discounts at local merchants, personal shoppers and gift wrapping and delivery. San Francisco's Maxwell Hotel is even less subtle: Its lobby is adorned with a bronze statue of a female shopper. The hotel also provides free foot massages for weary shopaholics and, instead of mints, places $25 gift certificates to neighborhood stores on guests' pillows. In Chicago, the Ritz-Carlton, which sits atop a mall, sells three times as many shopping-spree packages as it does romantic weekends.

Next destinations: For those with time and money to invest in real-world travel, *The New York Times* has identified the following Next destinations: Lhasa, Tibet (for peace and quiet); Tasmania (nature adventures); the Hindu Kush, Afghanistan (skiing); and Cambodia (beaches on the Gulf of Thailand).

Costa Rica-based Temptress Adventure Cruises is pioneering the concept of "soft adventure" cruises in Central America. These tours are for people who want to visit exotic destinations without the hassle and hurry of plane travel, but who also want to do more than just shop when they get there. "Our itineraries include cruises to remote, natural habitats where passengers can participate in guided tours through native village encampments, hike through primary and secondary forests, and enjoy various water sports in the Pacific Ocean and Caribbean Sea," says Sandra Jofre, vice-president of sales and marketing for Temptress.

Luxurious indulgence: Luxurious indulgence is back. And our renewed focus on finery is not limited to the privileged few. Even off-the-rack consumers are treating themselves to the relatively inexpensive props of a more luxurious age: cigars, martinis, pocket watches, and '40s fashion. What better way to escape the hustle and bustle of our everyday lives?

Luxury needn't involve conspicuous consumption, however. Today's trendsetters are happy to indulge in life's luxuries in the privacy of their homes. The appeal of a product now has more to do with quality and authenticity than with opulence. One example of a company that has mined consumers' twin desires for luxurious indulgence and reminders of a simpler time is Lush, a British cosmetics grocer. Lush sells fresh, handmade lotions and potions in retail outlets designed to resemble organic-food emporiums. Soaps, which are cut from huge cheeselike rounds and sold by the kilo (wrapped in white paper), are made primarily from fruit and vegetable extracts combined with essential oils. The indulgent products (including Skinny Dip, a violet-scented shower gel with cocoa butter chips and white Belgian chocolate) are kept in chilled cabinets to maintain freshness.

WHAT'S NEXT?

Culture prescriptions?: Researchers in Sweden have concluded that cultural activity can add years to your life, notes *Forbes FYI*. A team supervised by Lars Olov Bygren surveyed more than twelve thousand people about their lifestyles in 1982, 1983 and 1991 and discovered that those who regularly attended movies, concerts, plays and other artistic events—or rooted for their local sports teams—were half as likely to be among the 850 or so subjects who died during the period of the study. Such activities, Bygren speculates, influence longevity more than do education, income, physical activity or smoking, because they generate strong emotions, which stimulate the immune system. As more and more physicians accept the benefits of alternative methods of healing, expect "take in two operas/ballgames/plays and call me in the morning" to become a standard prescription.

On the fringe: Fringe festivals—thespian fairs made up of small performing companies doing everything from avant-garde performance art to juggling—offer a hefty dose of culture. Because of the relatively low cost of producing a fringe show, performers are free to do whatever they wish without requiring approval from funding agencies or boards of directors. According to *Utne Reader*, the movement was born in Edinburgh fifty years ago, when local performers angry about being left out of their city's international arts festival created a counterfestival to showcase their own work. Now the *Guinness Book of World Records* lists the Edinburgh Fringe (which draws more than half a million visitors each year) as the biggest arts festival in the world, and fringe festivals are popping up everywhere from Australia to South Africa to Hong Kong. New York City hosted its first fringe festival in August of 1997, and festivals debuted in Boston and New Orleans in 1998.

Beyond karaoke: Japan's list of cultural exports is growing: martial arts, bonsai, sushi, cartoons, sentimental songs, Tamagotchi. Without a doubt, though, the country's biggest cultural export of recent decades is karaoke. No bar for Asian business folk can hope to do good business without a karaoke system. For self-effacing Asians, karaoke has proved the perfect way to show off with an individualistic fantasy while remaining part of the group. So what's next? Be on the lookout for systems that take the fantasy a step further—not only putting the singer's voice into the mix, but also integrating his/her face into the accompanying video.

Mood foods: With all the conflicting information we receive each month on what we are and are not supposed to eat, it should come as no surprise that people are rejecting health specialists' advice in favor of comfort foods like macaroni and cheese or roasted chicken and mashed potatoes. Although comfort foods vary from country to country, they are almost always connected to childhood, to a time when we felt coddled and safe. And now there's scientific evidence that some comfort foods actually can affect us not just spiritually, but physically. "What you eat can affect your mood—whether you feel up or down," wrote Jean Carper in *Food: Your Miracle Medicine* (HarperCollins, 1993). "There's evidence that people often make unconscious food choices that change brain chemistry and put them in a better mood." So while the French might turn to creamy garlic soup (garlic can have a mood-elevating effect), the Chinese might opt for chicken soup flavored with ginger (in addition to having an antidepressant effect, ginger aids circulation and warms the body). Giving new meaning to the term comfort food, tomorrow's "mood food" will be enhanced with mood-altering substances such as aromatherapy scents and mild stimulants, depressants, or hormones.

Make-believe consumption: When overflowing closets and bulging waistlines are the norm, the time might be right for the ultimate in less-is-more marketing: make-believe consumption. The Associated Press reports that "conceptual dining" is being piloted in Tel Aviv, Israel, where Cafe Ke'ilu (loosely translated from Hebrew as "Cafe Make Believe") is serving up fat-free, sugar-free, cholesterol-free, substance-free food. Yes, that's substance-free, as in thin air. Owned by top-rated Swiss chef Philippe Kaufman, the cafe charges $3 to $6 for would-be orders of eel mousse, salad of pomegranates (in season), and ram's brain in lemon-lime sauce. It's about the ritual of eating, not the reality. If the cafe is successful, a franchise will open in New York.

In-home theaters: Although in-home screening rooms were once the exclusive province of Hollywood stars and producers, they're now becoming a common feature in large homes around America, regardless of the owner's occupation. These entertainment rooms typically feature a sophisticated stereo and large-screen home theater system with an overhead projector and multiple speakers. Some of these rooms feature theater-style draperies that operate electronically, lounge seating for as many as thirty people, and a full-scale bar. Other touches might include an old-fashioned popcorn or hot dog cart. Those movie buffs lacking the space for a full-size home theater can turn to Noise Cancellation Technologies for flat-screen speaker technology. In addition to offering high-quality audio, these speakers, which are less than two inches thick, come in a lightweight frame featuring a special acoustically-permeable material onto which a variety of prints and textures can be digitally imprinted.

Virtual beings: A modern rule of thumb in the digital revolution seems to be that if something looks and acts real, it's as good as real. At a minimum, it's entertainment. From Sony's Toki Memorial virtual dating game (which has been snapped up by half a million Japanese teens) to the cult status of computer-generated heroine Lara Croft (of the Tomb Raider video game) to the album sales of the virtual Web character Kyoko Date, the parallel universe of cyberspace is creating life forms of its own.

Pick 'n' mix nostalgia: In the movie *The Wedding Singer*, Adam Sandler romances Drew Barrymore to a soundtrack of '80s hits and a backdrop of the decade's barely dead fashions. Is it too soon to wax nostalgic for the decade of designer jeans? In the age of pick 'n' mix nostalgia, perhaps not. With the culture of an entire century on tap, trendleaders take inspiration from a vast palate of images and sounds. Consider Jennifur Brandt, twenty-two-year-old publisher of hip L.A. fanzine *Pesky Meddling Girls*. "Every day is a different era with me," Brandt told the Associated Press, "depending on what music I'm into at that time. . . . Or if I saw a really good '60s movie the night before, I'll have an insatiable urge to wear hip-huggers or bell bottoms." That might be followed by a week of '40s fashions. Subscribers to Brandt's fanzine range from rocker Marilyn Manson to designer Anna Sui to Warner Brothers Studios.

Way down south: These days the ends of the earth is literally the only place where the rich and famous can get away from it all. That reality no doubt has contributed to the celebrity influx in the remote wilderness of Patagonia, a region spanning a half million square miles of lakes, woodland, and mountains in southern Argentina and Chile. Fans of outlaw history might recall Patagonia as the place where Butch Cassidy and the Sundance Kid tried to evade the long arm of the law. Now celebrities such as George Soros, Sylvester Stallone, Ted Turner, and the Benetton brothers are buying huge plots of land in hope of escaping the long lenses of the paparazzi. According to *Electronic Telegraph*, the land rush is not popular among locals, who find themselves shut out from much-loved nature spots by newcomers' security measures. Nearly a sixth of Patagonia is owned by just 350 foreigners.

New music meccas: The connection between music and youth has long been established, and Anglo-American music in recent decades has had a tremendous impact on the development of youth culture around the world. These days, however, that influence is waning, as young people in Asia, Continental Europe, and elsewhere begin to take a more active role in the global music scene. Although the United States continues to account for more than a quarter of worldwide music sales, its days of domination appear numbered. And despite the recent upswing in Britain's music industry (thanks in no small part to Oasis and the Spice Girls), its influence is also on the decline. In 1985, artists from the United States and Great Britain accounted for 65 percent of music sales in Europe; by 1995 that percentage had dropped to 45. Due to aging markets in North America and Western Europe and economic uncertainty in Asia, the global music industry is expected to enter a period of slower growth over the next five years. While the market doubled in value over the past decade, a study by Market Tracking International predicts that retail sales of albums and singles will show real growth of only 26 percent through 2003 (rising from $40.2 billion in 1997 to $50.7 billion). Emerging markets such as Eastern Europe and Latin America will continue to show strong growth, but that won't offset slower sales in markets such as the United States, Germany, France and Japan.

Expect a showdown among the world's five largest record companies: Universal, Sony, Warner, BMG, and EMI.

Next, expect to hear more from local acts in Asia, Latin America, Africa and Eastern Europe. We'll also see a rise in world music, populated by the likes of Bulgaria's Folk Scat, Tibet's Yungchen Lhamo and Tanzania's Hukwe Zawose. The world's cross-cultural pollination continues.

CHAPTER 13:
Sports of All Sorts

*T*HE AUTHORS OF THIS BOOK have lived in just about every region of the U.S. (California, Connecticut, Florida, Maine, New Jersey, New York, Tennessee, Texas, Washington state, Washington, DC), as well as in Canada (Toronto) and Europe (Amsterdam, Milan, Paris). It's been interesting to see the degree to which sports help to shape local—and even national—identities. When Ira's family lived in Toronto, it seemed only natural that then eight-year-old Lily would become involved in competitive ice-dancing, a sport she likely would not have considered while living in New York. Ira's younger son, Nick, has a collection of a dozen or so jerseys from soccer teams in North America and Europe. Even though he's now living in Connecticut, he continues to follow AC Milan on satellite TV.

Sports arenas in various locales have also provided insights into an area's culture. Ira was in Toronto for two world baseball championships, both of which he watched as the world's most polite fans sat on their hands. In contrast, he took his older son, David, to New York's Yankee Stadium for his first baseball game. During the Fourth of July no-hitter, the seventy thousand New York fans made a continually deafening racket from inning seven onward. But that was nothing compared with the tumult the Matathias encountered at Milan's San Siro Stadium, where the building practically rocks from the orchestrated singing and dancing and shouting of 130,000 fanatics as they celebrate the fortunes of professional football's AC Milan (owned by media mogul and one-time prime minister Silvio Berlesconi).

Whether you're talking about soccer in Milan, hockey in Toronto, baseball or basketball in New York, bullfighting in Madrid or sumo wrestling in Tokyo, one thing is certain: Big-league sports are no longer just about the game and its fans; they're about big money. Go to any major stadium in the world, and you're likely to see business deals being conducted before, after, and during the game. Corporations are buying up luxury suites at stadiums in which to entertain clients and prospects. Championship tickets are thrown in to sweeten a deal. At New York's Madison Square Garden, it's not unheard of to see businesspeople plunk down in their seats, open their briefcases and laptop computers, and not look up until the end of the game, multitasking if you will.

Until recently, professional sports hadn't been a huge moneymaker in Europe, but that's all changing. Now major sports—and the concomitant advertising revenues, athlete endorsements, and merchandising opportunities—are beginning to hit the big time from Amsterdam to Zaragoza, Spain. The past few years have seen the birth of dozens of digital TV sports channels and pay-per-view events, escalating players' salaries and causing huge increases in bids for broadcast rights. When the World Cup went to France in 1998, organizers anticipated thirty-seven billion viewers for the sixty-four matches—more than twice that of the Atlanta Olympic Games.

In America, there are fewer and fewer professional sports venues that are not aligned with a corporate identity. All of the college football bowl games—a key component of many Americans' New Year's Day activities—now carry a corporate moniker. In contrast, while working on a sponsorship deal in the early days of the Madison Square Garden cable network, Ira remembers being unable to negotiate "dasher board" signage: Hockey officials and Garden executives deemed the approach "too commercial" for sports. Now even television time-outs have live sponsors for the in-person audiences—everything is branded, and the games' timing is based on the TV play versus the play of the sport. Go figure.

Around the globe, sports are turning profits for everyone from fashion designers, software manufacturers and publishers to equipment-makers and the athletes themselves. And this doesn't just apply to the top sports. According to a recent survey by the trade group the National Sporting Goods Association on sports participation, fishing is seventh in the top ten activities, with 44.7 million people participating in the United States And the market for snowboarding, popular throughout Europe, America and Japan, is now valued at $700 million. According to the National Sporting Goods Association, Americans spend $37.6 billion a year on sporting goods.

For a decade, Nike Inc. was particularly successful in tapping the desire of today's consumer to "Just Do It," a campaign that now is being augmented with the somewhat gentler tag line, "I Can." While the Oregon-based company commanded an impressive forty-seven percent of the American athletic shoe market in 1997 and has achieved a ranking as one of the world's top ten brands, alongside the likes of Coca-Cola and McDonald's, times are changing and Adidas is challenging Nike's dominance. The self-imposed goal of Nike today is to capture a greater share of the international sneaker and sports apparel markets. To do so, according to Nike CEO Philip Knight, will require one thing: establishing a greater presence in the world's largest sport, European football (soccer in the United States). Nike's efforts to unseat Germany's dominant Adidas AG have included Knight's $200 million purchase of the Brazilian national team. More recently the company launched a global events marketing division to showcase its athletes around the world. But the road ahead will not be easy. When Nike and Adidas competed for sponsorship of the All Blacks (currently the best rugby team in the world), the New Zealand Rugby Football Union chose Adidas—an indication of the edge that globally-oriented companies will have over their more nationalistic counterparts in culture Next.

Intensified competition among sporting goods retailers and

manufacturers is far from the only major story in sports today. Around the globe, technologies are redefining how and where games are played—and watched. The following highlights some of the primary trends taking place in sports.

- NEXT: ATHLETE OF THE MILLENNIUM: SWIFTER, HIGHER, STRONGER

In recent history, the breaking of sports records seems as dependent upon advances in equipment as upon improved physical conditioning. In the pole vault, for instance, the world record edged up a mere two inches between 1942 and 1960, hovering around sixteen feet. But with the replacement of rigid poles by aluminum, fiberglass and graphite composites in 1963, the record increased by two feet in three years and now stands at twenty feet, 1.75 inches. The latest technological advance to hold similar promise is the Superbike II, an ultrathin bicycle with a solid (not spoked) rear wheel that could shave several seconds off racing times. But every little advantage helps: In the 1996 Atlanta Summer Olympics, the American swim team wore synthetic suits that promised a lower drag than even smooth skin. Tiny striations reduce the turbulence produced during forward movement, much as the winglets on an airplane convert air turbulence into smooth flow.

Modern sports scientists also are mapping the human body's limits in an attempt to understand where improvement is still possible. At the United States Olympic Training Center, the swim team reaps the full benefit of these efforts: Swimmers are towed through the pool so they can determine where the drag on their body is greatest and then modify their technique to reduce that drag. The transparent bottom and sides of "The Flume"—a water treadmill that pumps sixty thousand gallons of water through a specially designed pool—make it possible for cameras to record a swimmer's every stroke. Data are then fed into a computer that calculates fluid force equations, with the result being a stick figure of the swimmer with vectors representing lift and drag. An added bonus: The Flume is housed in a hyperbaric chamber, thereby enabling swimmers to train at any "altitude."

And don't think the mental aspect of athletics is being ignored.

The zone. Flow. Harmony. The Zen moment. Whatever you call that optimal meld between mind and matter, it's no longer being left to chance among athletes. In countries around the world, almost every sport now consults psychologists to help athletes integrate mental focus with physical ability. Visualization, self-hypnosis, even tapes of simulated competitions with the voices of Olympic announcers all hone the mind-body link.

Sadly, the lengths to which athletes are willing to go to improve their natural abilities are perhaps best illustrated by the continued widespread abuse of expensive and dangerous performance-enhancing drugs. To detect abuse of steroids and other banned drugs, the International Olympic Committee designed a $3 million-plus testing program for the Atlanta Games, complete with the most sensitive mass spectrometer ever used in competition. Despite this effort, certain drugs might continue to defy detection. Two examples, as reported by *Newsweek*: Human growth hormone (hGH), a natural substance that fosters growth and muscle development in childhood and adolescence, is produced through genetic engineering. Despite astronomical costs (a one-year supply runs $20,000) and no evidence that the hormone improves athletic performance in adults, the black market for hGH is said to be booming. An international effort is under way to develop an effective screen in advance of the Sydney 2000 Games. Administered just before an event, another drug, called EPO (a synthetic version of the hormone erythropoietin), speeds the body's production of red blood cells to five to ten times the normal rate. The upside: More red blood cells in circulation let the body carry and burn more oxygen, resulting in a quick burst of energy. The downside: That same infusion of red cells can make your blood so thick that the heart stops in the heat of competition. Reportedly, twenty-four heart attack deaths have been caused by EPO. EPO recently caused a scandal at the Tour de France, when five cyclists and team officials were placed under investigation for using or helping riders to use it.

• NEXT: IT'S A WOMAN THING

On and off the playing field, girls and women are leading more active and sporting lifestyles, and manufacturers and retailers are scrambling to secure their share of the market. (According to Women's Sports Marketing Group in Massachusetts, one in three American women plays some kind of sport today, up from one in twenty-seven in the 1970s. Women also buy more than half of all merchandise sold at many sporting goods chains, including purchases for family members and others.)

The Women's Sports Foundation sponsors the We're Going to Win You Over! tour, which takes high profile female athletes to schools around the country to gain support for girls' sports. The tour, whose spokeswoman is Cheryl Miller, a coach in the Women's National Basketball Association (WNBA), also enlists Kristine Lilly, a gold medalist in soccer, and Liz Masakayan, a professional beach volleyball player.

Nike's push into the women's market includes its highly touted If You Let Me Play campaign and charter sponsorship of the WNBA. In addition, Nike was sole sponsor of the first two editions of a special girls' insert in *Sports Illustrated for Kids*. The sixteen-page editorial inserts, titled "Girls and Sports Extra," featured supplemental coverage of women's sports and female athletes. Finally, controversy raged over Nike's creation of a fictional women's high school team for their advertising campaign. (Nike suggests that the creation had nothing to do with fashioning a "mediable" team but rather was a pragmatic response to the understanding that amateur teams would lose their status if featured in an advertising program).

Sporting goods manufacturers are responding to this market surge by designing equipment specifically for the female figure. Women, for instance, have a lower center of gravity than do men, less upper-body and hand strength, smaller hands and feet and calves that extend farther down the leg than do men's. Spalding has brought out a line of fast-pitch softball gloves featuring narrower hand openings and fingers. The company also produces shorter-than-standard golf clubs with smaller grips, as well as smaller and lighter golf balls. Rawling has developed a helmet for softball players with a hole to pull a ponytail through. Louisville Slugger has developed lightweight bats for women. Rifle manufacturer Browning has come out with a twelve-gauge shotgun that weighs several ounces less than the men's version and has a stock that configures better to a woman's figure and hand. And Eddie Bauer, REI, and others are selling sleeping bags for women that are shorter than men's.

On the fly-fishing front, Robert Redford's 1992 film *A River Runs Through It* has been credited with spurring women's interest in the sport. Orvis, the oldest mail-order catalog in the United States, has introduced "Orvis for Women by Women," a line of waders, vests and hats designed by leading female fly-fishers.

• NEXT: NEW SPORTING ALTERNATIVES

Snowboarding is one of the strongest trends in today's sporting goods industry, having captured youth across Europe, North America and Japan. Worldwide, participation in snowboarding is growing at a rate of more than 30 percent annually, with snowboards and gear generating estimated wholesale revenues of more than $700 million.

According to a report in *Business Week*, the snowboarding craze is pitting small American companies against old-line European ski manufacturers such as Salomon and Volkl, both of which are experiencing flat or declining sales. In an effort to compete, European ski manufacturers are producing flashy snowboards under other names. Finland's Amer Group, for example, has been producing snowboards under the Oxygen label, while Volkl manufactures snowboards for the American brands Sims and Santa Cruz. A key factor that differentiates snowboarding from the ski industry is that approximately a third of snowboarding sales come from accessories such as grungewear and funky goggles. The snowboard company Ride even markets a line of condoms called Safe Ride.

Other extreme sports—including rock-climbing, paragliding, bungee-jumping, and heliskiing—also continue to grow in popularity among teens and young adults worldwide. The cable TV channel ESPN2 is devoted to such sports. In the United States, skateboarding and golf have become the biggest growth sports in recent years. There are today about 6.3 million skateboarders and 26.2 million golfers. Mountain biking has also become very popular. Again, Nike, in its ever-hip marketing quest, sought to bond with the extreme audience through a popular campaign that imagined the sensations associated with extreme performers being translated to more conventional sports.

- NEXT: STILL GOING . . .

The world's baby-boomers might be aging, but don't expect them to settle into rocking chairs anytime soon. The only concession many seniors are making to age is a move to less vigorous sports. Among the trends to expect in coming years, according to *American Demographics*:

- Safer Sports: Catering to people whose mindsets are somewhat younger than their bodies, savvy businesses are creating safer alternatives to the most dangerous sports. For example, in a new twist on climbing walls, an organization in Colorado recently opened the world's first ice-climbing park. It allows climbers of all ages to participate in this wintertime version of rock-climbing, but without dangers such as unstable ice.
- Grand Experiences: Kathie Davis, executive director of IDEA, an organization for fitness professionals, reports a surge in sports-specific training as middle-aged boomers apply their goal-oriented sensibilities to outdoor recreation. As boomers grow older, we can expect increased demand for activities that lead to a "grand experience," whether it be completion of an Ironman competition or the spotting of a bald eagle during a bird-watching hike.
- Spa Sports: As aging bodies lose their physical prowess, feeling good will become an increasingly important goal. From massages and steam baths to yoga and t'ai chi, we'll see a rise in the softer side of recreation.
- Companionship Clubs: By 2010, when the oldest boomers are age sixty-four, almost half of elderly homeowners in America will live alone, according to projections from *American Demographics*. One result might be increased membership in recreational clubs.

- NEXT: JUST WEAR IT

For many consumers, looking like an athlete is almost as good as being one. Companies are raking in money from casual clothing (at both ends of the price spectrum) that let even the most devoted couch potatoes feel sporty and active. High-end technical sports apparel has become a hot product. Materials such as Polartec, a polyester woven fabric used to make fleece, and Gore-Tex, a Teflonlike waterproof material, are being used in much of this winter apparel. Polartec, which started in 1984, topped $400 million in revenues last year. Gore-Tex made $100 million. Polartec recently funded a tie-in promotion with the IMAX movie *Everest*. The movie was a huge hit, grossing $2.4 million in two-and-a-half weeks while showing on only nineteen screens around the country.

Although soccer is not yet as popular in America as it is in the rest of the world, it is beginning to gain ground. The Sporting Goods Manufacturers Association estimates that participation in the sport has increased eleven percent to 18.2 million since 1993. In 1997, Nike made a ten-year deal with U.S. Soccer and spent $40 million on promotions for the 1998 World Cup to sell soccer stars to kids. Not surprising, considering that wholesale sales of soccer equipment was approximately $208 million last year.

Designer gear is happening all over the world. Upscale designers hoping to get a piece of the growing sports market are coming out with their own lines of athletic footwear. Among them are Ralph Lauren's Polo Sport, Tommy Hilfiger and Donna Karan. As reported in *Advertising Age*, Salomon Bros. predicts that the top six designer brands will account for seven percent of an $8.5 billion industry by the year 2000.

As in other industries, catalog sales are a growing category in the sporting goods market. Niche catalogs that have sprung up in the past few years include *Soccer Madness* and *Title 9 Sports*, a catalog specializing in women's athletic apparel. In addition, sporting goods catalogs are offering things such as branded seminars and travel adventures. L.L. Bean, for example, offers Outdoor Discovery Schools, which feature family-oriented skiing, canoeing and kayaking trips. Eddie Bauer offers guided trips to exotic locations around the world.

• NEXT: PLAYING IT SAFE(R)

No matter where in the world you live, chances are you're aware of a sports scandal. Recent scandals involving figures such as boxer Mike Tyson, Olympic figure skater Tonya Harding, and ex-football legend O. J. Simpson have made it increasingly risky for companies to tie their fortunes (and reputations) to celebrity athlete spokespersons/endorsers. Although top-of-the-line athletes such as basketball star Michael Jordan and golfing sensation Tiger Woods will continue to rake in endorsement dollars, companies already appear more cautious about the process. Kodak, for example, purportedly conducted extensive consumer research before signing the famously flamboyant basketball star Dennis Rodman to its roster of endorsers. The company went on to regret its decision in late 1996, when it found itself fielding calls from irate consumers offended by Rodman's outburst of profanity during a live postgame TV interview. Nonetheless, American advertisers continue to value the renegade images projected by stars such as Rodman, Dallas Cowboy Deion Sanders, and tennis ace Andre Agassi. Rodman, for example, currently earns approximately $10 million a year in endorsement contracts.

Outside the United States, athletes are more likely to be admired for their athletic prowess and good works than for their on- and off-court bad-boy antics. Going forward—in what we believe is an extension of our communal search for security—we'll see more and more marketers linking up with bona fide heroes, people who are using their celebrity for the common good. In Brazil, the most admired celebrities these days aren't flashy movie stars or singers, but athletes like Reynaldo who have risen from poverty to fame and fortune and who are using their money and prestige to help those at the bottom of the economic ladder. Tennis player Arthur Ashe, who died in 1993, had the new U.S. Open stadium named in his honor; Ashe helped create the National Junior Tennis League and Safe Passage Foundation. In a recent Gallup Poll, Michael Jordan was ranked ninth in a survey of the "most admired people living in the world today."

WHAT'S NEXT?

Sport/entertainment tie-ins: With sports continuing to be a cash cow, we'll be seeing all sorts of industries negotiating to get a piece of the action in the years ahead. One certainty is increased cross-licensing between sports leagues and entertainment companies. Warner Bros. (which has trademarked the phrase "Sports is entertainment") licensed its Looney Tunes characters with the National Football League in 1993, a move that has since been imitated in other sports by entertainment companies such as Disney and Marvel Entertainment. Disney's venture into the world of sports has been the most dramatic. In addition to producing Mickey Mouse basketballs and Donald Duck golf balls, the company now owns two teams (the Anaheim Angels and Mighty Ducks), Walt Disney World Sports Complex, and sports channel ESPN.

Virtual spectators: Fans unable to get to major games will increasingly have an opportunity to attend virtually, via Web sites that feature live camera feeds, commentary, continually updated statistics and discussion forums. The Olympic Games in Nagano, Japan, although generally panned as a TV event, were well covered by IBM's official Olympic Web site as well as by subdomains created by and for CBS. When Japan took the gold in ski-jumping, IBM's site registered 98,226 hits a minute; the hit rate for the entire Atlanta Games was surpassed in a day. To track Sydney's virtual progress, visit www.sydney.olympic.org.

Move over, snowboarding: As snowboarding becomes established, widespread, and perhaps even a tad demodé, a couple of newcomers are vying for honors as alternative winter sports. Skiboards are short, bi-directional skis that have points at both ends, thereby allowing skiers to jump forward and backward and perform some impressive stunts. Snowskating, a derivative of inline skating, is being promoted by Kent Rodriquez, inventor and sole manufacturer of snowskates and chairman and CEO of Sled Dogs Company. "We appeal directly to the inline skater," he says. "We have the potential to reach twenty-two million inline skaters who don't have a winter sport yet."

Electric bikes: Entrepreneurs are exploring the market potential of electric bikes, which can be pedaled like normal bikes or powered by unobtrusive, battery-driven motors. Although the bikes must be recharged every fifteen to twenty miles, they plug into normal electrical sockets. Prices typically range from $900 to $1,500. Two prospective markets: middle-aged and elderly cyclists, who generally love the exercise but loathe the hills, and urban commuters. Americans have purchased five thousand electric bikes since the product debuted in 1993, but sales are much higher abroad. The bikes are particularly popular in Japan, where parking spots are scarce.

Tomorrow's workout: Already new technologies are changing the face of health and fitness clubs around the world. One example: In an effort to keep their customers coming back for more, some gyms and health clubs have turned to FitLinxx, a company that uses technology to customize workout routines. The FitLinxx Training Partner records individuals' routines on different types of exercise equipment. Users enter a personal identification number at each workstation, which then provides a record of number of repetitions, seat settings and weight amounts. At each visit, users are also prompted to input information regarding lifestyle changes and indicate whether they are bored with their current routine; FitLinxx adapts workouts based on those responses. The results have been promising, with FitLinxx customers reporting dramatically increased membership-retention rates.

Boomer boo-boos: Increased participation in sports, particularly among aging baby-boomers, is proving a boon for the sports medicine industry, with sales of athletic tape and supports, bandages, and hot and cold wraps up across the board. Expect many product innovations in this area over the course of the next few years. One such product, introduced recently, is BIOflex, a neoprene biomagnetic support designed to speed recovery of muscle- and joint-related pain and injury. The product uses magnets to widen blood vessels, thereby allowing more blood to flow to the damaged area.

Walking, talking billboards: Expect to see more high-profile sports figures, including coaches, accept sponsorships from fashion designers. Olympic gold medal figure skater Tara Lipinski is a spokesperson for DKNY Kids. Donna Karan, the official outfitter for the 1998 U.S. Olympic and world figure skating teams, provided the official team warmups and other active wear for 250 skaters, coaches, and officials in the United States Figure Skating Association.

Soccer versus the NBA: Basketball's ascension to the world's favorite sport was tested when World Cup soccer hogged broadcasting schedules for World Cup 1998. The NBA's savvy marketing has made B-ball the cult sport among world youth, according to a recent survey of fifteen to eighteen-year-olds in forty-one countries. But soccer had its chance to win new fans with the France '98 World Cup tournament and succeeded, many would argue, magnificently.

Even before the World Cup, the popularity of soccer was on the rise in America. According to the Soccer Industry Council of America, eighteen million people played the game at least once in 1997. The number of truly dedicated players rose from 7.7 million to 8.5 million, and about three million kids under nineteen are playing the sport now.

There's no doubt that France '98 had hundreds of millions of six-packers lashed to their couches. But beyond that, there are three big questions waiting for answers: First, will soccer throw up any new stars as marketable as the NBA's finest? Second, will soccer's more parochial Old World barons get wise to the marketing strategy of the NBA and the threat it poses? And finally, which will prove to have more long-term teen appeal—ninety minutes with no guarantee of any goals, or forty-eight minutes of high-scoring, high-fiving action?

Globalizing games and gear: The National Football League has created an international division to market its brand of football outside America. NFL International is conducting research in Canada, Europe, Japan and Mexico to determine how best to educate consumers worldwide about American-style football. Plans for Europe include producing television packages of game highlights that contain brief, entertaining segments about the game and its rules, and creating football festivals that combine music, interactive games and football. And with Yankee football come boutiques that sell Yankee football gear, from jerseys with logos, to the actual playing "stuff"—pads, mouthguards, etc., etc. Watch for these products to become easily accesible, via the ultimate mall, the Web.

Sports to watch: Analysts predict that the most popular sports among American kids in 2006 will be basketball (including girls' basketball, spurred on by the recent debut of two American women's professional basketball leagues), ice hockey and figure skating, and golf (currently one golf course is being opened every day in the United States, and companies already are producing merchandise for junior golfers). Perhaps a real irony is that golf, especially golf on TV, is hardly an enjoyable sport to watch; Marian, for one, argues it's like watching a leaky faucet—yes, that exciting.

CHAPTER 14:

The Future
of Offices

"*W*HAT LEADERS MUST LEARN TO DO IS develop a social architecture that encourages incredibly bright people, most of whom have big egos, to work together successfully and to deploy their own creativity," wrote Warren Bennis in "Becoming a Leader of Leaders," a chapter he wrote in *Rethinking the Future* (Addison-Wesley, 1997), of which he is one of the editors. We, the authors of *Next*, have had the great luxury of working in office environments that encourage just such creativity.

Although we've embarked upon new adventures within the advertising industry, we have our roots within Chiat/Day, a virtual office environment—the first and (thus far) the only in our business, at least one involving so many hundreds of human worklives. Our virtuality began as an extreme experiment, one that bordered on revolutionary change and would ideally enable each of us to reinvent ourselves and our careers. As you read our story, we caution you that any change of this magnitude evokes a broad variety of personal reactions and consequences. It is necessary to continually reassess your goals and progress and to work to eliminate the bugs that are an inevitable side effect of any change.

Did our personal experiment with virtuality pay off? Yes. The simple truth is, when we were the Department of the Future, it simply would not have been possible for seven people (that's how many of us worked on our original Dutch team, a group that stayed together for nearly two years) to have provided a comparable level of service to our parent company on a daily basis if it were not for our virtual workstyle. The fact that the seven of us lived in three time zones meant that for an average of twenty hours a day, at least one member of our unit was reading, thinking, processing information, and generating strategies that were then passed along to colleagues in the next time zone.

As president of Chiat/Day New York, Ira had an opportunity in 1994 to be a part of an important milestone in its history. He was charged with ensuring the agency's smooth transition to a "virtual" office. In his words:

> As I write this from a cottage in Bellagio, Italy, and transmit it to Marian in Evian, France and to Ann in Tampa, Florida, I can't help but be aware of the extent to which our work environment has changed in a few short years. In late 1993 Jay Chiat outlined for me a vision he said had come to him, fully formed, as he skied down Telluride Mountain in Colorado. The essence of his vision was of an organization in which members were not constrained by physical or hierarchical restrictions, where each person would have access to the tools needed to create the environment in which he or she could work best.
>
> Having enjoyed the unique advantage of being a Macintosh beta site, the idea of using computers as a core business and communications tool was not new to us. Nor was the idea that walls and doors were barriers to the free flow of ideas. Jay had removed these barriers years ago, creating open spaces in which each employee maintained his or her own "workspace," complete with desk, Macintosh computer, file cabinet, etc. Approximately 70 percent of our physical plant was taken up by these personal workstations; the remaining 30 percent was collaborative (mainly conference rooms).
>
> In conducting an audit of space utilization, we found that at any given time some 50 percent of employees' private spaces were empty, while meeting spaces were always 100 percent occupied, often with queues for access. On any given day, some staff members were on vacation or sick; others were in meetings, at clients' offices, in production studios and so on. At no time was everyone at their desks.
>
> Our next step was to conduct a "storage audit"—figuring out what was in those endless rows of filing cabinets and other storage

units. Some of the "stuff" we found was legitimate "intelligence"—data related to client business. In many cases, though, we found that this information existed in multiple hard copies and—even more distressing—was not always shared with relevant staffers. We also found such items as last year's bad bottle of wine (proffered as a Christmas gift by a media supplier), scores of old newspapers, remains of meals long past their prime and so on.

In sum, even with an advantageous rental rate in our downtown location (versus Madison Avenue—the traditional, pricey home of the advertising industry in the United States), we were funding some very expensive closets!

Jay's vision was to restructure the office in a single-step change. Our space was to be physically organized the same way we were—by client team. Fifty percent of the office would be converted into a "project room"—a permanent facility in which current client activity and core team interactions would take place. An additional 20 percent of our space would be devoted to "temporary" project rooms, places in which to mount new-business pitches, work on campaigns, and hold private conversations. These temporary rooms could be booked electronically (for anywhere from ten minutes to ten weeks or more), so they would be available to function as private offices as needed.

Critical to this concept was the reorganization of information storage and retrieval. All paper documents were transferred to electronic files and stored on a central file server. Once there, they would be password accessible by every staffer, either through the in-office network or via modem-facilitated remote access. Beyond liberating "file space," this system ensured universal access to the agency's collective intelligence, allowing staffers to be productive anywhere, anytime.

What we had, then, was a fair exchange. Our staff members were asked to give up their private space in exchange for the freedom to work where they liked. As most of the staffers were young (median age twenty-four), we found the best model was the university. Groups came together for collaboration (in the manner of a lecture or seminar) and left with an assignment and a due date. No one told them how to do the work, how to schedule, where the resources were. Their responsibility was to deliver their best effort, on time. If you did well, you succeeded; if not, you failed. And that applied at all levels of the agency.

We even borrowed the idea of the "student union," creating a place in which staffers could meet, greet, and interact. This is also where each staffer's personal locker is located. It was interesting to watch the weekly paper dump, as people came to trust the virtual system and progressively gave up the security of the paper they had smuggled from the uptown office.

Our last step was to deal with all those phones that used to ring off the hook in unoccupied workstations. We simply cut the cords. Rolm provided a cordless PBX phone system that allowed portable telephony throughout the thirty-thousand-square-foot physical plant.

The result? In addition to cutting back our space requirements by nearly two-thirds, the transition to virtual infused the agency with a powerful rush of energy as employees became more adept at using technological tools to make their working hours more productive.

In the past couple of years, we've watched as others in our business and other industries have begun to adapt and adopt some of the fundamentals of Jay Chiat's vision. In that time, we've grown increasingly confident that virtuality will permanently alter the workplaces—and working styles—of the future.

A NEW WAY TO WORK

Think of the enormous changes that have taken place in the workplace in the past fifteen years. When Marian entered the workforce after college in the mid-80s, the use of fax machines was just becoming widespread, as they slowly replaced telex machines in America and abroad. Those businesses that relied on computers had them connected to an enormous mainframe, carefully guarded in a climate-controlled room. Secretaries and other assistants typed letters on IBM Selectrics, and important documents were hand-delivered by messenger.

Fifteen years later, even home offices are equipped with computers and fax machines. Typewriters are relics. Business documents are zapped practically instantaneously from office to office and country to country via modem. Personal couriers have largely been replaced by FedEx and DHL and other courier companies that "absolutely, positively" guarantee delivery overnight. And how many of us can't seem to make it across town these days without making a business call or two on our cellular phones?

As mentioned above, we don't just talk about virtuality—we have lived it. Ann O'Reilly and Christy Lane Plummer were Young & Rubicam's first virtual staff members. As senior members of Y&R's Brand Futures Group, they conducted all of their work virtually. Today Ann communicates with other members of the department through e-mail and instant electronic messages (and, much less often, by fax or phone). Until Ann and Christy flew to New York to meet with their new employers (mostly to convince Y&R that they really did exist), they hadn't seen Marian in years. And it was the first and only time Ann and Christy had met face to face and that either of them had met Ira.

To what extent will virtuality be embraced by other offices and industries in the years to come? We don't see a time—at least in the next few decades—when face to face contact will be eliminated. After all, most of us still place some credence in the value of a hand-shake and in building relationships over lunch or dinner as well as in a conference room. We do expect, however, to see a dramatic increase in the amount of business communication conducted virtu-ally, whether in intranet conference rooms or online chatrooms or via videophone.

Who's You?

The fact that our colleagues and co-authors, Ann and Christy, existed largely in the shadows has led to some interesting exchanges with clients. Following a presentation to Danish toy executives (regarding an American product launch), Ira and Marian referred to our "brilliant American researchers." One client responded, "You say your best people are in the States? That's excellent. When can we get them on our account?" We then had to spend the next five minutes explaining that these two members of our staff not only were already on the account but had actually handled all of the new-product testing and had generated many of the subsequent strategic recommendations. The two of us got used to fielding questions about our "imaginary" American employees.

And our Amsterdam-based team was equally curious about our faceless Americans. By means of introduction, our Dutch-Canadian researcher trainee, Friso Westenberg, sent digital pictures of the Amsterdam staff to Christy and Ann. A group e-mail sent in response ended with this postscript from Ann: "Thanks for the digital pics! None of you guys looks at ALL the way I imagined. Are you sure you didn't just go to the office next door and take random shots? :-)" And so it goes in the virtual world.

The move toward virtuality is the most dramatic example of changes in the workspace, but there are plenty of other, more subtle shifts:

• NEXT: ALTERNATIVE WORKSTYLES

Although many corporations would deny a trend toward virtuality, the reality is that they're already heading in that direction.

Intranet Explosion: Across North American and Europe, more and more companies are creating "intranets," internal company networks based on the same technology as the global Internet. Cordoned off from the public Internet via software programs known as "fire walls," intranets allow employee access while blocking (in theory at least) unauthorized users. Sample uses include data retrieval from networked computers, company services inquiries, and interoffice e-mail. Some analysts anticipate that the next big leap will be the creation of virtual corporations, enabling companies to reduce both physical plant and paper transactions.

Hundreds of companies, including AT&T, Levi Strauss and 3M, are making use of intranets. Pharmaceutical giant Eli Lilly, for example, has created an intranet that links approximately sixteen thousand workers—almost two-thirds of the company's worldwide staff. At Ford Motor Company, an intranet that links design centers in Asia, Europe and the United States helped engineers craft the latest Taurus. Fully 85 percent of American corporations that responded to a study by Cognitive Communications are implementing, piloting or planning an intranet; survey respondents included 162 Fortune 500 companies, together with some privately held corporations.

A recent study by Ernst & Young involving four hundred American executives showed that 72 percent of them were either building or planning to build an intranet site. Fifty-one percent believed that the intranet was the most important tool for building corporate knowledge. *Marketing Tools* discovered that there are more than twenty million employees on more than 200,000 network servers with intranet access. Intranet servers will outpace Internet servers four to one by the end of the century. The Business Research Group says that the market for network and systems management applications will reach $19.4 billion by the year 2000.

Telecommuting: Sometimes called teleworking or homeworking, telecommuting already is common in the United States and is being adopted in Europe too. According to the "Olsten Forum on Managing Workplace Technology" (www.olsten.com), 51 percent of North American companies now permit employees to telecommute through pilot and ongoing programs, with 74 percent expecting their use of telecommuting to increase this year. Telecommuters might work for a local company (perhaps splitting their time between the office and home), as freelancers or consultants, or even as employees of a company on the other side of the globe. According to market researcher Link Resources, 37 million American households—38 percent of the total—contain at least one person doing income-generating work at home. The fastest-growing segment of the telecommuting population (currently standing at 8.4 million) is individuals employed by corporations who work at home full or part time.

An estimated thirty to forty million Americans telecommute, to the benefit of themselves and the companies for which they work. AT&T and IBM are among the most prominent corporations to have instituted this practice. And the results have been good. AT&T estimates that it has saved $550 million since implementing telecommuting in 1991, and IBM is saving $100 million per year in its North American operation alone. In surveying employees in one of its divisions, IBM found that 87 percent believe their productivity and effectiveness have increased dramatically since they began telecommuting.

Hot desking and hotelling: "Hot desking" (having fewer desks than workers) is also becoming increasingly common around the world. Cisco Systems began implementing the concept of hot-desking in their offices worldwide. Using their New York office as a test facility, it was calculated that the company would save $7 million over a five-year lease. The program was implemented when it was discovered that employees were using their cubicles only 30 percent of the day. Secretaries and managers have kept their permanent offices and cubicles.

In a variation of hot-desking, some companies have adopted the practice of "hotelling." At each office, a concierge assigns desks on an as-needed basis. For most workdays, though, an employee's workspace consists of a state-of-the-art computer equipped with voice mail and remote access to computers, telephones. It's all about "connectivity."

Ernst & Young has implemented hotelling in its New York and Chicago offices, thereby cutting its physical plant by 25 percent. The offices now maintain one desk for every three workers. According to *Fortune* magazine, this accounting–consultancy firm expects to save $40 million annually once all of its offices are similarly reconfigured.

Flexible workdays: Among other signs of increased flexibility in the workplace is the growth of employee flex time, job sharing and alternative schedules (40-hour, four-day workweeks, for example). According to the U.S. Department of Labor, approximately 22 percent of professionals, managers, and administrative employees in the America have the option of varying their hours. And more companies are giving employees a set number of paid days off each year that they may schedule as they see fit (rather than the company dictating which holidays they'll have off). There's also a movement under way to make comp time (or earned time off) an alternative to overtime pay.

• NEXT: OFFICE OF THE FUTURE TAKES SHAPE

Expect to see significant changes in office design as the office of the future takes shape. Physical-plant changes are expected to encourage teamwork at the expense of privacy, with facilities such as centralized technology units, kitchens, lounges, and service centers featuring amenities such as dry-cleaning drop-off and pickup, takeout food (for meals at the office or at home), and day-care centers. Industry experts at the International Association of Corporate Real Estate Executives symposium in Tampa, Florida, agreed that the office of the future will have reduced space per employee (with workspaces made more efficient by technology) and will also be designed with more attention to the workers' day-to-day environment. Skylights, windows that open, and improved ventilation systems are some of the features expected to be incorporated in the next decade.

Also undergoing change will be office furniture, which will become both more mobile and more flexible. One example: Steelcase Inc.'s Personal Harbors. Costing $7,000 apiece, Personal Harbors are small, cylindrical booths with a door that can be closed. The interior space is large enough to hold a flat work surface, computer setup, phones, a file drawer and other standard desk items. There's also a whiteboard and built-in CD player. Unlike the ubiquitous cubicles of today, Personal Harbors offer both privacy and the ability to communicate with coworkers: The harbors are grouped around a large puzzlelike table that can be broken into several pieces. When harbor doors are open, employees can move in and out of the group space to talk to colleagues, participate in meetings or just listen in.

According to Special Interest Group on Computer-Human Interaction (SIGCHI), an estimated 80 percent of all salaried workers will work at video display terminals by the year 2000. "Cognitive ergonomics" will be the next big thing in office design. Based on the theory that there's a direct relationship between where you work and how you think, office space will be designed to maximize communication, creativity, and interaction.

• NEXT: WORKING ANYWHERE, ANYTIME

One of the great advantages (and disadvantages) of new technologies is that they have made the office portable. No longer tied to his or her desk, today's executive can conduct business at a client's office, in a hotel, on a plane—anywhere his or her laptop computer and modem can travel. This office-in-a-bag spells increased convenience, but also makes it even easier for work to intrude on personal life.

One result of new technologies is a growing population of "road warriors," the moniker bestowed by the travel industry on the growing number of business travelers who spend more time on the road than in the office—70, 90, even 100-plus days per year. This new class of superfrequent traveler represents the top one percent of people who travel for business each year. Still talked about at Hilton Hotels is the management consultant who stayed at the chain 330 nights in 1993—a record. (In 1994, Hilton estimated that the ten thousand customers who represent the top 1 percent of their frequent-customer program account for approximately 15 percent of all revenues from these customers, or approximately $60 million.) Perks accorded these road warriors by airlines and hotels include upgrades, admission to private lounges and housing on exclusive floors with around-the-clock snacks, and special attendants. The very best customers have even been awarded new cars, golf trips to Scotland, and tickets to the Grammy and Academy Awards shows.

In contrast to the home-oriented telecommuter, the road warrior takes advantage of new technologies to meet business obligations in other cities, other countries, and in the airspace between. The fact is, the technological gadgetry that made the home office a reality (and that was supposed to eliminate bothersome business travel) has had a freeing effect on personnel who were all but chained to their desks a decade ago. They now have the flexibility to go where business requires, packing the office in their bags much as they would have that reliable blue suit years before.

Rather than considering personal contact an old-fashioned formality, many futurists see increased travel as a sign that such contact is becoming more important. "[Road warriors] are the leading indicators of what's in store for the rest of us," says Paul Saffo, a director of the Institute for the Future, a California-based research foundation.

• Next: Never Out of Touch

Perhaps more than any other industry, telecommunications is in the midst of sweeping change. Telephone products are becoming more personal and more pervasive, as consumers come to expect 24/7 access to anyone, anywhere.

About a third of American adults are cellular/PCS phone users, and this instant connectivity has become downright cheap—about ten cents a minute—so that average usage has climbed to eighty-nine minutes per user per month this year, according to International Data Corporation. The majority of cellular/PCS calls are still made from the car, although an obvious Next is that cellular/PCS subscribers will use their mobile connections to replace landline service, especially between 8 A.M. and 5 P.M., when more than half of all cellular/PCS calls are made.

Whereas just a few years ago we relied on the telephone and mail service to keep in touch with colleagues and family, today we expect instantaneous communication and data exchange via cell phones, pagers and the Internet. Companies are scrambling to meet the demand for faster, more convenient, and more global methods of communication. NetworkMCI Contact fulfills the vision of a "one number world," in which a single phone number will "follow and find" subscribers wherever they are—if they want to be found. The system allows a computer to send and receive faxes, pages and e-mail; phone calls can be routed to the computer and digitized so a user can play them back. The service costs $70 a month.

GSM, a British telecommnications company, has introduced roaming capabilities for its pagers that enable users to receive pages while visiting France, Germany, Switzerland, Italy and the Netherlands. Microsoft's Bill Gates is formulating a plan to launch 288 low-earth-orbit satellites that would provide Internet access to any location on earth by 2002. The satellites would send data at sixty-four megabits/second downstream and two megabits/second upstream. A service from Germany's Bertelsmann AG will enable users to make phone calls, hold videoconferences, do online banking and exchange e-mail via the Internet. Customers who don't own a PC and modem will be able to use a specially designed telephone with a video screen and keyboard.

Our growing reliance on the Internet for both business and personal use has created a growth category for businesses that can provide Internet access in nontraditional locations.

AT&T is targeting the business traveler, having signed a deal with Hilton Hotels to provide free WorldNet Internet access software to Hilton guests in Chicago, New York, Los Angeles, and Washington, DC.

To provide Internet access for people on the go, Ohio's Diebold Inc. has created an ATM that allows bank customers to access the Internet for both banking and nonbanking information. Australia's WebPoint has already placed some kiosks, but plans to have five thousand Internet kiosks worldwide by the year 2000; twenty thousand users currently take advantage of the kiosks, which cost $1.34 per ten minutes.

In terms of making personal lives a little easier, home appliances will be equipped with microchips capable of accessing the Internet and downloading software to fix operational problems on their own. Smart buildings of the future will use fiber optics or wireless systems to carry as many as a hundred channels from a direct broadcast satellite, says Francis Friedman, president of Time & Place Strategies, a consulting firm in New York. Netpulse Communications has created Stairmasters and Lifecycles with built-in Web browsers, so diehards can surf the Internet or check their e-mail while unwinding from a long day. To enhance the deal, every minute online while working out earns one frequent flier mile on United or American airlines.

And a real estate company in the United Arab Emirates is building a wired mall, the first of its kind in the Middle East. According to project chair Mohammad Ali Alabbar, the complex will "bring buyers and sellers together with facilities like demonstration centers, where buyers can actually run real-life applications, and modern video conferencing to allow multimedia presentation, grouping buyers and sellers on different continents."

The authors' intelligence-gathering efforts go beyond Web surfing, "smart agents" and face-to-face and online market research. We also make an effort to work with smart folks around the world who can enrich our thinking by providing local perspectives. One, Stuart Harris, who has since joined our Brand Futures Group from an Amsterdam base, deserves our thanks for his brainfood on Asia and Western Europe, which has enhanced this book immeasurably.

We've chosen to introduce Stuart in this chapter because his career path has been a prime example of life Next:

Meet Stuart Harris: Living the Future

I started my working life just before the dawn of the Digital Age. When I took a position as a trainee journalist at the London office of the Reuters News Agency in 1979, manual typewriters, scissors, paste and telex operators were the norm. By the summer of 1980, most of the agency offices around the world had converted to computer terminals. As a correspondent in Italy in 1982 through 1984, I began hauling a "portabubble" terminal with an acoustic modem coupler that was the envy of my fellow journalists on off-base assignments. The same technology enabled me to report quickly from the floor of the London International Financial Futures Exchange in the heady Big Bang days of 1986.

Later that year, I quit my job after spotting an advertisement for a new service, e-mail, which I thought would give me an edge as a freelance translator—I would be able to work for clients in Germany, France, Italy, Spain and the Netherlands from the comfort of my London home. Unfortunately, Europe took a while to catch on to e-mail, and the only wired client I acquired lived just twenty miles away! Fortunately, he also became my biggest client.

Ten years later, I was working for the TBWA-Hakuhodo joint venture in Amsterdam when Marian and Ira swept into town and gave me a crash refresher course in cyberliving. After moving to Malaysia in 1997, my wife, Caroline, and I quickly came to rely on the Internet for news, general information, and staying in touch with family and friends. Working as a freelance collaborator on this book was a natural next step.
—*Stuart Harris, Kuala Lumpur, Malaysia (1998)*

• NEXT: INTERNET TELEPHONY

Without much fanfare, the Internet has begun to demonstrate its potential as a medium for carrying vocal data. Internet Protocol

(IP) promises to cut significantly into the revenues of traditional phone companies in the next decade. According to the International Telecommunications Union, IP telephony could eliminate the profits of American long-distance carriers by taking just 6 percent of telephone traffic. By 2002, the Internet could account for 11 percent of American and international long-distance traffic, up from 0.2 percent last year, according to IDC. Action Information Services suggested the Internet took close to $1 billion in revenues from telephone service providers in 1998 and predicts that this will rise to $3.5 billion by 2001.

As reported by *USA Today*, rates for IP are projected to be between five and 7.5 cents a minute. IP phone calls are cheaper, in part, because they are exempt from fees long-distance carriers must pay for access to the local networks, where all long-distance calls begin and end. Among the major telecom companies that are already in or have announced plans to enter the IP fray are AT&T, Deutsche Telekom, MCI, and Bell Atlantic. Companies can expect to cut their phone bills by 35 percent through IP technology, according to 3Com CEO Eric Benhamou.

• NEXT: NEW SECURITY NEEDS

Increased reliance on portable, or laptop, computers has led to a sharp increase in computer thefts. The television network MSNBC reported that 265,000 portable computers were stolen in 1996, 90 percent of which were never recovered. Safeware, an insurer of personal computers, estimated the losses to be around $1.4 billion, a 28 percent increase from 1995. And security products have been introduced, from the Master, a locking cable, to a device that produces an alarm whenever a computer is moved without its owner's approval.

Some companies have begun to warn employees to be vigilant while traveling (since airports are a prime target) and to back up files and activate passwords to protect sensitive materials lest they fall into the wrong hands.

A 1997 survey conducted by the Computer Security Institute for the FBI found that 75 percent of the companies that responded had been victimized by computer-related crime. The average loss per company was $401,600. Although such crimes are often costly, many companies do not know they have been victimized, says Scott Charney, chief of the Justice Department's section on computer crime and intellectual property. Because many companies won't report this type of theft for fear of damaging their reputations, the high-tech thieves are rarely caught.

Network security is one of the fastest-growing markets in America, according to the research firm Frost & Sullivan. The market attained more than a half-billion dollars in revenue in 1996, representing a growth rate of 217 percent over 1995. Rapid growth is expected to continue as the number of Internet and intranet commerce users expands. Internet-based e-commerce transactions and business use of the Internet and intranets are forecast to be the major drivers of the network security market.

WHAT'S NEXT?

Data dominance: Whereas today 90 percent of the world's telecommunications are "voice," digital transmission of data in the form of e-mail, fax, computer telephony and electronic commerce will grow to the point of overwhelming dominance. As noted by *Newsweek*, industry reports show that voice phone calls will account for less than 10 percent of all telecom traffic by 2002.

Number crunch: Toll-free numbers are growing at such a rapid rate in the United States that the new 888 prefix faces depletion after only two years. The volume of toll-free calls has grown from seven million in 1967 to nearly twenty billion last year.

USPS e-mail: The United States Postal Service offers official time and date postmarks so users can send certified and registered letters via e-mail.

Certified online transmissions: UPS (www.ups.com), the world's largest package distribution company, offers online document delivery via UPS Document Exchange. For critical or confidential documents, UPS OnLine Dossier utilizes encryption, digital certificates (to verify identity of sender and recipient) and third-party validation; it offers insurance for up to $100,000 in business losses. UPS OnLine Courier, for less sensitive documents, utilizes passwords and encryption. Both offer tracking and confirmation of receipt.

GTE call home: Home appliances will be equipped with microchips capable of accessing the Internet and downloading software to fix operational problems on their own.

Mobile wallets: Logica has teamed up with mobile phone operator Cellnet and Motorola to develop a "mobile wallet," a phone that can send and receive cash electronically. Customers can use the phone to pay for theater tickets, a pizza, or to transfer money between accounts, pay bills and view bank statements—perfect for today's busy road warriors.

Virtual dating: Videophone capabilities will offer a safe virtual meeting place for those who never liked kissing on the first date anyway. It means that reality and virtuality blur because the face and the voice become real. The play can be intense, but the silicon barrier survives, making it "oh, so safe."

Online utility monitoring: Utility companies will tap into businesses' electricity usage over the Web and send an instant online monthly bill. Cost-conscious customers can adjust their habits after periodically logging in to check the status of their bill.

Corporate campus: Blending of work and home will spur more corporations to create "campuses" complete with on-site child and elder care, health facilities (dentist, chiropractor, certified nurse practitioner), and personal services (dry cleaning, takeout meals).

Return of the "company town": High-tech companies will lure workers to subsidized apartments/homes/condos wired to the workplace.

CHAPTER 15:

The Future
of Work

*A*s WE USHER IN AN ERA OF GLOBAL MARKETS, automated production, and virtuality, we're not just seeing changes in the workplace, we're also seeing changes in the worker. The fact is, our transition from a nation-based Industrial Age to a global Digital Age will require new job parameters, new skills, and new approaches to how we conduct our day-to-day business—and plan our careers.

As we've already discussed, the authors and co-authors of this book have worked primarily virtually for the past several years, from home offices or on the road. We have also occasionally brought in contract workers to complete face-to-face consumer research projects or assist with specific client assignments. This blend of permanent employees and freelance help has given us the flexibility to expand our staff when needed, without taking on the expense of yearly salaries and benefits packages for a larger workforce than we need.

In an increasingly competitive world, companies no longer have the luxury of holding on to more employees than they need or workers who are not contributing fully to the bottom line— whether as a fault of their own or simply because their skills or areas of knowledge are no longer aligned with what the company needs. As a result, more and more companies are beginning to pay close attention to extending the value of their existing "human resources," recognizing that it is often far more expensive to recruit and train new workers than it is to maximize the value of the workers they already have. One of the buzzwords we've been hearing in the past couple of years is headlighting, which refers to companies taking a close look at where they want to be in the medium to long-term and determining what changes need to be made to ensure they get there. Texas Instruments has been doing some headlighting by listing, as much as a year in advance, which jobs are in jeopardy and asking those employees, "What do we need to do to broaden you to assume a new job inside or outside this company?" Workers and companies alike have come to find that if they don't spend time now preparing for the future, they might well find they have no role to play once they get there.

Today's university graduates, by and large, recognize that they cannot expect to stay with a single company for their entire career, and many have no desire to do so. Mergers, downsizing, and other broad business trends have created a work world that is far more fluid than it was for previous generations, as workers move from job to job, company to company and even industry to industry throughout their careers. The perceived decrease in company loyalty has resulted in employees who are far more inclined to take responsibility for their own success rather than pin their hopes on the achievements of any one organization. Those workers best positioned to succeed in the coming decades will be those who recognize that they must continually upgrade their skills and work to maintain or extend their competitive edge, for there is no guarantee that the organization they work for today will need their current skill set tomorrow.

In *Job Shift: How to Prosper in a Workplace Without Jobs* (Addison-Wesley, 1995), transition consultant Dr. William Bridges mapped out a vision of a work world in which just about all employees are temporary or contract workers. He believes that in coming years people will no longer *have* jobs, they'll simply *do* jobs. In essence, workers will build and run their own companies, packaging and selling their expertise at certain tasks. Ideally,

Bridges says, these workers will be paid by the task and get a slice of the profits. Among other benefits, "dejobbing," as Bridges terms it, will help companies avoid the increasing burden of health care and other benefits.

What is the attitude of young people about to enter today's business world? Overall, they appear optimistic, and they are evincing a strong desire to attain a balanced lifestyle and personal growth, as opposed to being willing to sacrifice all for a top salary or prestigious position. In 1997 Coopers & Lybrand (one of the biggest professional services companies—which began as a public accounting firm) released the results of a survey conducted among more than twelve hundred business students from thirty of the world's leading universities in ten countries: Australia, Canada, France, Germany, Japan, South Africa, South Korea, the Netherlands, the United Kingdom and the United States. The study found that "achieving a balanced lifestyle [and] having a rewarding life outside work" was among the top three career goals of 45 percent of respondents. This goal was followed by "building a sound financial base" (cited by 33 percent of respondents) and "having a position where I can work and travel internationally" (28 percent).

Nicholas G. Moore, chairman of Coopers & Lybrand, commented: "Apart from some minor cultural and geographical differences, we found that students all over the world share many common views on most aspects of life and careers. Students today have grown up in a world of international television, cinema, magazines, music and literature. Many have traveled throughout the world. The [Coopers & Lybrand International Student Survey] findings indicate that 23 percent of the students responding have international work experience. This is truly the world's first global generation."

Among other findings of the study: When asked what they considered the most important factor when looking for a first employer, 37 percent of respondents chose "ability to lead a balanced lifestyle." This was followed by "opportunities to reach management level" (31 percent) and "competitive salary" (30 percent). Students ranked their personal growth and development as more important than building a career, spending time with close friends and relatives and building a family. Seventy-four percent believe national borders will lose economic importance in the future. Sixty-six percent said business will have a greater influence than will politics on the future of the world. Seventy-three percent think "the global economy will strengthen and flourish in my lifetime."

The remainder of this chapter covers a number of trends we're seeing in our industry and in others as workers and organizations reinvent themselves to meet the challenges of a changing world.

• NEXT: AN END TO THE PERMANENT, FULL-TIME EMPLOYEE?

In North America, the temporary services firm Olsten Corporation has found that more than a third of firms employ temps in managerial or professional positions. Among firms using temps, 53 percent utilize accountants, 32 percent retain information systems specialists, 28 percent utilize human-resource professionals, and 27 percent use administrative professionals. Forty-five percent of firms surveyed by Olsten plan to increase their use of temporary employees during the next five years, and 51 percent intend to maintain current levels. Increased demand for temporary workers worldwide has created a boon for temp agencies. Adecco—the result of the merger of Adia SA of Switzerland and Ecco SA of France—for example, has more than twenty-four hundred offices in forty countries. The company notes that today's temporary worker tends to be older (median age 27.5) and to work longer at each assignment (median assignment length is now six weeks).

Middle management, however, seems to be the one area that has bounced out of this stagnation (while we once might have forecasted that they'd been burnt out, or outed and thrown out—all in the name of making changes) and is expected to steer companies through the next several decades. After years of being shed as corporate fat, middle management is staking its claim to the future. Today's supervisors need the same skills as upper-level executives and then some. This is a huge turnaround from just a few years ago, when middle management was being cut at a rate of twenty-three thousand employees per month. According to the

Department of Labor, last year the unemployment rate for managerial positions was only 1.9 percent. There is now a shortage of workers who are skilled enough to handle these new middle-management jobs.

The reasons for this newfound demand are encouraging. Some companies cut too many people back in the early '90s and are now looking to rebuild their staffs. There are more teams in the workplace consisting of fewer people, so there are more managers needed to supervise. A survey by Management Recruiters International determined that 56 percent of executives polled were planning to increase management and professional staff. "The demand for middle managers has never been higher," said Alan Schonberg, chairman of Management Recruiters International in an article in *USA Today* entitled, "Middle-management boom." Schoenburg added, "It's the highest it's been in the history of this company, which goes back thirty-three years."

The Department of Labor puts managers in the top ten occupations with the largest growth potential. Managers make up 14.2 percent of the workforce, compared to 11.8 percent eleven years ago. Managers in telecommunications, technology, transportation, construction, and financial services are in the greatest demand. This is not to say that these jobs are easy to get, because the standards have gone up as much as the job opportunities. New managers are expected to be strategic thinkers and visionaries. It is a time for cultivating leaderships in the middle ranks.

Although economists have been predicting the demise of Europe's cradle-to-grave welfare state for years, changes have been slow in coming. True, Sweden has made significant cuts in its social safety net, and Germany has placed some provisions of its postwar social contract on the bargaining table, but if labor protests in France a few years ago serve as any indication, the foundation of the welfare state is likely to stand strong, at least for the near term. One clear result has been high unemployment rates, fueled in part by employers' unwillingness to pay the high cost of hiring permanent workers. In Spain, for example, where unemployment has exceeded 20 percent, companies hesitate to hire permanent workers for fear of having to continue to support them in the event of layoffs. Spanish law dictates that laid-off workers are entitled to forty-five days' pay for every year they've worked. According to *Business Week*, when Gillette closed its Seville plant, the average employee took home three years' pay— and started collecting unemployment benefits that equaled as much as 90 percent of his or her old wages for four years.

Rather than shoulder the financial burden of permanent, full-time employees, many companies are turning to part-time and temporary workers. A survey of five thousand medium-sized and large firms in Europe revealed a strong increase in part-time and temporary work. Conducted by Cranfield University's European Network for Human Resource Management (Cranet-E), the survey pointed to increased flexibility among employers, as evidenced by their hiring of contract workers, allowing employees to telecommute and work flexible hours, and limiting overtime work.

As unions work to save jobs, limited work weeks are expected to become increasingly common in Europe. In the Netherlands, the four-day, thirty-six-hour week is catching on, despite the objections of many business leaders. Among companies that have already implemented this policy are Dutch retailer Koninklijke Bijenkorf Beheer (KBB) and banks Internationale Nederlanden Group and ABN AMRO. In France, the socialist government is enforcing a legislated thirty-nine-hour limit on work weeks with renewed vigor. Thousands of citations have been issued to companies that have employees working overtime without compensation; penalties can include fines as high as $1 million and jail terms of up to two years. Among companies cited were Electronics giant Thomson-CSF, home furnishings manufacturer IKEA, and retailer Auchan, all of which have been forced to introduce time clocks for managers. The law is intended to divvy up jobs among a larger proportion of the population.

"We're in a big economic shift from a mass production industrial economy to a knowledge and service economy," said Charles Heckscher, a professor in Rutgers University's School of Management and Labor Relations, as reported by *The Atlanta Journal-Constitution* in an article entitled "Contingency Workers Go Where They Are Needed." He continues, "This shift is at least as big a change as we saw in 1880 through 1920, which was the period of growth of the mass producers like autos and steels. We haven't even begun to see the impact of computers yet."

The era of nine-to-five jobs is gone, and employment contracts have been redefined. Full-time positions are now being taken over by contingency workers (consultants, independent contractors, and part-timers). Estimates on just how many contingency workers there are in the American workforce today range from less than 5 percent to 30 percent. It is estimated that this number will grow to 50 percent by 2005 due to advances in technology, which make it possible to work from anywhere.

Recently Lee Hecht Harrison/Human Resources Institute conducted a study called "The Changing Nature of Work." Of the ninety companies participating, 25 to 35 percent of their work was being done by contingency workers or outside contractors.

• NEXT: HUMANS REPLACED BY COMPUTERS

Analysts predict that in the coming century, employment as we know it is likely to be phased out in most of the industrialized nations of the world. For the first time in history, human labor is being systematically eliminated from the economic process. A new generation of sophisticated information and communication technologies, together with new forms of business reorganization and management, is wiping out full-time employment for millions of blue- and white-collar workers.

According to commentator Jeremy Rifkin, "The hard reality that economists and politicians are reluctant to acknowledge is that manufacturing and much of the service sector are undergoing a transformation as profound as the one experienced by the agricultural sector at the beginning of the century, when machines boosted production, displacing millions of farmers. We are in the early stages of a long-term shift from 'mass labor' to highly skilled 'elite labor,' accompanied by increasing automation in the production of goods and delivery of services. Workerless factories and virtual companies loom on the horizon. While unemployment [in the United States] is still relatively low . . . it can be expected to climb steadily over the next four decades as the global economy makes the transition to the Information Age."

Just as manufacturing jobs were taken over by robots in the 1970s, and accounting and finance jobs were taken over by batch-processing computers in the 1980s, middle-management jobs are under siege in the 1990s. According to a report in *Time* magazine, some analysts predict that by 2001, only one manager in fifty will be promoted in the U.S., compared with one in twenty in 1987. A key reason is advances in technology that have moved information out of the possession of management and into the general population. Most easily replaced by computers are those middle managers charged with assembling and analyzing large quantities of statistical data.

Andersen Consulting estimates that in just one service industry—commercial banking and thrift institutions—technological and management changes will have eliminated 30 to 40 percent of jobs in the 1990s. That's nearly 700,000 jobs. The number of banks is likely to decline twenty-five percent from 1997 to the year 2000. Technological innovations—including automatic teller machines and financial transactions conducted over the Internet, the use of electronic bar codes and scanners in retail outlets, and the promise of home shopping via interactive television—are significantly reducing the number of humans required to get the job done. The industries spawning these technological innovations are unlikely to generate additional employment, because—unlike the invention of the automobile, which rendered the horse and buggy obsolete but created millions of jobs in the process—the products and services created in the Information Age require fewer workers to produce and operate than did the products and services they replaced.

• NEXT: GROWTH OF SOHOS

As workers begin to rely less on corporate loyalty and more on their own skills, while also taking advantage of the opportunities new technologies afford, more and more of them are setting up shop on their own. SOHO stands for Small Office, Home Office, and is a very chic codeword for "free worker" and entrepreneur.

Thirty million American households have home offices, one third more than in 1992, according to market researcher IDC/Link.

Small offices and home offices are expected to increase from 34.7 million in 1997 to 40.2 million this year. Men and women work from home in approximately equal numbers, according to the Department of Labor, but women are more likely to work exclusively from the home. Sales of online information services to the SOHO market are expected to reach $2.5 billion by 2000, according to "SOHO Market Analysis & Forecast," a report from Cowles/Simba Information, a publication company and information provider. The study found that online marketing information and lead-generation services will be the largest SOHO sales segment.

More than 40 percent of people working from home will purchase office equipment, and they will spend, on average, approximately $2,500 on it. A survey commissioned by Smith Corona assessed purchase intentions of SOHOs and found that men between the ages of eighteen and twenty-four will spend an average of $3,100, compared to women of the same ages who will spend about $1,700. The most likely places for these customers to shop were office products retailers (19 percent), discount mass merchandisers (18 percent), consumer electronics stores (17 percent), computer retailers (12 percent), and warehouse clubs (10 percent).

Although many people think that working from home relieves work pressures, 75 percent of the respondents found that juggling business demands and personal or family issues to be "somewhat challenging" or "very challenging."

Eurostat, another European forecast venture, reports that approximately half of small-to-midsize businesses in Europe are one-person companies. The European nations with the highest concentration of small businesses are Mediterranean: Spain, Portugal, Italy, and Greece. Germany hosts the largest number of home-office workers in Europe, about 3.6 million in the western part of the country alone. Growth in the German SOHO market is driven primarily by entrepreneurs who have decided to establish their own small office-home office, usually in a particular professional field (e.g. real estate, accounting, information services) or to work as self-employed subcontractors for organizations or companies. Spearheading a trend among large companies to alleviate fixed costs through the promotion of home office work, IBM in

Germany has an estimated 25 percent of its staff working out of home offices.

• NEXT: SEARCHING FOR THE "EQUAL" IN EQUAL OPPORTUNITY

There is some truth to the Virginia Slims tag line. Women *have* come a long way. But as the following statistics demonstrate, the battle for equality is far from over.

American women are still struggling to gain power. Almost 90 percent of board seats on Fortune 500 companies are held by men (98 percent of them are white). Results of a survey done by Catalyst (a nonprofit organization that has worked to get women on boards for twenty-five years) found that women hold just 10.6 percent of the seats on Fortune 500 boards. Eighty-one of these companies, or 16 percent, have no women on their boards; 238, or nearly 50 percent, have only one; 30 percent have two; and 6 percent have three or more.

Among Fortune 500 companies, only two have female CEOs. Interestingly, the Catalyst survey also found that women hold 60 percent of the wealth in America. In fact, a 1997 survey by NASDAQ found that 47 percent of its shareholders were women.

Women use this economic power, but they do it quietly. In the last ten years, women have started companies at twice the rate of men. Fifty-eight percent of these women worked in the private sector, and 25 percent worked for medium to large companies, according to the NASDAQ study.

"Office girls" might be the stylesetters in Japan, but even the most powerful Japanese businesswomen account for no more than 7.9 percent of Japan's administrative and managerial workers, many fewer than hold the traditional secretary/stenographer/coffee-server positions. Despite the passage of equal-opportunity legislation nine years ago, Japanese employers frequently specify gender preference when advertising jobs. In a bid for greater opportunities, many Japanese women are working abroad. We found it very interesting that while researching a book about Japanese who are employed in Hong Kong, Sumiko Iwao, psychology professor at Keio University, found that whereas all of the Japanese men he interviewed had been transferred to Hong Kong by their employers, all of the women had come of their own accord.

In Europe, where women constitute 41 percent of the work-force, they earn up to forty percent less than their male counter-parts in manufacturing jobs and up to 35 percent less in service jobs. In the private sector, fewer than 2 percent of senior manage-ment jobs are held by women. Family-friendly benefits such as flexible hours and job-sharing are rarely available in non-Scandinavian countries.

In Britain, five years of campaigns by pressure groups have yielded moderate success: 41 percent of the hundred largest British companies today have a female board member, as do 12.8 percent of British companies overall. Women now claim about 2 percent of senior management jobs in Europe, ranging from Britain's 5.8 percent to Germany's 1 percent and Italy's 0.5 percent. In the United States, women account for half of the workforce and hold 10 percent of board seats and 5 percent of senior management jobs.

Although still significantly behind the United States with regard to opportunities for women, the tide in Europe might be turning. A well-established British program, Opportunity 2000, has convinced three hundred member companies to set voluntary numerical goals for promoting women. Among these member organizations, 32 percent of management spots are filled by women. One of the ways this program pushes change is by showing companies the financial benefits of women-friendly policies. According to *Business Week*, Opportunity 2000 con-vinced entertainment and leisure company Rank Group PLC to let new mothers phase in their return to work as a way of cut-ting recruitment and training costs. The result after five years: Rank saved $1.5 million by increasing its retention rate for skilled women from 20 percent to 80 percent. French women also are gaining ground in a number of business areas, having assumed positions of power in the medical and legal professions, the military and government. By 2000, women will make up 75 percent of new workers in Europe, according to the European Commission, and they will hold 50 percent of the slots in European business schools. One result: Companies might no longer have any *choice* but to hire women as managers.

Making their own breaks: Women in the United States own eight million companies today, up from three million in the mid-1980s. These businesses contribute $2.38 trillion to the American economy each year. These women represent a dramatic and revolutionary increase. Three agencies have compiled additional facts on women's breakthrough success—the U.S. Small Business Administration (SBA), the U.S. Census Bureau and the National Foundation for Women Business Owners (NFWBO).

- One in five employees, or 18.5 million people, work for a company owned by a woman.
- Three-fourths of companies owned by women in 1991 were still in business three years later, compared with two-thirds for all American companies.
- As of 1992 (most current figures available) 13 percent of companies owned by women were participating in international trade.

By 2000, women could own half of all businesses in the United States.

Minority women seem to be on an even faster track, when it comes to owning businesses today. Businesses owned by minority women, which today account for more than $184 billion in sales, are growing at three times the overall rate in America, according to a report by the National Foundation for Women Business Owners.

Race	Number of Companies Owned
Black	405,200
Hispanic	382,400
Asian, Native American, or Alaska Native	305,700

In Germany, one third of all start-ups are now woman-owned, up from 10 percent in 1975. Altogether, economists estimate, the 150,000 new female-run companies in Eastern Germany alone have created approximately a million new jobs and contributed about $15 billion to Germany's annual gross domestic product.

Researchers who study new-business growth in Germany say that companies run by women develop more slowly than those managed by men. One reason is that the profit motive isn't as strong among women entrepreneurs. According to government surveys, women cite earning profits as a fourth or fifth reason for setting up their own companies, after their desire to be self-sufficient and develop their own ideas. Male entrepreneurs cite profits as the number-one motive.

Technofemmes: Fifteen years ago in America, 70 percent of all personal computers were bought by men; today men and women are buying in equal numbers. A recent study by Lou Harris and Baruch College determined that 30 percent of the American population is online today. Although men still outnumber women online, the gender gap has narrowed to 54 percent of men and 46 percent of women, compared to 77 percent men in 1995. Women have become an important online target market. Search engine company Lycos (www.lycos.com) recently signed a two-year agreement with iVillage.com, the largest online women's site. Lycos is creating a new Women's Web Guide and an enhanced Home and Family Guide to integrate information with iVillage.com.

Women's involvement in technical careers also is growing. In response to studies citing the many obstacles girls face when attempting to pursue studies in math and science, a number of programs have been developed to encourage and support girls in technical fields. Among them is Camp T-Equity (pronounced "*tek-witty*"), based in West Springfield, Virginia, which helps young girls gain entrance into traditional male professions by opening doors of opportunity related to science, mathematics and technology literacy. Such efforts are beginning to pay off, as women by the thousands are achieving advanced degrees in technical subjects. For example, in the last fifteen years, American women have earned more than fifteen thousand Ph.D.'s in technical fields. Graduate schools in medicine and dentistry are routinely 50 percent female. More than 30 percent of graduate students in astronomy are women.

Once they've established a foothold in a male-dominated field, many women are doing their part to ensure that the climb is a bit easier for the women who follow in their footsteps. For example, Gillian Marcelle, an economist and lecturer at the University of East London, England, urges her fellow female technocrats to use their positions to help guarantee access, control and diffusion of technology to women worldwide by designing bureau systems and supporting library access to the Internet. Women in Technology International (www.witi.org) is one of a number of websites that further such efforts by facilitating and encouraging networking among technocratic women.

• NEXT: FINDING A JOB ON THE INTERNET

New technologies aren't just changing the way we do our jobs—they're changing how we find them. According to a survey released at the 49th Annual Society for Human Resource Management Conference and Exposition in California, approximately two-thirds of the six hundred human-resource executives surveyed indicate that they use the Internet for recruitment purposes. The majority began using the medium within the past year.

Whether you are looking for work or trying to fill a position, the Internet has become a valuable resource. CareerMosaic (www.careermosaic.com), for example, provides employment information in industries ranging from technology to health care, finance to the military. The Monster Board (www.monster.com) is also a valuable site. As reported by Newsbytes News Network, a recent survey found that fully 25 percent of job-seekers at The Monster Board site get at least one job offer, and those receiving offers get an average of three. Sue Zaney, the site's VP of product development and marketing, attributes the job board's high success rate to two factors: the growing diversity of job-seekers on the site and the fact that 44 percent of site users are "passive job-seekers . . . people who already have jobs but are willing to look for something better." Launched in 1994, The Monster Board was receiving in excess of two million visits a month by the time it celebrated its fourth birthday.

- ## NEXT: HOT JOBS FOR THE MILLENNIUM

As American companies compete to attract and retain talented workers in a tight job market, many employers are reshaping their work structures to be not only more flexible, but also more fun. The purpose is to improve employee morale, reduce stress, help manage conflict, motivate workers to be more productive and simply make the workplace a more enjoyable place to be. Companies uncertain of how to inject fun into their business equation can hire organizations like Playfair Inc. of Berkeley, California to give their managers tips on how to see their employees as complete human beings with outside interests and concerns. Playfair's approach emphasizes humor as an essential team-building technique. In Boston, Grand Circle Travel has appointed one of its employees "director of fun."

Which occupations will thrive in the next millennium? The following are likely to be on the upswing:

Personal Services: In an era in which time is an increasingly valuable commodity, we can expect all sorts of people to vie to meet our needs. Sample occupations include the following:

- Online moms: Entrepreneurs who do everything from sending e-mail reminders for anniversaries and birthdays to scheduling dental appointments and providing health-care pointers.
- Online researchers: Don't have time to search the Web for that critical piece of information? Hire someone to do it for you, perhaps keeping him or her on a retainer basis.
- Educational consultants: In addition to providing advice on which schools your children should attend, these consultants can create individualized education plans, complete with tutoring sessions, educational software picks, edutainment options, and so on.
- Babyproofers: Specialists who come into your home and make it safe for babies and active toddlers. Also expect a rise in in-home babysavers (such as infant CPR), massage and nutrition classes, as well as home security specialists who make sure one's home is protected from crime.

• Neighborhood nanas: Neighborhood drop-in centers for children will be increasingly common. These centers might be located in a home or in a variation of a day-care center.

• Home cooks: Expect to see a rise in businesses that deliver frozen home-cooked meals to families on the run. One advantage over takeout meals is that these can be prepared according to individual needs and tastes.

Business Services: The rise in contract workers, SOHOs, and temps will create many business opportunities. Examples:

• On-site repair services: When Ann's recently-purchased computer broke down, the manufacturer sent a technician to her home within three days to repair it. Expect such services to be available for all types of electronic equipment.

• Equipment lessors and business sites: Rather than invest in expensive equipment right away, savvy entrepreneurs will lease the needed equipment or rent a cubicle (or meeting space, as needed) from a business supersite. Also certain to grow are videoconference centers and technology consultants, who will advise small businesses on technological purchases.

• Skills trainers: The rapid pace of technological change, combined with the growth of contract workers, will create an increasing need for people who can train not only current employees of a company, but also freelance workers.

• Executive coaches: One of the latest twists on businesses devoted to helping busy people cope is the field of "executive coaches." At a cost of as much as $500 per month, coaches make weekly phone calls to clients to help them prioritize their goals and better manage their businesses and their lives. At the center of the field is Coach University, founded in Salt Lake City, Utah, in 1992. The training facility is entirely virtual, attended by five hundred students who participate in classes via teleconferences and download data from the university's website (www.coachu.com). The thirty-six-course curriculum costs $2,495 and graduates professional advisers who are part consultant, part therapist, and part friend.

And, of course, the Digital Age will clearly spawn new job opportunities for all sorts of high-tech specialists, including multimedia software designers and intranet coordinators.

WHAT'S NEXT?

Escalating competition: Worldwide demand for senior executives is soaring as a result of increasing economic confidence in Europe and North America, expansion of the financial services sector and growth of both consumer product and high-tech companies. Most in demand in Europe, according to a study by Korn/Ferry International, a global leader in executive search, are marketing, sales, advertising and public-relations professionals—a sign that the fight for the global market share is heating up among European companies.

We'll also see increased competition for highly skilled technical workers, who are already being lured from one company to another by million-dollar signing bonuses and the like. The International Technology Association reported that last year there were 190,000 vacant jobs at large and midsize companies in the United States. Aggravating the demand for technical workers is the fact that the number of college students graduating with degrees in computer science fell 43 percent between 1986 and 1994, from 42,195 to 24,200. This IT skills shortage is also being felt in Europe, where Logica's CEO announced that his company was unable to recruit sufficient staff, placing a number of lucrative contracts in jeopardy.

Sabbatical respites: Now that employers and companies are no longer wed for life, we can expect to see more widespread embrace of sabbaticals between career segments. Workers may choose to take a break from work for a number of reasons—to raise a family, go back to school, start a home-based business or another entrepreneurial endeavor, or simply to step back and take the time to consider in which direction they next want to go. We suspect that spiritual replenishment will be the focus of a growing number of voluntary sabbaticals, whether the time is used to give back to the community (by spending a year or two teaching in an inner-city school, for example), travel on a religious pilgrimage, or to achieve a life-affirming goal, such as climbing Mount Everest or bicycling across Europe.

As adjuncts to this trend, expect to see the growth of counseling sessions that help individuals plan for their financial security while they enjoy these occasional down years of rebirth and replenishment; extended working years, as individuals opt to put off their eventual retirement to take some time-outs earlier in life; and the emergence of partially paid sabbaticals as a corporate benefit in high-stress fields.

Nix the tie: Office dress codes will continue to relax, as boomers taking the corporate reins extend casual Fridays to the rest of the week. Look for men's designers and clothing retailers to increase their lines of "dressy casuals."

Electronic classrooms: Top-notch business training and development will be but a click away. We'll also see increased sharing of in-person training sessions, as companies see the benefits of dividing the cost of such sessions among corporate neighbors.

Telecommuting hubs: Telecommuters will form place-based workplaces that revolve around workers' philosophies and lifestyles rather than chosen professions.

Removable hard drives: Compact, portable drives will allow computer users to carry the brains of their computers with them (from work to home to temporary office site to airport lounge), insert them into available hardware, and get right to work.

Camp iworkformyself: Intensive entrepreneur camps will teach teenagers the skills they need to succeed in the next century.

Harassment insurance: As allegations of sexual harassment in the workplace continue to make headline news in North America, insurance policies guarding against such claims will become more common. Today, as reported by the Associated Press, more than seventy American companies offer employment practices liability coverage. One company, Hartford Financial Services Group, has sold approximately one thousand such policies since it began offering them a few years ago. The average company buying the policy has approximately forty workers and pays an annual premium of $3,000.

Career partnerships: Flexible working styles will inspire formal and informal partnerships between employees. As workers move from one job and one career to another, this steady partnership with a coworker will provide stability and increased flexibility, allowing both parties greater leeway than either might have if working alone in a corporate setting. Such partnerships also benefit the employer, ensuring a constant work flow even when one person is absent due to vacation, maternity or paternity leave, or an extended business trip.

Gender-blurred talking styles: Gender differences in communication styles are decreasing, according to a study by the telecommunications company MCI. The MCI "One Monitor" study found that men and women are abandoning stereotypical behaviors like the "strong, silent" male and the "emotional" female. The survey found, for example, that men and women today are equally likely to pay attention to body language when communicating in person, report similar tendencies to talk about their personal lives at work and prefer to give bad news in person (something men were thought to avoid). Watts Wacker, the futurist who conducted the study, commented, "As topics, forms and styles [of communication] continue to merge, gender communication myths will increasingly be broken. This trend will only be accelerated as gender-irrelevant communications styles develop for modern technologies—further disintegrating the communications barriers between men and women."

Fit for work: As job pressures increase, so do illness and absenteeism. Companies are now investing in initiatives that encourage employees to be fit and healthy. In addition to providing corporate gymnasiums or reduced rates at nearby fitness clubs, corporate managers are creating "lifestyle centers" that incorporate health screening and counseling, behavior modification classes, and healthful cooking courses.

No-work weekends: In a move that is certain to be emulated by other companies, accounting firm Ernst & Young has instituted a telecommunications ban on weekends. Employees have been instructed to resist the temptation to check e-mail and voice-mail messages between Friday evening and Monday morning. The new policy stems from concerns over employee stress and the firm's difficulty in retaining female hires.

CHAPTER 16:

Cyberbiz

SEVERAL YEARS AGO, John A. Quelch and Lisa R. Klein wrote, "The Internet promises to revolutionize the dynamics of international commerce and, like the telephone and fax machine, may be a major force in the democratization of capitalism. Small companies will be able to compete more easily in the global marketplace, and consumers in emerging markets, in particular, will benefit from the expanded range of products, services, and information to which the Internet will give them access." The article, titled "The Internet and International Marketing" and published in the prestigious *Sloan Management Review*, made other predictions that have begun to ring true. Today, according to a Mediamark Research study, 64.2 million U.S. adults are regular Internet users.

GLOBAL ROUNDUP: WHO'S ONLINE

Digital living is a chicken-and-egg affair. On the one hand, why bother going online if nothing of interest is there? On the other hand, simply by being online, users help determine that content moves forward. Users give shape to the online world click by click, trading patronage—in the form of membership, page views, click-throughs, and so forth—for the information, products, and services they desire.

Internet Usage High Among Senior Executives

While nearly half of all Americans are online, America isn't the only cyber-intense culture. What may be even more predictive is a survey finding from Andersen Consulting: Worldwide, 92 percent of top executives are online. That is, 92 percent of CEOs, CFOs, and CIOs had Internet access in 1998, up from 90 percent in 1997, with 83 percent going online at least once a week, up from 71 percent the previous year. In addition, 50 percent of senior executives described themselves as feeling comfortable using the Web, up from 36 percent in 1997.

Canadian executives lead the way, with 99 percent of its senior executives online. Ninety-eight percent of executives in the U.S. are online, down one point from the previous year. And 98 percent of Australian senior executives had Internet access in 1998, a huge rise from 80 percent in 1997. European executives are also getting wired: 97 percent of U.K. senior executives now have access; France follows with 95 percent; and the level of Spanish executives in cyberspace rose from 83 percent to 95 percent in 1998. Ninety percent of Italian senior executives are online, while Germany maintains its position as a laggard, with an access rate of only 82 percent. Even more stunning is the lack of cyber-involvement among Japan's most senior managers—78 percent of Japanese executives are online. This supports our hunch that the more keyboard-resistant senior managers are, the slower they are to embrace the Internet, which tends to require some typing.

American senior executives, however, were the most likely to shop online, at 65 percent; followed by Canada, at 48 percent; and Australia and the U.K., both at 39 percent. American and Canadian managers are the most likely to seek out travel information online (76 percent), followed by Spain (71 percent), and Australia (61 percent). Despite their comfort with computer-mediated communication and commerce, corporate titans are not embracing online brokerage as quickly—22 percent of the American CEOs, CFOs, and CIOs surveyed by Andersen use online brokers, and that was the highest level of involvement worldwide. Only 1 percent of Japanese CEOs, CFOs, and CIOs are participating in online brokerage. With this recognition that change is in the air, we approach the trends that are driving cyberspace's position as the next business frontier.

Mediamark reported that the number of American adults with access to the Internet either at home or at work rose by 16.3 percent to 83.7 million. Therefore, 42.2 percent of the total U.S. adult population (over eighteen) are regular Internet users, up 20 percent from the previous year. A study by the same group found that 53.5 million adults were regular Internet users in September 1997.

North America Leads the Way

Just a couple of years ago, when the Internet was still presented as a mysterious entity clouded with hype and hope, cautious marketers could reasonably ask, "Fine, but who's on it?" quickly followed by "Who's making money from it?" Today, the answer to both questions is, "lots of different people." User numbers are growing fast, and many smart retailers, both established and new, have shown that it's possible to do big business online.

According to market researcher IntelliQuest, nearly 70 percent of online households have shopped over the Internet in the last three months. In total, 23.5 million users (28 percent of those online) said that they made at least one online purchase during this first quarter of 1999. If they did not buy anything online, they used the Internet to research the range and availability of products.

Media Metrix notes an increase in Internet use at work. The latest figures for 1999 show workers view an average of 409.9 Web pages a month, an increase of 69 percent from last year. Additionally, workers spend an average of forty-five minutes a month shopping online—and forty-six minutes a month downloading pornography (although, as employers crack down on what employees do on company computers, and on company time, the porn number is likely to decrease).

Among other factors stimulating Internet sales are increasing demands on consumers' leisure time and the improvement of overnight and second-day delivery services. These factors spurred the growth of catalog shopping in the '80s and '90s, and are now leading people to shop over the Internet. Today, one in five visitors to specialty online stores are new users, according to ActivMedia, and revenue from sites specializing in gourmet food, personal care, and branded consumer products is rising steadily. Sales projections are skyrocketing: In 1999, sales are expected to be ten times what they were in 1998, and sales in 2000 are expected to be four times what they will be in 1999.

Greenfield Online just reported that 39 percent of American Internet users spend less time shopping in offline stores and malls—an extremely significant change, since those with online access have real clout, representing a whopping 60 percent of American consumer buyer power in 1999.

Consider the following statistics:
• Amazon.com reported revenue in excess of $293.6 million for the first quarter of 1999, up from $87.4 million for the same quarter in 1998. (Despite this, the company posted a loss of $61 million in the first quarter of 1999.)
• According to Jupiter Communications, despite a percentage increase of just two points, portal-driven retail sales will be $2.4 billion in 1999, climbing to $8.7 billion in 2002.
• Greenfield Online found that 70 percent of cyber-citizens who shopped for computer software did so online, while 71 percent consulted a local store, 40 percent used a catalog, and 46 percent visited a mall. In comparison, 49 percent of cyber-citizens bought software products online, 22 percent bought via a catalog, 68 percent made purchases in a local store, and 42 percent did their buying at a mall. Greenfield's findings reveal that, when shopping for books, 64 percent of cyber-citizens use the Internet, 29 percent use a catalogue, 63 percent visit a local store, and 58 percent shop at a mall. In comparison, 49 percent of cyber-citizens purchased books online, 23 percent used a catalog, 63 percent bought at a local store, and 42 percent purchased books at a mall.

• The Greenfield study also found that, when shopping for clothing, cyber-citizens definitely prefer malls and local stores. Still, 30 percent of cyber-citizens reported that they shop online for clothing and 38 percent of cyber-citizens use a catalog, while 70 percent use a local store and 75 percent shop at a mall. Just 18 percent of cyber-citizens buy clothing online, but that's not very different from the 22 percent who purchase through a catalog. In contrast, 66 percent buy at a local store and 68 percent buy at a mall. Still Delia's, the very "in" online boutique for teens, is making genuine waves among fashion-interested girls. (Indeed, *Good Morning America* just featured the authors chatting about how teens spread the word about the best new fashion sites—and since *Computer Economics* predicts that seventy-seven million user under eighteen years of age will be online globally by 2005. The potential is staggering.)

An audit of popular content provides a contextual perspective on digital living. And the numbers speak for themselves. The most recent Media Metrix study (February 1999) found Yahoo overtaking AOL as the top Website, with Geocities.com in third place. Based on examination of Web usage among forty thousand Americans, the number one Website is Yahoo.com, with almost 29.2 million unique viewers in January 1999.

In terms of unique visitors, next is aol.com with 28.9 million, followed by msn.com (20.2 million), go.com (19.9 million), Geocities.com (almost 18.9 million), Excite.com (15.54 million), Lycos.com (14.9 million), Microsoft.com (almost 14.2 million), and in tenth place Tripod.com (12.5 million).

The balance of the top twenty-five sites, in order of rank is: AltaVista.com, Hotmail.com, Angelfire.com, Xoom.com, Amazon.com, BlueMountainArts.com, Real.com, ZDNet.com, Hotbot.com, Snap.com, Weather.com, Infospace.com, eBay.com, ·MSNBC.com, and in twenty-fifth place, ICQ.com.

At the top of the Web properties list is the AOL Network with 37.9 million unique visitors, followed by Microsoft with 30.1 million, and Yahoo with 29.5 million. Other properties in the top 10 were Lycos (28.5 million unique users), Go Network (22.8 million), GeoCities (almost 19.3 million), Excite Network (18.2

million), Netscape (18 million), Time Warner Online (12.2 million), and in tenth place AltaVista (almost 11.2 unique visitors). The balance of the top twenty-five sites on the top twenty-five Web properties, in rank order, is Xoom.com, Amazon.com, BlueMountainArts.com, ZDNet.com, RealSite Portfolio, JUNO.com, Broadcast.com, CNET.com, Snap.com, the Weather Channel, Infospace Impressions, eBay, LookSmart, Go2Net, and, in twenty-fifth place, Viacom Online.

Who's Online in the U.S., and How

As soon as we nail down a figure for the number of interactive homes, we read a new study that reports a different total and forecasts a different rate of growth. For purposes of this book, we've settled on May 1999 statistics and projections from Datamonitor. It reports that there will be an estimated sixty-seven million interactive households across the U.S. and Europe by 2003, up from 10.3 million in 1998. Web TV will have a lot to do with this growth—the study estimates that the market for television-based Internet access will expand by 45 percent over the next five years. These new service providers will offer email and Web access, as well as interactive shopping and banking services. Digital television set-top boxes provided by broadcasters are expected to dominate the market over dedicated Internet access boxes provided by ISPs. (That's why the AT&T deals of late are so important to digital life now and next.)

Datamonitor predicts the number of set-top boxes in Europe will increase from 10.3 million in 1998 to 18.1 million this year, to an estimated 28.8 million in 2000, 41.2 million in 2001, 53.3 million in 2003, and 67.1 million in 2003. The report goes on to note that the number of dedicated set-top boxes was 800,000 in 1998, while interactive digital set-top boxes totaled 9.5 million. This year, dedicated boxes will number 1.4 million, and interactive digital set-top boxes will number 16.7 million. And the growth will continue, fast and furious. By 2003, Datamonitor predicts, dedicated set-top boxes will total 6.3 million, and interactive digital set-top boxes will number 60.8 million.

Europe

NORTHERN EUROPE

Increasingly, the Nordic region of Europe is becoming cyber central, with penetration levels in Sweden, Norway, and Finland approaching two and three times those of the U.K. and the Continent. *Business Arena Stockholm* reports that as of May 1999, 1.6 million Nordic consumers are buying online, with Swedes buying the most. There are currently 3.6 million Swedes online, with most of them using the Internet at least once a month; 950,000 of them (26.5 percent) have made an online purchase. These aren't new participants, either—76 percent of Swedish online shoppers have been online since 1997. And 56 percent of those online since or after 1998 have never bought anything over the Internet. Internet shopping appears to be a intermediate-level activity, with users preferring to get their feet wet—perhaps browsing, but not buying—before making a purchase.

The Cyber-savvy of Scandinavia:
- 1.6 million people have Internet access in Norway; 1.4 million of them go online at least once a month; and 250,000 have made an online purchase.
- 1.6 million consumers have Internet access in Finland; 1.1 million access the Internet at least once a month; and 200,000 have purchased online.
- 1.7 million Danes have Internet access; 1.5 million access the Internet at least once a month; and 250,000 have made an online purchase.

Business Arena Stockholm reported a mean purchase of over $120, typically for computer- or travel-related products. The study also highlighted the notion that cyber-shopping in Scandinavia isn't about low cost—there are very few purchases for $12 or under. This may change, however, since lack of interest for small purchases is likely due to unsuitable payment and delivery systems (for instance, shipping costs reward large purchases).

UNITED KINGDOM

Online usage is expanding in England. According to the U.K.-based NOP Research Group, the percentage of the British population who are online doubled from 9 percent to 18 percent from March to December of 1998, with an estimated ten thousand new users logging on for the first time every day. Lingering fears over security continue to encumber growth, however, particularly with respect to online commerce. According to a Gallup poll commissioned by De La Rue Systems, British consumers were more trusting of ATM (66 percent) and point-of-purchase (49 percent) transactions, while e-mail and Internet-based transactions bottomed out at 18 percent and a meager 7 percent, respectively.

THE NETHERLANDS

Not only are more Dutch jumping online, but they're doing it more often. A March survey by ProActive found that Dutch users log on an average of three days per week, with a typical session lasting nearly an hour. E-mail is still the most common activity, with 70 percent reporting that as their primary activity. However, searching for specific information and even aimless surfing followed close behind at 70 percent and 61 percent, respectively.

SPAIN

Online growth is slower in Spain. An AIMC study showed less than one percent change in usage levels—only five hundred thousand new users—from August 1998 to April 1999. On the bright side, Internet usage is highest at home (50 percent), where PC penetration hovers at about 26 percent. Notably, the study showed the Web is the most popular objective when dialing in, with 84.1 percent jumping online to surf, not just send and receive e-mail. However, both computers and Internet access continue to be stratified by class—upper- and middle-class users together account for over 64 percent of the online population.

BELGIUM

Brussels-based Initiative Media reports that, as of February 1999,

16 percent of Belgians are online. Users are heavily content-oriented, and tend to go with what they know—according to an InSites survey of new users, television and newspaper sites were used by 96 percent of the sample, radio sites by 94 percent, and magazine sites by 93 percent. Additionally, brand consciousness among Belgian Internet users tended to favor the known; brands without a strong Web presence continued to lead over brands known primarily in the online world.

Asia

CHINA

A recent report by *Computer Economics* predicts China will boast the second largest online population by 2005, with 71 percent of those polled who are not already online professing a strong inclination to get there soon. Additionally, a study by the Sinclair company estimated that only 70.8 percent of those with Internet access use it primarily for e-mail, while 85.6 percent use it to locate information on politics, society, technology, and science. PC penetration among existing Chinese users is also high, with 66 percent reporting access to a computer at home. Still, despite such rosy predictions, China's current Internet penetration remains below 1 percent, and Internet access is likely to remain the domain of middle-class urban dwellers.

TAIWAN

Online growth continues to be steady in Taiwan, where according to an ISOC estimate, over three million people—14.3 percent of the total population—are currently online. That number represents a 39 percent rise since June 1998, a gain matched by an additional 31 percent over the previous six months.

JAPAN

According to a Nikkei Market Access survey, there were fourteen million Japanese users online in December 1998. That makes Japan home to the single largest population of Internet users in Asia. A recent report from the DSA Group predicted that number to mushroom to twenty-seven million by 2002.

The DSA report also noted a number of demographic shifts that are beginning to change the face of Japan's online population. The most significant of these is the growth in the Internet presence of women, who now account for 40 percent of new users, compared with 21 percent the previous year. Opportunities in entertainment-oriented services and e-commerce are associated with this growth, as women tend to seek out these categories when dialing in. The majority of Japanese Internet users still are connecting from work, with the high cost of telephone use considered the major deterrent to home use. Users' average age is also increasing; previously dominated by younger professionals, the Japanese online population is growing older each year. (The report attributes this change to an increase in the adoption of local area networks by large corporations that tend to employ over-twenty-ones.)

While many respondents in the DSA study named online shopping—particularly convenience and access to foreign goods—as an incentive to gaining access, many complained that the Internet was too expensive and still too slow. Nonetheless, e-commerce is predicted to generate ¥1 trillion in revenues by 2001, five times the level of 1998.

SINGAPORE

By pure percentage, Singapore has the highest level of Internet usage of any Asian nation. Fourteen percent of Singaporeans are currently online, according to the latest Nielsen data, totaling 500,000 users. Paralleling rapid population growth, that number is expected to double by 2000. Next year, Singapore will become the first country in the world to use the Internet to help complete its next census.

INDIA

According to Reuters, only 0.01 percent of the Indian population is currently online. Low PC penetration levels tell part of the story—currently there are just 2.8 computers per one thousand inhabitants in India. Government incentives have been implemented to raise this ratio to ten PCs per thousand people by

2002. Even among those with the hardware, however, connectivity problems are keeping usage under par. Previously government-controlled, Internet service provision was privatized in November 1998. While nearly 100 national, regional, and local ISP licenses have been issued, bandwidth and infrastructure remain key problems affecting access.

AFRICA

While Internet penetration levels remain below even one-hundredth of a percent in all but a handful of African nations, predictions for the future by media and technology pundits are for rapid growth in developing nations as a whole, fueled mostly by the need for alternative economic channels in regions with insufficient infrastructure. Increased competition among shipping and delivery services, as well as improvements in Internet security, are expected to contribute to the future boom. Despite low usage levels, African governments are taking the Internet seriously—in Nigeria, both contenders for the upcoming presidential election established campaign sites on the Web.

LATIN AMERICA

As in Africa and parts of Asia where extreme economic diversity is the norm, access in Latin America currently is—and is likely to remain—limited to the middle- and upper-class segments of the population, where levels of PC ownership are highest. Issues related to telephony and infrastructure continue to hold sway—monthly service fees and toll charges make Latin Americans' monthly online bill roughly twice that of American users'. As a result, currently just one in five PCs in Latin America is connected to the Internet.

In a recent keynote at the Internet Commerce Expo in Boston, MIT Media Lab founder Nicholas Negroponte singled out Latin America as a key growth point for e-commerce into the next millennium, noting the Internet's potential to help companies sidestep local business and government infrastructural deficiencies. Again, however, such growth is likely to be limited to the professional segments of Latin American society. Growth in online commerce, however, is likely to find little resistance in Latin American shopping habits. According to an IDC Research study, most Latin Americans are accustomed to shopping out-of-market, and a Laredo Group study found that one in four Latin American Internet users have made a purchase. Many are predicting on e-commerce boom once PC penetration levels reach critical mass and infrastructural problems are resolved. Still, issues such as delivery and cross-border taxation are likely to persist.

COLOMBIA

IDC Colombia estimated there were a total of three hundred fifty thousand Colombian Internet users at the end of 1998, with this number expected to exceed five hundred thousand by the end of 1999. In terms of business use, IDC estimated that 80 percent of Colombian businesses had or were developing a Web site by the end of 1998, and 36 percent had or were developing e-commerce sites.

MEXICO

In December of 1998, MORI de Mexico reported half a million Mexicans would be online by 1999, a gain of more than 100,000 users over the previous year. Growth in the number of Spanish-language sites and search engines was cited among the contributing factors. PC penetration remains the key factor blocking growth; even among those who own PCs, MORI expects less than a quarter of them to be online by 2000.

Nexts Contributing to the Marketspace Opportunity

- **NEXT: ONLINE WINDOW-SHOPPING AS A PRECURSOR TO TRUE E-COMMERCE**

With many newbies hesitant to make purchases online, Internet window-shopping has become an important process for introducing consumers to the world of e-commerce. Comparing products, models, and prices is much easier online, even when the buyer intends eventually to buy over the counter. Given the opportunity to browse, look, and read product details in all their glorious minutiae without being hovered over, consumers feel more comfortable and capable of making an informed decision after time spent window-shopping online. The only thing missing is, of course, someone to answer questions immediately.

Research figures indicate that Internet users are getting wise to the window-shopping potential of the Internet:

- According to IntelliQuest Information Group in February 1998, although just 17 percent of Internet users make purchases online, nearly 60 percent of them shop online. Finding information about a product's price or features, checking on product selection, and determining where to purchase a product are the most popular shopping activities.
- According to a survey conducted by Greenfield Online among U.S. Internet users which concluded on January 6, 1999, 39 percent of Internet users spend less time visiting physical stores and shopping malls and more time shopping online than they have in the past. Among shoppers polled, 70 percent were likely to purchase computer software online and 64 percent were likely to shop for books online.
- An American Internet user survey found that 75 percent of adults who use the Web sought online product and investment information in the fourth quarter of 1997, up from 54 percent in the second quarter.

- ## NEXT : FRONT-RUNNING E-SHOPPING PRODUCTS ARE "KNOWNS" AND "UNDERSTOODS"

In time, virtually all goods and services will be available online. In the Internet's nascent stages, however, consumers are tending to purchase items that don't require looking or touching. According to Ernst & Young's "Internet Shopping" study, the best-selling products in cyberspace today are computers, software, books, travel, music, and magazine subscriptions.

Apparel is emerging as a popular choice as well, particularly among women, although this category has some way to go. According to the Greenfield Online survey of U.S. Internet users, only 39 percent of those surveyed were likely to shop online for textile goods.

The Greenfield study also found that 38 percent of cyber-citizens prefer to use a catalog, while 70 percent use a local store and 75 percent shop at a mall. Just 18 percent of cyber-citizens buy clothing online, but that's not very different from the 22 percent who purchase through a catalog. In contrast, 66 percent buy at a local store and 68 percent buy at a mall.

There are now 28 million parents online, according to CyberDialogue's most recent survey, "Families Online." Favorite goods for purchase online also consist of PC hardware and software, music, and consumer electronics. 18.6 million of them use the internet for research and fully 8.2 million of these users have made a purchase online. Out of an estimated 79.4 million U.S. adults online currently (IntelliQuest), online parental types are a niche force to be watched closely. CyberDialogue predicts that parents' "surfing habits are transforming the content choices on entertainment and shopping Web sites."

E-shopping is proving ideal in categories that traditionally have faced limited shelf space, including music, books, and videos. Unencumbered by the cost of real estate or the need to tie up capital in stock, cybersites are able to offer a far more diverse selection than can their offline counterparts. Amazon.com, for instance, offers Internet customers a selection of two million book titles. In comparison, traditional book superstores carry approximately one hundred fifty thousand titles. Similarly, Reel.com, the world's largest movie store, maintains a selection of more than eighty-five thousand film titles online. This breadth of selection is particularly appealing to those in search of hard-to-find titles. As a result, the top-selling movies on the Internet today aren't classics or blockbusters, but a mix of cult classics and offbeat films. Reel.com's ten best-selling new movies in 1998 were *Titanic*, *Lady and the Tramp* (Restored Edition, 1955), *The Rocky Horror Picture Show* (Special Edition), *The Planet of the Apes 30th Anniversary Box Set*, *Buffy the Vampire Slayer Collection*, *Teletubbies: Dance with the Teletubbies*, *Teletubbies: Here Come the Teletubbies*, *Barney's Great Adventure*, *Pocahontas II: Journey to a New World*, and *Boogie Nights*.

• NEXT: E-COMMERCE'S ENTREPRENEURIAL EDGE

Joining the e-commerce revolution doesn't automatically mean stratospheric increases in sales, as many established companies have discovered. E-shopping requires a different way of thinking—and one that might not come naturally to larger companies. In 1998 Internet-only start-ups have the advantage of being focused on their online business and having structured their operations accordingly. As noted in a recent report from the U.S. Department of Commerce, "These new Internet-only businesses had a head start of one to two years, during which they invested heavily to build a brand image and gain market share before super retailers like Wal-Mart, Barnes and Noble, The Gap, and J.C. Penney, equipped their Web sites with a sales capability."

It's interesting that only 15 to 20 percent of the impressive sales figures rung up in cyberspace thus far have gone to online sites of conventional retailers, according to investment company Piper Jaffray. Most were rung up in the travel and financial services industries and in business-to-business sales, noted *The New York Times*. The merchants finding the most success at selling online tend to be ones that exist only online (for example, Amazon.com).

Established companies, though, have every reason to hone an entrepreneurial edge in order to compete in cyberspace. Traditional retail already is finding that competition from online retail is making life tougher. The U.S. retail sector fired 55,393 workers in 1997 (up 32 percent from 1996), in part to cope with increased competition from online shopping business, according to a survey by outplacement firm Challenger, Gray & Christmas. Online commerce has a 4 percent higher profit margin than traditional sales avenues, according to Forrester Research.

Fortunately for larger companies, brand-name recognition gives Web sites a big boost. Ernst & Young's recent "Internet Shopping" study found, for instance, that 69 percent of online shoppers surveyed base their online buying decisions, in large part, on their familiarity with the company. Nearly three-quarters knew both the brand and the online store they were looking for when they made their last online purchase.

The Automotive Industry Now and Next

The automotive industry already is undergoing massive change even outside the Internet, with automakers revamping their distribution systems, large national chains entering the market, and dealers experimenting with changes in service. On top of this, the Internet is beginning to change the way consumers research, buy, and finance their new and used cars. This is particularly apparent in the States, where Internet usage is sufficiently common to make advertising and selling on the Internet economical for dealers.

We're seeing the same kind of evolution in car shopping that we have seen in other commercial applications on the Internet: new information-gathering habits, the creation of computer-mediated communities which provide first-hand information to prospective buyers, and ultimately, the actual transaction. Yes, people are buying cars via the Internet.

Equally important, we are viewing the efforts of each manufacturer to begin to establish one-to-one relationships with prospective owners, and owners. From detailed model information (which has the potential to save millions of dollars spent on brochures), to finance information and application, to elaborate owner retention programs, automotive manufacturers may be among those industries most in-tune with the unique ability of the Internet to provide connections to the brand.

According to Forrester Research, although in 1998 over two million consumers used the Internet to make a decision about purchasing a car online, by the year 2003 over eight million car purchases will be influenced, in part, by the Internet. They also estimate that 470,000 U.S. households will "purchase new cars entirely over the Internet, generating revenue in the amount of $12 billion." Already 61 percent of car dealers (representing *all* of the major car manufacturers in the US) have Web sites and two-thirds of these have staff members dedicated to smoothing out the still traumatically impersonal process of online car purchasing. Car purchases made online have, according to Forrester, four phases: "general research, dealer selection, payment plans and insurance, and finally sale completion." Customer service will continue to be a focus for the upcoming years with a potential build-to-order business competing for their parts of this online market.

NEXT: ONLINE AUCTIONS

The Internet is reinventing the barter industry and also creating a marketspace for business-to-business and consumer auctions. In fact, consumers are flocking to online auctions; they have come a long way from their original intention of selling PC stuff to geeks. The Internet Auction List counts more than fifteen hundred auction-related Web sites in more than forty product categories. The eBay site has become the world's largest virtual garage sale, boasting a community of more than eight hundred and fifty thousand people. Auctioning is also the latest feather in Amazon.com's expanding features cap.

But auction sites are not only swap meets for individuals, they're also being used as new distribution outlets where companies with excess inventory can reach eager customers. Companies with specialized goods and few local buyers often find consumers in the virtual world who are ready to snap up difficult-to-find items. Web auctions are a great place for buyers with very particular needs to find exactly what they want. Thanks to the Internet, bidding doesn't mean cheaper, it simply means greater capacity to bring far-flung buyers and sellers together.

WHAT'S NEXT?

Web hosts: Forrester Research estimates that building and operating a standard, in-house Web site costs $300,000-plus a year; the cost of an interactive site with shopping capabilities can reach $3.4 million. As an alternative, companies are using Web hosting services that install and operate sites for an average first-year bill of $42,000. The Web hosting business is expected to generate $5.3 billion in 2000.

Performance-assessment tools: InfoTEST International has launched what it calls the first business performance assessment method for measuring how corporate Web sites are meeting company goals in customer service, sales-lead generation, and sales, brand equity, and internal cost control. InfoTEST Benchmark features a standardized 1,000-point rating scale that combines quantitative and qualitative assessment techniques. The rating system and assessment guidelines can be downloaded free at www.imation.com/infotest.

Digital signatures: Forty U.S. states have enacted or are considering legislation to recognize digital signatures. The FDA began accepting digital signatures from drug companies last year. Since digital signatures can be an electronic signature copied into a file or a thumbprint translated into a unique electronic signature, there must be some universal standards set for using this technology in legally binding documents.

Not just for kids: With personal recreational time at a premium for the parental online users, it's not surprising that 73 percent use the Internet for fun compared to 63 percent of non-parents. Age makes a difference though—a whopping 83 percent of parents surveyed under the age of thirty-five surf for fun. (Source: "Families Online," CyberDialogue, 1999)

1:1 marketing online: According to the U.S. Direct Marketing Association, 48 percent of American direct marketers use online services for sales and marketing purposes. Web Screen Talk, a product of Sky Alland Marketing (www.skyalland.com), has broadened the range of customer interaction that can be achieved by online vendors. A step beyond automated response forms and generic "contact@" options, Web Screen Talk supports real-time customer service in the form of a streamlined private chatroom (an Internet equivalent to "operators are standing by") as well as a "Web Callback" feature that enables customers to schedule a convenient time to receive a follow-up call.

Automated customer service: Interacting with consumers online can be both blessing and curse. For example, Nike (www.nike.com) receives two thousand e-mails daily. To ensure timely response without heavy manpower investment, high-tech companies such as Aeromail (www.aeromail.com) and General Interactive (www.interactive.com) offer technology that reads, analyzes, and mass customizes responses to email.

Cyberscams: With the good comes the bad. In the U.S., federal and state regulators have announced that they are cracking down on marketers who tout business opportunity schemes over the Internet. As a first step, the Federal Trade Commission and North American Securities Administrators Association have issued warnings to two hundred and fifteen e-marketers, telling them that they must be able to back up all claims they make.

Euro cybergiants on the horizon: Look out, Amazon.com and Barnes & Noble. German media conglomerate Bertelsmann AG has announced plans to open a global electronic bookstore. BooksOnline will offer titles in major languages from all publishers at discount prices.

The check's in the hard drive: Although 6.9 million Internet users in the U.S. currently bank online, the number will swell to at least 24.2 million by 2002, according to a report by CyberDialogue. That is *triple* the current figure. While 62 percent of those currently banking online manage their investments there, 33 percent currently use online insurance information, 25 percent trade investments, 24 percent review mortgage information, and 16 percent have applied for a credit card online.

Online bargains: Aimed at filling some of the approximately five hundred thousand airline seats that fly empty every day, priceline.com solicits bids from leisure travelers looking for bargain fares. At www.priceline.com, customers insert travel dates, destinations, and the price they're willing to pay; the service responds with a "yea" or "nay" within an hour. A dozen U.S. and international airlines participate. Priceline.com initially focused on airline tickets but is expanding to include cars, home mortgages, credit cards, and computers. By fall 1998, priceline.com had also ventured into "name your own price cars," currently available in metro New York. They plan to expand into "name your own price home financing" and "name your own price hotel rooms" next.

CHAPTER 17:

Faux Money

"It is no accident that banks resemble temples, preferably Greek, and that the supplicants who come to perform the rites of deposit and withdrawal instinctively lower their voices into the registers of awe. Even the most junior tellers acquire within weeks of their employment the officiousness of hierophants tending an eternal flame. I don't know how they become so quickly inducted into the presiding mysteries, or who instructs them in the finely articulated inflections of contempt for the laity, but somehow they learn to think of themselves as suppliers of the monetarized DNA that is the breath of life."

—LEWIS H. LAPHAM, *Money and Class in America*

*L*OVE OF MONEY IS THE ROOT OF ALL EVIL, proclaims the New Testament. Not so, said English writer Samuel Butler, who asserted that it is the *want* of money that is the root of all evil. Somerset Maugham compared money to "a sixth sense without which you cannot make a complete use of the other five." And American economist John Kenneth Galbraith claimed that money "ranks with love as man's greatest source of joy, and with death as his greatest source of anxiety."

Suddenly money comes in so many forms—from plastic credit cards to certificates of deposit to e-cash—that it feels as though much of it doesn't really exist. We have no coins to jingle in our hand, no bills to pocket, no gems to admire under bright lights. Instead we have pieces of paper telling us that we have money out there—somewhere. Much of our wealth these days doesn't look like money, doesn't feel like money. We just have to hope it works like money when the time comes to spend it.

No matter where you live, money is changing. And so are the institutions that safeguard and manage it. In fact, you could make a convincing argument that no industry is being reborn, mutated, reorganized, and reconsidered at a greater rate than is the business of money. And this change is all starting with our neighborhood bank, the place where we keep our money, invest our money, borrow money and, perhaps most significantly, manage our money, since we all crave control in a world that's in constant flux. This feeling of control will become even more important in the world of Next, when the virtual bank will replace the branch, when smart computers will replace the oh-so-human beings who currently answer telephones, cash checks, and accept deposits.

Financial institutions have a history of success in persuading consumers to adopt new technologies, particularly when they're accompanied by the carrot of convenience. (ATMs, after all, were many people's first experience with a computer.) However, technology's incredible pace of change in recent years has led to wide gaps in consumer confidence levels. At the same time that early adopters demand the very latest in technological innovation (smart cards, PC banking, online investing), traditionalists are uncertain that new applications have been sufficiently tested and thus cling to the perceived security of face-to-face relationships. Increasingly, financial institutions are expected to be all things to all consumers, while also distinguishing their efforts by providing unmatched personalized service.

This chapter details some of the primary trends that will shape the way we conduct financial transactions in the near future.

• NEXT: THE INVISIBLE PAYCHECK

The best technological innovations are those that don't require our participation. Direct deposit fits that bill precisely. It's no surprise, therefore, that direct deposit is becoming prevalent around the world. By depositing salaries into employees' bank accounts electronically, employers reduce processing and delivery costs. Employees like the system because it eliminates delays, loss or theft, and trips to the bank. It's a service that plays perfectly into consumers' demands for convenience and simplification.

Direct deposit is being championed by a variety of organizations. Even the United States government (not known for simplifying anything) has joined the act. Since August 1996, all Social Security recipients applying for benefits must have their checks automatically deposited. By the end of this year, all federal payments, including salaries and other benefits, will be delivered electronically. The Treasury Department estimates that this conversion could save the government as much as $500 million over the next five years and eliminate 100,000 check forgeries and thefts per year.

• NEXT: HIGH FINANCE ON THE NET

Wired consumers aren't purchasing just books and airline tickets online, they've also discovered the value of Internet resources as an investment partner. In addition to researching potential investments, consumers can chat with fellow investors (both novices and veterans) and finance professionals in online forums, track stocks and bonds and even conduct investment transactions online. SRI Consulting in California predicts that while only 8 percent of United States households will use Internet investment services by 2002, those nine million households will represent 15 percent of all households with investments.

At present, investors can trade online via a company's proprietary software, through commercial online services, or directly on the Internet. The American Association of Individual Investors reports that direct investment over the Internet is the fastest growing segment of online trading, with 76 percent of online traders offering Internet service today, up from just 42 percent in 1995. Increased competition online has led to price wars, with some services offering trades for as little as $9.

Today there are more than fifty online brokerage houses in the cybermarket, up from twelve in 1995. A recent survey from *Barron's* determined that online trading accounted for 17 percent of all retail stock trades in 1997. According to Forrester Research, there are an estimated three million online trading accounts, and this number is predicted to increase to 14.4 million by 2002.

In general, personal-finance resources online are growing in both number and popularity. For instance, AOL's Motley Fool site records fifteen million visits each month (AOL keyword: Fool), and the Silicon Investor website (www.techstocks.com) draws thirty thousand daily visitors and sixty thousand monthly postings. Interactive activities range from the practical (online trading) to the educational (financial-planning worksheets) to the entertaining (contests). In addition to posting prospectuses and other literature on its website, Fidelity Investments (www.fidelity.com) has incorporated interactive planning tools. For example, a program asks questions to determine a respondent's investment timeline and attitude toward risk, then suggests appropriate investments.

Quote.com (www.quote.com), which bills itself as the Internet's leading provider of financial market information for serious investors, reports that its 195,000 registered users are predominantly serious investors and traders who conduct an average of forty trades per year and have an average net worth of $1.2 million. The typical user purportedly spends 3.5 hours per week on the Quote.com site.

Elsewhere on the Internet, investors able to describe their "perfect" fund can use software screening programs that search through a universe of funds for those that meet designated risk, return, and management styles. Mutual Fund Expert (www.steelesystems.com), for example, lists more than 10,950 mutual funds and 5,100 variable annuities. The Market News Center on AOL (AOL keyword: Markets) features most of the major United States and international indices (including the S&P 500, NASDAQ, Dow Jones Industrial Average, and the Japanese, British and Hong Kong), breaking news reports, reports on upcoming earnings, a guide to mutual funds and a guide to conducting company research.

These capabilities do not come cheap: Delivering Internet-based financial services can cost firms as much as $23.1 million, according to "Transaction Site Sticker Shock," a report from Forrester Research. "Financial companies are shifting their websites from promotions to transactions. Yet many of them are unaware of the rapidly escalating costs that lie ahead," said Karen Epper, author of the report. "As costs soar into the tens of millions, firms can no longer view the Web as an inexpensive, under-the-radar-screen venture."

• NEXT: THE FAUX BRANCH—ONLINE BANKING

Fifteen years ago, automated teller machines were just coming into vogue. Today, ATMs are such an integral part of banking in North America and elsewhere that at least one bank has begun charging a small fee to customers who wish to deal with an actual bank teller. Following the success of ATMs, a number of banks began to encourage their customers to pay bills, transfer funds between accounts, and conduct other transactions via telephone. That was followed by largely unsuccessful efforts to promote banking over the PC using proprietary software. Now some banks are offering one more option: banking via the Internet. Although we're only in the initial stages of this trend, a study by Coopers and Lybrand estimates that a third of all American households will use computers for some form of online investment or banking by 2004.

It's clear that many (if not all) banks consider the future of their industry to lie online. And they expect consumers to go where their money will be living—in cyberspace. A survey by leading management consultancy Booz-Allen & Hamilton revealed that major corporate banks plan to quadruple their Internet offerings by the year 2000 and that 42 percent of them plan to have advanced sites that offer complete interactive corporate banking. Booz-Allen projects that nearly 40 percent of corporate cash-management customers will use some form of Internet banking within the next three years.

An estimated two thousand United States banks have websites, and this number is growing rapidly. By 2000, 40 percent of all financial transactions are expected to take place online. Over twenty-four million Internet users in the U.S. are expected to bank online by 2002. This, acording to CyberDialogue, is a magnificent rise from 6.9 million a the end of 1998. Sixty-two percent of those who bank online handle their investments via the Internet, and 25 percent of banking customers trade investments in cyberspace.

In the United States, one big player in online banking is

America Online. AOL's Banking Center currently is partnered with more than twenty financial institutions, including American Express, Bank of America, Chase Manhattan, Citibank, Mellon, PNC, Sanwa Bank California, Signet and Wells Fargo. Each of these institutions has built a virtual branch accessible via AOL. In the United Kingdom, Dot Matrix is developing the Digital Online Terminal (DOT), a home-banking system that attaches to a television and communicates with a participating bank via a standard telephone line. Account holders will be able to view bank statements, pay bills online, make transfers between accounts, and make purchases over the Internet. The system will use a smart-card slot that accepts any standard card, including Mondex.

Focus: Online Banking in the U.S. Hits the Big Time

According to PSI Global, 52 percent of all online consumers believe that they will be banking online in the next year. Of the respondents in this survey, 27 percent use online bill payment, investment services or banking. This survey also shows that the majority of people who use online banking use only the minimum services such as calling up checking account balances and transferring funds. It was discovered that two thirds of these online banking patrons tried the product through a free trial offer. Citibank has taken this idea one step further and is offering $25 to new customers who complete bill payment transactions through their newly upgraded free online banking service. Citibank's enhanced Direct Access Internet Banking is now also available through AOL and Microsoft Internet Explorer. The goal of this marketing blitz is to get a million new customers using Direct Access. Online banking has been available to Citibank customers for fifteen years, but it was not until recently that banking through the Internet became available. Citibank was named Number One Online Banking Service in a recent survey. It has a complete range of financial offerings for its online customers, from bill payment to buying and selling stock. With more than three thousand locations in a hundred countries, that million-customer mark could catch up fast.

• NEXT: CASH GOES HIGH TECH

The time will most likely come when actual currency never makes it into the retail environment. Electronic cash (e-cash) is a totally anonymous, electronic debit card that uses an embedded computer chip. It's intended to replace currency (not credit cards or checks). This innovation has huge potential given that whereas an estimated 82 percent of the value of daily U.S. dollar transactions occur in electronic form (e.g., credit-card purchases and bank transfers), approximately 85 percent of the actual financial transactions are in cash. Examples of e-cash at work include pre-paid phone cards and metro and bus debit cards. Vending machines and other self-service devices generally are used as the introductory step.

Like e-cash, smart cards are embedded with a computer chip that tracks consumer spending and stores information, such as product preferences and spending history, about customers. A smart card is considered more secure than e-cash, since it won't work without a personal identification number. Among other applications, the technology can be used for electronic supermarket coupons, paperless airplane tickets, and electronic medical records.

Ironically, high-tech cash (including e-cash and smart cards) is something that's still Next in computer-obsessed America, although Europeans are already living a life of plastic smart money. The vast majority of consumers in Denmark, for instance, handle almost all bill payments and major transactions electronically; debit cards have largely replaced checks. Among other concerns hampering the adoption of smart cards in the United States are the products' untraceability (which might benefit tax evaders and drug dealers), difficulty in taxing cyberspace transactions (where did the transaction take place?), questions surrounding who should issue e-cash (unlike currency, e-cash becomes worthless if the issuing entity goes bankrupt), and the potential for counterfeiting.

In all likelihood, smart cards will rise above these concerns and become standard practice throughout the world. The advantages for businesses and consumers are simply too strong to ignore.

A study by Killen & Associates entitled, "Non Banks' Smart Card Strategies: New Opportunities to Increase Sales and Profits," found that telephone companies are ideally positioned to apply smart cards to capture a significant share of the booming market for electronic cash and Internet payments. Killen sees these markets growing from a worldwide total of 250 million transactions in 1996 to twenty-five billion in 2005. Because providers will aggressively introduce and market stored-value cards (cash already deposited against purchase—also known as prepaid) and smart cards, 30 percent of these payments will be made by smart cards by 2005, the company reports.

Smart cards offer myriad applications. Monaco, for example, has created a smart-card loyalty system for visitors to the country's hotels and casinos. It's intended to encourage repeat visits to Monte Carlo. Users accumulate points every time they make a purchase at a participating store. Points can be exchanged for cash discounts on merchandise or applied toward a range of reward schemes, including discounted meals and airline tickets. Airlines are sure to be close behind in devising innovative frequent-flyer schemes facilitated by smart-card technology.

WHAT'S NEXT?

Consolidation craze: Look for a growing number of bank consolidations, particularly outside the United States. *The Economist* reports that as American banks have consolidated over the past decade, their costs have decreased from 67 percent to 56 percent of income, making them among the most efficient in the world. By contrast, the average expense ratio is 65 percent among German banks and 70 percent among French banks. Outside Britain, Europe is severely overbanked. Whereas the United States has one branch for every forty-seven hundred people, Italy has a branch for every twenty-nine hundred citizens, Germany has one for every two thousand and Spain has one for every eleven hundred. Since competitors today must make it in the global arena, expect the rest of the world to join the consolidation craze.

One-stop shopping: As in the telecommunications industry, one-stop shopping is essential to reach finance customers who don't want multiple relationships with vendors and who want to facilitate the transfer of funds between checking and savings accounts, mutual funds, certificates of deposit and other accounts. Miguel Velhinho, our colleague based in Lisbon, Portugal, notes that in his country, hypermarkets already have blurred the distinction between shop and bank by providing products and services such as in-store bank branches and credit cards. The key to finance Next will be convenience, whether that convenience comes via Internet access or by the ability to switch funds between accounts while picking up the week's groceries. (That is, until Net Grocer becomes your preferred purveyor of groceries...)

Internet-affiliated charge cards: Block Financial, a division of H&R Block, and Visa International have created WebCard Visa, a credit card for Internet users. Cardholders enjoy unrestricted access to account data and can download information directly into word-processing, spreadsheet, database, or personal-finance software such as Quicken. Account numbers never appear online, and the card has a competitive interest rate and no annual fee.

Online machinations: To root out potential stock manipulations related to orchestrated hype or outright fraud, the National Association of Securities Dealers has announced it will conduct routine searches of online sites for any mention of stocks experiencing unusual trading activity.

Investment clubs: Across America and in parts of Europe, people with limited disposable incomes are joining investment clubs. Participants typically contribute $10 to $50 a month and collectively invest the pooled funds. More than half of all such clubs have a better average annual return than Standard & Poor's 500-stock index each year.

Bible-based investing: In conjunction with a rise in spirituality, we're seeing an increase in Bible-based investing. The practice is grounded in the Judeo-Christian principle of stewardship, under which you are obligated to make the best use of resources entrusted to your care. Under its tenets, bankruptcy is a sin, as is investing in so-called sin stocks. Mutual funds that have been established to cater to the beliefs of specific Christian denominations include the Domini Social Equity Fund, which excludes companies involved in alcohol, tobacco, gaming, weapons making and nuclear power. Organizations specializing in Bible-based financial advising include the Timothy Plan's network of Christian Financial Consultants and the First Affirmative Financial Network. Among other investment guides available is one titled *God Wants You to be Rich* by Paul Zane Pilzer (Fireside, 1997).

Socially responsible investing: On a broader scale, consumers are insisting that the companies in which they invest maintain certain standards of conduct. The bottom line is no longer their sole concern. Shareholder requests have led Shell, for example, to release two new reports to investors, one on environmental preservation efforts and the other on human rights.

Multiservice ATMS: Within a few years, multiservice ATMs are expected to dispense not only cash, but also stamps, phone cards, travelers checks, and theater tickets. Sprint has even contracted with EDS to provide long-distance services through ATMs. Users receive a receipt bearing Sprint's logo, an 800 number and an access code. NatWest's ATMs in London have begun to dispense advertisements along with cash.

Bartering: Bartering is back. Perhaps as an offshoot of our desire for simplification, in addition to being a cost-saving device, the barter industry is experiencing 15 percent annual growth and has reached $8 billion in annual trade. The concept of bartering— exchanging goods and services without cash—is ancient, but bartering in its modern form reemerged in the 1960s and is experiencing steady growth. Barter transactions in the United States and Canada were estimated at $9.1 billion in 1996, up from $5.3 billion in 1990, according to the International Reciprocal Trade Association. IRTA estimates that in 1997, the barter industry conducted $20 billion in transactions worldwide.

At the center of the industry is the National Association of Trade

Exchanges, an association of business owners and professionals who have joined together to trade surplus goods and services. Members provide products and services to other members in exchange for trade dollars (which have the equivalent of cash dollars). Further growth of the industry is expected to be fueled by the Internet, which has opened up global trading and communication possibilities that were once unthinkable. With expansion being the buzz in the barter industry, expect to see smaller, independent exchanges consolidate into larger, more sophisticated electronic clearinghouses.

New access to investors: A couple of years ago, Destiny Pictures, a startup film-production company in Los Angeles, offered stock in a low-budget movie over the Internet for $100 per share. Within a few months, more than 150 people from around the world had ordered $15,000 worth of shares in the erotic thriller *Intimate Stranger.* (Not exactly a blockbuster, was it?) Look for other innovative investment opportunities online—and subsequent regulation.

Innovative investment ideas abound on the Internet. You just need to know where to look. On the Internet today there are more than a hundred investment clubs where people can research potential stock buys, meet people who know the market, or even learn how to start their own club. One site with useful research tools is Invest-o-rama (www.investorama.com).

Eye-scanning: New Jersey-based Sensar Inc. will soon offer ATM manufacturers an alternative to passwords and PINs. When a customer inserts a bank card, a camera locates his or her eye and takes a digital image of the iris. In less than two seconds, the resulting "iris code" is compared with one initially provided by the customer. No match, no money. Sensar has run tests in unnamed banks already.

On-site screening: Deluxe Corporation, the largest check printer in the United States, has joined with credit scoring company Fair, Isaac & Company and data warehouse Acxiom Corporation to create the "debit bureau" credit-rating system. Deluxe will gather information from banks about bounced checks and payment problems. Acxiom will combine that data with other financial information and pass it along to Fair, Isaac, which will use it to generate a credit rating. Retailers will soon use the system at point of purchase to determine whether to accept an individual's check or debit card. The service also will be marketed to banks to help them decide whether to open a checking account for a particular person and, if so, under what terms.

• NEXT: MORE BANKRUPTCIES ON THE HORIZON

1.4 million Americans declared bankruptcy last year, which is one in every seventy households. And the number continues to rise. But while bailing out of debts on a personal level seems to be gaining in popularity, business bankruptcy seems a less appealing option, and grew at a rate of just 1 percent last year. (In comparison, personal bankruptcies were up almost 20 percent.) This also spells a subtle next in terms of an increasing divide in values between Americans who can walk away from their personal debts, by declaring themselves unable to pay them, and Europeans who consider it a terrible action, akin to total failure.

• NEXT: MONEY MATTERS

While it's not new it is next: Money is increasingly associated with security. And money is also associated with freedom. As *Roper Reports* noted, money means security, independence, freedom, comfort, being able to help your children, pleasure, something to leave heirs, achievement, contribution to society, control, power, and status. Most meaningful, though, is that the greatest rise in "value" is "contribution to society" and "something to leave heirs" illustrating an increased sense that money means one can make a mark on life in this century and beyond.

CHAPTER 18:

The Future
of Media

> People don't actually read newspapers, they get into
> them every morning like a hot bath.
>
> —MARSHALL McLUHAN

• NEXT: THE END OF DEAD-TREE MEDIA?

Video may have killed the radio star, but will the information age
be the final coup de grace for the embattled publishing industry?
Discount chains are driving mom and pop bookstores out of the
market, while online vendor Amazon.com steals market share
from the giant brick-and-mortar establishments. Meanwhile, to
stay competitive in the global marketplace, the publishing industry is consolidating like crazy—the most publicized example being
Bertelsmann AG's acquisition of Random House. It is becoming
increasingly clear that the future of print is subject to two oppos-
ing forces. On the one hand, lower prices, greater access to rare
and out-of-print books, and cyber-retailing are making this a consumer's market. On the other, the more conglomerated print publishers become, the less they are able to stay in tune with hyperlocal consumer markets. The biggest problem for publishers then,
may not be one of sales but of inventory, as cartloads of remain-
ders are shipped back to the warehouse.

This is not the case in digital media, where vendors learned
from the made-to-order computer model (pioneered by the Dell

Computer Corporation) and started purchasing books on a per-order basis. But mired in Gutenberg-era tradition, publishing companies are slow to adapt to such paradigm-altering change. Barnes & Noble and Borders Books, for example, learned how much market share they were giving away the hard way as Amazon's valuation soared past the market cap of both of those bookstores put together.

Whether or not concrete media (that is, books and newspapers) are ever going to be replaced by their digital descendants, one thing is clear: The way people read is evolving. "Media is not a zero sum game," says Paul Saffo, a director of the Institute for the Future in Menlo Park, California, told the *Consumer Research Study on Book Purchasing*. "Just because a new medium arrives doesn't mean an old medium dies out. We still have writing in an age of word processing; we still have reading in an age of video. That will continue, but the nature of reading will change as it has changed all along." As consumers pick and choose which media best suit their needs, a number of innovative new trends in book and newspaper retailing may ensure that the "print edition" not only survives, but even expands its reach.

• NEXT: DIGITAL PUBLISHING

The death of the author! The death of the novel! Death to dead-tree media! As early adopters snatch up e-books to download libraries of free e-text off of the Internet, even the Amazons of the world may have some nail-biting to do about the future of print. But industry analysts started preparing the eulogies long before the advent of the digital age. And despite all of their doomsday braying, the paperboys are still making their rounds.

True, e-books will allow for quick, cheap downloads of virtually any book (in or out of print) and may eat into publishers' profits. But the new wave of portable, lightweight electronic "books"—among them NuvoMedia's Rocket eBook and SoftBook Press' SoftBook—are still beset with the typical problems of first-generation products. The glowing LCD displays, for example, don't come close to the clear resolution of ink on a page. They are too heavy, have a too short battery life, and are still prohibitively expensive ($499 to $1,500 for color), according to the *San Jose Mercury News*. Of course, in the electronics market, prices fall faster than the Dow; models priced as low as $199 will undoubtedly be next year's stocking stuffers.

The upside is that these devices may eventually do as much to popularize reading among youthful digerati as Oprah's Book Club has among women. Kids are increasingly hard-pressed to abandon their interactive 3-D video game consoles to delve into a staid, 2-D medium. But interactive experiences that are half audio book, half video game, might do much to bring kids back to the library (itself soon accessible from home as a digital repository offering online downloads).

Having learned the lesson of early adoption from the Internet, publishers are jumping on the e-book bandwagon. HarperCollins, McGraw-Hill, Penguin Putnam, Random House, and Simon & Schuster are among those promising to convert some of their books to a compatible electronic format. Still, they aren't giving owners of e-books a price break; most downloads are the same price as the paperback version. Authors are optimistic as well, viewing online distributors as a way to increase royalties and bypass publishing houses, which tend to move at a glacial pace.

E-book makers are conservative about the reach of their market, at least for now. "It's not a consumer business we're aiming for," says James Sachs, CEO of SoftBook Press, in *Business Week*. "It's a professional information business—financial services, pharmaceuticals, law firms." Sachs expects professional publishers to begin selling their publications in electronic form sometime in the coming year.

But the electronic reading tablet is only one part of the digital publishing revolution. Other innovations coming down the pipe include print-on-demand technologies, Internet distribution systems that send books in either Adobe Acrobat (pdf) or PalmPilot formats, and "digital ink." The latter is perhaps the most sci-fi of them all. Digital ink is made up of tiny, charged particles in a dye. The particles change position when they're exposed to an electric charge, thus changing the shape of whatever is written or drawn. Being able to change the text with an electronic zap means that texts will be more like works in progress than final editions—with everything from outdoor billboards to college textbooks updating themselves in real-time.

Digital ink is a natural outgrowth of digital publishing. And both applications present an enormous opportunity for publishers and advertisers as print media seeks to customize its content for hyperlocal markets without multiple print runs. "That's where the real opportunity for digital printing comes in," says Forrest P. Gauthier, CEO of Varis Corp. in *American Printer*, a trade magazine. "Digital technology's real strength is when each page in a document is different—total page composition based on demographics. The objective is to create a document that meets exactly what the end-user's need is. . . . Digital printing, combined with variable data or database publishing, has the ability to create a custom document at press speeds. That's where we believe the printing industry can go."

Such customization is raising the eyebrows of retailers too. J.C. Penney & Co., for one, is eager to start testing digital ink signs, says Edward Sample, the retailer's manager of systems support and technology. He already has seen a prototype that changed from blank to the words *J.C. Penney* and back, and he looks forward to printed signs bearing eye-catching moving messages or counting down the days to the arrival of a new line of sportswear. Associated Press reports that a company called E Ink of Cambridge, Massachusetts, hopes to start marketing the changeable signs this year. With letters two inches to four feet tall, signs would cost $100 to $5,000, depending on the number of letters to be displayed, says E Ink vice president Russ Wilcox.

If what's happening in North America has any bearing on what will happen in the rest of the world—and with regard to cyberspace and media consumption, it does—TV programmers had better get poised for decreased audiences once online services get into full swing. Seventy-eight percent of respondents to a study by Forrester Research said they make time for PC use by spending less time in front of the TV. For the most part, viewers are not giving up their favorite programs but are cutting down on channel-surfing. Although frequent PC users could watch a lot less television without dramatically changing overall viewership, the attrition of these more affluent and better-educated viewers is likely to make the medium less attractive to some advertisers.

Newspaper publishers already are taking steps to stay competitive in a wired world. A recent report from the Newspaper Association of America confirms a downward trend in advertising and circulation. This is not a new trend: in 1996, only 59 percent of adults in America read a daily paper, down from 64 percent in 1995. In the same period, Sunday readership dropped from 72.6 to 68.5 percent. This trend is particularly evident among young people, with only 45 percent of eighteen to twenty-four-year-olds and 47 percent of twenty-five to thirty-four-year-olds reading a daily paper in 1996, down from 55 and 56 percent, respectively, in 1994. Given current trends, respected journalist John Morton has predicted that the newspaper industry will essentially expire in the next thirty years or so as consumers turn to the Internet, TV and radio for their news.

Customized News

The proliferation of Internet-based media and other online sources means competition not only for newspapers and magazines but for TV (network, cable and satellite) and radio as well. It seems inevitable that news will become more customized as consumers gain the ability to configure an individualized diet made up of niche-market publications, Usenet newsgroups, "push" newsfeeds, cable news programming, and other sources. Result: Nations might become increasingly fragmented in the absence of a handful of standard sources of news. There was a time when workers gathering at their place of employment could be relatively certain that they had all watched the same TV newscast the night before and read the same newspapers that morning—and afternoon. That assumption is no longer valid.

Is the customization of news and information channels a bad thing? Not necessarily. For many people, customized news is more convenient and useful than traditional sources. Each of this book's authors subscribes to at least one customized news source, whether it be NewsHound, PointCast, or some other Internet-based venture. We receive a continuous flow of information on trends we're tracking and other topics of interest without combing through dozens of publications. Ann, for example, starts most workdays at the NewsPage website (www.newspage.com), where she scans headlines and reads work-related articles. When she joined the service, she indicated which topics she was interested in, and her daily menu is drawn from that list. She also receives a daily guide to articles available at the CNET site (www.cnet.com) as well as regular alerts from Wall Street Journal Interactive (www.wsj.com) regarding industries in which she has expressed an interest.

On a more personal level, Ann recently joined the Food Allergy Network's "alerts" mailing list (www.foodallergy.org/index.html). She is notified immediately via e-mail whenever the network learns that a manufacturer has recalled or sent out a warning about a product that contains an unlisted ingredient. (In most cases, the company in question covers the cost of sending out the alerts.) Since Ann's son is allergic to peanuts, this direct newsfeed is a valuable resource; it ensures that she gets information she'd be unlikely to receive from the national TV news and might have overlooked when reading her local paper. This program's value was proved recently when Ann received an e-mail warning her of a product recall involving the medication she keeps on hand in case her son has a severe allergic reaction. The e-mail reached her hours before her pharmacist's phone call.

That's the upside of customized news.

What will happen, though, if people begin to restrict themselves to highly tailored news to the exclusion of general-interest news sources? The same targeted resources that allow for the building of online communities among the elderly, gays and lesbians, Stateside Europeans, environmental activists, and the like also can provide a steady flow of narrowly cast news and information to political extremists and conspiracy theorists. It's already difficult to tell fact from fiction on the Internet, and rumors are spread at blinding speed. In 1997, we saw journalist Pierre Salinger go public with "facts" purportedly showing that TWA Flight 800 was downed not by a mechanical malfunction but by friendly fire from a U.S. Navy surface-to-air missile. His source? Internet newsgroups.

Some Americans claim that the media have perpetuated the 1998–99 sexual scandal surrounding President Clinton, and they don't want to hear anymore. Yet television ratings and newspaper circulations have been at peak rates. NBC's *Meet The Press* ratings were a full 50 percent higher the week in January when the scandal broke versus the week before. *Good Morning America* reached its second highest ratings in a decade the morning Hillary Clinton appeared to defend her husband.

We've already introduced you to Matt Drudge, of "The Drudge Report", who has hundreds of thousands of readers each day on his website. He also purports to be the one who forced the story about President Clinton and the twenty-four-year-old White House intern into the open. True or not, this was one Internet rumor of global proportions.

The vast array of information channels available to consumers today means each of us is responsible for selecting his or her own media diet. It's up to the individual consumer to determine whether his or her diet is rich in nutritious news from top-notch journalists or made up of nothing but tabloid reports, extremist e-zines, and other forms of junk news. Neighbors who choose vastly different media diets might find that their world views have little in common. There's also the possibility that the market will cease to support the high-cost apparatus that is the foundation of objective journalism, as audiences become increasingly fragmented and subscription and advertising moneys are further divided.

A Truly Global Medium

Cyberspace will be the first medium to become truly global; as such, it is subject to debate over everything from freedom of the press to copyright infringement to the risks and rewards of cultures becoming blurred through common sources of news and entertainment. Although he has visited China many times since, media mogul Rupert Murdoch, whose News Corp. bought the Star TV cable network in 1993, attracted the most attention from Chinese officials that very year, when he made a speech in London saying that technological advances such as satellite television were "an unambiguous threat to totalitarian regimes everywhere." China's leadership promptly forbade individuals to buy satellite dishes, which had been selling at a fast clip. Since then, sales have quietly resumed, but the damage had already been done. According to *The New York Times*, Murdoch's efforts to repair ties to Beijing—which included eliminating the BBC news service from Star TV's broadcast—have yet to win over government officials. Oddly, an unintended consequence of Murdoch's remarks was that Beijing started encouraging the growth of cable networks, until then very small, because leaders are convinced they can control the content of cable better than that of satellite broadcasts. Star TV is believed to be losing at least $100 million a year, primarily because unknown viewership figures (it does not collect subscription fees) prevent the channel from selling sufficient advertising.

This chapter takes a look at some of the other major trends we're seeing in media today, with a focus on how various industries are responding to this upstart competitor, the Internet. We actually thought about titling this chapter "You Are What Influences You" because as consumers gain access to more and more means of communication, the marketing communications future will be grounded in the idea of "message layering," or approach consumers in as many ways as possible.

Paul Woolmington, president of international media operations at The Media Edge, shared his insights with us. "The new media order requires us to put consumers and customers at the center of our media- and content-rich universe," he says. "From this vantage point we will be better equipped to select the most potent communication and media channels. These new rules of engagement require us to take a much broader view, use sharper media tools, break and remake the rules through better 'consumerized' strategies."

Woolmington adds, "Prime time, as we have traditionally known it, is being slowly but surely redefined—redefined in the minds of ever-fragmenting audiences with regard to when, where, how and in what format they want to receive and interact with their own, more personalized, media content."

The core strategic challenge for tomorrow's marketers will be to ensure a consistent, uniform presentation of the brands in their steward, recognizing the appropriate roles of each "layer" of the communications plan in generating a coherent, effective whole. We watch with particular interest as marketing communications practices jockey for position as the custodian of the layering strategy.

• NEXT: GLOBALLY BRANDED NEWS

We've come a long way from the age of the town crier, Gutenberg's printing press and Ben Franklin's almanac. Today, we want information delivery, like every other aspect of our lives, to be *fast*. The terms *instantaneous* and *real-time* convey expectations that are far removed from those implied during the days of Edward R. Murrow's "See It Now" or even the *60 Minutes* of today. (Seven days after the fact is anything but "now.")

The press has risen to the occasion. CNN, for one, has become an important worldwide source of information. CNN's coverage of the Persian Gulf War generally is considered to be the seminal moment in the network's coming of age as the preferred source for breaking coverage of world events whenever and wherever they occur. The venerable news divisions of ABC, NBC and CBS did not cede their hegemony as the source authority in television news. Rather, CNN steadily chipped away at their domination through dedicated brand-building. It brought to bear an unmatched combination of focus (24/7), reach and credibility (sometimes in the form of "name" talent secured from traditional sources, but more often by rigid reporting standards and legitimate global credentials)—and harnessed the necessary technology to yield seamless and timely delivery. Today, CNN has new competition, in the form of Britain's BBC World Service. Tomorrow, the rate at which information will span the globe will mean that competition can come from anywhere around the world. In our opinion, the Operation Tailwind nerve-gas story in 1998 undercut CNN's legitimate global credentials and reputation for rigid reporting standards for the long haul—changing again the psychic landscape for globally branded news next.

• NEXT: HYPERLOCAL OFFERINGS

We discussed earlier how consumers' media menus are growing more individualized as a result of the much broader selection of information sources. As we count down toward the millennium, we expect to see companies lay the groundwork for sponsor-supported Web pages customized to individual consumers who fall within specific demographic markers. Rather than waste time surfing the Internet for sites that are relevant to their interests and needs, consumers will be able to fill out an online questionnaire, specifying their areas of interest. From those choices, cyberconsultants will design a personalized Web page filled with links to an individually tailored assortment of ever-changing sites. Once a personal Web page has been designed, it will be constantly updated and revised to reflect 1) new and improved options available on the Web, 2) customer feedback, and 3) the amount of time the customer spends at each linked site.

A few years down the road, we expect to see this customization concept extended to local television news reports. Viewers will be able to tailor their nightly news broadcast from a menu of options, specifying, for example, whether they wish to receive the total sports broadcast, just news on certain teams or no sports news at all; whether they want just local news or national and/or international news; and whether they are more interested in financial reports or human-interest stories. It will even be possible for viewers to specify that they do not want to receive news of a violent or sexual nature or even any "bad" news. Hyperlocal news segments will also be available, as towns and communities provide footage of local events.

One of the most important implications of this trend will be that the increased segmentation of households and individual viewers will allow for hypertargeted advertising. At the same time, national media organizations will struggle to stay relevant for a mass audience as resources shift to local news operations.

• NEXT: OTHER MEDIA GET WIRED

Newspaper journalists are bemoaning the demise of their medium. A survey by the American Society of Newspaper Editors found that journalists tend to be dissatisfied with the quality of their own newspapers and believe newspapers are losing importance. According to a report in *Editor & Publisher*, 64 percent of the one-thousand-plus journalists surveyed by the Association of Newspaper Journalists said they only occasionally or rarely consider their papers a "good read," and only 36 percent find them "usually very interesting." A majority (55 percent) think newspapers will play a less important part in life ten years hence than they do now.

In a bid to keep pace with the rapidly changing world of information retrieval, more than fifteen hundred commercial newspapers have staked a site on the Internet thus far. Internet-based ad sales are expected to grow to more than $5 billion by the year 2000, but for now many publishers are building their sites with the expectation that they will be losing money in the short term. Time Warner's Pathfinder, for instance, was said to be losing between $5 million and $10 million a year before it died in 1999. Parent companies are agreed to take early losses with the expectation that growing reliance on the Internet will push a paying audience—and advertisers—their way in the months and years to come, but they're anxious about getting into the black (and far outta the black hole).

Of course, not everyone can afford to be in the red for so long. Companies whose pockets are not quite so deep are being displaced in what has come to be known as the "great Web shake-out"; significant news domains such as Out and Politics Now, for example, have closed their sites in the face of serious financial losses. Nevertheless, the Newspaper Association of America reports that more than a third of online newspapers made money last year. An additional 24 percent of online newspapers run by traditional media companies expect to be profitable within four years. The big moneymakers to date have been classifieds, display advertising and job listings. We expect competition among content providers to increase even more, as companies choose to build their brands via their own content-heavy Web sites, rather than simply place ads on other organizations' sites.

By most indications, there's a clear audience for online publications. The research firm NPD Group reports that sixty percent of Web users surveyed frequently read newspapers and/or magazines online. Nearly 40 percent of the 1,527 respondents read an online daily newspaper. Among other findings: Nine out of ten respondents who read print and online newspapers rated the two comparable in terms of accuracy and reliability. Of magazines read online, computer titles are the most popular (read by half the sample), followed by entertainment (36 percent), news (also 36 percent), business (24 percent), sports (15 percent), and women's magazines (11 percent). Approximately a quarter of the participants who read online publications said they would be willing to pay for a subscription to online computer magazines, newspapers, business magazines and/or sports magazines. Subscriptions to entertainment magazines, however, would be purchased by only 13 percent.

Who's reading newspapers? Well, according to a 1998 study by the Newspaper Association of America, readers of daily newspapers are more likely to be fifty-plus, white and male. Also, and perhaps more interesting, given the Big Next of The Global versus Hyperlocal paradox, is that people who've lived in a given community for ten-plus years are almost twice as likely to read newspapers regularly. Homeowners read newspapers more often than do renters. And those with a strong sense of local identification are regular newspaper readers. Women are less likely than men to be regular newspaper readers, perhaps because America's women are more overloaded with home/work demands. The NAA study revealed that women claim to have only four hours of free time during the week and seven on Sunday, whereas men have almost five hours during the week and nearly nine hours of "personal time" on Sundays. (And if local is a strong *Next* for the newspaper business, it won't surprise anyone that the most interesting item in the newspaper is weather, followed by community and neighborhood news.)

• NEXT: LESS INTEREST IN POLITICS AND GOVERNMENT

While people might be reading newspapers with some level of enthusiasm, despite the fact that total newspaper consumption has fallen over the last twenty years, they're not following politics and government most of the time. In 1998 a Pew Research Center study revealed that only 36 percent of Americans reported they follow politics and government most of the time, down from 46 percent in 1994. And when it comes to what political issues *do* catch our eyes and ears—and thus what's going to be covered more completely by media in the future—potential regulation of health maintenance organizations is it. Americans see this issue as very important to the country (69 percent) and to themselves (60 percent). You'd never know it from the number of newspapers and magazines and television journalists jawing on in late September 1998 about Monica Lewinsky and President Bill Clinton, but high-profile government investigations generally interest few Americans—only 18 percent say they are important to the country, and only 17 percent call them important to themselves personally.

• NEXT: THE CONVERGENCE OF TV AND PC CONTENT

In the summer of 1998, a merger of astounding proportions was completed that might change the face of the computer and the TV as we know them. AT&T, the nation's largest phone company, stunned the world with its forethought when it bought TCI, the nation's second-largest cable company. AT&T has committed to helping TCI upgrade all of its lines for high-speed data transmission. With this kind of clout behind it, @Home—a high-speed Internet service provider partlly owned by TCI—hopes to avoid problems such as the busy signals and call terminations that have plagued AOL. "All the things that the Internet was supposed to be, it hasn't been yet," @Home's Jake Moffat said. "We finally are offering what the Internet was supposed to be." This is the wake-up call for the 4,700 Internet service providers who hope to remain in this ever-changing industry.

Television executives are also taking the growth of the Internet seriously, as is evidenced by their efforts to get a piece of the action. In July 1996, Microsoft and the National Broadcasting Company launched MSNBC (www.msnbc.com), a twenty-four-hour, online cable TV network. Core programming originally included three prime-time hours: a news talk show, a new-media and technology show and an hourly evening newscast with interview and discussion segments. The network has contributed some serious talent to help ensure the initiative's success: NBC News anchor Tom Brokaw, former *Today* host and current *Dateline NBC* anchor Jane Pauley, and Washington chief Tim Russert have regular MSNBC gigs; Brian Williams is the chief anchor.

The cablecast TV offering is closely linked to its companion website at msnbc.com, which provides archived content (to provide depth) and offers a host of interactive facilities, including viewer ratings of on-air content and opinion polls. MSNBC might well be what "convergence" looks like.

Microsoft also is appealing to a more narrow audience via its recent Web programming partnership with BET (Black Entertainment Television).

Hoping to compete with MSNBC in the category of computer-mediated news reporting is ABCNEWS.com (www.abcnews.com), an alliance between ABC News, Starwave, Netscape Communications, and America Online. The online news service provides up-to-the-minute local, national and international news, as well as sports, entertainment, business and technology news. The venture has a reach of sixteen million, including the twelve million visitors to AOL and four million visitors to Netscape. ABCNews.com will draw on the worldwide resources of ABC News, including ABC News Radio and ABC's affiliate newsrooms.

In a bid for a global audience, CNN Interactive (www.cnn.com) has launched a twenty-four-hour news and information service on the Web that includes regional products. The CNN site's once over-loaded World News section has been broken into separate sites for Europe/Middle East, the Americas, Asia-Pacific and Africa. CNN Interactive averaged ten to twelve million hits a day in 1997, with two-thirds of all users based in the United States.

Clearly, we can expect to see more interaction between TV and the Internet in other parts of the world as well. If the North American model is any guide, Web sites will increasingly offer more in-depth analysis, interviews, and background materials than would ever be practical in a TV broadcast forum.

• NEXT: CYBER-RADIO

Radio has also entered cyberspace. Thanks to technology such as RealAudio (www.realaudio.com) and Xing Technology Corporation's StreamWorks (www.xingtech.com), listeners are able to hear "streaming"—or uninterrupted, live, or prerecorded sound—without having to download the full audio file. Bloomberg News Radio, the twenty-four-hour report from WBBR AM 1130 in New

York City, is available at www.bloomberg.com/wbbr/index.html. The news broadcast is delivered in real time at most modem speeds via Streamworks. Minneapolis-based net.radio (www.netradio.net) is the first live, twenty-four-hour-a-day, Internet-only radio station. The eclectic mix of vintage rock and cyberchat has attracted an audience from as far away as Australia, Germany, Israel and South Africa.

CNET radio (www.news.com/Radio/Index), a free daily audio news service exclusively for the Web, covers computers, the Internet, and online services. The Monday through Friday segments run approximately eight to ten minutes each. To encourage interactivity, CNET has incorporated a "your turn" forum, which allows listeners to speak out—literally—on the Web. Listener comments are recorded on dedicated phone lines and then translated to RealAudio segments that can be accessed by other online users. Launched on the Web in June 1995, CNET radio immediately attracted more than 200,000 registered members within the first four months.

• NEXT: DISPOSABLE NEWS

In cyberspace, content is rarely permanent, as users reject yesterday's pages in favor of the latest and greatest. As a result, much of the information produced for the Web and other digital media is disappearing almost as fast as it's created. Among the reasons for the disappearance: Site operators run out of money or time and disconnect their websites or newsgroups from the Internet, and changing technical standards make older websites unreadable. Journalist Denise Caruso, writing for *The New York Times* News Service, observed, "Over the last two decades, an historic shift has occurred as an enormous amount of human endeavor—culture, commerce, communication—has moved from the physical world into the realm of electrons. Text printed on paper, the most persistent fossil of human thought, can still be read and appreciated centuries later. But a thought recorded only as electrons vanishes forever when the last machine that created it finally dies or when a publisher purges all the files from what once was the Web server." Just as much of recorded music didn't make the transition from vinyl to CDs, a significant portion of current Web content is likely to fall by the wayside during the transition to the next generation of Web protocols. One possible way to prevent this is through the use of "Web spiders," software programs that methodically index and archive the entire textual contents of the Web daily.

WHAT'S NEXT?

Land of the giants: Industry mergers are continuing to concentrate power in the hands of a few media giants. We can expect cross-marketing with these companies to be an essential component of marketing communications in the early millennium. Also increasingly common is newspaper "clustering," as newspaper companies buy and sell properties to achieve greater concentration of ownership. In the United States alone, more than 120 dailies changed hands in 1996, according to *American Journalism Review*. Advantages of clustering include lower operating costs, shared news coverage and feature sections and increased advertising revenue (by offering a bigger circulation package, clustered papers can attract more advertising moneys than a single daily could hope to obtain).

Nothing but talk: Consumers' seemingly insatiable desire for news and information is forcing formatting changes in radio, just as consumers' desire for entertainment is edging hard news out of TV broadcasts. Growing listener interest in news talk radio is illustrated by the popularity of nationally syndicated personalities such as Rush Limbaugh and Larry King and by the willingness of Infinity Broadcasting Corporation to keep shock jock Howard Stern on its payroll despite handling over $1.7 million to the Treasury Department in 1995 to settle indecency charges brought against Stern by the FCC between 1989 and 1994. Nearly 1,100 American radio stations specialized in talk and news in 1994, up 175 percent from 1989, making it the fastest-growing radio format. Other non-music formats being adopted by stations include all-sports and all-self-help.

European cable: In Europe, cable still seems new, maybe because its reach is just now achieving critical mass. Net revenues for Western European cable operators are expected to grow to approximately ECU8.4 billion by 2005, according to CIT Research Ltd. The fastest growing markets include France and Eastern and Central Europe. Cable operators in Poland, for example, are expected to triple their revenues by 2005.

Educative marketing: Remember when we used to pick up newspapers for news and information and expect nothing but account balances in our utility bills? No more. Nowadays everyone wants to inform us—print advertisements contain recipes and "fast facts," inserts placed in the envelope alongside our bills contain information on keeping our home at a moderate temperature, protecting our children from bug bites, and keeping the dog's coat shiny. Who needs schools when we have marketers?

Hypertargeted press: As newspapers grow more successful in decoding user demographics, readers can expect targeted zoned editions and tailored ads. "We started out geographically, with zip codes, which made inserting ads easier," Eric Wolferson, VP for technology at the Newspaper Association of America, told the *San Francisco Examiner.* "Now advertisers want even narrower niches, so we're [using] database technology that allows us to have household-specific designations." Eventually, says Wolferson, "you and your neighbor will get different newspapers," with the majority of differences in the ads. A house hunter's newspaper, for example, would feature all available real-estate ads for as long as the reader is in the market for a home.

Increased personalization: Digital printing—which weds computer-generated content with high-speed copiers—eliminates the economies of scale associated with offset printing, making it easier to turn a profit when publishing books in small quantities. Print times are reduced to a few minutes, enabling on-demand printing, a cost-effective alternative to warehousing and stock overruns. Using Xerox DocuTech printers, Simon & Schuster (www.sscp.com) produces more than 125,000 customized books per month. Possible implications: books printed at the bookstore while you wait, ongoing updates from authors, greater chances of being published for unknown writers, and for those in marginal categories, an end to out-of-print books.

Audience feedback: To improve newsstand sales, *Men's Health* is inviting readers to vote for preferred cover text and graphics at www.menshealth.com. Instantaneous feedback means that broadcasters and publishers can more accurately tailor their content to meet the changing needs of their audiences.

Media filters: To stave off information overload, consumers will depend on a variety of trusted sources to help differentiate between worthy and unworthy.

CHAPTER 19:

360 Degree Branding

---

*W*HEN YOU LOOK AT THE PRIMARY CAUSES of business failure over the last decade, resistance to change routinely emerges as a culprit. This bodes ill for entrenched traditionalists, for change is one of the few constants businesses will find in the global marketplace in the year 2000, according to an Economist Intelligence Unit (EIU) survey of ten thousand business executives in North America, Europe and Asia. In marketing we're experiencing that much-overused phrase *paradigm shift* as we work to reinvent our industry to keep pace with rapid changes in communication and consumerism. One result of increased globalization and developments in new media is a push to prepare ourselves for the future by evolving and taking advantage of emerging technologies and cross-border marketing opportunities. By getting in on the early stages of these developments, we're in a good position to foresee and profit from emerging forces among consumers and markets.

What's in Store for Business

Business trends, by their very nature, tend to travel more slowly than do consumer and marketing trends. Many more organizations talk about fundamental change—throwing around buzzwords such as change agents, value migration, and business ecosystems— than actually succeed in making genuine transformations. To be effective, programs to bring about basic corporate change must fulfill two requirements: They must be linked to performance objectives, and they must be created and managed by people who have an understanding of both the current and preferred business structure.

In much of the developed world today, companies are coming to terms with the notion that the business environment isn't changing, it *is* change. As we discussed in earlier chapters on the emergence of the virtual office and the new worker, technological developments over the last two decades are in no small way driving organizations to reevaluate how they do business. One clear sign that the business world is focusing on future shifts and opportunities rather than dwelling on past results is the increasing number of companies eliminating the "review of operations" sections of their annual reports in favor of essays on growth potential and strategies for taking advantage of changes in their businesses and industries. As Les Segal, president of *Addison Corporate Annual Reports*, told *The New York Times*, "The whole business world is changing so fast that investors don't want to look backward; they want to look forward."

In the EIU survey of market place 2000, 67 percent of European respondents stated that their companies' organizational structures will undergo great change by the year 2000; 62 percent expect great change in their corporate cultures. "It is very hard to win in a status quo environment," commented respondent Rob Cawthorn, CEO of French pharmaceutical firm Rhone-Poulenc Rorer. To keep his organization in a "desirable state of flux," Cawthorn (now retired) took steps to prepare his executives for a company in which "authority is pushed down the line and an entrepreneurial approach is encouraged throughout the company."

As we move forward in an era of increasing entrepreneurialism, we can expect heightened efforts to close the gap between top executives and their employees. These efforts will be both psychological (executives dressing more casually, for example) and structural (executives working in the same room as their underlings rather than being ensconced in private corner offices).

We cover business trends specific to advertising and marketing later in the book, although we do warn you that we're marketers first and foremost, so we see the world through different eyes than if we were, say, auditors or finance directors.

• NEXT: KEEP IT SIMPLE, STUPID! (THE KISS PRINCIPLE)

Awareness that consumers are overwhelmed by the product choices they face has spurred companies in a wide variety of industries to simplify their product lines. According to the consulting firm Kurt Salmon Associates, almost a quarter of the products in a typical American supermarket sell fewer than one unit per month. In contrast, 7.6 percent of all personal-care and household products account for 84.5 percent of sales, according to Paine Webber Inc. Responding to the overkill of duplicate brands and unmanageable product lines, Procter & Gamble has slashed its product roster by a third since 1990. Nabisco Inc. has cut its new-product launches by 20 percent and is taking approximately 15 percent of its existing products off the market. Toyota has simplified its car design by stripping vehicles of unnecessary parts.

Today most "new" products are simply copycat versions of old products or line extensions that bring no meaningful new features or benefits to consumers. In general, although copycat products might eventually carve out a small piece of the market, it's the innovative products that are the big winners when it comes to generating sales. According to Market Intelligence Service Ltd., marketers introduced a total of 25,261 new products last year, but only 7 percent of them were genuinely new. In certain industries, though, it was not a record-breaking year; food launches were down 5.9 percent (10,416 new products), beverages dropped 2.8 percent (3,424), and miscellaneous products were down by 37.7 percent (291). Health and beauty aids were up 14.2 percent (9,371), household products increased 49.9 percent (1,177) and pet products were up 31.1 percent (582). Of these product introductions, however, only 5.8 percent were considered different from existing products.

These trends, like the merger-and-acquisition mania that has invaded the advertising industry, lead us to wonder whether the marketplace has turned away from the invention, entrepreneurship, and innovation that have historically driven the industrial engine toward the art of the deal. Has finance replaced creative genius as the driving force? Is this bean-counting style what's Next, especially in the near term? (Unfortunately, we believe "Bean Think," mixed with prudent financial management, is indeed what's Next in many businesses.)

• NEXT: THE URGE TO MERGE

Chrysler married Mercedes. Novartis was born when Ciba married Sandoz. America Online acquired CompuServe then Netscape, and Disney now owns ABC-TV. Blurred, blended, acquired, absorbed—there are a lot of new competitive styles springing from a basic philosophy that big is sturdier than medium-sized. And in most economies and markets, this is true.

Until the last few years, Europe has avoided mergers, preferring instead to concentrate on local markets, even at the expense of profits. The globalized economy is making that practice ever more unrealistic, however, and European companies such as Daimler-Benz and Novartis are joining the mania associated with blending and merging and acquiring. Among other factors driving the merger movement: fear that the United States and Asia will muscle European companies out of entire markets, global pressures for industrial efficiency, and the increasing number of European companies falling into foreign hands. Industries deemed most likely to consolidate in Europe include air travel, auto, banking, and pharmaceutical.

One of the most important factors driving mergers around the world is the desire (and need) for global expansion. In a Watson Wyatt Worldwide survey of top executives in twenty-three countries, 46 percent of the respondents cited global expansion as their company's primary business strategy over the next five years. The survey "Competing in a Global Economy", included responses from executives at 2,143 companies. Of those who responded, 40 percent were CEOs; more than seventy-five participants were members of the Global Fortune 500.

On average, global executives estimate that 30 percent of their customer base is international today. As the focus of global expansion intensifies over the next five years, they expect that percentage to increase to 38.

Percentage of Customer Base Expected to be "International" in Five Years:

Sweden	55%
Canada	50%
Germany	50%
United Kingdom	43%
Mexico	41%
Hong Kong	38%
United States	29%
Japan	22%

"The recent economic woes in Asia have only heightened interest among leading executives in serving global markets," commented George Bailey, global director of the Human Capital Group at Watson Wyatt. "Currency devaluations and falling stock markets seem to have made companies *more* determined to expand internationally, not less."

• NEXT: THIS DOES NOT COMPUTE— INFO OVERLOAD IN THE '90s

According to "Dying for Information?," a survey of thirteen hundred managers in Australia, Hong Kong, Singapore, the U.K., and the United States (conducted by Benchmark Research for Reuters Business Information):

- Thirty-one percent of managers receive enormous amounts of unsolicited information.
- Forty-nine percent feel they are unable to handle the volumes of information received.
- Thirty-eight percent waste substantial time trying to locate the right information.

- Forty-seven percent say collection of information distracts them from their primary job responsibilities.
- Fifty percent take work home or stay late as a result of having to deal with too much information.
- Sixty-one percent report that their personal relationships have suffered as a result of information overload.

In another study, also commissioned by Reuters, telephone interviews with one thousand people in Germany, Hong Kong, Singapore, Ireland, Great Britain and the United States determined that information might be the drug of the decade. "Dataholics" are springing up all over the world, thanks to the wealth of information available via the Internet.

- More than half of those surveyed "craved" information.
- Nearly 50 percent said that if information were a drug, they would know someone who was an addict.
- Seventy-six percent thought that information was addictive.
- Fifty-four percent claimed to get a "high" when finding the information they were looking for.
- More than 50 percent could not handle the amount of information accumulated.
- Ninety percent of parents want schools to do more to prepare the next generation to handle this information overload.

What are the key factors contributing to information overload? They include the Internet (48 percent of respondents to the study above believed that the Internet would be the prime cause of information overload in the next two years), telephone/fax, pagers, PDAs (think Palm Pilots), the cable-sparked explosion in TV news, the rise in special-interest news, and the expansion of network news offerings.

According to these Reuters studies, Information Fatigue Syndrome might bring about decreased efficiency in workers by creating high levels of stress and illness, paralysis of analytical capacity, inability to make decisions, and the tendency to blame others. Other symptoms include a lost sense of proportion, an inability to determine the relative importance of one piece of information over another, a loss of confidence in news sources (73 percent of respondents to a *Time*–CNN poll reported being "skeptical about the accuracy" of the news they're getting), and an increased need for branded content (information businesses and consumers can trust), and information filters.

This spells opportunity for marketers and purveyors of certain products and services, but the overall implication is disturbing. If we can't combat information overload in these early stages of the Digital Age, what might the state of our businesses be five or ten years down the road?

• NEXT: STRATEGIC PLANNING BACK ON THE FRONT LINES

After more than a decade of downsizing to raise productivity and efficiency, companies are returning to strategic planning in a bid to increase profits. Business strategy is now the most important management issue and will remain so for the next five years, according to a survey by the Association of Management Consulting Firms.

"The increased focus on shareholder values that developed in the late 1980s and became acute in the early 1990s has had a profound effect on the way business is conducted—on the motives behind the actions and the impact on the consumer," says Toronto-based adman Laurence Bernstein. "As the focus of business and marketers shifted from sales improvement to share price improvement, product development, marketing planning, personnel development and other issues, everyone became more focused on the short-term. Rightsizing (or downsizing), the fundamental expression of corporate reengineering, resulted in fewer mid- and long-term programs. Those managers and employees left were (and still are) hard-pressed to accomplish their immediate functional tasks, leaving little opportunity for strategic planning and development."

Bernstein continues, "Marketing was especially hard hit, as new-product development, market-share investment, etc., fell by the wayside. As a result, traditional industry leaders allowed smaller, less accomplished companies to introduce leading-edge products, grow their market niches, and so on. Large corporations are now scrambling to become more current (they seem to have missed a technological wave) and many seem to be floundering. There will probably be a flurry of small and medium company buyouts in the next few years, as companies realize that their focus on 'core competencies' in a climate of intense technological change was fundamentally flawed."

Today's breed of strategic planning is different from the '80s version in that the process is no longer confined to the senior elite. The trend toward democratized planning calls for input from all levels of the company as well as from customers and suppliers. Finland's Nokia Group, for example, involved 250 employees in a strategic review in early 1995, according to *Business Week*, and the company's top executive team now holds monthly strategic meetings. One result: the creation of a "smart car" unit in Germany to develop products for the auto industry. In the United States, the jelly and jam company J.M. Smucker enlisted 140 employees (seven percent of its workforce) to devote nearly 50 percent of their time to a major strategy exercise for more than six months. Additional input was solicited from all 2,000 employees. At the conclusion of the project, the company anticipated that the resulting initiatives would double its $635 million in revenues over the next five years.

• NEXT: QUEST FOR COMPETITIVE INTELLIGENCE

Long accepted in Europe, snooping is now taking hold in the United States, according to a report by *Business Week*.

Need the lowdown on a competitor? Want to go into a meeting knowing everything about your counterpart, from her career history to her golf handicap? An expert in business intelligence can deliver the answers. There's no skulduggery involved, just the systematic gathering and analysis of information.

The Financial Post reports that the market for business intelligence is booming. The Palo Alto Management Group Inc., in California, estimates that the worldwide market for collecting and analyzing information, including systems, software, and in-house expenditures, will be $113.5 billion by 2002. The number of providers is growing, too: The U.S.-based Society of Competitive

Intelligence Professionals, which started in 1986 with twelve members, now has about six thousand five hundred members.

Following the 1996 Economic Espionage Act, the FBI set up the Computer Investigations and Infrastructure Assessment Center to help companies defend themselves.

Reasons for the growth in industrial espionage are manifold: Economic globalization requires better intelligence to anticipate threats from abroad and penetrate overseas markets. The quickening pace of technological change and deregulation makes it more likely than ever that companies will be blindsided by a competitor, who can take the lead with a single innovation. And digging up information on rivals' products and strategies is facilitated by the Internet and CD-ROM databases, which contain information it once would have taken days or weeks to ferret out. Assisting in such searches are companies such as Real World Intelligence Inc., which offers customized software developed for the CIA.

Building Brands in Cyberspace

As we've noted repeatedly, knowledge is power. But more than that, as futurist Alvin Toffler has said, knowledge is the most democratic source of power. As the world becomes more wired and more people are connected to the global Internet, knowledge that was once restricted to the economic and political elite will be accessible to anyone with a computer and modem.

In our view, every business today must compete in two worlds: the physical marketplace and the online marketspace—a virtual world of information, entertainment and interaction. Activities that take place in the marketspace mirror those that traditionally have occurred in the marketplace, but that does not mean that the process of creating value is the same in both worlds. New consumers who log onto the Internet are looking for instant solutions and for direct and efficient interaction with the brands among which they must choose. In the face of information and sensory overload, these consumers will turn to a trusted face in the crowd—choosing the brand with flawless credentials, a continuous history, and the drive and ability to anticipate the consumer's needs.

What some analysts have failed to notice is that the power of the Internet goes far beyond shopping, entertainment and research. Of even greater impact will be the Internet's role as a vehicle of persuasion. The world was stunned by the mass suicide of members of the Heaven's Gate cult in California. The group's ties to the Internet immediately became fodder for an oftentimes uninformed discussions of the "dark side" of the Net. People who likely had never even logged onto the Net immediately began to decry its base nature, warning of its sinister power to brainwash the weak-minded into doing all manner of dastardly deeds.

Ten Realities of the Next Millennium

1. If you know the marketplace, you can own the marketspace.
2. Any company that establishes a site on the Internet automatically becomes a multinational company.
3. New-product announcements on the Net will generate immediate demand, making it more difficult to conduct slow test-as-you-go rollouts.
4. Geekspeak, the jargon of the technologically fluent, is the newest international language, and it has a better chance of survival than does Esperanto.
5. Thanks to Usenet and other online forums, the distinction between news and gossip is becoming increasingly blurred.
6. Everyone, no matter what age or income level, has the potential to be influential in cyberspace. Conversely, those who wield great power in the "real world" find themselves on a far more level playing field when they come online.
7. Privacy is an increasingly rare—and treasured—commodity, and consumers will pay a premium to ensure that personal information remains just that. Companies that can't be trusted with personal data are less likely to be trusted in any other category.
8. New technologies are giving small and midsize companies far greater access to consumers than they have ever before enjoyed. Established corporations would do well to watch their backs.
9. The homogeneity of traditional media images and messages will break down as ethnic and other minority groups gain a greater share of voice via the Internet.
10. The Internet is turning the population into creators of content as opposed to mere consumers of it.

Already, most companies are utilizing the enormous power of the Internet in three ways: as a conduit of information to and from consumers, as a vehicle for consumer and market research, and as a platform for cyber-persuasion. We'll look at each of these in turn.

• INFORMATION PIPELINE

A corporate Web site can be nothing more than an electronic version of a product brochure. It can tell the consumer what a product is, how much it costs, and where you can buy it. But the potential of a Web site as a conduit of information is far greater. An effective site will offer an opportunity for interaction with the consumer. It will provide a mechanism for customer service, whether in the form of e-mail, a bulletin board or a chatroom. (Note: A recent study by Jupiter Communications suggests that servicing customers via online chat could cost as little as $.25 a transaction, compared with $1.25 per phone transaction.) And it will take advantage of opportunities to garner personal information from consumers visiting the site. Some Web sites do this by requiring basic demographic information before allowing the user to access the site's full content. Other sites gather user data by means of entertaining surveys and message boards. In addition to being useful for general marketing purposes, this captured data can be used very effectively to target individual site visitors with product information.

One of the great advantages of advertising online is the ability to tailor ads to individual consumers. By using DART technology from DoubleClick (www.doubleclick.net), for example, site managers can increase the odds of achieving a click-through by delivering advertisements based on known information about the site visitor. A visitor who had indicated upon registering at the site that she is a tennis player who travels extensively and plans to buy a new computer within the next twelve months can be targeted with ads from sponsors such as Adidas, Samsonite, and Gateway 2000 when she logs onto the site. A visitor from London or Helsinki or Boston can be targeted by companies doing business in those locales. Some sites tailor ads to each visitor's computer platform (Macintosh, Windows, or DOS) so as to be sure of peddling only those products that are technologically compatible.

To fully appreciate the implications of this targeted advertising, imagine if TV commercials and magazine ads were different from household to household, consumer to consumer. An amateur athlete watching local TV news might be targeted with an ad for Nike athletic shoes, while a gardening enthusiast down the street could receive instead an ad for Ortho lawn-care products. Of course, this has long been the quest of marketers. Procter & Gamble began producing soap operas nearly a half-century ago to target homemakers. And the increasingly targeted magazines available today are attempting to reach everyone from gourmets to golf enthusiasts to Nintendo addicts. Still, the Internet has an edge in that it is able to verify interest in a product or category through such means as ClickWise, and can produce and disseminate a much greater variety of ads than would be practical in other media.

Recognizing the potential of cybermarketing, more than 90 percent of top advertisers in the United States have established one or more websites. And a study conducted among the 125 member companies of the Association of National Advertisers Inc. found that more than half already sell or plan to sell products and/or services via the Internet, and approximately a third advertise on other companies' websites, with advertising expenditures averaging $250,000.

• CREATING AN ONLINE DIALOGUE
WITH THE NEW CONSUMER

Using cyberspace as a vehicle for consumer and marketing research is something the authors of this book know a great deal about. Marian is widely credited with having invented online focus groups (she co-founded American Dialogue: Focus Groups in Cyberspace, a forum on AOL, with Jay Chiat in 1993).

In our work, we continue to rely on cyber-research, regularly conducting online focus groups and one-on-one interviews and sending out e-polls on behalf of a variety of clients. For example, while still with the multinational advertising agency TBWA, the four of us conducted an intensive research project in the United

States on behalf of one of the world's most important toy companies. Participants, who were recruited online, filled out e-polls and detailed questionnaires. They even visited a specially constructed website to view a product in development. The entire project was conducted electronically, which meant we were able to use participants in all areas of the country without incurring one dollar in travel cost or even the expense of renting research facilities. And because these children and their parents were able to participate in the study from the comfort of their homes and on their own time, we were able to recruit the busy, relatively affluent families who are the product's target.

In the years we've been conducting online research, we've become convinced that this convenient and relatively inexpensive forum is the most time- and cost-effective way to access consumers of all ages, in a variety of occupations, in many parts of the world. In addition, citizens of cyberspace (particularly outside North America and Scandinavia) are widely regarded as change leaders, people who are ahead of the curve. As a result, although online research might not always be scientifically representative, it is predictive of trends and attitudes that are making their way toward the mainstream.

Research conducted in cyberspace can be qualitative and/or quantitative (although, given current penetration rates, "quantitative" data will almost certainly involve a skew). Online focus groups are like their real world counterparts in that a moderator leads a session based on a formal discussion guide; they are unlike real world groups in that participants enjoy a certain amount of anonymity, which often alleviates embarrassment and facilitates honesty. (This came in particularly handy when we were asking teenage girls to discuss their problems with acne.) Transcripts are available immediately following the group, and clients can be invited to "sit in" on the sessions.

E-polls—another research staple for our group—are a cost-effective, timely means of obtaining answers from a broad consumer sample to a well-defined set of questions. Although there are limitations with respect to length (for obvious reasons, shorter polls yield a greater participation rate), respondents can easily be recontacted for participation in a follow-up poll or interview addressing more in-depth questions. Given an average poll-completion time of no more than fifteen minutes, our experience dictates that a sample size of three hundred typically can be secured within five days of aggressive distribution.

• THE ART OF CYBERPERSUASION

A third critical way in which marketers can reach the new consumer online is by means of cyberpersuasion. By this we mean more than simply building Web sites that attract consumers and keep them coming back for more (although the potential benefits of building such a community online should not be under-estimated). What we are referring to instead are the ways in which a corporate presence can be established throughout the Internet. Whether using newsgroups, chatrooms, online forums or e-mail, marketers have valuable opportunities to connect with their customers and build their brands in cyberspace.

In our work with clients, we often talk about "whisper campaigns," a means by which a message can be spread to an online audience without becoming intrusive—and thus unwelcome. The best whisper campaigns are conducted by people who genuinely have their fellow cybernauts' best interests at heart. By way of example, when we were conducting some background research for a client in the animal health-care field, we visited a forum on America Online for pet-lovers. One of the message boards was devoted to the topic of coat and skin problems common to household pets. (Yes, some of these online forums get very specific!) A new flea-control product had recently been introduced, and many of the visitors to the board were searching for information regarding the product's safety and effectiveness. Some participants were also relating rumors they had heard about various negative side effects associated with the product. What caught our attention was the presence in this forum of a former veterinarian who now works in public relations for the company that makes the product in question.

He did his job perfectly.

Whenever someone posted a question or rumor about this product, the company representative responded within twenty-four hours. He stated his affiliation with the company as well as his former position as a private-practice veterinarian. He then answered the question or squelched the rumor, providing specific data from research projects that had disproved whatever the rumor happened to be. The reason this company rep was so effective was that he was a member of this online community. He didn't just answer questions pertaining to his company's products; he also provided advice on all sorts of ailments and conditions in his capacity as a trained veterinarian. So instead of being regarded as a corporate shill, he was valued as a trusted member of the community. His company benefited from his presence there—and so did the pet owners and animal-care professionals who frequented the site.

One of the first companies to feel the potential backlash of the Internet was Intel. As you might recall, the company had a problem with its Pentium computer chip a few years back. It attempted to respond to e-mail complaints by issuing a notice online that the "bug" in its Pentium chip was rare and would cause problems for only a minute percentage of users. IBM responded by posting a notice on its Web site that contradicted Intel's claims (and later refused to ship any computers that contained the defective chip). The result: Intel issued a recall and replaced the chip.

Since that time, many companies have used the persuasive powers of the Net or been the victim of them—sometimes both. In 1997, for example, a rumor circulated on the Internet that American fashion designer Tommy Hilfiger had made some racist comments on *The Oprah Winfrey Show*. The result was a cry for a boycott of Hilfiger's products (which was heard both on and off the Internet) that spurred the company to fight back, using the same Internet to fight the rumor-mongers. It created a memo contradicting the rumors and circulated it in popular Internet newsgroups. This incident serves as a reminder that smart companies don't only work to spread their message in cyberspace; they also monitor Internet content and take whatever actions are necessary to protect their brand.

The remainder of this chapter takes a look at some of the important (or just plain interesting) trends we're seeing in marketing efforts aimed at the new consumer. Most have in common the attributes of personalization, multiple channels of communication and innovative techniques designed to break through the clutter and chaos surrounding consumers.

• NEXT: IMAGE IS LOTS OF INTANGIBLES

In 1998, Roper Starch reported that "most Americans continue to have at least a moderately favorable opinion of most large business corporations (67 percent, on par with the average of four previous surveys in 1997 and 1998). But a little luster has been lost in terms of small businesses, with 85 percent saying they have a favorable opinion of most small business companies, off four from the average since the beginning of 1997." This study goes on to note that some individual companies have also seen their images suffer. For example, the strike at General Motors led to a loss of their market share. In a world in which virtually everything communicates, it's not surprising that virtually everything influences our attitudes toward brands. This might also explain why most advertising is intended to convince people to switch brands. In a different Roper Starch study, it was reported that people do start using new products such as fast food, diet soft drinks, instant coffee and cold breakfast cereal based on what they find out from advertising.

• NEXT: INCREASED EMPHASIS ON ONE-ON-ONE MARKETING

Mass marketing is obsolete. Changing demographics, new distribution channels, intensified competition, additional media channels, new technologies and declining advertising effectiveness have combined to make personal marketing a must.

Around the world, we're seeing innovative marketers step up to the plate, customizing their offerings to extend the impact of their messages on targeted consumers. In Great Britain, American Express uses special software to personalize offers to cardholders based on their purchasing history and demographic data. Sports enthusiasts might receive a special discount offer from a local sporting goods store along with their monthly invoice. These personalized inserts have achieved an impressive "take" rate of just under 40 percent.

Loyalty cards are a marketing technique used to build databases that a company can refer to in order to customize marketing tactics. Wal-Mart has used their database to determine buying patterns, which in turn helped them improve product placement. For example, they discovered that people who bought cold medicine tended to also purchase orange juice. By placing a juice display in the pharmaceutical aisle, they increased their orange juice sales, according to Audits & Surveys' findings.

Teleco Ameritech has taken an unusual position. It has designed a system to block annoying sales calls. Privacy Manager gives customers a way of identifying telemarketer calls even if there is an ID "block" in place. Privacy Manager intercepts unknown callers and asks them to record their name and affiliation. It will then call the customer, allowing him to accept or reject the call. The system, which works only on those lines equipped with caller ID, costs $3.95 per month. Telemarketers, though, claim that many consumers are receptive to sales calls. According to the Direct Marketing Association, telemarketing calls generated $209.5 billion of consumer spending in 1998, and $272.7 billion of business-to-business spending.

MicroMass has created products that will allow health-care companies to personalize their marketing efforts to their diverse consumer groups. The products will eventually cover all mass media channels, including the Internet, print, e-mail, phone and fax lines. IntelliWeb, the first product, creates either a single page or an entire website based on information provided by each website visitor. This allows a company to tailor its messages.

In the increasingly competitive airline industry, American Airlines representatives now call their most valuable frequent flyers before their flights both to thank them for choosing American Airlines and to see whether there's anything they can do to make the trip more comfortable. British Airways has installed new software that will allow them to record frequent fliers' preferences (favorite magazines, beverages, and meals) so they can greet these customers with the items on boarding. (Flip side: If you make passengers feel that Big Brother knows them too well, people become uncomfortable; customization is okay, but invasion of personal privacy is the ultimate *no* for most of us, even in the name of customer service.)

• NEXT: RENEWED FOCUS ON DEVELOPING CUSTOMER LOYALTY

With more women in the workforce and the increased need for men and women to juggle the responsibilities of work and home, many consumers are growing frustrated by the retail shopping experience. Key complaints: inadequate selection, high prices, poor service and inconvenient hours and locations.

Innovative retail techniques: To attract and retain today's discriminating consumers, retailers are turning to innovative strategies. Hyperefficient operators (e.g., Wal-Mart and Home Depot), based on the French hypermarket concept, are expanding their offerings while shrinking prices. Specialty stores (e.g., Sunglass Hut, PetsMart, and Babies 'R Us) are seeking to dominate narrow categories by means of deep selection and low prices. Large companies are staking a claim to convenience by bringing the mountain to Mohammed. Examples: in-mall McDonald's, bank branches in supermarkets, and travel offices and post offices in department stores.

Retailers are also attempting to reinject fun into the shopping equation. Borders Superstores, for example, include CD listening stations, kids' reading areas (regularly featuring puppet shows, storytelling and other events), in-store cafes, and live entertainment. Home furnishings retailer IKEA attracts busy shoppers with in-store dining, and play areas for children.

It's interesting to note the potential of Internet retailers to take advantage of each of these strategies. Consumers in search of the bargain prices they associate with hypermarkets and other discounters can scan the Net for the lowest prices on a variety of products with services such as Whats4Sale (www.whats4sale.com), CompareNet (www.compare.net/), PriceHunter (www.pricehunter.com), and KillerApp Computer Channel (www.killerapp.com). And there is no better place than the Web to locate specialty products. Among other highly specific sales sites already online are Lens Express (contact lenses) at www.lensexpress.com, Any Watch U Want (wristwatches) at www.anywatch.com, The Hat Shack (www.hatshack.com), The Pepper Plant (www.pepperplant.com), and Cheese Cake City (www.cheesecakecity.com).

Corporate concierges: In an effort to strengthen customer loyalty, many companies are offering concierge services to valued clients. As reported on the INSIDE 1to1 website (www.1to1.com/), these services might range from scoring tickets to sold-out events to finding a hard-to-locate product to getting a car serviced. Many of these companies outsource the service, relying on organizations such as San Francisco-based LesConcierges (www.lesconcierges.com) and Washington, DC-based Capitol Concierge (www.capitolconcierge.com), which maintain the high-tech databases and call-center infrastructures necessary to handle consumer requests around the clock.

While the corporate concierge business has traditionally been local or regional, it is now going national and, for some clients, global. According to INSIDE 1to1, American Express, Visa, MasterCard, Diner's Club and General Motors are just some of the big names that have adopted concierge services as a value-added amenity. Companies in an array of other industries—including telecommunications, airlines and insurance—are considering such services as well.

New ways to reach youth: As superstores continue to edge smaller operations out of the market, manufacturers are under increased pressure to produce a greater variety of products more quickly. This is particularly evident in the toy category. Today just four retailers—Toys 'R Us, Wal-Mart, Target, and Kmart—account for approximately two-thirds of American toy sales.

With limited retail shelf space a growing problem for some manufacturers, alternative distribution routes are evolving. For example, Bright Ideas (now owned by Addison Wesley) uses consultants to demonstrate and sell educational software in consumers' added another distribution channel by launching Bright Schools, a hands-on workshop that shows teachers how to integrate software into their classrooms.

Increased retail competition in the children's market is also spurring the formation of all kinds of creative production and marketing partnerships. Preschool-toy giant Fisher-Price and computer manufacturer Compaq, for example, are collaborating on a line of compu-toys geared to families with kids under age seven. Kraft Foods Inc. and cable network Nickelodeon have entered into a deal whereby Kraft will spend $10 million on advertising on the cable network, while also offering coupons on twenty-five Kraft "kids' food" brands for Nickelodeon-branded toys.

In coming years we can expect to see familiar toys being sold on shelves right next to related software packages, offering a variety of choices that appeal to children with different learning styles.

Join the club: A broad variety of companies have begun to encourage multiple sales and brand loyalty by inviting kids and parents to join special clubs. The Book-of-the-Month Club has begun a division for children aged six months to ten years. The Books of My Very Own Club features a low-cost introductory book package and monthly mailings of books geared to the child's age group. There's also a club featuring books by Dr. Seuss: (The Beginning Readers' Program by Grolier Books). In the sports apparel category, Kids Foot Locker and Nike teamed up to offer the Future All-Stars Club. Kids who signed up received a free Michael Jordan or Gail Devers poster along with a "letter of encouragement." The LEGO Builders Club, offering discount coupons and a LEGO magazine, is one club that builds loyalty while also soliciting consumer feedback from kids.

An increasing number of companies don't even wait for the child to be born before targeting parents with club memberships. Carnation, for example, offers expectant mothers a Disney Babies Mom-to-Be planner, information on child care, and discount coupons for Carnation products. Supermarkets have also been targeting expectant parents, mailing discount coupons, product samples and other incentives to parents who sign up for their "baby club."

Service with a smile: In Europe, consumer dissatisfaction with the retail process very often has as much to do with poor service as with long lines or lack of parking. The European attitude about service has often baffled visitors from North America and Asia. The key to understanding the surliness, sloppiness, and general unhelpfulness of many European service workers is the mindset that the job exists for the benefit of the person doing the serving, not for the benefit of the person being served. A logical consequence of this has been the tendency of stores to close at hours convenient to the staff, even if customers are knocking at the doors.

The fact is, Germans find the idea of service demeaning. They are far from alone in Europe (with the honorable exception of professional waiters and bar staff in France and Italy). But the demise of many older industries and the rise of service-based industries is forcing Europeans to rethink their attitudes toward service. Customers might have accepted grudging service in the past, but as competition increases, their preference is likely to go to businesses providing service that is both competent and friendly.

Those we spoke to in Spain, Italy, Germany and Sweden anticipate greater emphasis on the quality and variety of services in their countries.

• NEXT: GLOBAL BRANDING

Satellite television, Hollywood movies, and cross-border marketing efforts have created a world culture with implications for brand strategy, market intelligence, and management techniques in every business that hopes to be international. In a world in which national borders present few obstacles for the winds of culture, advertising and media, marketers are now called upon to make sure their brands are marketed in a way that is most relevant—and least offensive—to every nation in which they are sold. One of the world's best-known brands, Levi's, has tackled this mission by building a Web site (www.levi.com) that delivers one overriding message: Unity crosses borders. Visitors to the site can view Levi's advertisements from all over the world while absorbing messages such as, "Many voices, many cultures, many venues, one message: Levi's jeans, true originals for true originals," and, "Around the world, down the street, across points of view, Levi's jeans are there."

Launched in 1983, the Swatch watch company has grown into

the most successful maker of wristwatches of all time. The watches are now available in seventy-two markets worldwide. In addition to a global print advertising campaign, the company spreads its message through innovative marketing promotions. In one example, Swatch ran a promotion in conjunction with the Museum of Byzantine Civilization in Thessaloniki, Greece. Anyone wearing Swatch's commemorative watch for the exhibit of the treasures of Holy Mount Athos was granted free admission.

Swoosh. Not just the sound of a tram careening by you on a street corner in Amsterdam, but also the symbol that runs the length of the cars. American-based Nike has managed to make its geometric logo one of the most recognized symbols around the globe. By plastering its logo on billboards, phone booths, all forms of mass transportation and the shoes and clothing of top athletes worldwide in just about all sports, Nike has become synonymous with athletic excellence—and marketing savvy. (Interestingly, as we were completing this book, Nike had begun to drop the swoosh in some of its advertising, replacing it with "NIKE." This would appear to be an attempt to shake up its advertising in the face of increasingly gloomy financial news.)

- ### NEXT: CREATING THE AD BIZ IN A PARALLEL UNIVERSE

"Internet spending is real. It does reach an upscale demographic. The Internet is eroding TV use. It is measurable," says Rich LeFurgy, chairman of the Internet Advertising Bureau Board (IAB) and senior vice-president of advertising for ABC News/ESPN Internet Ventures. Net-based advertising revenues continue to grow: IAB reports that revenue topped $906.5 million for 1997, with fourth quarter revenues of some $330.5 million marking the eighth record-setting quarter in a row. "It was definitely a breakthrough year for Internet advertising," said LeFurgy. "When we compare advertising revenue for the television industry in equivalent dollars for its third year, the Internet is slightly ahead, at $907 million compared to television's $834 million."

For now, American companies dominate the market. Jupiter Communications predicts that non-U.S. online revenues will reach $704 million in the year 2000. By comparison, the American market is expected to reach $5 billion-plus in that time. Dresdner Kleinwort Benson, the investment bank, expects the value of British advertising on the Internet to reach $450 million by 2001.

According to a study by Coopers & Lybrand, ninety percent of all Internet advertisement spending is generated by five categories: computing products, 30 percent; telecommunications, 22 percent; consumer-related businesses, 17 percent; financial services, 11 percent; and new-media businesses, 10 percent. For now, banner ads continue to be the standard, but new advertising business models and formats continue to evolve. Among recent developments: "in-lines" or "one liners" (visitors performing a search are presented with a simple sentence, such as "Buy a new car at a great price—click here"; the line appears as just another entry on a list of search results); ad-supported e-mail; and ad-supported chatrooms.

Although the medium is developing at a rapid pace, we still have a long way to go before optimum use is achieved. A study by *Ad Age* and Mediamark Research Inc. found that marketers still use two-way technology to deliver primarily one-way messages. Nearly three-quarters of respondents use interactive technology to provide information about their company, 48.2 percent use it for promotion, and 45.8 percent use it as a public-relations tool. In contrast, only 37.2 percent use interactive media as a basis for one-to-one marketing—and even fewer conduct electronic commerce.

A number of organizations are taking steps to facilitate and encourage online advertising. Audits & Surveys (www.surveys.com) and CyberGold (www.cybergold.com) have formed an alliance to help online advertisers gauge response to their ads and develop responder and nonresponder profiles. The new service combines Audits & Surveys' polling and sampling programs with CyberGold's incentive arrangements, which reward consumers for responding to ads and surveys. The combined effort is intended to elicit demographic and lifestyle data and to probe consumers with regard to how online advertisements influence or fail to influence purchases.

- ## NEXT: CONTENT IS KING
  FOR BRANDS

Although less obvious than banners and other forms of advertising online, branded content provides a valuable opportunity for companies to build their brands in cyberspace. By luring consumers with information on everything from parenting to classic cars to the fight against breast cancer, companies are able to associate themselves with a positive message or cause while also gaining access to a steady stream of potential customers.

OshKosh B'Gosh, which has focused recently on clothing for kids, has created the OshKosh B'Gosh Genuine Parents Club at its Web site (www.oshkoshbgosh.com/cgi-bin/dp/gpcintro). Among other features (including store locators and a gift gallery), the site posts a newsletter containing parenting tips, gift ideas, and kids' fashion trends. Parents who join the free club are given a gift subscription to *Parents* or *Child* magazine.

Procter & Gamble also is attempting to align itself with parents online. P&G has entered into a multiyear advertising deal with ParentTime, a joint venture of Time Warner Cable Programming and Procter & Gamble Productions. The site (www.parenttime.com) is designed to "inform and entertain parents and expectant parents." Contributors include sex guru Dr. Ruth Westheimer and authors William and Martha Sears (*The Birth Book* and *The Discipline Book*); Dale Burg, Carol Boswell and Ron Barrett (*How to Mom*); and Adele Faber and Elaine Mazlish (*Liberated Parents and Liberated Children*).

The Adidas webzine (www.adidas.de) features sports news, profiles of and interviews with Adidas-sponsored athletes, and information about Adidas-sponsored events. The webzine is offered for six markets: Germany, Spain, Sweden, Switzerland, the United States, and the United Kingdom, with each edition focusing on local sports heroes and issues.

Johnson & Johnson's website (www.jnj.com) is devoted to "caring." Information is provided on topics such as infant care, issues related to motherhood and breakthroughs in health-care products. There is also a link to the Library of Healthcare Information, a list of organizations that provide support for new parents.

- ## Next: Innovative Branding and Image-Building Techniques

In-school marketing: Despite the controversies surrounding it, in-school marketing is becoming increasingly common, as cash-strapped schools welcome equipment, materials, programming and products from companies eager to reach the youth market. In America, Channel One continues to beam satellite news programming and sponsors' advertisements into secondary-school classrooms in exchange for providing the schools with free satellite and video equipment. Other companies enter schools more subtly, with lesson plans and materials on topics such as nutrition and recycling. The inclusion of product logos, marketing messages and—some charge—biased information, continues to infuriate many parents and educators.

Shape shifters: Warning: It's no longer just Video News Releases we have to watch out for. These days, organizations of all kinds are working to get their message across to us without letting us know they're behind it. A few examples:

- With $100,000 in federal grants from the National Science Foundation and the Department of Energy, a group of scientists recently tried to reshape their profession's geeky image by commissioning the writing of a prime-time TV show that, they hoped, would do for scientists what *ER* is doing for doctors. So far, there have been no takers for the series.
- Among some organizations, an increasingly common practice is "greenscamming," giving environmentally friendly names to groups on the other side of the battle. Two examples: Friends of Eagle Mountain, organized by a mining company that wants to create the world's largest landfill, and Northwesterners for More Fish (since dissolved, we're happy to report), created by companies accused of depleting the fish population.
- Whereas root beer provides a taste of nostalgia for many boomers, it's being pitched to younger male consumers as "The foam that goes straight to your brain." The slogan, for PepsiCo's Mug brand, accompanies ads that appear primarily on MTV.

- To give startups a fighting chance in a market that favors unique, personalized products, mass-market giants are opting to distance themselves from certain of their products: Miller Brewing Company's Red Dog beer was launched as a microbrew of Plank Road Brewery. R.J. Reynold's Moonlight Tobacco Company markets cigarettes under the brand names Politix, City and Northstar in selected markets, with scant mention of their parent company. Detroit heavyweight General Motors distanced itself from Saturn by setting up shop in rural Tennessee and packaging its offspring as a small-town enterprise.

• NEXT: MUSIC AS A MARKETING TOOL

Eager to tap into the lucrative hip-hop market, manufacturers are forming alliances with big names in rap. Most successful thus far has been fashion designer Tommy Hilfiger, who lured rappers into the fold with free wardrobes. Last year, Hilfiger used hardcore rappers Method Man and Treach (of Naughty by Nature) as runway models. Luxury-goods maker Louis Vuitton has also jumped onto the hip-hop bandwagon, with print ads featuring pioneer deejay Grandmaster Flash.

The use of CDs as premiums and promotional products is also on the rise, with recent releases of music compilations from companies such as Godiva, Ralph Lauren, Pottery Barn, and Fila. Intended to build customer loyalty by delivering the stores to customers' homes, these compilations also allow retailers to develop a brand image based on a signature sound. Philip Morris has raised the ire of tobacco foes by creating a record company, Woman Thing Music, to promote its Virginia Slims brand. In addition to giving away CDs with cigarette purchases, the company is sponsoring a series of concerts. CDs produced by The Body Shop raise money for causes the company supports; compilations have included "Protect Respect: Artists Who Care About AIDS" and "Voices Against Violence" (female artists).

Tying together three areas of keen interest to young folks—music, fashion, and beer—Anheuser-Busch produced a Budweiser-branded tour in Great Britain that coincided with the company's launch of a line of branded clothing. In an example of the new emphasis on integrated marketing, Kahlúa, a coffee-liqueur brand, teamed up with the British band M People, first sponsoring a global tour and then branching out to include on-bottle CD offers and radio promotions, including Kahlúa Groove, a branded radio program.

• NEXT: MEGA MOVIE MARKETING

From action figures to prepaid phone cards to breakfast cereal to toothbrushes to pajamas, toys and other merchandise tied into blockbuster movies have become a huge business in the past decade. Universal Studios reports that licenses from *Jurassic Park* alone generated $1 billion in sales. Ira Mayer, publisher of *The Licensing Letter* in New York, told the *Los Angeles Times*, "Up until 1991 or so, licensing was an ancillary revenue stream, a bonus that went straight to the bottom line. Now some films wouldn't even get made unless they get this licensing agreement out front." By the time the remake of *101 Dalmatians* was released, Disney had licensed a grand total of seventeen hundred product tie-ins. A Cruella de Ville tennis visor, anyone?

According to *The Licensing Letter*, licensed products generated $73.23 billion in 1997, up one percent from 1996. More than $16 billion of that came from entertainment such as movies. By early 1998, studios had already plotted their course through the next year, when the first installment of the new *Star Wars* trilogy would be released. As expected, *Star Wars* dominated movie merchandising for weeks in spring 1999.

• NEXT: CEOs AS CELEBRITY SPOKESPEOPLE

Corporate executives with the personality and credibility to serve as spokespersons would do well to try their hand. With five hundred commercials to his credit, Dave Thomas, founder of Wendy's Old Fashioned Hamburgers, has emerged as one of America's most recognizable corporate spokespersons—second only to basketball star Michael Jordan.

At the same time, however, companies are increasingly alert to the potential downside of real-life spokespersons (Dave Thomas's recent heart attack, for instance, wasn't the best advertising for the company's product). Tying a brand to the fate of any celebrity appears risky in this era of fallen stars such as O. J. Simpson and boxer Mike Tyson.

Consumers are also rejecting celebrity endorsements in cases in which there is not a logical fit. In conducting a series of online focus groups for a parenting product, we were told time and time again by the parent participants that they would not accept a celebrity spokesperson for the product because most celebrities are too busy (or uncaring) to be good parents. To be effective, an endorser must somehow be linked in consumers' minds to the product category. Rock star Tina Turner, for example, has been a big hit in ads for Hanes hosiery because she is well known for her great legs and active lifestyle. She would be far less effective endorsing a credit card or automotive company.

Who else sells right now? For better or worse, the authors propose the following list, our top ten, in random order: Fergie, Richard Branson, the baseball duo of McGwire and Sosa, Calista Flockhart, Alan Greenspan, Nelson Mandela, Chelsea Clinton, Steve Jobs, and Katie Couric. Obviously, many on our list aren't available for endorsements. But it gives you insight into how we think promotions really work—as in who influences who!

WHAT'S NEXT?

The General Business Scene

Ethical consumption: American companies are working hard to make ethical consumption profitable. The world's first "eco-home department store" is open in Macungie, Pennsylvania. Home & Planet specializes in environmentally friendly home and garden accessories from reclaimed sources such as recycled glass, bicycle parts and textile scraps. Some other examples of eco-friendly products are:

Mitchell Gold uses sustainably harvested wood to create sofas and chairs for companies such as Pottery Barn, Crate & Barrel, and Restoration Hardware. In addition to cotton and linen, the company's slipcovers are available in hemp and recycled soda bottle fabric.

Earth Friendly Products from Venus Laboratories are made from "plant-based ingredients and . . . packaged in biodegradable, environmentally safe materials." The company, which targets young families concerned about their children's health, has increased its product line from four items in 1993 to thirty-four, including furniture polish made from olive oil and window cleaner made from vinegar.

Europeans with a social conscience used to vote socialist and regard the idea of "consumers" and "consumption" with distaste, but socialism lost, and Europeans are proud consumers now. In the future these urges will express themselves as ethical consumption, with a warm glow as part of the added value.

In past years, German consumers have been particularly militant, refusing, for example, to buy drinks in plastic bottles (glass good, plastic bad) and boycotting Shell in protest of its proposed sinking of an oil platform in the North Sea. "Fair trade" and "sustainable production" products are widely available, and not only at Body Shop stores. In Denmark, consumers can buy eggs produced in cages at 1,00 Kroner (about $.16) each or "happy eggs" at 2,83 Kr (about $.44). These eggs are produced in *voilieres*, and on the pack are the farmer's name and picture and a description of how happy the chickens are. The Euro perspective is that companies will have to be increasingly careful about the ethical implications of their actions, which will open up opportunities for agents to help them source (identify) and initiate business relationships with ethically impeccable products.

Corporate philosophers: There's still hope for liberal arts majors! As reported in *Slate* (www.slate.com), "The job market for academic philosophers is as desperate as ever, but deep thinkers now have a range of alternative careers. A French outfit, Philocit, offers pricey 'philosophical consulting' to companies looking to add Heideggerian heft to their marketing strategies. (Clients can subscribe to Philocit's telephone-consultation service for $2,600 per year.)"

Wired CEOs: If you want to catch the attention of business executives ten years from now, don't rely on traditional news channels.

Ninety-one percent of American executives surveyed by Deloitte & Touche—the accounting, tax and consulting firm—expect the Internet to be an important business news source for them in 2005, while only 50 percent expect to get their news from daily newspapers. Following the Internet, the next most important sources of news, according to executives, will be the corporate intranet (80 percent) and e-mail (74 percent).

The Brand Biz

Thoughtful convergence: Convergence isn't just about making everything digital; it's also about connecting people to brands in ways that leverage insights into consumer patterns—all without being mistaken for Big Brother. "Brand convergence" is about brands bonding because their combined power is greater than the sum of their parts. Case in point: Citibank's Driver's Edge card, which enables Ford Citibank members to earn points toward the purchase or lease of a new Ford vehicle.

Business-to-business convergence is next. In the coming months and years, we can expect more alliances among investment banks, management consulting firms, public accountancies and even advertising agencies and public-relations firms. All are selling knowledge—and in this age of brand zeal, knowledge is the only bankable power.

Anti-advertising backlash: With all the branded babble thrust at modern consumers every day, who can blame them for being a bit jaded? In the online arena, techies are even devising ways to get around banner ads. Cybersitter software has launched WWW Advertising, a filter that prevents browsers from loading banner ads on numerous Web sites. The company says the feature helps its 1.2 million users save bandwidth and avoid intrusive pitches.

Warning to marketers: This backlash will get worse before it gets better. A survival tactic for smart marketers: Talk smart to smart people about smart brands.

Discreet branding: Discretion is the better part of branding. Intel inside is far more honorable than Microsoft everywhere. Discretion doesn't mean an absence of branding; what it means is steady branding without being intrusive or overpowering. Today's mantra should be, "More is not always most memorable, and quantity isn't a substitute for quality." While others were peppering the world with multiple thirty-second commercials, Ford sponsored the American network television debut of the award-winning film *Schindler's List* in 1997. No commercials aired—not even during the intermission. Sometimes, the best way to call attention to a brand is by being very, very quiet.

Brand action marketing: Jupiter Communications (www.jup.com) contends that a strategy that exploits interactivity to simultaneously develop a brand and drive consumer action is the key to successful online marketing initiatives. Peter Storck, director of Jupiter Online Advertising Group, warns, "Brands are choosing an either/or strategy in which they focus on brand building *or* direct marketing initiatives. This ignores what makes online different from other media—interactivity." According to Jupiter, successful brand action marketing consists of six component tactics: media, retail enhancement, customization, promotions, sales service and support, and distribution and transactions.

Digital coupons: Chicago-based CoolSavings (www.coolsavings.com) offers personalized coupons via the Net. The company, launched in March of 1997, has 900,000 members, each of whom has completed a personal-preferences profile. CoolSavings has drawn more than thirty national advertisers—including McDonald's, Blockbuster and Barnes & Noble—that target customers geographically, demographically or by stated preferences.

Microbrands: Narrowcasting (show me what matters most to me, and make me a niche of one next) will enable microbrands (a brand just for a few of us or maybe just for you!) to create and then own niche categories (e.g., climate-customized furnishings or do-it-yourself materials). While small is not necessarily better, in this age of narrowcasting, small is definitely possible and flexible.

Heritage trail: Watch for brand spokespeople who focus on the legacy of the brand—and expect these individuals to be members of the brand's employed ranks rather than celebrity endorsers. It should have come as no surprise that Anheuser-Busch's spot featuring family members made its way onto a recent best-of list. Schwab Online has begun featuring its Gen X employees—to connect their consumer peers to the Schwab brand.

Fast marketer: One product we hope to see is a magazine in the style of *Fast Company* written expressly for marketers that would offer insights into change agents for those who steward brands.

CHAPTER 20:

Next Now

_____

We Can Run But Cannot Hide

*A*MERICANS ARE INCREASINGLY more vulnerable to many things: the state of the Japanese banking industry, political unrest in the Balkan region, even the mental (or physical) wherewithal of Boris Yeltsin. Following the U.S. missile strikes in Afghanistan and Sudan, and after Capetown's Planet Hollywood restaurant was bombed by terrorists focused on punishing the chain's American partners (who include Bruce Willis and his estranged wife, Demi Moore, and Sylvester Stallone), the Associated Press reports that America's film industry is genuinely terrorized—and on high alert. Actors fear that they and their loved ones as well as the employees and patrons of their businesses could become terrorist targets.

For Islamic fundamentalists, the products of Hollywood, running the gamut from films and movie theaters to clubs, restaurants, and theme parks, are easily distinguishable symbols of everything American. They are also proof of American encroachment into everything, everywhere. In effect, fantasyland is feeling increasingly vulnerable as it finds escaping reality harder and harder to do. Then again, so are all Americans, as the news media pump stories of avowed enemies into our homes, 24/7. Abdul-Bari Atwan, Palestinian editor of the Arabic daily *Al-Quds Al-Arabi,* has been widely quoted in the press for his take on terrorist Osama Bin Laden: "He loves publicity. He wants to pass a message to Muslims all over the world, and he needs the media to do it. Bin Laden is isolated from the outside world and living in a dangerous environment. His only outlet is the media."

And fear of Muslims just gives a face to a mounting sense that our increasingly multicultural society isn't what we were expecting, for Now or for Next. America isn't going to be white much longer, and today could be the beginning of a society defined by intermarriages and a blending of cultures that make it difficult for race-counters to keep score. Or it could mean a balkanized society—increasingly polarized, with culture pockets dotting the landscape. Reality is probably somewhere in the middle. But as the U.S. struggles to redefine itself and its increasingly multicultural population, signs of ethnic diversity abound.

Globally Speaking: There's a myth that's been propounded recently by some U.S. think tanks that the world's population explosion is over. In terms of our total numerical clout, and the clout of our closest allies, things aren't looking up. Yes, there will be a decline in some parts of the world (most notably, Europe), but we'll be seeing huge growth in less-developed regions of the world. In Asia, for example, we're seeing the population boom from approximately 3.5 billion in 1996 to nearly five billion in 2030. And while North America will grow from only around 299 million to 374 million during that time, Latin America will positively explode, increasing from 484 million to almost 720 million. We'll see similar shifts in the United States, with the African-American and Caucasian populations in decline at the same time that Hispanics and Asians are on the rise.

	Population (thousands)		Percent change
	1996	2030	
World Total	5,767,774	8,371,602	+45
Less-Developed Regions+	4,592,734	7,159,455	+55
Least-Developed Regions#	94,511	1,267,202	+113
More-Developed Regions*	1,175,040	1,212,147	+3
Asia	3,488,027	4,956,764	+42
Latin America	484,301	719,858	+49
Europe	728,777	690,090	-5
North America	299,252	374,063	+25

(+) Less-developed regions comprise all regions of Africa, Asia (excluding Japan), and Latin America and the Caribbean, and the regions of Melanesia, Micronesia, and Polynesia.

(#) As of 1995, the least-developed countries, as defined by the United Nations General Assembly, comprise forty-eight countries, of which thirty-three are in Africa, nine in Asia, one in Latin America, and five in Oceania. They are also included in the less-developed regions (Source: United Nations publication (ST/ESA/SER.A/166), Sales No. E.97.XIII).

(*) More-developed regions comprise all regions of Europe and North America, Australia/New Zealand, and Japan.

Living in the Digital Age

Underlying many of today's most significant trends is the advent of a wired world (and obviously a wired U.S.—since this is one of those areas where America leads—provided you discount the Scandanavian countries). The penetration of these technologies is enormous when you consider that targeting people by a common product they use (e.g., a cell phone) is potentially more effective than targeting people by their geographic location. One of the most interesting tidbits we've read recently is that India, in a bid to ferret out its legions of income tax evaders, has implemented an innovative plan: Under the assumption that a person who can afford a mobile phone must be wealthy enough to pay tax, revenue officials have begun warning mobile users that they must pay their taxes within a month (or prove they have already done so) or face punitive action. The result: Mobile-phone subscriptions plunged nearly 50 percent in less than sixty days after this policy went into effect.

This story highlights the degree to which the middle class the world over has adopted new technologies. Cell-phone use is reaching incredible proportions, with the Asia-Pacific cellular and PCS subscriber base alone expected to reach 221.5 million by 2002. In Norway, cellular-phone penetration already exceeds 25 percent, and Israelis—who rank first in the world in terms of per capita cell-phone usage—average thirty-seven minutes per month for every person in the country. Another communication tool, the pager, also is becoming more and more popular. Analysts estimate that by the end of the decade sixty million Americans will be using pagers (up from thirty-nine million in early 1999). The biggest growth opportunities for paging, however, are in emerging markets, including Eastern Europe, India, Indonesia, and Latin America, where market penetration is less than 1 percent. Overshadowing both these technologies, of course, is the Internet, with estimates placing the global population of users at more than 115 million.

As we mention throughout this book, several factors—including repressive governments, high telephone rates caused by limited lines, and cultural separations between work and home—account for the disparate Internet adoption rates between nations and between different generations within the same nation. But despite such barriers, we believe that the Internet will take hold globally within the next decade. Why? Because computers are now about communicating, rather than about technology. The Internet will spread as computers leave the workplace and enter the home and as price and "enough Internet" (i.e., e-mail and limited surfing) make alternatives such as Web TV more attractive. And that's a marketplace shift that *matters*.

More Fear (Living at Hyperspeed)

One result of having weathered scandal after scandal in the past few decades is that we've grown more cynical. By 2010 we'll be even wiser to the ploys of politicos, preachers and priests, teachers, and, yes, advertisers and marketers, since new media keep springing up (most recently a magazine which is making headlines, Brill's *Content*, in part for reporting on alleged leaks from Independent Counsel Kenneth Starr's office) to inform us that marketing and media are almost one and the same. (Believe it or not, we'll be bombarded even more with advertising messages in the coming years!)

Add to the stress of info overload the uncertainty that our quickly changing world brings. All of us will have worries—about our futures, our countries, our jobs, our cities and towns, our schools, and violence down the street and overseas. We'll be looking for things we can hold on to, things we can trust.

One of the interesting dichotomies we see in today's consumers is their simultaneous embrace of new things and fear of change that is too rapid. They want everything to be smaller, better, faster—but only if it fits comfortably within the world they're used to. They place an enormous value on physical and emotional safety and covet "classic" products they can trust. People in many parts of the world including the U.S. are undergoing a shift from a therapeutic to a prophylactic perspective. We're no longer certain that we can "fix" whatever might go wrong. (Think Y2K. No one understands it, no one thinks it can really be "fixed," and more and more people really fear its implications.) As we attempt to take advantage of the benefits of new technologies and other conveniences, we remain acutely aware of the potential pitfalls. And in a world traveling at hyperspeed, it's a brave (or delusional) person who never has questioned whether he or she can keep up.

More Ritalin Nation

Media consumption by sound bite is a reality of contemporary America (and, increasingly, other parts of the world as well). MTV is considered the pioneer of this form, but the love affair with sound bites has been going on in all media forms: CNN's *Headline News* gives us the world in a half hour (every half hour, 24/7); in print, we have *USA Today*—news from around the nation in colorful, condensed form; and round-the-clock radio news, such as our favorite, WINS-AM in New York City ("Give us 22 minutes; we'll give you the world").

Today we're already hearing analysts decry Americans' short attention spans, particularly concerning politics and economics. Tomorrow we can expect to see an even wider chasm between the emaciated majority of the population and those few who continue to dine on hearty media diets that come complete with global perspectives and analysis. Tragically, trusted sources of such perspectives and analysis will become far fewer, as economic realities continue to force news organizations to emphasize entertainment over education. *The New York Times* reported a wholesale overhaul in the news-gathering operations of the three major television networks (that is, more newsfeeds, more affiliations), who recognize that they can never compete with 24/7, dedicated channels, and that costs of "bringing you the world" are prohibitive. With more students being taught the fundamentals by means such as puppet shows, computer games, and videos, what are the odds that upcoming generations will generate demand for hard news and in-depth coverage? As noted earlier about the metamorphosis of media when confronted with "new media," it is precisely a desire for more depth that newsmagazines and even the TV networks are counting on (the nightly news carries fewer in-depth stories; TV news "magazines" are still cheaper to produce than entertainment; and we now have at least one network devoting one hour of its prime time fare to magazine format every night of the week).

Our collective attention span is shrinking. If a book's too complicated, we put it down. If a video has a slow part, we hit fast-forward. We're also becoming expert at multi-tasking. Why do one thing when we can do three or four things at once? In *Electric Language: Understanding the Message* (St. Martin's Buzz Edition, July 1998), Eric McLuhan writes, "So why is it impossible to take one thing at a time in the world we live in? The global village is not a place where one thing happens at a time. Everything happens there at once [multi-tasking]. What we must have in order to survive, therefore, is a means of coping with an all-at-once world. At electric speed, everything happens at once: there is no sequence, and everything that happens influences everything else, at the same time."

Among other results of our diminished attention span will be the growth of serial life partners. Already many baby-boomers are admitting that the institution of marriage doesn't work for most people their age. When one presses a boomer, male or female, who has been married for more than a couple of years, one quickly learns of lustful yearnings (acted upon or not) outside the marital bedroom. Being denied these extramarital dalliances—or made to feel guilty for participating in them—makes boomers feel fenced in.

At the height of the "Bill & Monica" controversy, *Time* magazine reported that 26 percent of Americans believe that infidelity is an unavoidable part of married life today, compared to 72 percent who say it is avoidable. Married men and married women disagree about when the line is crossed—64 percent of married men and 74 percent of married women think that having a sexually explicit conversation on the phone constitutes cheating. In fact, 75 percent of married women think kissing someone else is cheating; only 59 percent of married men agree. What's Next is the role of the Net in adultery: 72 percent of married women and 62 percent of married men think having a sexually explicit conversation on the Internet constitutes cheating in a marriage. What's still unclear for Next, though, is whether divorce rates will rise or the implication will be decreased interest in exchanging marital vows, making serial monogamy that much easier to enter and exit.

Even more stunning are findings from the most recent sex survey of ten thousand respondents from Australia, Canada, France, Germany, Hong Kong, Italy, Mexico, Poland, South Africa, Spain, Thailand, the U.S., and the U.K. commissioned by The London International Group, manufacturer of Durex condoms. Americans, for one thing, seem to have the most free time for lovemaking, both in terms of length of sessions and (as runners-up) in terms of frequency.

- Hyperspeed is now. Result: Average time spent making love dropped by forty-two seconds, to 17.2 minutes from 17.9 minutes last year. Americans spent the most time, an average of 28.1 minutes per session. As a Reuters report noted, "Those from Thailand were the speediest, spending an average of 10.4 minutes per session."
- Paris might well remain the city of romance. The French had sex more often than those of other nationalities—141 times a year. We Yankees ranked second in frequency, reporting an average of 138 sessions annually. As with the economy, Asians seem to be suffering most: Respondents in Hong Kong reported the fewest sexual encounters yearly at fifty-seven.

- The survey also found infidelity fairly common, more so among Americans than among other nationalities. Reuters reported, "Half of Americans admitted having more than one sexual relationship at a time. At the other extreme, only 22 percent of Spanish respondents reported lapses in fidelity."

An array of public events, most notably the scandals erupting around President Clinton, has brought the issue of infidelity into the open. (But since we're living at hyperspeed, by 2010 the Clinton scandals will seem like ancient history, as long past as Watergate seems now.)

Although not everyone will be bedding their interns, in an era in which people entering the workforce are likely to have five or six careers over a span of five or more decades, we'd be naive to assume that one's shifting needs will be met by a single life partner. Given the unprecedented rate of change in our world, people now live multiple "life spans." And the recently announced breakthroughs in cellular research suggest that one's "productive" years might soon extend far beyond what the average person experienced during the 20th century. Will second, third, and even fourth families become increasingly common? Will movement from one "life" to the next be prepared for and celebrated? How will long-term financial planning be influenced by the knowledge that one's life—and one's partners—will undergo radical shifts every decade or so? The social, economic, and commercial ramifications are extraordinary.

If Only the Good Times Could Keep Rolling

In many ways, what's Next here in the U.S. is more hurry up and wait. The American economy has been booming for what seems like forever. Today's youngest teenagers have enjoyed robust times since the day they began first grade. There have been few divisive interests other than abortion (and in some places the debate about school vouchers) to mobilize their parents to do their civic duty and vote, and the events that have begun to shape this generation's worldview are decidedly American-centric: Terrorism in Oklahoma City turned the spotlight on the left–right struggle, and abortion-clinic bombings ensure that most teens will enter the pro-life versus pro-choice debate. The terrorist attack on the World Trade Center, and the ongoing media coverage (even more than a decade later) of Pan Am Flight 103, guarantee that anti-Arab sentiments will bubble just below the surface.

It didn't much feel like a multicultural melting pot in New York City during Labor Day weekend 1998. Police used pepper spray on rally organizers, and demonstrators threw bottles at the stage as Khallid Abdul Muhammad finished his racially charged rhetoric at the close of the so-called Million Youth March. (Although attendance fell 990,000 short of Khallid Abdul Muhammad's target, he and fellow organizers immediately began talking about switching venues for the next march to accommodate more participants.) Then again, what could have exploded into a riot simply simmered, with black versus white, Muslim versus Jew, and rich versus poor being the unspoken challenge at a time when fundamentalists call for the end of heresy and heretics argue that morality is personal rather than public. It's much easier to focus on McGwire taking down Maris's record than it is to figure out how the holy wars of the Middle East will ever be peacefully resolved.

Okay, So?

In rereading what we've written so far, we can't help but feel some angst and pessimism as well as some techno-induced overdrive, the proverbial hyperspeed that drives those of us who are doing Next now. Could it be that all is not well as we wind down the 20th century? We've had lots of hard lessons these last few years.

What do the early returns tell us about this new generation? How have they been shaped by the defining moments of their lives? Last winter the Louis Harris market research organization completed a study of college freshmen on behalf of Northwestern Mutual insurance company. Press releases note, "Top line results of the survey show a certain 'sense and sensibility' about this group—a well-balanced mixture of mind and heart. On the one hand, the sensibilities of Generation 2001 students appear to be alive with idealism, optimism, and a vision of a better world. On the other hand, they also appear to be well grounded. This generation is not so blindly idealistic or optimistic as to deny the realities of life or the challenges and issues we all face." Overall the study found that college-enrolled eighteen- and nineteen-year-olds (the prime age of second-semester freshmen) are "extremely motivated toward realizing their hopes and aspirations for a bright future for themselves and for America. Already they have established specific goals for themselves. They are truly confident they'll be able to afford the kinds of lifestyles in which they were raised."

David Krane, executive vice-president of Louis Harris, summarized the findings of the Generation 2001 survey by saying, "All new generations build on the experiences of the previous generations. Look at this group and you'll see some common threads from the past as well as different qualities. Generation 2001 students are not as radical as those in the 1960s, nor as materialistic as people in the 1980s," he said. "If Gen2001 is going to change society, it will do so by working within the system. Where some might say these students are naive, others would say that what is most surprising is that this group seems particularly enlightened—and even mature—when it comes to certain aspects of their lives."

Generation 2001 Survey: Facts and Figures at a Glance

- Almost 100 percent of Gen2001 students believe they will get to where they want to be in life. Technology is cited most often as the biggest advantage about being a member of Gen2001, followed by better career opportunities and more educational resources and opportunities. Crime and violence are cited most often as the biggest disadvantage or special problem Gen2001 faces, followed by drugs and AIDS/HIV.
- When it comes to values and lifestyle, the majority (85 percent) says there is a difference between themselves and their parents. Grandparents are trusted most by Gen2001, followed by parents; Gen Xers are trusted the least. Honesty and integrity are the attributes Gen2001 students admire most about a per-

son. Moms are most admired, followed by dads. More than 90 percent say they are satisfied with their appearance.

• Ninety-six percent plan to marry, at the average age of twenty-six, and 91 percent hope to have children—on average, three.

• Almost two-thirds of Gen2001 students say it's their financial responsibility to care for parents when they become elderly and unable to care for themselves.

• More than three-fourths disagree that money buys happiness. Almost three-fourths of Gen2001 students have volunteered in the past year, with most (92 percent) saying it is likely they will volunteer for a charitable organization in the future.

• Almost 90 percent believe in God; three-fourths believe in life after death; the majority attend religious services; almost half say religion will be more important in their future.

• Regarding careers, medicine gets the most votes, followed by teaching, business, and engineering. Regarding jobs, top requirements are having idealistic and committed coworkers and doing work that helps others. Two-income households are going to be important to 82 percent. Owning a home and life insurance are the two vehicles cited most often as very important to financial security.

• Fifty-six percent say the country is headed in the right direction; 42 percent say the wrong direction. Fixing education is a top concern of 96 percent. Ninety-four percent intend to vote. Thirty-three percent say they're Democrats, 31 percent say Republicans, 24 percent Independents. A majority (55 percent) holds a negative view of the current state of race relations; 43 percent expect things to improve by 2001.

• Nearly three-fourths say it's likely in their lifetime that a person of color will be elected president; 64 percent think it is likely that a woman will be elected president.

Generation Gap

The Harris findings surely reinforce a sense that pervades much of America: The young are acting much older, and the old think they're still young. Consider the dignity of young Prince

William and compare it to his father, Prince Charles. Although now deceased and thus elevated in many camps to sainthood, Princess Diana didn't behave any more maturely.

Chelsea Clinton's poise during the summer of Monica and the media also speaks much to the upside we're banking on as Gen2001 matures. Or will they go the way of their parents and begin to struggle with delayed adolescence as they turn twenty, twenty-five, thirty, and older?

In fact, America's obsession with the doomed figure of Princess Diana, who took on mythic powers in life and has retained them after death, raises many other trends we're observing:

- Fear of Islam: The barnstorming led by the father of Dodi Fayed, Mohammed Al-Fayed, the owner of Harrod's among other mega-businesses, has highlighted Anglo-American fears of everything Middle Eastern.
- Age of desirability: Goldie Hawn remains a sex symbol, even if her daughter, Kate Hudson, is scheduled to be the biggest star of the new millennium but doesn't seem to be cutting into her mother's attractiveness as a "young" woman.
- Conspiracy theories abound on everything: Hillary Clinton has blamed a vast right-wing conspiracy for many of the First Family's problems. Mohammed Al Fayed has blamed a conspiracy that originates in or around Buckingham Palace (which he claims would never have wanted the future King of England to have a Muslim stepfather or half-siblings fathered by an Arab dad) for the death of Dodi and Diana. Even corporate conspiracy rumors abound, as recently reported in *USA Today* when it did a business feature on conspiracies—real and perceived—against big corporations. For example, rumors about Procter & Gamble's links to Satan are more than a decade old.
- Invasive journalism is no longer the most coveted type of coverage; in fact, the West is overloaded with tabloid-style information.

America's boomers are the worst offenders of the Peter Pan principle: Never grow old. Remember when toys and fantasy play were for children and grownups tackled more serious pursuits?

Welcome to the '90s, when kiddies are stuck with developmental toys and after-school language classes, while Mom and Dad are off catching the waves on their top-of-the-line Jet Skis. It seems that self-indulgent yuppies have given way to the so-called mature adolescents, middle-aged boomers who aren't quite ready to put away their toys and settle into the seriousness of adulthood. We told you this generation wasn't planning to grow old without a fight!

Warning: Change Isn't Always Good

Wall Street Journal writer Bill Buckley asked Marian what businesses she thinks will fall away by 2010. "I think focus group facilities will suffer," she responded. "We can conduct significant actionable market research online today, and by 2010 most of the Western world will be connected to the Net, and, thus, genuinely representative samples should be easily accessed via e-mail, instant chat, and other methods of connectivity. Further, the entire business of market research and business intelligence will change dramatically because business professionals and others increasingly will be prepared to pay a premium for 'actionable information' versus the overloaded clutter of everything out there." In effect, people who have jobs like ours will have revolutionary tools—and these tools might well ensure they stay smarter and more stressed, since 24/7 surely drains even the most energetic folks. (We both laugh about the fact that our friends and associates in Holland have the ultimate cop-out for whenever they feel stressed—they go "overloaded" and take time off—with pay—until they feel fully rested. Perhaps this is why a country the size of the state of Florida is the fourth most significant economic superpower. Nobody living and working in Holland needs to worry about burning out.)

So what else will change? Marian also told the *WSJ*, "Private schools and private tutorial programs also will be hurt, because 'enhanced education' will be easily accessible via interactive devices. And book publishers will find that, while content still makes profits, the Byzantine business of bringing books to market over a sixteen-month process will be replaced by 'on-demand' publishing. Video stores, too, will cease stocking inventory, since movies, in whatever form they're sold, come 2010, will be printed when the consumer steps up, really or virtually, to place the order."

And we both note that real estate owners might be the most dramatically affected, since we'll emphasize home/work spaces and flexible architecture and we'll need far fewer storefronts once considerable commerce migrates into the virtual environment of *unreal* estate.

A Topic on Which We Cannot Agree: The Future of Advertising

Mass advertising might well have died a slow, tortured death by the middle of the next decade. (Then again, we tend to embrace change faster than most, although this debate about advertising is one that Marian and Ira see somewhat differently. Marian claims advertising in America will be *dead*. Ira says it will be diminished rather than replaced by direct messaging.) But the through-the-line, one-to-one messaging solutions—artful persuasion—will become marketers' mainstay activity. Inventing desire will remain the name of the game, but by 2010, we'll know so much about the consumer that we'll be able to identify all of his or her hot buttons.

Paying With What?

A cashless society is coming, and fast. When you consider the far-reaching effects of ATMs on global currency, euro-anxiety seems a bit overdone. Who could have imagined a world in which our Chase Manhattan or Marine Midland cards could get us cash in a township in Johannesburg, from a local bank in Hong Kong, from a till in Cambridge, England, or Billund, Denmark, or in Pest, Hungary. In this world of NYCE, CIRRUS, etc., where American Express and Visa and MasterCard are the equivalent of money, it's no wonder we just expect our e-cash to be accepted no matter where we are.

One must note, though, that the gap between the first and third worlds on this matter means further inequities. Yankees can play with global currency floats on their business expense accounts and between credit cards, while the poorest in the U.S. and around the world have no sense of how to navigate such financial waters—not to mention no faith in any fiduciary institution. Today, perhaps more than ever before, knowledge truly is power. And the financial services category demands a savvy consumer, otherwise you're simply a victim of everything from fine print to the premiums you're forced to pay as a consumer laggard.

Interestingly, while the U.S. has the lead in Internet adoption and other high-tech categories, we've allowed European banks to eclipse us in terms of consumer-friendly technologies. Marian's ABN-AMRO bank in Holland, for instance, let her pay using a smart chip (Chipknip) on a MasterCard-looking ATM card. She'd periodically load the card to ensure that she'd never have to struggle for change to make a phone call or to log on for her e-mail at the public pay terminals that are increasingly scattered around upmarket neighborhoods in Amsterdam. Ira's BT phone card (he has spent a lot of time in the U.K. over the last few years) also has a smart chip, which lets him use the £20 investment intelligently, again ensuring that he doesn't lug around a pocketful of heavy coins for those vital phone calls we all place on the street.

Marian suggests that "pinning" (using personal identification numbers) for purchases is much more efficient, but this is still the exception in the U.S. Also, the recordkeeping that comes with paying by ATM-style card (direct debit) means you run up lower finance charges and can manage your money more effectively. But it also means Big Brother knows all, so forget the off-the-books babysitter or dog-walker. In Holland we called such "secret" payments, "black payments," and they actually command a discount because they are so advantageous to the small-time operator. In countries with enormous value-added tax, cash might become king because with cash there can be secrets, provided payments remain small enough to stay not only below the radar screen but below the radar waves themselves.

Conclusions—Or More Questions?

In our opinion, true convergence is the genuine blurring of life and work, home and office, family and friends, as well as all the techie blending of PC and TV, freezer and cooker, education and entertainment.

We'll have much more time for our fantasy lives in 2010, since the highly connected world ensures we can manage a 24/7 existence. That's the only way we'll be able to fit in the respites and escapes we'll need as alternative fuel to get us through the pace (a.k.a. hyperspeed) of our highly connected days and nights.

• NEXT: EXPERIENCE COLLECTING

We introduced the experience economy as a what's Next for the world. But for Americans experience collecting is a definite Next. Why? Two seemingly conflicting impulses drive experience today: a focus on creating full, flexible, diverse lives; and a quest for simplicity and control in an ever-changing world. The first contributes to an à la carte approach to life (Think "Arm's Length Communion"). We sample thrills by taking adventure vacations; we graze among cheap luxuries, such as storefront massages. At the same time, we crave continuity. Picture frames, video cameras, and all manner of keepsakes help us package and relive experiences as memories.

We need to keep the experience collector and the new economy in mind at all times as we're thinking about the citizens of the world. Experience collectors and collectors generally are different but similar, as global citizens and road warriors are. Their ways of life and work are similar and they share common needs and wants, but the twain ain't the same. Experience collectors live to savor the moment as "memory" (think "memory as sound-bite"), whereas collectors have pride of ownership: They enjoy the tactile and emotional satisfaction of collecting things versus memories. The June/July 1998 issue of the *Harvard Business Review* featured strong insights into the experience economy.

To paraphrase the article, first there was agriculture, then manufactured goods, and eventually services. Each change represented a step up in economic value—a way for producers to distinguish their products from increasingly undifferentiated competitive offerings. Now, as services are in their turn becoming commoditized, companies are looking for the next higher value in an economic offering. Leading-edge companies are finding that it lies in staging experiences.

To reach this higher level of competition, companies will have to learn how to design, sell, and deliver experiences that customers will readily pay for. An experience occurs when a company uses services as the stage and goods as props for engaging individuals in a way that creates a memorable event. And while experiences have always been at the heart of the entertainment business, any company stages an experience when it engages customers in a personal, memorable way. As we mentioned already, Virgin Atlantic offers its travelers more than just an airplane flight from Point A to Point B. Old Navy provides a unique shopping experience for Americans of all ages—part kitsch, part competitive pricing, and part deep stock and a broad range of sizes and silhouettes.

What the Future Holds

Perhaps we need to explore scenarios in which the future goes on hold. We note five things that we believe could slow progress. As important, there is an infinite number of scenarios that could lead to a brave new Next—anything from the discovery of life on Mars to the resignation of one or more of the leaders of world superpowers to an all-out religious war to a massive Y2K meltdown.

Some things might extend the American spirit of isolationism and desire to ward off the future:

- A global psychoeconomic depression, which might result from the postpartum blues of millennial celebrations
- Increased religious angst, placing technology at the center of the war between those who embrace change and those who believe the traditional is the best and only way to go
- Natural and unnatural disasters that leave us believing there is some force of ill will out there plaguing and punishing ordinary man (the proliferation of media makes bad news so much more vivid than ever before)
- A true (or perceived) techno-meltdown in relation to the Y2K problem, which leaves the techno-averse convinced that the past was better than progress

• Persuasive forces becoming so pervasive that we end up feeling as though life has become mass manipulation paid for by the almighty dollar, or some other currency of power. Turning off becomes the last line of defense...

The potential problems of the brave Next world leave us ambivalent about whether life is better Now and Next or whether it was finer in simpler, less challenging (slower) times.

More significantly, we think there is an antisocial component to life today that makes us uncertain about whether "progress" is taking us in the right direction. If we evolved toward losing our capacity to make the tough phone call when we discovered answering machines and voice mail, will e-mail make for an added dimension of fearfulness breeding fearfulness? What happens when we stop knowing how to manage, with eye-to-eye contact or voice-to-voice, down to the cracks and deep pauses, the tough face-offs of life? Also, will we become such a high-tech world that our downtime will feel more pressurized, if for no other reason than that downtime is a self-select (you're not picking up your e-mail, voice mail, pages)? In a culture already filled with guilt, it seems there will be yet another predicament preying on our sanity.

Reality Check

By now the news seems almost surreal. If we were Armaggedonites, we might be seeing the handwriting in all of the craziness that seems to be flooding the premillennial airwaves. As it is, there's suddenly a collective angst blowing through the United States, as talk of recession is balanced with a Next debate over family values, at a moment in history—the first one—when more children have unwed mothers than wed mothers. Take this for a spot check on the now (remember that Marshall McLuhan urged, "Know the now," for it is the best map for the next journey).

Is all this news and analysis good for us? We're all overloaded with the minutiae of the moment and yet crave understandings of what's behind the massive changes shaking our fundamental way of life to the very core. Madonna, the quintessential trendsetter, became known as the Material Girl nearly a decade ago. And *The*

Wall Street Journal takes us full circle on the isolation versus globalization and spiritual core versus material matters, with its look-see, "From Small Towns to Big Cities, America Is Becoming Cultured" by Douglas A. Blackmon. "At a crossroads Texaco station, where a strip of pavement curving through the Ozark Mountains meets Highway 62 on the way to Yellville, a flashing yellow sign beckons weary travelers. 'Two Hot Dogs $1,' reads the first line. 'Propane Gas,' the second. And the third, all in red capital letters: 'CAPPUCCINO.' Poured from a machine into the same foam cups used for Coca-Cola and Mountain Dew soft drinks, the steamed milk and java here doesn't make the same impression as the stuff Starbucks sells. But the Ozark concoction in this town of 319 people is a humble harbinger, nonetheless, of a revolutionary transformation of American culture."

But the most important finding of this thought-provoking news feature is, as Ira notes, if you accept that exposure will lead to desire, it is not surprising that as we find new means of information dissemination (more media, Internet, zines), these kinds of things will find themselves migrating from style centers to rural environments. Isn't this precisely what we say is the value of trend-tracking? Measuring the movement from the cutting edge to Main Street anywhere is what we've been doing for years. And this book is the measurement of Next—from a Now standpoint.

Many accuse us of being negative. The reality is, we're bullish on Now and Next, but since we've been living the future, we also know all too well that, regardless of the century, Now is more real than Next, Next is more romantic than Now—and change is inevitable.

CHAPTER 21:

Generation 2001

WE HOLD AS A BASIC TRUTH the idea of America as a "melting pot" that embraces and engages the influences of many cultures. This sense has no doubt enriched our culture. It is equally true that our "Americentric" view of the world—the idea that "Americanization" and "globalization" are synonyms—has been our prevailing view since the dawn of the Industrial Age. We're convinced that our immediate future will prove the folly of that view. And where is the future-day Paul Revere to warn us, "The Euros are coming"? (And will somebody tell him to warn our allies on the other side of the pond, the Brits?)

Americans have a mounting sense that our increasingly multicultural society isn't quite what we were expecting. America isn't going to be white much longer, and today could be the beginning of a society defined by intermarriages and a blending of cultures that make it difficult for race-counters to keep score. Or it could mean a balkanized society—increasingly polarized, with culture pockets dotting the landscape. The reality is probably somewhere in the middle. But as the United States struggles to redefine itself and its increasingly multicultural population, signs of ethnic diversity abound. A recent report by the Roper Center for Public Opinion Research indicates that while minority culture is increasingly familiar to mainstream Americans, 68 percent of blacks see racism as a big problem; only 38 percent of whites agree. The good news, though, comes from a Louis Harris poll, that found that about half of all blacks and whites believe that by the time their kids become their age, race relations will be much improved. And even though black employees in 1999 report that they feel a sense of discrimination in the workplace, a clear majority of all adolescents insist that they have an equal chance to master their universes in the future.

Uberview: X and "Why" Equal Tomorrow

Much has been made of Generations X and Why's desire for constant stimulation.

"I get bored easily. I need something on all the time—TV, music, something." —A fifteen-year-old girl from California [Quoted in the *Star Tribune* (Minneapolis)]

Such cravings, combined with a perceived underachievement, have saddled members of Generations X and Why with the rap of being passive reactors to the purportedly bionic efficiency of their boomer parents. In addition, Xers were the first to be diagnosed with such "millennial" afflictions as attention deficit disorder and chronic ennui—widely thought to be symptoms of an Information Age in which kids are weaned on computers, consumer electronics and the high-octane programming of MTV.

Doomsayers cite such reports as indicators that future generations won't have the skills required to lead us in the next millennium. Others maintain that Generation X's and especially Generation Why's ability to "surf" new technologies and enjoy ever more networked, virtual and holistic forms of entertainment is a mark of progress. Many, including youth-culture guru Douglas Rushkoff, consider these abilities to be an evolutionary leap that will come to define the culture of the next millennium. In his book, *Playing the Future* (HarperCollins, 1996), Rushkoff argues that a decreased attention span will make Xers and Whys (whom he dubs "Screenagers") smarter consumers and better prepared to adapt to what is to come. He writes, "The child of the remote control may indeed have a 'shorter' attention span as defined by the behavioral psychologists of our prechaotic culture's academic institutions. . . . But this same child also has a much *broader* attention *range*. The skill to be valued in the twenty-first century is not length of attention span but the ability to multi-task—to do many things at once, well."

Their multitasking evolutionary skills firmly in place, Generations X and Why are increasingly seeking out all-consuming, cathartic entertainment experiences that involve multiple electronic devices. A twenty-four-year-old man from California, when asked what things symbolize his generation, said, "Music CDs, computer CDs, and CD-ROMs. All of these things are related to technology and [we are] ever craving the bombardment of sensations."

As youthful trendsetters establish multitainment as *the* lifestyle of the future, they are ushering in what many are calling the experience economy, a concept we introduced earlier. Needless to say, the move toward this experience economy is dependent on the market penetration of consumer electronics. With unemployment at record lows and, despite turbulence in the market, consumer confidence high, Generations X and Why have access to the cash they need to become the most important and influential market for the consumer electronics industry. According to the Consumer Electronics Manufacturers Association, eighteen- to twenty-six-year-olds are the most likely population segment to be interested in technology (eighty-three percent of men and 78 percent of women).

The Teen Scene Will Mushroom

The number of teenagers in the United States is mushrooming at levels not seen since their boomer parents were teens in the '60s. Nielsen Media Research reports that today's thirty-one million-strong generation of teens will grow to thirty-five million by 2010. And they're burning through cash faster than the music industry can burn CDs, spending $122 billion of their own and their parents' money each year, according to Nielsen Media Research, not including family purchases, such as cars and computers, which they also influence. All this amounts to a viral consumer trend in which young adults are both buying electronics for themselves and also influencing their (less-savvy) parents' purchasing decisions.

However, these young people are also balance-seekers who oftentimes crave escape from the info-noise of our age. It's not unusual for multitasking teens to have the TV and stereo on while they talk on the phone, participate in an online chat, or compose e-mail. "I'm holding the phone chatting while listening to the stereo with the remote in my hand. That's what you'll find me doing every night." An eighteen-year-old from New York City said, "we're also using stereos and computers to retreat from the world, escaping into private, fantasy-filled oases."

In other words, Generations X and Why's relationship with technology is not one-dimensional. They can be just as ambivalent about new technologies as are their analog parents. They fear that consumerism run amok will damage the environment, and they express concern about the depersonalization brought on by new millennial technologies.

A twenty-year-old woman in New York City said, "[My] fear of the future is the uncertainty of losing the familiar to the unfamiliar."

Ultimately, Xers and Whys crave security and are wary of anything that threatens to disrupt their sense of home. According to a nineteen-year-old woman in New York City, "My house [is] my favorite hangout because it's never crowded and noisy, it's always clean, warm and friendly."

In the wake of events in Columbine High School in Littleton, Colorado, we can only assume that visceral fears in any public space will continue to grow. Consider that places like post offices and fast food outlets became our initial focus of "safe zones." When fear invades our schools, we need to wonder where, if any place, provides the basic comfort that comes from an absolute assurance of safety.

About this Book

*T*HIS BOOK IS THE WORK of several individuals, spun through the voices of two who trekked the planet, and was made possible only through the support of our multinational employer, called Young & Rubicam. In November 1997, just three weeks before the Dutch edition of this book was unveiled, Marian, Ann, and Christy joined Y&R as its Brand Futures Group. Later that week, before she had even settled into her new workspace, Marian left for Helsinki, to address the marketing community. Two weeks later, she and Ira were back in Amsterdam to celebrate publication of *Trends Voor De Toekomst*, the original title of this book. In the meantime, Ann O'Reilly and Christy Lane Plummer launched Brand Futures Group's line of products at Y&R, including a weekly newsletter called *Future Dialogue;* our in-depth sector analyses, *Futurescopes;* and *BrainSnacks*, weekly compilations of thought-provoking quotes, survey findings, and miscellaneous data.

As publishers around the world began signing on for updated versions of *Trends* (now called *Next*) in a variety of languages, Ira and Marian went to work revising the manuscript, which they then handed over to Ann and Christy (and later Nancy Arnott, Stuart Harris, Merritt Walters, Amy Woessner, and Shoshana Berger) for their input—the goal being to produce the most timely product possible in the most narrow window imaginable (a trademark of our collaborations). Thus, any errors are Ira's and Marian's, and are the benign byproduct of what happens when people need to trust their instincts when honing conclusions.

Electronic links are truly the backbone of this book, since so much of it has been culled from discussion groups, chatrooms, Web sites, and articles and reports found on the Internet—as well as conversations with fellow cybernauts and e-polls conducted amongst our global trend scouts. Though *Next* still has its origins in our original Dutch edition, it benefits from a more global perspective, thanks in large part to extensive analyses offered by our colleagues at Y&R Inc. offices and companies, around the globe: Yoshitaka Abe, Stephanie Abramson, Anne Ainsley, Jennifer Alexander, Edward Appleton, June Blocklin, Maggie Brennan, Barbara Bruinsma, Adrian Day, Joe Dedeo, Daryl Elliott, Lisa Epstein, Maria Evangeli, Daisy Exposito, Leslie Gaines-Ross, Adolfo Garro, Peter Georgescu, Sophie Glovier, Claudia Gonzalez, Lola Gonzalez, Jemma Gould, Arianna Grigoriadis, Jonathan Holburt, Louisa Holland, Sonja Huerlimann, Lara Hussein, Zoya Ivanova, Barbara Jack, Meridith Jamin, Jaime Kalfus, Nikki Karani, Daniel Ko, Philippe Krakowsky, Tammy Lechter, Sharon Lee, Marco Lombardi, Steven Lyons, Mila M. Marquez, Scott Marticke, Richard McGowan, Liz McKee, Cristina Merrill, Kate Milano, Melissa Miller, Dominique Missoffe, Fernan Montero, Jennifer Moore, Karen Ng, Lia Nikopoulou, Todd Ochsner, Stewart Owen, John Partilla, Mary Peng, Jim Pharo, Angela Pih, Tim Pollak, Julie Rothhouse, Mike Samet, Stan Stefanski, Mark Stroock, Sachin Talwar, Kamila Tischler, Katarina Varenius, Han van Dijk, Miguel Velhinho, Ed Vick, Jim Williams, Paul Woolmington, and Mike Zeigler.

WHAT'S NEXT?

The authors also are grateful to a number of people with whom we worked while in Europe, especially Fleur Dusee, David Matathia, Willemijn ter Weele, and Friso Westenberg, our staff at the Department of the Future, who made our international adventure so deeply personal, as well as professionally expansive.

The people we met in Amsterdam taught us how truly satisfying a global village can be. We're also grateful to Amsterdam for the unique place it holds as an embracer of change, albeit with pragmatism and a sense of "so prove it." If the Dutch media hadn't sparked to us, our own futures might be so much less interesting. We made many friends and acquaintances in Amsterdam, and realize that the people who are Amsterdam helped us make the myth of our trend-tracking accuracy real by trusting our hunches about what's Next so that the media would test us again and again.

Leonard Orkin of Kaye, Collyer was a godsend in sorting through our past, present, and future agreements regarding the publication of *Next*. Sheri Radel has managed our lives as we run in eleven directions, to 61 countries, and build our futuring consultancy. We owe her one—or more!

BORN AT CHIAT/DAY

This book took root because Chiat/Day, our former employer, believed in the future. Jay Chiat gave us the most important professional legacy we could dream of: confidence to evolve in revolutionary ways; quirky, unconventional working styles to ensure that good enough is never enough and a tradition of forcing change into and up organizations.

Finally, we want to acknowledge the opportunities and support we enjoyed during our two-year international odyssey with the DOF: Laurie Coots, Colette Chestnut, Gavin Heron, Jonathan Hill, John Hunt, Reg Lascaris, Robin Lauffer, Alasdair Ritchie, Velda Ruddock, Keith Smith, Tom Spikerman, and Perry Valkenburg.

SEP 9 9